Library of
Davidson College

OXFORD HISTORICAL MONOGRAPHS

Editors

M. G. BROCK BARBARA HARVEY
H. M. MAYR-HARTING H. G. PITT
K. V. THOMAS A. F. THOMPSON

THE OXFORD ECONOMISTS IN THE LATE NINETEENTH CENTURY

BY
ALON KADISH

CLARENDON PRESS · OXFORD
1982

Oxford University Press, Walton Street, Oxford OX2 6DP
London Glasgow New York Toronto
Delhi Bombay Calcutta Madras Karachi
Kuala Lumpur Singapore Hong Kong Tokyo
Nairobi Dar es Salaam Cape Town
Melbourne Auckland

and associate companies in
Beirut Berlin Ibadan Mexico City

Published in the United States by
Oxford University Press, New York

© Alon Kadish 1982

All rights reserved. No part of this publication may be reproduced,
stored in a retrieval system, or transmitted, in any form or by any means,
electronic, mechanical, photocopying, recording, or otherwise, without
the prior permission of Oxford University Press

British Library Cataloguing in Publication Data

Kadish, Alon
   The Oxford economists in the late nineteenth
century.—(Oxford historical monographs)
   1. Oxford Economic Society   2. Economics—
Great Britain—History—19th century
   I. Title
   330'.0942   HB103.AZ
ISBN 0-19-821886-9

Library of Congress Cataloging in Publication Data

Kadish, Alon, 1950-
   The Oxford economists in the late nineteenth
century.
   (Oxford historical monographs)
   Bibliography: p.
   Includes index.
   1. Economists—Great Britain—Biography.
2. Economics—Great Britain—History—19th
century.   3. Oxford Economic Society—Biography.
I. Title.
HB103. A3K3   330'.092'2   82-3573
ISBN 0-19-821886-9   AACR2

Typeset by V.A.P. Ltd.
Printed in Great Britain
at the University Press, Oxford
by Eric Buckley
Printer to the University

To the Hellners

PREFACE

J. K. Ingram, in his *History of Political Economy* (Edinburgh 1888), concluded his survey of the work of the Historical School in England with the optimistic comment — 'If, as we are told, there exists at Oxford a rising group of men who occupy a position in regard to economic thought substantially identical with that of Toynbee, the fact is one of good omen for the future of the science.' This book is an attempt to provide a collective social and intellectual biography of this group of young men during the first years of their professional careers. The study is not the result of an earlier interest in the history of economic thought. It has emanated from an interest in the dynamics of the relationship between the individual scientist and his environment as reflected in his theoretical work. More specifically it sets out to examine how various environmental circumstances and an individual's biographical experience and personality are integrated in the work of the individual social scientist in creating a theory about a certain social reality. Thus, rather than concentrating on similarities in structure or contents of various theories or on the way a certain economic phenomenon is reflected in various theories, the focus of this work is the theorist himself. Circumstances are considered on the basis of biographical relevance, be they intellectual, scientific, or material. Theory is considered as the product of an individual scientist and a school of thought as a conscious corporate entity.

As a result, the study is not contentiously structured. It does not set out to prove or to disprove the results of previous work in the relevant fields. Although some of the findings and conclusions may differ from those of existing works, especially in the history of economic thought, no attempt has been made to refer directly to these potential controversies. It will also be noticed that relatively few references are made to secondary works; this omission might be excused on the basis of the following considerations. First, very little use has been made of the relatively few works available on the Oxford economists, and therefore no mention is made of works that have not been of direct use, even if consulted. Secondly, I have been extremely fortunate in locating a mass of previously unused primary material not found in the secondary works. Finally, a somewhat complicated narrative, encumbered by numerous references to primary sources, would become even more unwieldy if I were to compare the various findings and conclusions with other studies which do not share my basic approach.

Lack of satisfactory research on some of the historical developments relevant to the early careers of the Oxford economists—notably the foundation of Toynbee Hall, the early history of the Oxford Extension movement, and the foundation of the London School of Economics—has forced me to try to fill the gap without, I hope, too many diversions. However, on some issues in which modern scholarship is sadly wanting, such diversions have not been practically possible. There are no satisfactorily detailed studies on many related lines of enquiry. These include the influence of the developments in constitutional history on economists, detailed examination of the relations between economists of English and foreign schools — mainly the German historical and the American schools—and a comparable study of similar developments at other English universities: mainly Cambridge, London, and Glasgow. The existence of an Oxford group of young economists was not in itself unique. Contemporaneous groups may be found in other British universities, and a study of their composition and development is likely not only to fill some gaps in our knowledge of the period but also to allow a better understanding of the development of the study of economics and related scientific disciplines. Hence, although the study naturally magnifies the work of a small group, it does not claim to cover the whole scope of late-Victorian economics, nor does it pretend to describe the most important development in the field. At the same time it is felt that the findings may justify a reassessment by internal historians of the importance of the Oxford economists.

I am especially grateful to Professor Yehuda Elkana who first set me on this track of enquiry, to my Oxford supervisor, Professor Peter Mathias, whose faith in the subject and continuous support helped me to see it through, and to Professor A. W. Coats, who opened my eyes to numerous aspects and implications of the work which I would otherwise have overlooked. His unfailing kindness and responsiveness have made the task of an outsider easier as well as more pleasant.

I have received much valuable feedback and sound advice from Professor Klaus Hennings and from Stuart Marriott and John Wood, for all of whose friendship I am grateful. Valuable advice and kind encouragement have also been received from my examiners Dr R. M. Hartwell and Professor T. W. Hutchison.

This work owes much to the co-operation and generous help received from numerous librarians and archivists. I am especially indebted to Mrs Macdonald of Oriel College, to Mr Quinn of Balliol College who helped to an extent I had no right to expect and to the librarians of the Radcliffe Camera for their infinite patience. I would also like to thank a fellow Wolfsonian, Mr Oliver Nicholson, for locating the Price MS at Trinity College, Oxford.

It is with gratitude that I acknowledge the kindness of Mrs Barker, Mrs P. V. W. Gell, and Dr S. Llewellyn Smith in allowing me to study their family papers. I am especially indebted to Mrs Diana Farr for her friendship and enthusiasm in tracing the Cannan family history and to Mrs S. Argyle for invaluable help at The Oxford University Press.

Finally, this work has been made possible by the generous financial support of Wolfson College, the Institute of Historical Research of the University of London, and the Hellner Foundation. It is to the latter that this work is dedicated.

CONTENTS

Chapter		Page
1	The Making of an Economist	1
2	The Oxford Extension Movement	76
3	Economics Courses in the Oxford Extension	115
4	The Debate on the Study of Economics—Initial Moves	126
5	The Debate—Oxford Variants	153
6	Oxford Economists and the Chair	172
7	The Debate—Marshallians and Dissenters	209
8	The Alternatives Facing the Dissenters	242
9	Some Conclusions	276

APPENDIX: Members of the Oxford Economic Society 1886–1891: Academic Record ... 292

BIBLIOGRAPHY ... 294

INDEX ... 309

1
THE MAKING OF AN ECONOMIST

In November 1878 William James Ashley, the son of a journeyman hatter, was elected Brackenbury Scholar at Balliol College, Oxford. Had it not been for the scholarship system, he, most likely, would never have gone up to Oxford.[1] Having won a scholarship, he was for ever grateful for the absence of the stigma of poverty in a system based, as it was, on merit rather than on need. Not only did the scholarship make an Oxford education financially possible, it also conferred considerable distinction 'which no other system could there secure for him. He, the scholar, is known by all to have won his place by his brains, in a keen competition with men who have enjoyed every social advantage, and he is respected accordingly.'[2]

On entering Balliol, Ashley found that he was one

of a number of quite poor men, sometimes from the very humblest of classes, who combine with first class abilities (so far as any human tests can ascertain) the enjoyment of an income which enables them to dress like their associates, to have comfortable rooms, and to give all their working time for four years to the studies of the place.[3]

William James Ashley, born on 25 February 1860, was one of eight children of whom only six survived infancy, William James being the eldest survivor. His father, James Ashley from Wrexham, was a devout Baptist, a teetotaller who did not smoke or play cards, and to whom Liberal politics combined with temperance were manifest in religion and philanthropy. His wife came from Gloucestershire and was of Welsh descent. Neither seems to have had much of an education and the Ashleys' home in Bermondsey in south London, devoid of

---

[1] Anne Ashley, *William James Ashley, A Life* (London, 1932), p. 10.
[2] W. J. Ashley, 'Scholarships at Oxford and at Harvard', reprinted from the *Harvard Monthly* 1(1900), in id., *Surveys Historic and Economic* (London, 1900).
[3] Ibid.

books (except for Dickens), was one of little cultivation.[4] William attended two privately run schools, then a large Wesleyan elementary school which was under government inspection, and finally St. Olave's Grammar School in Southwark. On Sundays he attended a Congregationalist Sunday School and at the age of fifteen he became a full member of the Baptist Church. For the whole of his life he remained an active churchgoer, moving gradually towards the Church of England, and in later years his sermons, delivered as a lay preacher, were collected under the title *The Christian Outlook; Being the Sermons of an Economist* (London, 1925).

School revealed in him a lack of interest in the natural sciences; the Darwinian theory of evolution alone caught his imagination. At the age of sixteen, he decided to sit for the Balliol Brackenbury History Scholarship which had been won three years earlier by another St. Olave pupil, T. F. Tout (1855–1929). With his mind set on history, Ashley attended a series of Extension lectures delivered in Clapham by S. R. Gardiner and was coached for the scholarship examination by Tout during the latter's vacations from Oxford. Even the fees paid for Tout's coaching were a considerable financial burden on the family. James Ashley was temporarily out of work, a new mechanized process having rendered his skill redundant.

It was therefore obvious that a scholarship was essential if Ashley was to go to Oxford.[5] He failed at his first attempt in 1877, but won an internal St. Olave scholarship of £30, followed in 1878 by a £50 per annum school scholarship and an exhibition awarded by a parochial trust worth £50 per annum for four years. The sum of £130 per annum was barely sufficient for an Oxford education.[6] Nevertheless, having tried again for the Brackenbury, Ashley was admitted to St. Edmund Hall, from where he moved to Balliol a few weeks later when the results of the scholarship examination became known.

[4] W. J. Ashley, 'Jowett and the University Ideal', reprinted from the *Atlantic Monthly*, July 1897, in Ashley's *Surveys Historic and Economic*.
[5] Fees at St. Olave's were £6.6s.0d. per annum. See Charles Eyre Pascoe, *Where Shall I Educate my Son?: A Manual for Parents of Moderate Means* (London, 1887), p. 59.
[6] In an article, 'The Future of English Universities' in the *Fortnightly Review*, March 1883, James Bryce computed the expense of an Oxford education to be £140–£200 per annum.

The relative financial freedom did not ensure automatic social acceptance. The growth in size of the annual intake of students (fifty-eight in Ashley's year) seemed to promise better social integration, for as the college grew,

> the undergraduate body became more and more composite in social origin—from the earl down, or up, to the clever son of the artisan. Jowett's dream was that the earl and the artisan's son should fraternise; but as a matter of fact, they did not. It was notorious in Oxford that Balliol was one of the most cliquy of colleges. . . . [Jowett] failed to realise that a large and diversified college is incompatible with real acquaintance with one another on the part of the undergraduates. No quantity of college songs or tutorial 'tea and toast' can make headway against the centrifugal forces.[7]

It is no accident that Ashley is rarely, if ever, mentioned in the memoirs of his Balliol contemporaries. It was observed at the time[8] that 'the old rule of "like consorts with like" which holds good of all society, is especially true of the society of Oxford . . . generally speaking, a man falls into a groove or set with which he thinks, talks, and acts, and beyond which he makes few intimate acquaintances.' Public-school men, upon coming into residence at Oxford, would look up old school friends at other colleges or of other years. They would usually join the school's university club and start their university social life on the basis of public-school acquaintances. The student intake at Balliol in Ashley's year[9] consisted of the usual high proportion of public-school men (ten from Eton alone), and a strong contingent of Scots (seven) who were usually older than the average undergraduate since most of them had already attended a Scottish university. The rest included some privately educated men who, although they had difficulties in adjusting to the academic discipline of the place, had few problems in finding their social place.[10] Some of the grammar-school men were Indian Civil Service candidates usually seeking the company of their fellow candidates. Finally there was a small number of grammar-school men such as Ashley, for whom a university education had to serve as the last training

---

[7] Ashley, 'Jowett and the University Ideal'.
[8] An Oxford Tutor, 'Young Oxford', in *Fraser's Magazine*, May 1881.
[9] Sir Ivo Elliot (ed.), *The Balliol College Register 1833–1933* (Oxford, 1934).
[10] One such person in Ashley's year was John St. Loe Strachey: see his *The Adventure of Living; A Subjective Autobiography* (London, 1925).

they would receive for a job. For a career other than taking Holy Orders or becoming school masters, such men were dependent on obtaining a double First. They could not, for instance, afford, upon leaving Oxford, to read for the Bar, to enter politics, or to become journalists. After graduating they would have to find a job almost immediately and start earning a living, and the better they performed in Schools the better chance they had of doing this. Furthermore, men such as W. J. Ashley, M. E. Sadler, W. A. S. Hewins, and others, were bound to their family background socially as well as financially. More often than not they became engaged to girls they knew from home, whereas public-school men of a more well-to-do background tended to marry sisters of friends from school, college, or the Inns of Court. Although long engagements were quite common, there was, upon graduation, a certain added urgency in the task of finding a secure source of income which would allow marriage. As a result, university days for men like Ashley were a period of intensive work, in the course of which he had to overcome the disadvantage of the lack of a public-school training in classics, essay writing, and so on.

'An Oxford Tutor', writing in *Fraser's Magazine* in May 1881, surveyed the social life of the University. He found that each college had its rowing and cricketing sets, its reading set which would organize theatricals, poetry reading, etc., one or more debating societies (another public-school tradition), and a 'fast' set interested primarily in horse riding, fashionable dress, card games, and gambling. A young man of Ashley's background did not play games, nor could he afford the time. He lacked the cultivated taste for reading plays and poetry. Although interested in political issues, he was not used to the form in which debating societies were run. Therefore, despite the apparent egalitarianism, Ashley did not belong to any of Balliol's debating or literary societies and did not play games. He took no part in the Oxford Union debates, and only in 1883, after obtaining his degree, did he become a member of the Liberal Radical Palmerston Club.

Ashley's college tutors were A. L. Smith and J. F. Bright, whose lectures he found 'incorrect in substance and stimulating

THE MAKING OF AN ECONOMIST

in expression'.[11] Another young man to come under A. L. Smith's influence some two years after Ashley, was Edwin Cannan[12] who entered Balliol on 29 January 1881. Cannan, like Ashley, took no active part in undergraduate life, for reasons significantly different from Ashley's.

Edwin Cannan's grandfather, Thomas Cannan[13], was born in 1789. He was educated at Edinburgh University and was employed for a while as a travelling tutor to a young nobleman, then as tutor to the Ogilvie family and as Minister of New Spynic, Elgin. In 1826 he obtained, through Lord Selkirk, the more lucrative ministry of Carsphairn, Kirkcudbrightshire, where he died in 1832. In 1818 he married at Knocknalling, Kirkcudbrightshire, Margaret Kennedy, daughter of David Kennedy of Knocknalling. Margaret, born in 1797, bore Thomas Cannan eight children of whom David Alexander — Edwin's father, born in 1820 — was the second son and fifth child. The family on both sides was of Scottish ancestry. Margaret Kennedy could boast an ancestor, Alexander of Stirling, killed at Culloden fighting for Prince Charles Edward. It was one of Alexander's daughters who moved south to Kirkcudbrightshire and married Robert Kennedy of Knocknalling. The Cannans had always been Covenanters, with one martyr (James) for an ancestor, and they piously cultivated the virtues of learning and thrift. While at Carsphairn, Thomas Cannan took in some pupil-boarders. He had the reputation of being a severe disciplinarian and a good preacher. He was a Liberal in his politics and the only minister in the district to approve of the Catholic Emancipation Bill in 1829. After his death Margaret Cannan, left with seven children (one had died in infancy) and an annual income of £100, moved to Kirkcudbright, settling in a house, the rent for which was paid by a Kennedy relative. The children were all sent to the Kirkcudbright Academy where David Alexander, at the age of twelve, won prizes in Latin and in 'accounts' (arithmetic).

[11] Anne Ashley, *William James Ashley*, p. 19.
[12] Cannan's other college tutor was E. Abbot.
[13] Notes by Edwin Cannan for a family history are in the Cannan family papers. Another source of information is Rita Cannan, 'In Memoriam; Maria Louisa Cannan, An Old Gallovidian (1819–1911)' in the *Gallovidian*, Summer 1912.

In 1842 the family moved again, to a small house near the London Road Station in Manchester, where David Alexander found employment in the office of the McConnel and Kennedy Mill, owned by one of Margaret Cannan's uncles — John Kennedy. David's poor health forced him to leave Manchester, and during the early 1850s, probably with some help from the Kennedys, he moved to London. For a time he worked with Edwin Chadwick for the General Board of Health and although plans for his employment by the board never materialized, they remained close friends over the years.[14] Eventually David became the London representative of a Manchester hardware firm and in 1853 married Jane Dorothea Claude (born 1822) of Ambleside, who taught at a Sunday School in Manchester and was the friend of one of David's sisters.[15]

Following their marriage, David and Jane Dorothea Cannan left for Australia. David was to represent his firm and promote the sale of corrugated-iron huts, now in demand as a result of the Victoria gold rush. In 1854 Jane Dorothea's uncle, Charles Guillaume Claude, died in Chile leaving her some £9,000 or £10,000, which provided a comfortable source of income for the young couple independent of David Cannan's business skills.

Although the Australian venture was successful, the parent firm in Manchester collapsed. David Cannan, after winding up affairs for the Australian creditors, returned to England in 1857 with his wife, settling at first in Richmond near the home of Edwin Chadwick. It was at Richmond that their son Charles (named after his great-uncle Charles Claude) was born in 1858.[16]

The family seemed unusually susceptible to consumption. Thomas Cannan had died of it. It was also the cause of David's poor health, so that upon the family's return from Australia he did not seek new employment. By now Jane Dorothea's health too had begun to deteriorate, and in 1858 the family moved first to Bournemouth, and when she did not improve, to

---

[14] Another fellow worker of Chadwick some years earlier was Joseph Toynbee, Arnold Toynbee's father.
[15] May Wedderburn Cannan, *Grey Ghosts and Voices* (Kineton, 1976), p. 24.
[16] The Cannans had a daughter, born in Australia, who died in her infancy.

Madeira, where Edwin was born on 3 February 1861. His parents expected a girl whom they intended to name Rachel after Mrs Chadwick, but instead they named their son after Chadwick himself. Thirteen days later Jane Dorothea died.

David Cannan and his two young sons moved back to Bournemouth where they were joined by his older sister Agnes. He chose to live virtually as a pensioner, taking some interest in local-government business and acting as treasurer to the Scottish church of which he became an elder. In 1864 Agnes died and her place was taken by another sister, Margaret, who had previously tutored the granddaughter of John Kennedy, the mill owner, while the family was residing in Europe. Edwin grew up 'a sweet, endearing little fellow' whose early education seemed somewhat unpromising, marred as it was by his obstinate refusal to master the letter B. (Some years later he was to develop a similar aversion, when learning the multiplication table, to the number 7 and, refusing to say it, would always pass on to 8).[17]

On 6 August 1868 David Cannan remarried and his sister Margaret returned to Manchester to live with her mother. David's new wife, Eliza Matilda Hicks Weekes, kept a boys' school — Aschan House — to which the family now moved and in which Edwin was enrolled. Unlike Charles, who was of robust constitution, Edwin was a 'delicate' boy, 'too small to be regarded as of any account in games' and at pony riding unable to 'master the art of "rising in a trot" with a tendency to fall off rather frequently'.[18] The ever-present fear of his contracting tuberculosis resulted in a prolonged period of over-protectiveness. As a child he seemed much concerned with holding his own among his peers, although his only recollection of being bullied 'was once having my head mildly punched for being a "Radical" about the time of the 1868 elections.' The combination of the constant fear for his health, the loss of his mother and Aunt Agnes, and the over-protective Aunt Margaret, to which were added his colour blindness and tone deafness, serve to explain to some extent his later social shyness and a tendency towards introversion.

[17] Edwin Cannan, 'Pages from an Autobiography' in the *Clare Market Review*, vol 16, no. 1, 1935. The whereabouts of the original MS are unknown.
[18] Ibid.

By the end of 1869 David's second wife had died, and Aunt Margaret returned from Manchester to keep house for him and look after the children. In September 1870 Charles entered Clifton as a boarder, while Edwin remained in the care of his father and aunt. During the winter of 1875–6, as Edwin was nearing his fifteenth birthday, it was decided that he should join his brother at Clifton, but fears for his health being as strong as ever, the whole household moved to Bristol and Edwin was entered in January 1876 as a day boy. During the following year both brothers did well at school. Edwin came third in the Upper Third, second in the Lower Fourth, and top in the Upper Fourth, and Charles won a scholarship to Corpus Christi College, Oxford. Upon leaving Clifton, Charles, accompanied by his friend J. E. King went with David Cannan on a tour of West Ireland, where on 8 August 1877 David died in Limerick. Charles went off to Oxford and took charge of the family's financial affairs, while Edwin was left in the care of his aunt. Thus the Cannan brothers, despite having come from a line of 'poor relations' ended up with a private income which they managed, at least to some extent, from a relatively early age.

Clifton was then dominated by the character and ideals of its headmaster, John Percival, who in December 1880 became the Master of Trinity College, Oxford. Percival was a faithful disciple of Dr Arnold, and Clifton at the time was described as a colony of Rugby.[19] The spirit of the school was dominated by Liberalism and Broad Church. Percival aimed at producing young Christian gentlemen inculcated with a strong sense of duty. In a sermon given at Trinity College, Oxford, he divided undergraduates into two classes:

(1) the Whites, hard working scholars, steady conscientious men (preferably teetotallers and non-smokers), destined to be clergymen, schoolmasters, writers on Social Reform, philanthropic manufacturers of great municipal activity, or Radical Members of Parliament; (2) the Blacks, hunting men, betting men, frequenters of billiard-rooms, taverns and houses of ill fame— 'the sporting, the low toned, the lewd, the cynical'.[20]

[19] O. F. Christie, *Clifton School Days 1879–1885* (London, 1930), p. 106; see also id. *A History of Clifton College 1860–1934* (Bristol, 1935); and Q [A. T. Quiller-Couch], *Memoirs and Opinions, An Unfinished Autobiography* (Cambridge, 1944).
[20] Christie, *Clifton School Days*, pp. 23–4.

At Clifton Edwin was undoubtedly a 'white' when it came to his politics, his aversion to tobacco, and his later interest in social and municipal activity. He did quite well at Clifton, but failing to obtain a scholarship in the Exeter–Trinity group,[21] he entered Balliol on 29 January 1881 as a commoner. His Aunt Margaret moved with him to Oxford, into a flat at 24 St. Giles so that, although a public-school man, Edwin Cannan lived apart from university or college life.

In 1891, after Margaret's death, Edwin for a while took in his cousin, Gilbert Cannan, who left a somewhat unkind but technically accurate description of the life at 24 St. Giles in his book, *Little Brother*,[22] in which Edwin is used as the model for the character of George Laurie, a Cambridge specialist on Greek coins. George Laurie was described as living with his aunt in a three-roomed flat: two rooms were bedrooms and the third 'a large room looking out on the gloomy churchyard, which served as dining room, living room, and study. This was lined with books of all ages and languages.' George (Edwin) was described as fanatically temperate: 'He carried *not* doing things to a horrible extreme', a person to whom fiction was 'light-minded and improper' and poetry 'madness'. Although this seems rather harsh towards Cannan (who was colour blind and tone deaf), it is true that in his later years he took no interest in art, music, or the theatre.[23]

According to Gilbert Cannan, Aunt Margaret

> never let it occur to him [George Edwin] that there might be any other way of living, and fed him that cardinal Laurie [Cannan] quality which makes us [Cannans] all think everybody else is wrong, and every other way than our own of doing things fantastic. He lived in the same lodgings for twenty years, rarely went abroad, dined out perhaps twice a term, spent about a third of his income, and regarded all knowledge not connected with Greek coins [in Cannan's case, economics] as useless.[24]

As an undergraduate Edwin adopted a simple daily routine which would remain basically unchanged for the rest of his life — work in the morning, a walk in the afternoon (or in later

---

[21] His examination papers are in the Cannan notebooks, Balliol College Library.
[22] Gilbert Cannan, *Little Brother* (London, 1912), mainly pp. 69–95. See also Diana Farr, *Gilbert Cannan, A Georgian Prodigy* (London, 1978). Mrs Farr is Charles Cannan's granddaughter.
[23] Interview with Lord Robert Hall, 13 Mar. 1979.
[24] Gilbert Cannan, *Little Brother*, pp. 69–70.

years, cycling, driving, or gardening), and in the evening 'his aunt used to sit in the great chair . . . while he worked until ten o'clock, when they had a little improving conversation before she retired to bed'.[25]

In his room George (Edwin) kept some books, on subjects other than economics, mostly devotional 'but among them were the poems of Tennyson and Henry Taylor and Aubrey de Vere, and a few works of fiction, including Hawley Smart and George Eliot. There was a set of Jane Austen's novels, but the pages had never been cut.'[26] It was roughly during that period that Edwin developed the habit of spending his afternoon walks, examining the accuracy of the positions of milestones and the location and origins of various local landmarks. He became a self-proclaimed expert on the paths and byways of the country around Oxford.[27]

In 1882 Edwin obtained a Second in Classical Moderations and he probably intended to read for an Honours degree. However, during the spring of 1883 his health seriously deteriorated[28] and, instead, he took a Pass degree, following which he left with Aunt Margaret for a trip around the world passing through the Cape, New Zealand, and Cape Horn.[29] Upon their return they moved back into 24 St. Giles where Edwin began work on his essay on the Duke of Saint-Simon for the Lothian Prize.

The circumstances of Edwin Cannan's intellectual development are clearly unique and his career retained a certain singularity which is traceable to these circumstances. His development may be contrasted with that of his older brother, Charles, who, after becoming Fellow and Dean of Trinity College (he was brought there from Corpus Christi by Percival), was elected Secretary of the University Press.[30] Or it

---

[25] Ibid., p. 79.
[26] Ibid., p. 76.
[27] Ibid., pp. 82–3; see Cannan's letter in the *Oxford Magazine*, 7 Dec. 1904.
[28] His notebooks in Balliol College Library include a table of daily activities during the Easter and Trinity terms of 1883, in which the period 13 May—12 June is entered solely as 'ill'.
[29] From the trip one letter to his brother (addressed as 'Dear Don') dated 18 Feb. 1884 has survived in the family papers.
[30] Some of the differences between the two brothers are brought out by May Wedderburn Cannan (Charles's daughter) in *Grey Ghosts and Voices*.

may be compared with that of two contemporaries from a relatively similar social background with an interest in social and economic problems—Michael Ernest Sadler and Hubert Llewellyn Smith.

Michael Ernest Sadler, born on 3 July 1861 in Barnsley in the West Riding, was the son and grandson of general practitioners.[31] The family traces its ancestry to the fourteenth century, counting among its members some men of prominence and including in the family's history a baronetcy which survived until 1706. According to M. E. Sadler's son, Michael Sadleir, the absence of socially eminent family members after the early eighteenth century is probably due to a lack of ambition combined with little talent for business and a tendency to become spenders rather than savers.

One exception was Michael Thomas Sadler (1780–1835), Fellow of the Royal Society, MP for Newark and Aldborough, and a pioneering reformer of conditions of labour. On his advice his nephew and namesake Michael Thomas Sadler (1801–72) — Michael Ernest's grandfather — established a medical practice in Barnsley in 1832. In 1835 his wife died and the young widower, left with three children, immersed himself in campaigning, in the style of Edwin Chadwick, for local improvements in public sanitation. Another issue which at the time lay heavily on his mind was religious dogma, concerning which he had growing doubts. These doubts were passed on to his eldest son—a third Michael Thomas Sadler (the father of M. E. Sadler)—who as a result, declared himself unfit to take Holy Orders and left instead for London to study medicine at the University.

Young Michael Thomas did well in his studies and for a time it seemed as though he was heading towards a successful medical career in London. But his father's practice in Barnsley was disintegrating and the loyal son returned home as a junior partner. The return to Barnsley meant the sacrifice of a promising career with its accompanying social advancement; nevertheless, the young man retained his vision of a way of life different from that of a provincial general practitioner which he passed on to his children. Through considerable financial

---

[31] Michael Sadleir, *Michael Ernest Sadler; A Memoir by his Son* (London, 1949).

sacrifice he obtained for them a better chance of realizing that ambition.

In 1860 he married Annie Eliza Adams who came from a strict Methodist Lincolnshire farming family. Thus religion remained a central factor in the Sadler household, the children being brought up in a spirit of religious and material severity with the aid of Michael Thomas's only sister, Aunt Lizzie, a convert to Roman Catholicism.

At the age of ten, Michael Ernest was sent off to school, first to North Hill House in Winchester and then, in the autumn of 1875, to Rugby. His schooling constituted a major financial strain on his father who was still struggling to rebuild a ruined practice. With an expense of no less than £120 per annum,[32] to obtain scholarships was financially necessary as well as a moral duty, in the light of the boy's Wesleyan upbringing.

Scholarships did not come without effort. Michael Ernest's son summed up his father's scholarly limitations by stating that 'his talents were not those of an "accurate scholar". The present, with its ever changing colour and atmosphere, was too vividly a delight to him to permit a pursuit of learning for learning's sake. He never lost the eager excited interest in some new idealism.'[33]

Michael Ernest evidently enjoyed Rugby and, having been away from home from an early age, did not find Rugby traditions objectionable. Upon leaving school he defended fagging on the grounds that 'none of fag's duties are debasing, and none arduous. Their very multiplicity warns a boy what unnecessary trouble he may give his own servants by-and-by by exacting too frequent attentions; and, above all, most fags learn that it is pleasanter to serve a master who says "Thank you" than a master who does not.'[34] He himself joined wholeheartedly in the spirit of the school. In the sixth form he became house- and form-master, and he contributed enthusiastically to a short-lived school magazine. Not being robust, he

---

[32] Pascoe, *Where Shall I Educate My Son?*, p. 6. At Rugby nine scholarships were up for competition anually, worth between £80 and £20. The sum of £120 did not include travel expenses and pocket money.

[33] Sadleir, *M. E. Sadler*, p. 24.

[34] M. E. Sadler, 'Rugby School—The School Life' in Charles Eyre Pascoe, *Everyday Life in Our Public Schools* (London, 1881).

was not very active in games although he developed the habit of walking, which was to remain with him as a favourite form of leisure.

Vacations were spent at home in Barnsley where Sadler became acquainted with university extension work through the lectures of R. G. Moulton whom Sadler described in later years[35] as 'a gardener bringing water to a thirsty garden. His pupils were but a handful. But he opened windows in their minds. He made them love poetry more. He shared their love of music. He showed them new standards of scholarship. He made an isolated group of booklovers feel companionship with groups elsewhere.' This model of Extension teaching would remain with Sadler in later years when, as the Oxford Extension's secretary, he insisted on the importance of the Extension's reaching small towns as well as the great industrial centres.

In 1880 hard work won Sadler a Classical Scholarship at Trinity College, Oxford. The scholarship, and a number of exhibitions he won at Rugby, brought his annual income to £170, which was supplemented by his father by another £30 per annum, a sum which allowed him a modest lifestyle with few luxuries, provided that he did not entertain much or indulge in expensive forms of recreation.[36] His relative poverty 'imposed quietness', while 'the absolute necessity of a good degree compelled hard work.'[37] Nevertheless, he was soon drawn into a number of political activities which 'distracted' him, and although he obtained a First Class it was secured 'by no more than a narrow margin'.[38]

Compared with Ashley, Sadler, at the outset of his university education, suffered less from social isolation. As might have been expected, upon coming up he joined the Oxford Old

[35] Introduction by M. E. Sadler to W. Fiddian-Moulton, *Richard Green Moulton; A Memoir* (London, 1926), p. 8.

[36] Cf. J. G. Lockhart, *Cosmo Gordon Lang* (London 1949), p. 31, in which Lang (Balliol 1882) is quoted as writing that 'in spite of all sorts of social distractions I like to think that I never spent more than £200 a year and that I left without a penny of debt.' See also Anthony Hope, *Memories and Notes* (London, 1927), p. 57, and Sir Charles Mallet, *Anthony Hope and his Books* (London, 1935), p. 38.

[37] Sadleir, *M. E. Sadler*, p. 29.

[38] The view taken by L. L. Price, (a Trinity undergraduate, one year Sadler's junior) in 'Trinity College, Oxford, 1881–1885', unpublished MS, Trinity College, Oxford.

Rugbeians as well as various political debating societies including the Union. It was Price's recollection that Sadler

> brought from Rugby assured distinction as a speaker, and our Head, Dr. Percival, I believe, went to hear his first triumph at the Union. His progress was easy and unopposed to the Presidential chair of that Society and certainly he had a rich gift of graceful eloquence which could be impassioned. At the time we seriously conceived the forecast that going into politics he would rise to be eventually Prime Minister.[39]

At that time the Union was politically under the virtual control of the Tories and socially dominated by a small number of colleges, foremost amongst which was Balliol.[40] Thus Sadler's swift rise to its presidency was no mean feat. By Michaelmas 1881 he had already been elected sub-treasurer and his election to the presidency came in Michaelmas 1882, after which he remained a member of the Committee till Michaelmas 1884.[41] He first spoke at the Union a short while after entering Trinity, in favour of B. R. Wise's motion 'That the first duty of the present Government is to redress the grievances of Irishmen by some large measures of conciliation and reform'. (The motion was lost.) His own first motion, moved on 10 March 1881, was 'That in the opinion of this House the Higher Education of Women will conduce to the well being of the country'. It was won by a majority of fifteen. All through his Union career Sadler defended consistently, although with rare success, the Liberal Government and its policies. In this he joined forces with a small group of Liberals within the Union which included L. T. Hobhouse, W. Hudson-Shaw, Oliver Elton, A. H. D. Acland, D. J. Medley, and from 1884 H. Ll. Smith. It was Price's observation that Sadler 'associated naturally with leading intellectual men of other Colleges, especially of Balliol, and with those politically minded.'

Yet, despite appearances, Sadler was not known for his social grace. According to his son, his 'eager response to personal intercourse went [with] a blend of shyness and preoccu-

---

[39] Price, loc. cit.
[40] Charles E. Mallet, *A History of the University of Oxford*, vol. 3 (New York and London, 1968), pp. 458–9.
[41] *Proceedings of the Oxford Union Society, Michaelmas 1870–Easter 1884* and *Proceedings 1884–1890* (Oxford, 1891).

pation with whatsoever problem or speculation happened to fill his mind at the time which rendered him at once ill at ease and remote in general mixed company.'[42] Furthermore, at times his manner was distinctly unpleasant. In one instance, after taking a leading part in the foundation of the Trinity College Gryphon Debating Society, at a later meeting he

> rather scornfully 'pictured' us in a patronising jest as moths 'fluttering round a candle' and getting our 'wings singed' . . . . Some of us were moved in return or retaliation to find then in his whole make-up a spice at least of rhetorical gloss or specious affectation . . . We were actually provoked by passing wrath into some suspicion of his effective customary use of ostentatious earnestness, however real and spontaneous that might be as a rule. Easily, impressively, forthcoming it also might be tainted on occasions by design. In our exasperation, which we thought justified, it might seem mingled with, if nor marred by some deceptive pretence.[43]

Although the anger of fellow members of the Gryphon Society was short-lived, Sadler's occasional rash statements and quick temper resulted in later years in some unnecessary quarrels, at least one of which was with W. A. S. Hewins, a fellow Oxford economist.[44]

Another trait Price detected in Sadler was his relative impressionability when brought into contact with strong personalities. He noticed that Sadler, having been privately coached by R. Macan for Greats, altered the M in his signature to the likeness of the form used by Macan.[45] By inference it may be argued that at least his early career reflects the strong influence of men such as A. H. D. Acland or Arnold Toynbee, who were to a considerable extent the political and ideological mentors of the circle of earnest young men to which Sadler belonged.

A minority in the Union, the University Liberals, whether undergraduates or young dons, gathered to discuss liberal politics and social ideas in the Palmerston Club and in the younger Russell Club. Founded on 1 May 1877, the

---

[42] Sadleir, *M. E. Sadler*, p. 28.
[43] Price, loc. cit.
[44] Sheffield University Library, Hewins papers, 42/154–219. The papers consist of Hewins's minutes of a meeting with Sadler and the draft of a letter to Sadler following accusations by Sadler of Hewins's mismanagement of a meeting at Keble Hall during the 1889 Extension's summer meeting.
[45] Price, loc. cit. The M in question was written M.

Palmerston Club aimed at 'the consolidation of the Liberal Party in the University of Oxford'.[46] It consisted of thirty-five undergraduates as well as a number of honorary members who were either old members who had graduated or specially elected members of the University. When Sadler joined the Club in November 1881, its honorary members included T. H. Green, Arnold Toynbee, T. C. Snow, Sidney Ball, and A. H. D. Acland, all of whom were dons and active supporters of the Liberal Party. It was at a meeting of the Club that Sadler first heard Toynbee lecture on reform. Toynbee stated his belief in the value of state intervention in the form of factory legislation based on T. H. Green's concept of the state, as opposed to the standard doctrine of *laissez-faire*, and Sadler was gratified to hear his great-great-uncle Michael Thomas Sadler mentioned as one of the pioneers of this form of state action.[47] It was Toynbee's influence that clinched Sadler's conversion to the brand of social and economic reform advocated by practical-minded Oxford Idealists. Like many of his contemporaries committed to this type of reform, Sadler did not seek its philosophical justification — indeed few of those who followed the example of T. H. Green were much concerned with the finer points of his philosophy. Most, if not all, of them were, to begin with, advocates of Radical Liberalism and it was mainly through personal contact with men such as T. H. Green, Arnold Toynbee, Sidney Ball, A. H. D. Acland, A. Sidgwick, and others that they became involved in particular reform schemes,[48] adopting and developing their ideological reasoning.

How such influence was exerted is illustrated by a small group, half of whom were Balliol undergraduates and the rest 'kindred spirits from the outside', who gathered for informal

---

[46] Rules and lists of members of the Palmerston Club are in the Bodleian Library, Oxford. C.A. Oxon 4°600, b,146, 8°1127.
[47] Sadleir, *M. E. Sadler*, p. 31.
[48] For T. H. Green's personal influence see Lewis R. Farnell, *An Oxonian Looks Back* (London, 1934), p. 44; Walter Sichel, *The Sands of Time* (London, 1923), p. 126; the Revd. P. A. Wright-Henderson, *Glasgow and Balliol and Other Essays* (Oxford, 1926), pp. 44–5; Arthur J. Ashton, *As I Went my Way* (London, 1924), pp. 60–2, in which Ashton summed up Green's influence by stating that 'to be a good man was to live in the spirit in which Mr. Green lived. That was all, but it was everything'; James Bryce, *Studies in Contemporary Biography* (London, 1903); and L. A. Selby-Bigge, 'Practical Oxford', in the *Contemporary Review*, May 1894.

discussions at A. H. D. Acland's home in North Oxford.⁴⁹ Acland was at the time a Student and Steward of Christ Church (1879–83), from 1882 the Senior Bursar of Balliol, the Secretary of the Oxford Extension, and an active promoter of co-operative education. The dozen or so young Liberals who collected around him, known as the Inner Circle or the Inner Ring, and to outsiders as the Upper Suckles, went from the discussion of various social issues into active participation in the various schemes in which Acland had involved himself. The membership of the circle included, besides Sadler, Cosmo Gordon Lang, J. A. Spender, Bolton King, W. Hudson-Shaw, C. E. Mallet, and L. T. Hobhouse. Their ties with Acland remained strong even after their graduation, and Sadler's career up to 1895 owes much to Acland's support.

A different outlet for liberal views as well as the flourishing interest in the arts was the *Oxford Magazine*, founded in January 1883. In its early days it was described, somewhat acidly, by Charles Oman as 'very "high brow", very liberal in politics, very "progressive" in academic matters, in short (as we used to say) "very Balliol".'⁵⁰ Its founders included Sadler himself, W. Hudson-Shaw, Anthony Hope Hawkins, and Cosmo Gordon Lang, all of whom were members of Acland's circle, as well as Oliver Elton of Corpus and D. S. MacColl of Lincoln. The Magazine's first editors were mostly young dons, including Charles Cannan, then at Trinity.

Membership of the various groups within a given type of 'set' usually overlapped, and young men actively interested in social and political issues tended to belong to more than one group or society. Many of the colleges had their own 'Aclands' with their own circles of earnest young men. One such don was A. Sidgwick at Corpus Christi College who had been a master at Rugby and became an Oxford don in 1879, where he kept in touch with some of his Rugby pupils, including Sadler. A photograph taken in 1886,⁵¹ of the Corpus Pelican Essay Club,

---

⁴⁹ Sadleir, *M. E. Sadler*, p. 68; Hope, *Memories and Notes*, p. 73. Mallet, *Anthony Hope and His Books*, p. 31, note by Sir Hugh Orange in the Bodleian Library MS Eng. Misc., c. 552.
⁵⁰ Charles Oman, *Memories of Victorian Oxford* (London, 1941), p. 41.
⁵¹ The photograph as well as the family papers are in the possession of Dr Stephen Llewellyn Smith, the youngest son of Hubert Llewellyn Smith.

shows him in a group including L. T. Hobhouse, Oliver Elton, and H. Ll. Smith, who in that year took a First in Mathematics and won the Cobden Prize.

Hubert Llewellyn Smith's ancestors had been mostly yeomen or small tradesmen, and since the seventeenth century, Quakers on both sides.[52] His paternal grandfather, John Clare Smith, kept a small grocer's shop in the Old Market of Bristol, with his family living in the apartment above it. During the early part of the nineteenth century, wishing to expand his business, he established contacts with farms in the district of Mendip which was then regarded as remote countryside. Success led to the purchase of a farm in the neighbourhood of Woodborough which supplied the Bristol shop with produce while providing the family with a holiday resort.

John Clare Smith had nine children, five of whom survived infancy. The youngest but one — Samuel Wyatt Smith — gradually took over the running of the family business and eventually inherited it upon his father's death in 1853. He married Louisa, daughter of James Scholefield of Kingsholm, Gloucester, and entered into partnership with her brother in a wholesale tea business. Their success led to the sale of the grocery business and the family moved to the suburb of Cotham where on 17 April 1864, Hubert Llewellyn Smith was born. Although Samuel Wyatt was not as active as his father in local Quaker affairs he chose to bring up his family within the Quaker community, and although the family moved again in 1867 into a larger house, it remained in a neighbourhood of well-to-do Quakers.

Hubert was Samuel Wyatt's youngest child. He had two older brothers—Clare and Arthur (who was an invalid)—and a sister Louey to whom Hubert was very close. In September 1875 the eldest son, Clare, was sent to Clifton, but he stayed only till July 1876[53] and no other son was sent here. It seems that despite Samuel Wyatt's relative success in business, after his death the family could not afford the expense of sending all the sons to Clifton. Instead Hubert was sent to Bristol Gram-

---

[52] Ll. Smith family papers, a fragment on family history by H. Ll. Smith.
[53] F. Borwick (ed.), *Clifton College Annals and Register 1862–1912* (Bristol, 1912) and information provided by Dr Stephen Ll. Smith.

mar School, where tuition for a day boy was not more than £12 per annum.

At school Hubert did exceptionally well. He was the last head boy under John William Caldicott's headmastership.[54] Caldicott was an autocratic teacher and a strong disciplinarian. In politics he was a Radical with 'an acute eye for practical reform',[55] and his political views may well have influenced young Hubert. The school's curriculum emphasized classics and mathematics[56] in both of which Hubert excelled, winning an impressive number of prizes and certificates annually. On the other hand 'the work done in History brought little risk of being biased by contemporary politics, for it stopped at the Wars of the Roses.'[57] Thus it was not until he came up to Oxford that Hubert encountered the use of the historical approach in the study of current issues. School examinations provided his first encounter with J. E. Thorold Rogers who, when Hubert was in his final year, examined for the school in divinity, classics, and English, subjects in all of which Hubert was awarded certificates.[58] In addition, in 1883 he came third in the Public Schools' Examination of the Royal Geographical Society, for which he was awarded a gold medal, with honourable mention for physical geography.

Hubert Llewellyn Smith entered Corpus Christi College as a Scholar on 19 October 1883 — the same year as L. T. Hobhouse. By 1886 he had obtained a double First in Mathematics, but having as an undergraduate developed an interest in social and economic issues, upon graduation he relegated mathematics to a position of secondary interest, to be used as a tool rather than as a field of enquiry. Upon entering the University, he was quick to join the Oxford Union and the Corpus Debating Society. At the Union he spoke for the first time on 31 January 1884 against H. D. Leigh's motion 'That, in the opinion of this House, the antagonism of present parties is prejudicial to Social Reform'. He was heard fairly regularly

---

[54] C. P. Hill, *The History of Bristol Grammar School* (London, 1951), p. 129.
[55] Ibid., p. 85.
[56] Ibid., p. 129.
[57] Ibid., p. 88.
[58] Ll. Smith family papers, newspaper cuttings. When in the sixth form Ll. Smith was awarded two prizes and seven certificates in one year.

afterwards, although not too frequently, in defence of the Liberal Government and its policies and later against the Tory Government. In 1887 for two terms (Lent and Easter) he was elected a member of the Union's Committee and it was during 1887 that he moved his only two motions — in favour of free education and 'That, in view of the wide-spread evils caused by Drink, the prevalence among all classes of the practice of Total Abstinence is to be heartily desired.'[59]

Llewellyn Smith was slightly more active in the Corpus Debating Society,[60] which was open to all members of college, serving on its Committee in the Lent Term of 1885 and as its president in the Michaelmas Term of the same year. It was a much lighter affair than the Oxford Union, much of its time being spent on carrying points of procedure to absurd and often hilarious extremes. Ll. Smith was at one time ruled out of order for 'allowing his eyes to wander over the books in the adjacent shelves' instead of 'attending to the matter before the House'. (The ruling was appealed against, put to the vote, and overturned.) When the Society did get round to actual debates the subjects raised were similar to those raised in the Union.

The position taken by L. T. Hobhouse and H. Ll. Smith in these debates reflects the mainstream of young Oxford Liberalism. Oxford Liberals were divided over the Home Rule controversy. In 1888 many of the older Liberal dons such as Benjamin Jowett, Henry Nettleship, W. A. Spooner, and A. V. Dicey joined the Unionist League. On the other hand, most of the younger Liberals supported Gladstone,[61] to whom a letter was sent in 1887 signed by men such as Thorold Rogers, E. Cannan, L. R. Phelps, and W. J. Ashley, stating their 'earnest conviction of the justice and expediency of the Irish policy you have adopted and promoted: a policy whose aim is to satisfy the natural and unmistakably expressed desire of the Irish people for a separate and subordinate Parliament . . . to ensure the safety and increase the strength of the Empire.' Following the

---

[59] *Proceedings Michaelmas 1884–Easter 1890*. The first motion was lost by twenty-three votes, the second by the president's casting vote.
[60] Corpus Christi College, *Minutes of the Proceedings of the C.C.C. Debating Society Commencing November 1873*.
[61] Bodleian Library, G.A.Oxon 4°600; b.146, papers of the Oxford University Home Rule League and of the Union League.

letter, the Oxford University Home Rule League was founded in support of a form of Irish self-government and in opposition to Coercion Acts. Its vice-president was A. H. D. Acland, its assistant secretaries included Sadler, T. C. Snow, and L. T. Hobbouse. W. A. S. Hewins was college secretary for Pembroke, and members included L. L. Price, Sidney Ball, O. M. Edwards, L. R. Phelps, Edwin Cannan, and W. J. Ashley. Some of the young Liberals' support of Gladstone's Irish policy went back to his land reforms. However, support for Home Rule did not automatically lead to total opposition to Chamberlain's brand of Radicalism, and on 12 February 1887 Hobhouse, with the support of H. Ll. Smith, moved unsuccessfully in the Corpus Debating Society 'That apart from the question of Home Rule, this House approves of the Radical Programme'. It is also evident that Chamberlain's Radicalism was not as yet closely identified with imperialism since, on 3 May 1884, H. Ll. Smith, with the support of Hobhouse, moved, also unsuccessfully, 'That this House strongly condemns the line of foreign policy usually known as Imperialism'.

A more exclusive society to which H. Ll. Smith belonged was the Corpus Pelican Essay Club, whose membership was restricted to fifteen.[62] The Club met on alternate Fridays to hear and discuss a paper given by one of its members. H. Ll. Smith failed to get elected to the Club on his first attempt on 6 February 1884 (when Hobhouse was elected), but was elected more than a year later, on 6 November 1885, becoming, in 1886, first secretary and then president.

It was probably from the Pelican Club that he took the idea of starting a small economic club at Corpus called the Adam Smith.[63] The Club, started during May 1885 (before Ll. Smith was elected to the Pelican), was more a voluntary study group than a debating society. After deciding on a subject, its members would divide among themselves the relevant economists' works, and it was through his preparation for 'The function of Capital as an agent in production' that Ll. Smith

---

[62] Corpus Christi College, *The Pelican Essay Club Minute Book*.
[63] Ll. Smith family papers, H. Ll. Smith to his sister, 17 May 1885, the *Pelican Record*, vol. x, no. 4, Dec. 1910. Unfortunately the whereabouts of the Club's minute book are unknown.

became acquainted with criticisms of the wage-fund theory put forward by Thornton and Walker.

On the whole H. Ll. Smith seems to have been more successful than Sadler in adjusting to Oxford and its social life. He took to rowing and mixed socially with relative ease. With Hobhouse he belonged to the same set as the Hon. Charles James Stanley Howard, later to become the tenth Earl of Carlisle, at whose home he was to spend some vacations after obtaining his degree. According to his friend Hobhouse, Ll. Smith's only fault was a lack of confidence in his abilities, of which Hobhouse wrote to Ll. Smith's mother, 'he takes a ridiculously low estimate'.[64]

Ll. Smith's interest in various social and political issues was not confined to participation in debates. His letters home mention attending a university meeting on the 'Housing of the Poor' addressed by Octavia Hill,[65] and an active interest in the University East End Settlements — Toynbee Hall and Oxford House in Bethnal Green.

After delivering two lectures on Henry George's *Progress and Poverty* in London to a restless and vociferous audience, Toynbee collapsed. On 9 March 1883 he died at his mother-in-law's home in Wimbledon. In the eyes of many of his friends he had died a martyr to the cause, and on 15 April 1883 they convened at Balliol to consider a suitable memorial which would continue his work of converting England's working classes to gradual and peaceful material and moral progress, with the help and guidance of England's middle class.[66] At the meeting it was decided that money should be collected to finance a series of lectures, at Oxford and elsewhere, on economic and social subjects, to be named the Toynbee Lectures. It was intended that the lecturers employed would be of 'ability and practical experience, who sympathise with the spirit of Mr. Toynbee's work . . . there is reason to hope that these lectures may exert a lasting influence and tend to promote zeal for the study of social questions, as well as union between various

---

[64] Ll. Smith family papers, L. T. Hobhouse to Mrs Ll. Smith, 20 May 1887.
[65] Ll. Smith family papers, H. Ll. Smith to his mother, *c.* 1885.
[66] Phelps papers, A. L. Smith to L. R. Phelps, 12 Apr. 1883. The meeting was initiated by Alfred Milner and P. L. Gell, both close friends of Arnold Toynbee.

classes in the cause of social reform'.[67] A committee, including M. E. Sadler as one of its secretaries, was set up to administer the funds.

Not all Toynbee's friends were of the opinion that the lecture scheme was the most appropriate memorial. During the summer of 1883 an alternative scheme was put forward and soon adopted by a group who represented the growing interest at Oxford in new and direct forms of improving the living and working conditions of working men in general, and the residents of London's East End in particular. This interest was largely due to efforts of the Revd. Samuel A. Barnett, vicar of St. Jude's, Whitechapel, who since the mid-seventies had been recruiting young Oxford men to help with community work in the East End. The original group of recruits had included Toynbee, A. L. Smith, A. Sidgwick, L. R. Phelps, Henry Scott Holland, and Sidney Ball, and they in return, as young dons, kept the interest alive and supported Barnett's work.[68] Some, like Toynbee, resided for short periods in Whitechapel and occasionally lectured there. Others, like James Bonar, stayed in the East End for longer periods, helping in the day-to-day community work. And some, including L. R. Phelps and Sidney Ball, supported Barnett from Oxford in his East End work as well as in his efforts for church reform through the National Church Reform Union.

Generally speaking, these young dons advocated two spheres of action. Most of them belonged to various local branches of the Liberal Party and various societies campaigning for specific legislative measures, including the Oxford Reform Club, the Oxford Branch of the National League of Young Liberals, the Oxford Liberal Association (of which A. Sidgwick was president during the period 1886–1911), and at various times the Home Rule League, the Free Trade League, and *ad hoc* committees supporting issues such as the Licensing Bill (1908), Women's Suffrage,[69] etc. Greater emphasis was laid upon per-

[67] 'Memorial to the late Arnold Toynbee', *Oxford Magazine*, 9 May 1883.
[68] Henrietta Barnett, *Canon Barnett; His Life, Work and Friends* (London, 1918), vol. i, pp. 302–8.
[69] Bodleian Library, G.A. Oxon b.164, papers related to the activities of the Oxford Reform Club, the Free Trade League, Committees in support of Women's Suffrage, and the Licensing Bill. Bodleian Library, G.A. Oxon. 544, papers related to the activities of the Oxford Liberal Association.

sonal involvement in specific schemes and organizations such as T. H. Green's work in promoting local schools, Poor Law Guardianship in which Spooner, L. R. Phelps, A. L. Smith, and A. H. D. Acland were active, and attempts, mainly during the early eighties and nineties, to organize agricultural labourers first in the National Agricultural Labourers' Union and, after the success of the Dockers' Strike, in the Dock, Wharf, Riverside and General Workers' Union.[70] They encouraged promising young Oxford undergraduates to take an active part both in the local branches of Liberal activity and in special projects; in the early eighties no project was as popular as the East End Settlements.

On 25 May 1883 the Revd. S. A. Barnett addressed a meeting of the Palmerston Club, presided over by M. E. Sadler, and on the following Sunday he preached in Balliol Chapel.[71] On both occasions he dwelt on his usual theme of social reform and the personal contribution that might be made by Oxford men. But later the same year Barnett went beyond the promotion of the existing practice of temporary individual residence in the East End and developed the idea of a more centralized scheme on similar lines and on a larger scale. Having been told of a group of men at St. John's College, Cambridge, who were seeking to operate as a group in a manner different from the existing college missions, Barnett developed the idea of creating a centre in the East End which would provide residence for university men who wished to take part in local community work and facilities for community activity ranging from lectures and classes to meetings on local political issues.[72] This type of plan for community work received further amplification when, during October 1883, Andrew Mearns published *The Bitter Cry of Outcast London* which called for the establishment of district mission halls less sectarian in nature than the existing missions.

---

[70] Pamela Horn, 'Agricultural Trade Unionism in Oxfordshire', in J. P. D. Dunbabin (ed.), *Rural Discontent in Nineteenth Century Britain* (London, 1974). Report in the *Oxford Magazine*, 7 Feb. 1883, of a meeting of NALU, chaired by J. Percival and addressed by A. Sidgwick.
[71] *Oxford Magazine*, 23 and 30 May 1883.
[72] Henrietta Barnett, *Canon Barnett* i. 309.

Some of Toynbee's friends, including S. Ball and P. L. Gell, found the idea of a settlement of the type advocated by Barnett a more appropriate memorial to Toynbee than the lecture scheme, which Ball felt would fall 'miserably short in the way of performance'.[73] Gell and Barnett set out to draw up a detailed scheme for a settlement, hoping to persuade the memorial committee to adopt it instead of the lectureship scheme.[74] As it happened, they faced some strong opposition from within the committee and perhaps more importantly from Mrs Charlotte Toynbee.[75] Arnold Toynbee's widow was somewhat vague about why she thought the settlement scheme was a bit 'hazardous', but she clearly liked the lectureship scheme better and at least one member of the committee — Milner — thought that this was a good enough reason to support it.[76] There was also some feeling of resentment towards Barnett as expressed by Milner in a letter to Gell: 'As for Barnett, he is simply a professional grabber for the East End. Why the dickens should the thing be specially for the East End . . . any other of the towns that received Toynbee well and that he was fond of have more claim.'[77]

The issue was not confined to the Senior Common Rooms. In addition to the various political and debating societies and Acland's Inner Circle, during Michaelmas 1883[78] Sidney Ball started the Social Science Club which some years later he described as relatively sentimental but at the same time practical. His aim was 'not propagandism but knowledge of facts and actual difficulties. For the obstruction [to the progress towards socialism] in Oxford is not so much want of sympathy as of elementary knowledge.'[79] The Club was in fact a list of names of Oxford men interested in social questions who would be invited to meetings organized by Ball, usually to be addressed by a guest speaker.[80] It was a potential source of recruitment for organizing undergraduate support for the

[73] Gell family papers, S. Ball to P. L. Gell, 5 Nov. 1883.
[74] Ibid., S. Ball to S. A. Barnett, 10 Nov. 1883.
[75] Phelps papers, Mrs Toynbee to L. R. Phelps, 28 Nov. 1883.
[76] Gell family papers, A. Milner to P. L. Gell, n.d.
[77] Ibid.
[78] Notices of meetings in the *Oxford Magazine*, 24 Oct. and 7 Nov. 1883.
[79] LSE, Graham Wallas papers, S. Ball to Wallas, 18 Sept. c.1887.
[80] Herbert Samuel, *Memoirs* (London, 1945), p. 13.

settlement scheme as well as a meeting ground for young men who shared an interest in practical approaches to questions of social reform.

The feeling among the circles of Oxford men interested in social questions during that Michaelmas Term was expressed in the *Oxford Magazine* in O. M. Edwards's report on William Morris's address to the Russell Club on 'Democracy and Art':

> The question has been asked 'Is the new Oxford movement to be a socialistic one?' and if this be interpreted to mean 'Is the most living interest of Oxford now that in social questions?' the answer must be distinctly, 'Yes!'. Oxford has turned from playing at the Middle Ages in churches, or at a Re-Renaissance in cupboards; and a new faith, with Professor Green for its founder, Arnold Toynbee for its martyr, and various societies for its propaganda, is alive amongst us.[81]

The Toynbee Memorial Committee met on 17 November and decided to approach the subscribers to the Memorial for their views on the appropriate use of their money. The various possibilities listed included both the lectureship and the settlement schemes. After the committee meeting, another informal meeting was held in Sidney Ball's rooms in St. John's, organized by Ball, Acland, and Sidgwick, and attended by some of their young 'protégés,[82] to hear Barnett describe the details of the settlement scheme.

The settlement was envisaged as a non-sectarian centre for community work operated by young university men in temporary residence and supervised by a salaried warden. The ideals behind it were expressed in a manner closely resembling Toynbee's emotional appeal to the working classes in his 'Progress and Poverty' lectures:

> A university settlement will at any rate keep alive and consolidate the interest between a centre of education and centre of industry. . . . It will meet the sorrow and misery born of class division and indifference; it will bring classes into relation; it will lead them to know and learn of one another, and those to whom it is given will give. Settlers may look to ideals higher than that of self helped respectability — an ideal that stops not short till beauty, knowledge, and righteousness are nationalised, and every noble source of joy is opened to the people.[83]

[81] *Oxford Magazine*, 21 Nov. 1883.
[82] Lockhart, *Cosmo Gordon Lang* p. 39; *Oxford Magazine*, 21 Nov. 1883; S. A. Barnett, 'Settlements of University Men in Great Towns', in S. A. and H. Barnett, *Practicable Socialism, New Series* (London, 1915).
[83] *Oxford Magazine*, 21 Nov. 1883.

During the meeting it was agreed that an independent effort should be made to launch the settlement scheme. Rather than setting up a university committee, the work should be started by a college (Balliol) or by a small number of college committees. The young men present felt certain that the settlement was a practical solution to the urgent problem of the widening gap between the classes. In a letter to the *Oxford Magazine* Cosmo Lang argued that 'a set of university men, animated by practical zeal, could not fail . . . to hinder selfishness and revolutionary extremes.'[84]

During the rest of the Michaelmas Term Cosmo Lang and M. E. Sadler, elected for the purpose during the meeting in Sidney Ball's rooms, organized a number of meetings at which the settlement scheme was discussed.[85] Nevertheless, when the Memorial Committee met on 9 February 1884 it decided on the basis of the subscribers' recommendations to entrust the money to seven trustees who would use it to endow annual lectures in Oxford and elsewhere with the purpose of promoting 'the investigation and diffusion of true principles of Political and Social Economy'.[86] As for the settlements, the Committee felt that the plans 'as yet could not provide a sufficient nucleus' for the work envisaged.

Despite the Committee's decision, work in support of a settlement continued independently of the official Memorial. During February 1884 the scheme was given national publicity through the publication of an article by Barnett in the *Nineteenth Century*.[87] The final touch was added on the occasion of the memorial service to Arnold Toynbee held at Balliol Chapel on 10 March 1884, at which the Revd. S. A. Barnett delivered the sermon. The settlement was to be named Toynbee Hall,[88]

---

[84] Ibid. See also W. F. [Curtoys] 'University Settlements' in the *Oxford Magazine*, 28 Nov. 1883.

[85] e.g. in a meeting of the Social Science Club on 1 Dec. 1883 reported in the *Oxford Magazine*, 5 Dec. 1883.

[86] *Oxford Magazine*, 13 Feb. 1884. The trustees were A. Milner, the Earl of Dalhousie, H. S. Foxwell, H. Sidgwick, A. H. D. Acland, W. Markby, and R. Spence Watson.

[87] S. A. Barnett, 'University Settlements', reprinted in S. A. and H. Barnett, *Practicable Socialism* (London, 1894).

[88] Mrs H. Barnett, 'The Beginning of Toynbee Hall' in S. A. and H. Barnett, *Practicable Socialism, New Series*.

which would establish it in the minds of most Oxford men as the main popular memorial to Toynbee.

Support of the Hall was organized nominally by a General Committee of the University[89] which elected an Executive Committee. In fact the actual work of collecting funds for the building and then for the operation of the Hall, and of recruiting helpers and residents, was done by the college associations run by college secretaries. Members of the General and Executive Committees were mainly instrumental in lending support to the respective college associations and in addressing various meetings aimed at widening support for the project.[90] Amongst the Executive Committee were A. H. D. Acland, Sidney Ball, and L. R. Phelps. It was therefore to be expected that members of the various Liberal political clubs, the Social Science Club, and the various 'Inner Circles' would take an active part in promoting the Hall. The same names would reappear on the membership list of the Oxford Economic Society and later as the editors of, and contributors to, the *Economic Review*. In 1887 the Executive Committee included W. J. Ashley, M. E. Sadler, W. G. Smith, L. T. Hobhouse, and W. A. S. Hewins. Membership of the various college associations included H. Ll. Smith, W. J. H. Campion, H. W. Blunt, O. M. Edwards, and T. C. Snow.[91]

Toynbee Hall did not remain the only Oxford settlement in the East End. There were those who thought that it was too secular and that there was room for a similar settlement with a greater emphasis on religious work within a given parish, combined with educational and social work. Toynbee Hall had been mainly a Balliol project; Christ Church, Magdalen and Trinity already had urban missions. So a separate initiative was started, mainly at Keble and New College, aiming at the foundation of a settlement which would combine the functions of a college mission and Toynbee Hall. The result was Oxford House in Bethnal Green, which differed from Toynbee Hall only in the expectation that visiting and resident university

---

[89] Later in 1884 a Committee was started at Cambridge including J. R. Seeley, H. S. Foxwell, and W. Cunningham.

[90] Phelps papers, Cosmo Lang to L. R. Phelps, 27 Feb. and 25 Apr. 1884.

[91] Papers related to the Universities' Settlement in East London in the Bodleian Library, G. A. Lond. 8°527.

men would take an active part in 'conducting and assisting in services in mission rooms and elsewhere'.[92] Although there were differences of opinion between some of the supporters of the two projects concerning the advisability of introducing the 'denominational spirit' into a movement of social reform,[93] most of those who supported the one supported the other. Thus H. Ll. Smith saw no contradiction in being his college's secretary for the Toynbee Hall project and taking part in the entertainment of a group of working men brought to Oxford by Oxford House.[94]

By early 1883 Sadler had become one of the main figures of the Palmerston Club and in March 1883 he was elected its president. Shortly before that, on 9 February 1883, he had proposed, and succeeded in securing, the election of his fellow undergraduate L. L. Price to the Club. Price had already been an inactive member of the Union (as were Ashley and Cannan). During the term before his election to the Palmerston Club, he had witnessed 'the unchallenged rapid rise of Sadler to the Presidential Chair' of the Union.[95]

Langford Lovell Frederick Rice Price was born on 20 July 1862, the second son of the Revd. Aubrey Charles Price, MA, of Clapham Park, London. His family background, compared with that of contemporary Oxford men who became actively interested in economics, provides a curious blend of circumstances. He was not the first member of his family to go up to Oxford, nor was his the first generation of Prices at Oxford. His grandfather, Aubrey Charles Price—vicar of Chesterton in Oxfordshire—had been a Scholar at Winchester and had sent his three sons there: Aubrey Charles, George Frederick, and William, all of whom proceeded to New College, Oxford.[96] L. L. Price's father — Aubrey Charles Price, born in 1829 — entered Winchester as a Scholar in 1844. At New College he was a Fellow from 1849 till 1857. He was awarded his BA in

---

[92] Bodleian Library, G. A. Lond. 132, papers related to Oxford House. See also W. A. Spooner, 'Notes for Autobiography', MS New College Library, Oxford.
[93] Lockhart, *Cosmo Gordon Lang*, p. 40.
[94] Llewellyn Smith family papers, H. Ll. Smith to his sister, 17 May 1885 and 1 Feb. 1885.
[95] L. L. Price, 'Supplementary Memoirs', ch. V. MS in Oriel College, Oxford.
[96] J. B. Wainewright, *Winchester College 1830-1906; A Register* (Winchester, 1907), pp. 94, 101.

1853 and during the same year he took Holy Orders. During the period 1854-6 he was employed as Curate of St. George's, Bloomsbury, and it was during the same period that he met and married (on 8 October 1856) Camilla, daughter of Langford Lovell Hodge of Upper Seymour Street, Marylebone, former Member of the Assembly and Puisne Baron of the Exchequer of Antigua. She was described in her son's memoirs as 'literally a saint. Unquestionably she was an ideal Christian. Her piety was impeccable . . . Her temper was wonderfully forbearing.'[97]

Price's was a family of clergymen — his grandfather, his father, his father's brother George, who died while at New College in 1861 (as did the youngest brother, William, in 1858), and his mother's brother Henry. All belonged to the Church of England except Aubrey Charles who, as a Low Church Evangelical, had moved to the Free Church. Langford Lovell grew up in an atmosphere dominated by the issues of verbal inspiration from the Bible, sudden conversion, immediate redemption, justification by faith, sacrificial atonement, and eternal punishment. Aubrey Charles was a popular preacher and a dedicated Liberal. His son shared his political convictions and read the lessons in his church, but the relationship between the two was strained. Whereas he 'adored' and 'revered' his mother, his relationship with his father was by his own admission 'imperfect'. As Aubrey Charles grew old, especially after the death of his wife, he suffered progressively from a 'grave disorder weakening the brain' which led to the development of suicidal tendencies and to his death in 1897, at least to some extent, by his own hand. Home, which after his wife's death was kept by his two daughters Mary and Ethel, was not a happy place. The family had never been wealthy; when Aubrey Charles and Camilla married they had to borrow money for furnishing. Although at times his income was good he had a tendency to live beyond his regular means, thereby perpetuating a state of economic hardship.

The Price brothers—another Aubrey Charles, born in 1858, and the younger Langford Lovell — were educated first at Clapham Grammar School and then at Dulwich College where

---

[97] Price, 'Supplementary Memoirs'.

both became editors of the 'Alleynian'.[98] Aubrey Charles entered Dulwich in May 1871 as an Exhibitioner and left in 1876 for Pembroke College, Oxford, as a Scholar. Langford Lovell entered Dulwich in 1876 as a Scholar and later as an Exhibitioner, and in 1881 left for Trinity College, Oxford, as a Scholar. It was due to both brothers' success at winning scholarships and exhibitions that the course of their education was an uninterrupted one. Nevertheless money was an ever-present problem which, in L. L. Price's view, caused his older brother to become 'parsimonious to a fault'.[99]

At Dulwich, in addition to becoming editor of the school's magazine, L. L. Price became school captain in 1880. However, in spite of his success at school and his membership of various debating societies at Dulwich and Oxford, he was basically 'a rather shy man, who did not make friends very easily'.[100] He took part in college and university life, but did not become as well known within the University as Sadler and some of the other members of the Inner Circle.

Price entered Trinity College, Oxford, in 1881, having won an open Classical Scholarship in the Trinity–Exeter group— this after competing unsuccessfully for scholarships at Pembroke and Corpus Christi Colleges. As a Scholar he joined the small group of not much more than a dozen scholars at Trinity who enjoyed the privilege of a separate table in Hall and relatively easy and friendly intercourse with the college dons[101] and its Head, Dr Percival. He managed to obtain a 'satisfactory' First in Moderations and was among the first half-dozen in the Finals in Greats.

Price, according to his own account, had developed an early interest in economics. Every year he bought *Whitaker's Almanack*, and in retrospect, he was content to 'court the fancy that that persistent habit betokened an enduring as well as an original fondness for statistics'.[102] He was one of the very few of his contemporary Oxford economists to have been trained by

[98] T. L. Ormiston, *Dulwich College Register 1619–1926* (London, 1927), pp. 104, 144.
[99] Price, 'Supplementary Memoirs'.
[100] W. D. R[oss], 'L. L. F. R. Price' in the *Oxford Magazine*, 27 Apr. 1950.
[101] Price, 'Trinity College, Oxford 1881–1885'.
[102] L. L. Price, 'Memoirs and Notes on British Economists 1881–1947', MSS in the Royal Statistical Society, London, and the Brotherton Library, Leeds.

Alfred Marshall during the latter's short term at Balliol. In his memoirs Price described Marshall's lectures as being

> somewhat discursive, based, so far as they were based at all, on notes, and not embodied in any formal written shape, and there were frequent, apparently extempore, digressions, seemingly prompt at the moment. But the discourses (or observations) were vividly alive and wonderfully instructive. One went away each time with something stimulating to think over. It might indeed puzzle or seem hard, but it was hard grit.[103]

Marshall was impressed by Price's ability and for some years considered him the 'ablest of the pupils he had to do with'.[104] Upon his election to the Cambridge chair, Marshall remained in touch with Price and took an active interest in his career, a privilege no other contemporary Oxford economist enjoyed.

After obtaining a First in 1885, Price spent the summer campaigning for the election to Parliament of Henry Mather Jackson in Monmouthshire.[105] Following the elections (and Jackson's failure) he returned to Oxford and was soon asked by Sadler to join the Extension as a replacement lecturer on trade unionism at Ashton under Lyne.[106] About the same time he was composing his essay for the Cobden Prize Essay competition of 1886, in which he came second (*proxime accessit*) to H. Ll Smith.[107] Despite the precarious income offered by the Extension work, Price preferred it to private tutoring or school teaching. According to his own account, he turned down two offers of private tutoring for aristocratic families and an offer by Percival of an assistant-mastership at Rugby. In 1888 his income was finally secured when he was elected Treasurer at Oriel College.

Following the foundation of Toynbee Hall and Oxford House there was a noticeable increase in the interest of Oxford undergraduates and dons in social issues. One result was that Sidney Ball found it necessary to bring in help in organizing the meetings of the Social Science Club. For the purpose he chose a young Pembroke undergraduate—W. A. S. Hewins—

---

[103] Ibid.
[104] Ibid. According to Price, Marshall had written thus to Percival in 1888.
[105] L. L. Price, 'Miscellaneous Reminiscences', MS in Oriel College, Oxford, ch. 2.
[106] Ibid.
[107] Price, 'Trinity College, Oxford 1881–1885'. Price's brother, on the other hand, upon obtaining his Oxford degree, became a schoolmaster.

who for a time was to bear the title of Secretary of the Social Science Club.

William Albert Samuel Hewins, born on 11 May 1856, was the second child and first son of Samuel Hewins (1833–99), an ironmonger of Bushbury, Staffs., and Caroline, née Green, of Bampton, Oxfordshire. Albert was one of six children, three sons and three daughters, and the Hewins household, not uncommonly, combined material austerity with a strict religious upbringing. In 1886 he wrote to his parents from Oxford:

> It is pleasant to think that 'the life is more than the meat'. By the force of circumstances, we have been compelled to think a great deal about the 'meat' which is sad. The 'life' must be our chief concern, it is grand to think noble and beautiful thoughts, to look with a clear eye into God's universe, even though we die of starvation. This is not sentimentalism but eternal truth.[108]

In his autobiography he attributed his first interest in economics to the material difficulties he witnessed at home:

> the depression of trade in the late seventies and early eighties . . . involved great hardships and I wanted to know the reason. From that time until I went to Oxford I read many economic books but they did not help me. I disliked their theoretical outlook, their materialism leavened with sentiment and their remoteness from real events. . . . I wished to make life worth living for all those people troubled with great anxieties owing to the breakdown of the industrial machine; to bring about an end great enough to give them dignity and a meaning.[109]

The search for the right combination of viable means leading to a more moral as well as a materially more comfortable future of the community as a whole was the focus of much of Hewins's intellectual development. He found inspiration in the works of Charles Kingsley, Ruskin, and Carlyle and through them developed an affinity towards Christian Socialism. But their work, with its clear concept of what was wrong with the present state of society and its vision of what society should be like, did not provide, to Hewins's mind, a clear exposition of the means for transforming society. So that whereas as a young man he felt fairly confident that he knew what the desirable ends of progress were, he was much perturbed by the relative uncertainty as to the means.

Albert Hewins was educated at Wolverhampton Grammar

---

[108] Hewins papers 16/8. W. A. S. Hewins to his parents, 17 Oct. 1886.
[109] W. A. S. Hewins, *The Apologia of an Imperialist* (London, 1929), pp. 14–15.

School. During his final year he was school captain and won prizes in classics and in mathematics. His report card for Michaelmas 1883 ranges from 'had done his best . . .Good Progress' in mathematics to 'Excellent work' in classics.[110] The Hatherton Scholarship to Pembroke College, Oxford made the jump in fees from £4.10s.0d. per annum[111] to the cost of an Oxford education possible. Nevertheless it did not put an end to financial concern. Upon coming up he purchased the cheapest furniture he could find and was careful to keep his battels down to less than £30 per month during winter and less than £25 per month during summer.[112] Although he joined a number of societies he was still not entirely integrated into Oxford society. In May 1886 he wrote home: 'I shall spend most of my afternoons this term in the fields round Oxford, alone if possible.'[113]

In 1885 Hewins joined the Guild of St. Matthew, seeking the ideal combination of Christian ends and social action. The Guild proved a disappointment since its main concerns were religious and missionary. Out of its three objectives only one touched upon social issues: 'to promote the study of Social and Political Questions in the light of the Incarnation'. Hewins found that he was out of sympathy with the Guild's ecclesiastical view and that its economics were 'too general, vague, and sentimental'.[114] His search for a more realistic approach to the solution of economic and social problems led him to take an active part in Sidney Ball's Social Science Club, through which he was brought into touch with a group of young dons including L. R. Phelps, W. J. H. Campion, and Robert Ewing, all clergymen actively interested in social research.[115] Through his friends John Carter and W. J. H. Campion, he was also drawn to the *Lux Mundi* group—young High Church clergymen who were to start the Oxford Branch of the Christian Social Union at Pusey House.

Like H. Ll. Smith, Hewins chose mathematics as his subject

[110] Hewins papers 41/11, 41/217.
[111] Pascoe, *Where Shall I Educate My Son?*, p. 64.
[112] Hewins papers 10/3, 41/29, 41/36.
[113] Ibid. 10/16, W. A. S. Hewins to his parents, 2 May 1886.
[114] Hewins, *Apologia*, pp. 15–16. See also Hewins papers 42/174, letter from J. Carter.
[115] Hewins papers 41/68, W. H. Johnstone to Hewins, 18 Dec. 1886.

and in the same way his interest soon shifted. Having obtained a Second in 1887, he decided to remain at Oxford and read for another degree in history under the tutorship of C. H. Firth who was then a lecturer at Pembroke. Firth directed Hewins's attention to seventeenth-century economic history and was impressed by his work to the extent that in 1895, he wrote to him that in his seven years of teaching at Oxford Hewins had been his only student of any merit.[116] Hewins remained at Oxford during the long vacation and was urged by Firth to go to Germany for a year. He seems to have hoped for exemption from college fees so that he might manage financially on coaching students, with some help from his fiancée's family.[117] But College would not waive the fees and by January 1888 all he had were two students.[118] As a result he was forced to abandon his plan to read for another degree and instead to seek employment, preferably at Oxford, where he could continue his research independently.

During 1887 Hewins was admitted to the Oxford Economic Society, a small body of young graduates and dons interested in research on economic questions, founded on 20 October 1886 at a meeting in W. J. Ashley's rooms in Lincoln College.[119]

Ashley's training as a historian was mainly influenced by Stubbs's writings and the teaching of A. L. Smith. At that time a historian's training was thought to be incomplete unless he spent some time studying in Germany.[120] Ashley was no exception. Having decided to concentrate on English medieval history he went to Germany for the first time, with some financial help from Jowett, in 1880 (and again in 1883 and 1884) to attend Reinhold Pauli's lectures at Göttingen.[121] It was through

[116] Ibid. 44/104, C. H. Firth to Hewins, 23 Nov. 1895, L. L. Price, 'W. A. S. Hewins', in the *Economic Journal*, 1832.
[117] Ibid. 41/93, 41/148.
[118] Ibid. 41/156, 41/158.
[119] Cannan papers, vol. 905, E. Cannan, 'The O.E.S.', MS Bodleian Library G.A. Oxon. 4°602, b.147, Notices of meetings, rules, and lists of members. Another list of members is in the Hewins papers 41/155.
[120] H. A. L. Fisher, *An Unfinished Autobiography* (Oxford, 1940), p. 59.
[121] Anne Ashley, *W. J. Ashley*, p. 19. On Pauli he wrote in Sidney J. Low and F. S. Pulling (ed.), *The Dictionary of English History* (London 1884), p. 1107: 'Few modern historians have surpassed Dr. Pauli in intimate knowledge of the original materials for English history, and in sound critical judgement in using them.'

Pauli that he was introduced to Sidney Ball who was also at Göttingen attending Lotze's lectures.[122] Ashley was greatly impressed by German historical scholarship, especially in constitutional history, but it was not until he came under Toynbee's influence that he was introduced to the works of the German historical school of economics.

Upon obtaining a First in Modern History in 1881 Ashley hoped to remain at Balliol for two more years and read for a second degree in Greats, with an emphasis on philosophy. However, this proved financially beyond his means and, instead, for the next four years he made a living by writing some articles for Low and Pulling's *Dictionary of English History*, and by coaching, 'uncertain at the opening of each term whether I should have enough pupils to pay for my lodgings'.[123] In 1882 he won the Lothian Prize for his essay on *James and Philip von Artvelde* (London 1883). This, his first published work, bears the marks of A. L. Smith's teaching, the influence of the German school of constitutional history, and the emergence of Ashley's own concept of history.

A. L. Smith directly influenced Ashley and Cannan as well as many other Balliol history students. According to their contemporaries, Charles Mallet and Anthony Hope, 'no one could resist the short tough man in the faded Balliol blazer, with a shaggy face like a Skye terrier's in a high wind; who on almost any subject seemed to be eagerness and sympathy incarnate, and whose vitality and humour swept every form of littleness aside.'[124] His teaching is representative of a young generation of Oxford history dons whose work differed significantly from that of the older generation represented by E. A. Freeman. It combined a wide range of influences including T. H. Green's Idealism, Mazzini's concept of duty, and Comte's vision of uniting the human studies into one science of society, to create both a methodology and an ideology according to which history was the essential training for any man who wished to under-

---

[122] W. J. Ashley, *Scientific Management and the Engineering Situation*, Sidney Ball Memorial Lecture, 28 October, 1922 Barnett House Papers No. 7 (Oxford, 1922).

[123] Ibid. He coached mostly in constitutional history and political economy as required for a paper in the School of Modern History.

[124] Mallet, *Anthony Hope and His Books*. See also Fisher, *An Unfinished Autobiography*, p. 85, and Strachey, *The Adventure of Living*, p. 132.

stand the present. In A. L. Smith's view,[125] the study of history was passing from its romantic to its scientific stage. Its aim was critical rather than the amusement of the reader, and the study of the past was undertaken from the standpoint of the present. Furthermore, no subject could be treated scientifically unless its study was prefaced by a history of that subject. A scientific theory, according to the criteria laid down by Comte, was 'a body of generalisations from facts, which enable us to predict fresh facts'. These generalizations could not be derived by any means other than induction from historical facts.

As for the actual way in which the history of a subject should be approached, A. L. Smith taught:

> No one can now study history without asking first (1) what is the true *historical method*; what should history aim at being, what is the real use and *value of history* and what are its limits; what can it teach and what can it not teach.
> Secondly (2), what is the *meaning of human history*, what general lesson if any can be read in it; what law can be seen in the succession of one historic stage to another.

Laws, then, described the course of historical development rather than the mechanics of historical events. History was not mechanistically determinable. It could not be reduced to a combination of static factors whether human or external (such as climate, food, soil, etc.) nor, scientifically, could heavenly intervention be brought in as an explanation. History, to an ever-increasing extent, was determined by conscious moral action. This observation in itself was a law of historical progress since progress was understood to manifest itself in an overall ascent of corporate conscious moral action. Progress meant that in human affairs less and less was left to chance or to individual action, and that evolution to an increasing extent was determined by general causes. It was a law of historical development which did not permit the use of historical incidents for contemporary analogies, nor did it accept a deductive analysis of history—for example, the use of psychological analysis to describe ever-present human motives and modes of action. Historical analogies were impossible since progress and evolution made each age essentially different from the other. Static deductive psychological analysis was impossible because

---

[125] A. L. Smith, 'The Science of History', lecture notes, in Balliol College Library.

man's nature, as well as his social and moral character, were in a constant state of change.

All human creations such as institutions or ideas were regarded dialectically as bearing a direct relation to the circumstances in which they were created. According to A. L. Smith, when a historian wished to examine a certain theory he required 'a real philosophic grasp of the political and social conditions and literary influences which produced it and a similar grasp of the various results which historically can be traced back to it'. His dialectics, therefore, were not purely material since ideas were identified not only as products of historical circumstances but also as historical agents in their own right, worthy of historical investigation as much as any other historical agent. Institutions, as well as the theories that governed and justified them, were not universal and must not be accepted on an *a priori* basis. It was the duty of each generation to examine its institutional and theoretical heritage and to keep, change, or abandon it according to its needs. Such an examination could only be a historical one since judgement could not be passed without the knowledge of the original circumstances in which institutions and theories were formed, the needs they answered, and the record of their performance. It had been noted by the mid-nineties that this dialectical approach was linked with a certain loss of interest in 'solving the great speculative problems':

> We have betaken ourselves to seeing whether we cannot get a little further and deeper in our conception of the practical concepts of life. . . . if there is any direction in which Green's spirit still animates any among us, it is in the direction of an attempt to make institutions reveal their true meaning—an attempt to remove the obstructions which render property, law, and society itself stumbling blocks, instead of stepping stones.[126]

This was not due to any rejection of Green's Idealism. Indeed there were dons who continued to develop his philosophical theories, including David Ritchie at Jesus and R. L. Nettleship at Balliol. Young dons, however, as well as students, were content with a certain notion, vague as it may have been, of the principles of Green's philosophy. Their main concern was with its applications.

---

[126] Selby-Bigge, 'Practical Oxford' p. 734.

A. L. Smith, in effect, adopted Comte's vision of a unified study of society and its use in forecasting the future on the basis of inductively obtained generalizations. At the same time he pointed out that a unified social science with a generally accepted methodology was yet to be created. The historian was thus left to widen the horizons of historical investigation to include more forms of human activity without significantly changing his methodology. There was no sense of the inadequacy of history. According to Stubbs,

> [History] presents, in every branch, a regular developed series of causes and consequences, and abounds in examples of that continuity of life, the realisation of which is necessary to give the reader a personal hold on the past and a right judgement of the present. For the roots of the present lie deep in the past, and nothing in the past is dead to the man who would learn how the present comes to what it is.[127]

It was a positivistic view in its implicit assumption that historical facts could be given only one valid interpretation, and relativistic in that it did not assume one definite system of laws governing all human action regardless of time and place, beyond a loose concept of certain wide generalizations describing the general course of human development. Prediction, therefore, was restricted to the identification of general trends and an analysis of their nature based on their history and present state.

This view of history, which is well represented in Ashley's work, was contrasted by him with the more conservative view held by the historian E. A. Freeman.[128] In Ashley's view, 'there can be little doubt that the thought of slow but never ceasing change, of the appearance of new conditions out of the bosom of the old, a thought set before us in different forms by Hegel, Darwin and Comte, is dominating the most typical historical work of the day.' Whereas in Freeman's approach, Ashley went on, 'the continuity of history [except for the influence of the Roman Empire] was very apt to be . . . only geographical. Such and Such things had happened centuries ago in such a

---

[127] W. Stubbs, *The Constitutional History of England; In its origin and development* (Oxford, 1875), p. iv.
[128] Ashley's review of W. R. W. Stephens, *The Life and Letters of Edward E. Freeman* in the *Nation*, 18 July 1895, reprinted in Ashley's *Surveys Historic and Economic* (London, 1900).

place, and accordingly . . . we ought to regard with such and such views events happening there now.'

In Ashley's view, not only did Freeman hold to a static view of history which allowed for historical analogies provided that they were set in similar physical circumstances, but he rejected the notion of the intelligibility of history: 'History to him was full of the irrational or the unrational, and to a generation that sees, or thinks it sees, more and more meaning in the world outside man, his utterances concerning mankind could not but be unsatisfying.'

Ashley reasoned that it was the English love of precedence that made the search for analogies especially dear to the English historian. In an ever-changing world this was of no practical value. But the search for precedence should not be confused with the study of origins which was also motivated by the problems of the present. How the present motivated the study of the past was demonstrated in Ashley's Lothian Prize Essay in which he argued:

> An increased sense of dangers attending the modern industrial system, contemporaneous as the growth of that feeling has been with a deeper research into the development of institutions, has begun to turn man's minds to the social arrangements of the mediaeval world, and to that banding together of men for mutual help which is known as 'the guild system'.[129]

Ashley's concept of history as a slow and steady process of evolution placed him in opposition to two popular historical theories of his day: Thorold Rogers's view of the development and decline of the guild system and the German Mark theory with its application to English constitutional theory.[130] Both were based on the concept of a historical golden age — the golden age of the English labourer and the golden age of individual liberty within the ancient tribal community. History, according to these two theories, was not a process of gradual and continuous progress, but rather of a cataclysmic nature. Argument in favour of the existence of a golden age of the English labourer or of a population of independent freeman, followed by a period of repression and long centuries of increas-

---

[129] W. J. Ashley, *James and Philip van Artvelde* (London, 1883), p. 2.

[130] e.g. in E. A. Freeman, *The Growth of the English Constitution from the Earliest Times* (London, 1872).

ing degradation, established two different precedences. The main purpose of the advocates of a 'golden age' theory was to present contemporary reform as the restoration of ancient rights—primarily a romantic view of history. However, in the course of doing so they established class antagonisms and conspiracy as historical phenomena which were likely to recur. They offered a convenient but entirely misleading label to any opposition to the reforms they supported. Their theories were not only factually wrong, they were dangerous in that they served to perpetuate class antagonism.

Ashley attacked these theories in a series of reviews pubished during the eighties and early nineties.[131] His position on the matter was summarized in his Introduction to the translation of Fustel De Coulanges, *The Origin of Property in Land* (London, 1891). In it he restated some of his basic notions of the nature of the study of history. He quoted with approval De Coulanges's claim: 'Of late years people have invented the word *Sociology*. The word *history* had the same sense and meant the same thing, at least for those who understood it. History is the science of social facts; that is to say, it is sociology itself.'[132] He justified his own work by stating: 'The study of economic history is altogether indispensable if we are ever to have anything more than a superficial conception of the evolution of society.'[133] On the other hand, he had realized by then that appearances were deceptive and that some might confuse analogies with the results of proper historical research when used in contemporary controversies.

> Although a principle motive for . . . inquiry will be the hope of obtaining some light on the direction in which change is likely to take place in the future, it will be wise for some time to come for students resolutely to turn away their eyes from current controversies. There is a sufficient lesson in the topic we have been considering. The history of the mark has served Mr. George as a basis for the contention that the common ownership of land is the only natural condition of things; to Sir Henry Maine it has suggested the precisely opposite conclusion that the whole movement of civilization has been from common ownership to private. Such arguments are alike worthless, if the mark never existed.[134]

---

[131] Most of them were reprinted in Ashley, *Surveys Historical and Economic*.

[132] W. J. Ashley, 'Introductory Chapter on the English Manor', in Fustel de Coulanges, *The Origin of Property in Land* (London, 1891), p. xii.

[133] Ibid., p. xliii.

[134] Ibid.

Thoroughness in research and caution in its application would guarantee the historian from the fate of the supporters of the mark theory—relatively quick invalidation.

A. L. Smith's teachings on the nature and methodology of history were of direct influence on Ashley and Cannan. The same, or very similar, views were adopted by Sadler, Ll. Smith, Price, and Hewins through the influence of their respective college tutors. The adoption of such a concept of history was not restricted to the influence of a history tutor on a history student. It was part and parcel of a wider *Weltanschauung* in which the general principles of Green's Idealism, accepted more or less unquestioningly, were applied, with a combination of additional influences (e.g. Mazzini, Comte) to academic work and, in the form of a political and social ideology, to practical issues. This influence was due not solely to the logical soundness of these ideas or to their suitability to the needs, beliefs, and personalities of the 'converted' (a term used by Cannan to describe A. L. Smith's influence on him[135]) but also to the personal inspiration of certain dons. An outstanding example of such an inspiration was Arnold Toynbee (1852–83) whose views demonstrate both the academic and the practical application of the new ideology.

During the period following his graduation Ashley began to attend Toynbee's lectures and it was on the basis of his and Bolton King's notes that Toynbee's 'Industrial Revolution' lectures were eventually reconstructed.[136] From Toynbee Ashley learnt of the relativistic-historical approach to economic theory and of the study of economic phenomena as a historical process. Following the lectures, Ashley asked Toynbee for advice as to how he might develop his interest in economics. It was Toynbee's view that Ashley should 'take some one subject, e.g. wages, and, beginning with Adam Smith, read in chronological order, what each noteworthy English economist had said upon the subject, and see if you can make out the way in which various doctrines have arisen and have been modified'.[137]

[135] Edwin Cannan, *The Economic Outlook* (London, 1912), pp. 10–11.
[136] Mrs C. M. Toynbee, 'Prefatory Note' to A. Toynbee, *Lectures on the Industrial Revolution* (London, 1908).
[137] W. J. Ashley, review of F. C. Montague, *Arnold Toynbee*, in the *Political Science Quarterly*, 1889.

Ashley adapted Toynbee's advice to his own interest in English medieval history by treating medieval economic theory and economic activity in the way advocated by A. L. Smith in the field of political theories and institutions; whereas the line of enquiry suggested by Toynbee was eventually used by Cannan in the early stages of his work on the development of economic theories after Adam Smith.[138] Toynbee had added to other influences in directing Ashley towards the 'historical investigation of social development, and . . . the direct examination of existing phenomena'.[139]

As well as receiving academic advice, Ashley was drawn into Toynbee's circle and joined in the promotion of some of the causes Toynbee had adopted, including the National Church Reform Union.[140] The Union aimed at national moral regeneration through the democratization of the Church of England's government at the parish level, which would lead to the greater involvement of communities in church affairs. The Union sought to introduce the ideal of democracy through corporate social action at the community level into church reform with the belief that, despite all its shortcomings, the Church of England as a national institution had a vital role to play in ensuring the moral progress of the nation. Disestablishment and disendowment would only destroy what might be a national agent of moral improvement.[141]

Of Toynbee's friends Sidney Ball, P. L. Gell, L. R. Phelps, and in London the Revd. S. A. Barnett were active in the Union. Although politically it proved to be of relatively little weight, it did not lose its power as a cause and, at least for some years, Ashley retained his interest in church reform through the Oxford University Society for Promoting Religious Union.[142] It

---

[138] Cannan, *The Economic Outlook*, p. 17.

[139] W. J. Ashley, review of F. C. Montague.

[140] Phelps papers, S. Ball to L. R. Phelps, 28 Jan. 1882, on organizing a meeting of the National Church Reform Union. W. Garwood and Ashley are referred to as 'working and active members'; Ashley to Phelps, n.d., *c.* 1882; S. A. Barnett to Phelps, 21 Mar. 1883, in which Ashley is suggested as a possible candidate for organizing a visit of school teachers to Oxford.

[141] For the Union's programme, see Albert Gray and Canon Fremantle (ed.), *Church Reform* (London, 1888).

[142] There is a record of a meeting of the Society in Ashley's rooms in Lincoln College on 30 May 1886: Bodleian Library papers related to the Oxford University Society for Promoting Religious Union.

was not a movement created by Toynbee, but one in which the involvement of his friends owed much to Toynbee's enthusiasm. In retrospect Ashley admitted that in many points Toynbee's academic work and practical proposals were preceded by Comte, Cliffe Leslie, F. A. Walker, Bagehot, Mundella, and Sedley Taylor, but it was Toynbee's direct personal influence that had led Ashley to become interested in economic history and theory and in the adoption of a certain approach to social reform.[143]

In his 'Industrial Revolution' lectures Toynbee tried to establish the concept of gradual and continuous progress on a factual basis. Specifically he was concerned with the progress of the working classes in England since industrialization. He followed two lines of argument: (a) factual proof of continuous working-class material progress during the recent stages of industrialization; and (b) refutation of the various theories that argued otherwise. If it could be shown that the material condition of the working classes had improved through industrialization and that the process was likely to continue within the present system, or even be helped through certain modifications, then there was nothing fundamentally wrong with the system that might necessitate its replacement by revolutionary means. From the theoretical aspect, if the theories that describe a state of poverty and class antagonism as a constant state within the given system were proved to be based on false assumptions and to be factually invalid, then there was no theoretical justification for a revolutionary change of system. Thus Toynbee's investigation of the Industrial Revolution was undertaken with an eye to the ideological controversies of the early eighties.

Toynbee argued that history was not mechanistically determined, as Spencer's interpretation of Darwin would have it, but rather, and to an increasing extent, that it was determined by conscious human action. The mistery inflicted on the lower classes was not the inevitable outcome of the working of natural laws. It was the result of self-seeking action of the dominant classes acting in ignorance and the short-sighted pursuit of self-interest or, in some cases, the working of particular circumstances peculiar to a certain place and age. This was

[143] W. J. Ashley to Brentano, 25 Mar. 1913, in H. W. McReady, 'Sir William Ashley; Some Unpublished Letters', in *Journal of Economic History*, 1955.

directed not only against Spencer's general view of history with its defence of all existing misery and injustice,[144] but also against any attempts to present generalizations based on certain peculiar circumstances as universally valid, such as, according to Toynbee, the law of diminishing returns, the 'Iron Law of Wages', and Ricardo's theory of rent. Contrary to Spencer's view, nothing was inevitable, and the refutation of a static view of economic relations indicated that change was possible.

Toynbee set out to prove not only that economic and social conditions were constantly changing, but that, since industrialization, change meant improvement. Since 1864, he argued, the growth of population had not outstripped the means of subsistence;[145] no wage could be shown to be fixed so that it could not be increased or diminished at a long-range steady rate;[146] and although historically 'rent has risen, there is a good reason to suppose that in the future it may fall; that interest has not fallen much; and that the standard of comfort and the rate of wages, both of artisans and labourers — of the former decidedly, and to a certain extent also of the latter, has risen.'[147]

Toynbee was careful to point out that to argue the possibility of progress within the existing industrial system was not to defend the faults within the system: 'The more we accept the method of historical inquiry, the more revolutionary shall we tend to become in practice. For while the modern historical school of economists appear to be only exploring the monuments of the past, they are really shaking the foundations of many of our institutions in the present.'[148]

In his attempt to defuse revolutionary theories Toynbee chose to adopt some of their terminology and use it with an altered meaning. Two key terms were 'revolution' and 'socialism'. Toynbee argued that there were two essentially different types of 'revolution' and 'socialism'. There was a continental type of revolution — for example, the French

---

[144] A. Toynbee *Lectures on the Industrial Revolution*, lecture 5.
[145] Ibid., lecture 10.
[146] Ibid., lecture 11.
[147] Ibid., lecture 13.
[148] Ibid., lecture 5.

Revolution, which achieved democracy through violence, terror, loss of property, suspension of all individual legal rights, and a period of repressive reaction. In contrast, there was an English type of revolution—for example, the Glorious Revolution depicted by Macaulay and the Whig historians, bloodless, gradual, and continuous. Toynbee adopted Macaulay's notion of English history as the history of progress, in which one could speak of successive stages of one great revolution.[149] The Industrial Revolution was such a stage and it was only through an overall historical perspective that one realized that it was another major step in the direction of democracy and prosperity. Symmetrically there was a continental socialism—the revolutionary creed advocated by Rodbertus, Lassalle, and Marx, which called for the destruction of the present state of society through revolutionary means. There was also an English brand of socialism, which advocated gradual change through reform. With this differentiation in mind, Toynbee had no difficulty in declaring himself a socialist and a revolutionary.

Toynbee supported a wide range of reforms including factory legislation, readjustment of taxation, municipal action in the improvement of working-class dwellings, enforcement of sanitary laws and the Building Acts, working-class representation on all boards and town councils, etc. He enthusiastically defended and supported trade unionism, co-operative societies, industrial partnership, conciliation boards, and all forms of conscious corporate working-class action. At the same time Toynbee was a firm believer in self-help: 'We have not abandoned our old belief in liberty, justice, and self-help but we say that under certain conditions the people cannot help themselves, and that then they should be helped by the State representing directly the whole people.'[150] State intervention was in principle justified as representing the whole people, whereas in practice it was to be resorted to only after the failure of self-help. In some spheres the need for state help seemed to Toynbee to be relatively obvious—for example, in factory laws and education. However, he and many other like-minded radicals, had put great faith in the potential of working-class

[149] e.g. in Macaulay's review of Sir James Mackintosh's *History of the Revolution* in Lord Macaulay, *Reviews, Essays and Poems*, vol. 2, (London, 1876).
[150] Toynbee, 'Are Radicals Socialists?' in *Lectures on the Industrial Revolution*.

self-help action. It was not until the nineties that economists, witnessing what they believed were the limits of working-class self-help, began to seek a more comprehensive form of state intervention.

Toynbee's concept of progress was essentially a moral one in which material progress was the necessary means. This point needed to be constantly emphasized to both the working class and the middle class. In this Toynbee was something of a preacher for, when he called upon university men to give of their time in the service of the lower classes, he did not ask as a working man might, demanding his share of the nation's wealth, but as a missionary seeking the intellectual and spiritual elevation of the lower classes through the means of material improvement, corporate action, submitting to collective interests, etc. When addressing working men Toynbee felt it necessary to stress the underlying purpose for which he and the others pledged themselves to work in their service: 'We demand increased material welfare for those who labour with their hands, not that they may seize upon a few more coarse enjoyments but that they may enter upon a purer and higher life.'[151]

In his moral stance Toynbee incorporated one of the basic principles of John Ruskin's teaching. For some time, when still an undergraduate, Toynbee had belonged to the small circle which met weekly in Ruskin's rooms in Corpus. This he 'won' by virtue of his exertions as foreman during the final stages of Ruskin's Hinksey Road project by means of which Ruskin hoped to convert Oxford from sport to the gospel of labour. He may have adopted from Ruskin the basic notion of the inalienability of economics from ethics but he had soon drifted away from Ruskin's circle. Having come under the influence of T. H. Green, his economic views developed independently of Ruskin's. Ruskin tended to emphasize the evil in the present state of society and although his vision of the desirable form of society was of one morally superior to the present one, his means for achieving this state were unrealistic and unacceptable. During the early eighties Ruskin was still a cultural hero,

---

[151] Ibid. The address was delivered early in 1882 to working-class audiences in Newcastle, Bradford, Bolton, and Leicester. In the same vein he ended his 'Progress and Poverty' lectures: *Arnold Toynbee, Progress and Poverty; A Criticism of Mr. Henry George* (London, 1883).

and young men such as Hewins and Sadler still flocked to his lectures.[152] But his more vituperative statements were treated with careful scepticism, even by his admirers. Something of a legend in his own time, his name came to signify to Oxford's young economists the importance of the moral perspective of economic issues. Beyond this his direct influence was on the wane.

As a rule Oxford's young economists shared Toynbee's sympathy towards the aims of socialism. While rejecting much of the revolutionary socialists' analysis of society, they recognized the reality of the grievances from which it originated. This approach is evident in an early attempt on the part of W. J. Ashley to describe to his future wife his 'economic faith'.[153] He differed from 'what are usually known as Socialists in England' in his rejection of Marx's *Mehrwerth* theory, in his belief in gradual evolution as opposed to rapid radical change, and in his argument that the importance of the vices of the employers and capitalists as a class should not be exaggerated while the vices of other classes are being overlooked. Socialists, he argued, left agriculture out of their theory, along with all forms of non-factory industry. The socialists' analysis of factory industry, based on the abstract economics of Ricardo and Cairnes, was valid where its theoretically presupposed conditions, such as complete freedom of competition and superfluity of labourers, were in existence. But, as Toynbee pointed out, the socialists' theories could be criticized by a refutation of the validity of the abstract economic theories on which they were based, theories which were shaky, since most of their presuppositions did not actually exist.

Ashley professed faith in the future of trade unions, factory legislation, co-operative societies, etc. He found cause for optimism in a trend he detected in private industry which seemed to lead towards socialization through the replacement of individual entrepreneurs by corporate companies, the growing importance of the managerial echelon, and the emerging distinction between profit earned by skill and profit won by the mere investment of capital. Finally, he saw a gradually increasing role for state intervention in industry through supervision

---

[152] One of his lectures is described in M. Sadleir, *M. E. Sadler*, pp. 32–3.
[153] Anne Ashley, *W. J. Ashley*, pp. 34–5.

of working conditions (e.g. Factory Acts), intervention in industrial relations (e.g. the Employer's Liability Bill), and in some cases the undertaking of industrial services (e.g. Parcel Post).[154]

Quoting from Tennyson's 'Of Old Sat Freedom';

> All the past of Time reveals
> A bridal gown of thunder-peals,
> Whenever Thought had wedded Fact.

Ashley admitted that it was not impossible that eventually, when a new order was born, it would be born in violence. But that, to his mind, was not the present case nor was it likely to be so for the next fifty years. Under the present circumstances 'barricades are useless and therefore criminal.'

Ashley drew two sets of conclusions which he defined as the work of the economist and the work of the politician. The economist, bearing in mind the main contemporary issues, should concentrate on economic history and detailed examinations 'of modern industrial life *in the piece*'. The politician should, at the same time, concentrate his efforts on the establishment of the wage policy of state enterprises on the principle of a fair wage rather than of competitive wages, on the extension of state ownership to railways, waterworks, and gasworks, and on increasing municipal ownership of land and houses.

By implication Ashley based his 'programme' for immediate political action on the findings of scientific investigation aimed at determining the means most likely to achieve the ideological goals in which both the economist and the politician believed. Political action, then, was to be guided by scientific investigations into economic history and current aspects of the industrial system, assuming that not only did the politician and the scientist share the same ideology, but that the politician had faith in the value of the economist's findings. This dependence (which, although theoretical, did not seem to Ashley improbable) of the politician on the economist served to justify the economist's work in terms of his duty as a citizen. By the same token, economic investigations that did not result in practical recom-

---

[154] Compare with the more radical form of state intervention advocated by Ruskin in the preface to *Unto This Last* (London, 1862).

mendations for action were, from society's point of view, useless and unjustifiable.

The cohesive nature of Ashley's *Weltanschauung* may be demonstrated by his ability to justify his choice of the direction of scientific enquiry by means of an internal as well as an external line of reasoning. The study of economic history and current aspects of the industrial system led to practical recommendations since, as A. L. Smith had argued, it was the only valid method known by which social activity could be scientifically investigated. The combination of the two lines of reasoning led Ashley to believe that here was more than just a method for arriving at a truth. It was the method for arriving at what he considered to be the most important of historical truths. This combination of external and internal reasoning is evident in a letter written by Ashley in 1886 to his future wife:

> I care for history and economic history in particular because it tells me of the life of the people . . . In 'constitutional' history one is bound constantly to generalize, to try to discover the *meaning* of institutions, their growth and decay, their relation to one another. And thus one gets into the way of regarding the whole human history as having a meaning, as not being purposeless, as moving to some goal. To see that this is true in such little bits of history as one knows, makes one hope that it is true in those facts nearer our own times where we are too near the events and have too little information to be able to judge.[155]

Ashley had reached the point at which his moral, social, and political convictions combined with his university training to produce his first independent research programme. This in turn resulted in the first part of the first (and only) volume of *An Introduction to English Economic History and Theory* (London, 1888), dedicated appropriately to the memory of Toynbee. The cohesion of his *Weltanschauung* was such that any one component could be used in support of the other. Ideology and scientific methodology could support the choice of subject for research. The findings of his research could in turn support his ideology and prove the value of the methodology. The independence of his programme is indicated not only by its place in his own cohesive *Weltanschauung*, but also by its combination of the professional influences of the 'A. L. Smith type' of methodology, Toynbee's emphasis on the history of economic

---

[155] Anne Ashley, *W. J. Ashley*, p. 33.

theories and institutions, and Ashley's interest in English medieval constitutional history, to create a programme for independent work.

After four failures Ashley was finally elected in February 1885 to a Fellowship at Lincoln College, with lecturing responsibilities in history and political economy to Lincoln and Corpus Christi College undergraduates. Although the Fellowship gave Ashley economic security, he soon found that it allowed him too little time for independent research, which added to the frustration of teaching a programme determined by what he considered an anachronistic examination system.[156] In retrospect, reflecting upon his experience as a Fellow, he concluded:

> We may be pretty sure that the English universities will never become primarily places of original investigation or homes of learned leisure. There is the crowd of undergraduates to deal with somehow, there is the obvious benefit that can be conferred upon the students, and the influence for good that can be exercised through them upon the nation. On the other hand it can hardly be maintained that Oxford does as much as might fairly be expected of her for the advancement of knowledge; and it is scarcely seemly for her to be so very dependent for fresh ideas and new conclusions upon German universities and 'private scholars'.[157]

The college tutors had become no more than overworked schoolmasters. In addition to their duty to instruct their own college pupils, the inter-college lectureships significantly increased their teaching responsibilities. They were soon burnt out, unable to produce any work of original scholarship. Ashley did not belittle the importance of a don's work in educating undergraduates, but he designated research as a first priority and his conscientiousness as a teacher prevented a working combination of teaching and research. The same point was made by Ll. Smith in 1888 during a term he spent at Rugby as a replacement mathematics master. In a letter to his mother he wrote:

> I enjoy the school life very much. I think I told you before that for a *permanency* I think it would tend to be very absorbing both of the interest and of the energy, and so cut off from any things I should be sorry to be cut off from. To

---

[156] Marshall Library, Cambridge, Ashley to Seligman, 20 Jan. 1887, and a letter, n.d., from Toronto (copies).

[157] W. J. Ashley, 'Jowett and the University Ideal'.

make it thoroughly successful, all the powers must be concentrated on it, and the real school master rarely has time or energy for much else. But I do not know of anything for which I would be more ready to make the said sacrifice if I had to make it.[158]

As a result, young men of Ashley's commitment towards research were on the look out not only for a job but for a job which would allow them to fulfil their duty as scientists through research.

Although institutionally Oxford was not equipped to stimulate and maintain research, Ashley and some fellow dons sided with M. Pattison in taking the view that research should be an essential aspect of the University if it was to be a truly national institution. Some felt that there was a particularly urgent need for research into economic and social issues. The expression of their concern was the foundation of the Oxford Economic Society. In 1860, during his first tenure as the Drummond Professor of Political Economy, Thorold Rogers, with some fellow dons, founded the Oxford University Political Economy Club.[159] It was a combination of a dons' dining club and a debating society, in which membership was restricted to 'graduates of the University of at least three years' standing'. It met twice a term to dine and discuss an economic issue of which prior notice was given. Some of its members taught political economy in their respective colleges. Others, such as W. A. Spooner and L. R. Phelps, were also active on the Board of Poor Law Guardians (a third of which was composed of university members) and as such were interested in practical social issues[160] to the extent that in time they came to be considered as authorities on questions of pauperism. Nevertheless the overall standard of debate was considered, even by some of the members, to be amateurish and it was not until the late eighties and early nineties that the younger economists were admitted as members.[161] Thus the Club did not and could not

---

[158] Ll. Smith papers, Ll. Smith to his mother, 30 Mar. 1888.
[159] Bodleian Library, G. A. Oxon, 8°258, 4°499, papers related to the activity of the Oxford Political Economy Club.
[160] Bodleian Library, G.A. Oxon.b.105, statement by L. R. Phelps, 30 Apr. 1882, and W. A. Spooner, 'Notes for Autobiography', ch. 5, MS in New College, Oxford.
[161] In any event, the introduction of new members was a slow process since they could only be elected when a vacancy occurred and then only one member could be elected per meeting.

fulfil the role of stimulating an interest in research which was being expressed by young graduates wishing to pursue an independent and systematic course of study.[162]

The rules of the Oxford Economic Society limited its membership to twenty-five graduates. In fact, although the official list of members came close to that number, it included some undergraduates considered promising by college tutors who were members of the Society. Actual attendance never reached the full number of members and it was computed by Cannan never to have reached a higher annual average than 11.5 per meeting.[163] Officially the Society was run by a committee which in 1888 consisted of W. J. H. Campion, L. R. Phelps, Sidney Ball, Edwin Cannan, and W. J. Ashley. In reality it was managed by the Secretary, the first one being Ashley who was replaced on 23 October 1888 by Cannan, after Ashley's election to the Toronto chair. The Society met once or twice a term to hear a paper given by one of its members, usually on his current subject of research, a paper which in some cases was the first attempt of a member to present a professional paper on an economic subject. According to the list of papers given, the most active members were Cannan (three papers), Ashley, Sadler, Hewins, and Robert Ewing of St. John's (two each). Most papers were on issues currently being debated, including income tax, regulation of shop hours, the cost of free education, regulation of wages, etc. Ashley and Hewins contributed papers on economic history and there was at least one guest speaker, who held forth on 'Greek Ideas of Political Economy'.

Members of the Oxford Economic Society as a group were relatively isolated from groups of economists elsewhere in England and most noticeably from the Cambridge economists around Marshall. The voluntary aspect of this relative isolation was expressed in a letter written on 20 January 1887 by Ashley to Seligman, who had been an active promoter of the American Economic Association.[164] This letter, written a few months after

[162] Graham Wallas papers, S. Ball to Wallas, 18 Sept. (*c.*1887). The Oxford Economic Society is probably the more 'academic' society (compared to the Social Science Club) referred to by Ball.

[163] Cannan papers, E. Cannan 'the O.E.S.'. According to Cannan average annual attendance per meeting since 1886 was 11, 11.15, 9.83, and 7.6.

[164] Marshall Library, Ashley to Seligman, 20 Jan. 1887 (copy).

the Society's foundation, described its work and membership. In it, Ashley, doubtless with the knowledge of the Society's committee, wrote:

> it has occurred to some of us who are acquainted with the existence of the American Economic Association and who know such work as that appearing in the Political Science Quarterly . . . that it would be well if in some way we could join forces with the American [Economic] Association. We feel the American Association is doing most excellent work, for it is giving the results of German thought as seen by men who understand the English orthodox teaching and English and American circumstances (which is not always the case with the Germans themselves) besides, of course, dealing with actual American questions in a way worthy of our imitations.

Although there is no record of official affiliation being established, Ashley's letter reflects the high regard Oxford economists had for the work done by their American contemporaries, mainly members of the Association group which called itself the 'new school'. F. A. Walker's work on wages was received at Oxford with enthusiasm and described by H. Ll. Smith as striking . . .

> the key note of the new school of Political Economy; we find a return to facts, a searching examination of the premises, a keen analysis of the conditions under which they are really true, and under which they are plausible but false . . . Walker's book on the "Wages Question" is the best extant refutation of the old theory of the Wages Fund, and the best real analysis, saturated with illustrations from real life, of the real wages problem.[165]

R. T. Ely's work was received with similar approbation, to the extent that around 1891 he was considered for an Oxford honorary degree, a proposal to which Marshall was strongly opposed.[166] Thus Ashley's frequent choice of American periodicals for the publication of his articles during the nineties was not entirely due to geographical convenience.

The Society brought together within an institutional framework a group of young men who had more in common than a technical choice of the field of economics for further research. They shared a similar cultural and social background, they came under similar influences at Oxford, and

---

[165] H. Ll. Smith, *Two Lectures on the Books of Political Economy* (London, Birmingham, and Leicester 1887), pp. 162–3.

[166] Phelps papers, Marshall to Phelps, 23 Apr. 1891. Marshall's main argument was that Ely was not worthy of such an honour.

they chose to pursue their interest in economic and social issues along similar methodological lines, with a similar and related choice of subjects. So that although the Society ceased to exist after 1891, its members appear in the lists of the Oxford Extension Movement as some of its main organizers and lecturers in economics, in the initiative that led to the formation of the Oxford Branch of the Christian Social Union, and in the lists of editors and contributors to the *Economic Review*. Membership in the Society represented the nucleus of a school of thought as a corporate entity although the Society itself was of a generally limited significance.

Of the Society's members Cannan had the most pronounced leanings toward economic theory. Economics seems to have been for him, at first, an intellectual exercise which he pursued in relative isolation. However contact through the Society with the work of his Oxford contemporaries resulted in adding other dimensions to his work, mainly the study of historical and contemporary issues. Although Cannan's earliest work was purely theoretical, when Ashley suggested to Campion in 1890 that the planned *Economic Review* should have a periodical synopsis of legislation on social questions, Cannan seemed the obvious choice to undertake such work.[167]

Cannan's theoretical concepts developed mainly through his early rejection of Fawcett's synopsis of J. S. Mill, and at Oxford of J. S. Mill and Adam Smith whose work he had studied for Finals.[168] His relative approval of Jevons was, at least to some extent, due to Jevons's style of criticism of the work of the 'old' economists. In 1906, reviewing the publication of Jevons's *Principles of Economics*, Cannan wrote:

In 1883 Jevons' vigorous attacks upon Mill would have been attacks on the economics of the day, which would have caused horror on the one side and acute delight on the other. Those of us who were young then would have hailed with applause the pages which begin with the caustic observaton, 'Mill expounds the theory of capital in four fundamental propositions, all false'.[169]

---

[167] Phelps papers, W. J. H. Campion to Phelps, 3 Aug. 1890.
[168] Cannan, *The Economic Outlook*, pp. 10–11. Cannan notebooks, Balliol, a table computing his daily reading for his Pass degree during the period 15 Oct.–17 Dec. 1883 includes thirty-three hours of Adam Smith.
[169] E. Cannan, Review of W. Stanley Jevons's *The Principles of Economics* (London, 1905) in the *Economic Review*, April 1906.

Cannan's approach to theory (see p. 156 ff. below) was set within the historical-relative concepts as expressed by his college tutor, A. L. Smith. By the time he became Secretary of the Oxford Economic Society his papers on theory could be considered to reflect the ideological consensus of his fellow members. In his second paper to the Society (the first as Secretary) on 'Communism in relation to Production',[170] read on 27 November 1888, Cannan set out to prove that the common opinion, which rated communism as inferior to private enterprise and economic systems aimed at the production of wealth, was false. He rejected the view that communism would result in a population explosion by arguing that whereas 'at present the prudence when it exists at all is the prudence of individuals; under communism it would be the prudence of the society. No question of morals is involved.' The same was true of the validity of the basic utilitarian presupposition of the identification of individual self-interest with the good of society. This was clearly disproved by experience, as in the case of the proverbial individual engaged in trade whose interest was not always identical with 'the interest of that trade, considered in a corporate capacity'. It was also disproved in the case of a trade in relation to society as a whole, since 'under the institution of private property the self interest of the whole of the individuals engaged in any trade at any particular time is frequently that the productiveness of industry in that trade should *not* be great'. It was the opposite of the main contention of individualism which had been proved to be true. The interest of individuals, when correctly understood, would lead them towards more widespread corporate action.

Cannan saw no reason to suppose that communism would result in a loss of the will to work. On the contrary, he detected in the present system of free enterprise a growing tendency to base wages on 'time' rather than on 'piece', a system in which 'except for a wish not to lose his place or his chance of promotion the worker's interest is to do nothing'. A change to communism might in fact bolster the working man's will to work by entrusting him with some of the owner's and manager's

---

[170] Cannan papers, vol. 900, E. Cannan, 'Communism in relation to Prodcution'. The paper is based on an essay submitted for the Cobden Prize.

responsibilities and by ensuring his basic comforts and services: 'to those who work without hope of obtaining anything more than their daily bread almost anything except food may be given without diminishing their industry provided of course it is not exchangeable for food.'

Finally he dealt with the common notion that progressive income tax would undermine the incentive to workers to earn money by further exertions:

> No one ever heard of anyone in this country giving up working for fear he should raise his income above £100 a year and consequently have to pay a higher rate of income tax! There is nothing to show that the motive of industry would be relaxed by progressive taxation of a much more drastic kind than that which already exists in the most civilised countries.

If the positive influences on Cannan's rejection of the claims of individualism in the paper to the Oxford Economic Society are not easily discernible, they are more fully presented in his paper 'The Bearing of Recent Economics on Individualism, Collectivism, and Communism', read to the London Fabian Society on 5 July 1889.[171] In it Cannan endeavoured to state his social idealogy as a 'derivative from recent economic research and theory'. His opening statement established the relation between historical relativism, social ideology, and economics: 'The historical spirit has made so much way in recent years that no one now expects any particular organisation of industry and society to be described as the best for all times and places'.[172] Each age had to work out the forms of social and economic organization best suited to its needs. Therefore change, with the reform of existing institutions, was a constant issue.

As for the nature of change, Cannan came to express the 'Toynbee spirit' as based on scientific investigation: 'Modern Political Economy has become historical, and consequently does not believe in revolutions. What are called revolutions are not enormous changes suddenly effected, but merely some striking incident in the course of long continued change'.[173] If

---

[171] The paper was published as 'Economics and Socialism' in E. Cannan, *The Economic Outlook* Cannan's connection with Sidney Webb is discussed below, p. 268.
[172] Cannan, 'Economics and Socialism', p. 53.
[173] Ibid., p. 68.

change was neither total nor sudden the issue was whether society moved towards greater communism or towards greater individualism. Since advocates of both systems claimed that political economy proved their contentions, it was worth while examining what political economy actually had to say on the matter.

By the term 'communism' Cannan meant what Toynbee had called 'English Socialism'. It seems that Cannan had tried to go a step further than Toynbee in defusing radical terminology through adopting it. However, he must eventually have realized that his use of 'communism' was bound to be misunderstood, and when he published the paper in 1912 he changed its title to 'Economics and Socialism'. Like Toynbee and Ashley, Cannan found that revolutionary socialism was based on the works of the 'old' economists—Ricardo, Malthus, and to some extent J. S. Mill,[174] — which he found unacceptable. On the other hand, he was eager to demonstrate that modern economics was a different matter. 'The mere opinion of the old economists is not now of much importance'[175] and the only reason for discussing it was in order to uncover the theoretical fallacies of revolutionary socialism.

Modern theory, Cannan maintained, rejected the claims of individualism and supported the view that progress depended on increasing communism (i.e. socialism or collectivism). This he found to be especially true of Jevons's theory of value, and J. E. Cairnes's theory of non-competing groups. Content to ignore Jevons's utilitarian philosophical premises, Cannan hailed the gradual acceptance of Jevons's theory of value as 'perhaps the most important change which has taken place in Political Economy during recent years'.[176] Its importance was due not only to its accuracy but also to its social implications: 'If each additional given quantity of any commodity is less and less useful to a person, it follows very clearly that, so far as individuals have the same power of enjoyment, inequality of wealth is an economic evil, possibly a necessary evil, but still in itself an evil. To the old economists inequality was not in itself

[174] Ibid., pp. 71–3, 74–5.
[175] Ibid., p. 55.
[176] Ibid., p. 59.

an evil.'[177] To the modern economist, 'every approach to equality, or, strictly speaking, to equality modified by differences of need, when not accompanied by counteracting evils, is seen to be an economic good. As everyone knows, inequality modified by differences of needs is the true and only rational basis of communism.'[178]

According to Cannan, Jevons explained why value was dependent on supply and demand, whereas Cairnes explained why the differences in earnings between different employments depended on supply and demand,[179] i.e. on the 'relative numbers of individuals who devote themselves to the several employments'. Given equality of opportunity, the state of labour would have corresponded to Adam Smith's 'equality of advantageousness'. Differences of earnings from one occupation to another, indeed the choice of occupation, was due less to differences in skill and more to 'hereditary castes of labour'. As long as actual equality of opportunity did not exist, complete freedom of competition within the labour market was a fiction. This freedom could not therefore be expected to develop in a system of free enterprise.

Cannan did not consider Cairnes an economist who warranted the kind of praise he had for Jevons. Although his theory was of considerable value, Cairnes himself 'had an extraordinary talent for stating the simplest truths in languages so inflated as to impress the great class which most erroneously believes that the only useful political economy is that which is difficult to understand.'[180]

Modern theory, then, justified the identification of progress with communism. To this Cannan added his rejection of the 'old' economists, including his previously developed criticisms[181] of the distinction between productive and unproductive labour and his theory about accumulative and non-accumulative wealth. Approaching the 'old' economic theories from a

---

[177] Ibid., p. 61.
[178] Ibid., pp. 61-2.
[179] Ibid., p. 65.
[180] Ibid., p. 65.
[181] In his first paper to the OES, 'The Capital of a Community', read on 1 Mar. 1887: see Cannan notebooks, Balliol College. A second version of the paper, called 'The Two Wealths' is in the Cannan papers, LSE, vol. 899.

theoretical point of view, Cannan found them untenable and added that they could probably be further disproved factually by history and statistics. What he termed the 'pessimists' case was, therefore, groundless and socialists would have to 'cease to complain of an imaginary "subjection of labour to capital", cease to represent the existence of private property in the means of production as the cause of extreme poverty, and cease to expect a national regeneration from the extension of mercantile institutions worked by the State.'[182] (The last point was related to an argument outlined earlier in the paper in which Cannan maintained that the viability of a policy of free trade was not dependent on the acceptance of individualism.)

Poverty was not caused by private property but by inequality in earnings, which in turn was the result of 'ignorance, vice, and weakness of mind and body'.[183] These primary causes created a vicious circle perpetuating both moral and material poverty. Therefore the aim in eliminating 'ignorance, vice, and weakness of mind and body' was the material and spiritual progress of the nation. This could be done by a combination of individual and state action, the end result of which would be on lines closer to communism than to individualism. In this a better distribution of wealth was but one of many means and it did not necessitate immediate or drastic change in the structure of society.

Cannan's paper indicated some of the main directions he chose for further research, in all of which the repudiation of the 'old' theories was a central theme. These included the study of theory from both a current and a historical-relativistic point of view. 'Old' theories were found wanting when considered from the critical point of view of modern theory. A historical examination of the way in which the 'old' economists' work corresponded to specific circumstances explained why these theories could not be applicable beyond the environment in which they were created. Unlike Ashley, Cannan did not embark upon a detailed historical examination of the periods considered, nor did he examine in depth the operation of economic theory as a historical agent. His main concern was the refuta-

---

[182] Cannan, *The Economic Outlook*, p. 81.
[183] Ibid., p. 85.

tion of the 'old' theories from a present-day perspective; he added to the force of his argument by examining specific doctrines in the light of history and statistics. His intention was not purely destructive: he wished to see the 'old' theories, and the revolutionary ideology based on them, replaced by more accurate theories which inevitably supported his vision of gradual progress. The faults he found in the 'old' theories were the issues he tackled in his 'positive' works.

The certainty of gradual and continuous progress is also evident in L. L. Price's early intellectual development. An early paper on 'Statistics and Whitaker's Almanac for 1883'[184] lacks any traces of Marshallian theory. It reflects a simple Baconian faith in facts as the basis of all knowledge. By facts Price meant both contemporary and historical facts. A careful study of statistics and the history behind them could not fail to lead to rather obvious conclusions:

If the mere figures of the statistical tables are taken into consideration and from these sweeping deductions are drawn then indeed nothing is so misleading as statistics. But if the antecedent history of statistics, and the causes of which the figures are merely the effect, are subjected to the microscope of the investigator then solid and valuable knowledge may be and frequently is obtained. And in many cases statistics are the only means we have of lifting the veil and discerning the influences which are at work on society hastening or retarding progress of civilisation; narrowing or widening the gulf between the classes; advancing or hindering the spread of education; the decrease of pauperism and the fellowship of mankind.

It was Price's contention that facts thus examined could not fail to impress one with the continuity of progress within the present system. He concluded his analysis of *Whitaker's Almanac* by declaring:

The two thoughts which have ever and again forced themselves upon me while collecting the material for this paper[185] are the wonderful progress which has been made already, and still more wonderful advances which we may expect in the future. I can scarcely conceive any more wholesome study for a stern unbending Tory than the examination of statistics, for he cannot fail to recognize the grand irrecusable law of nature, as true in politics as in everything else, that movement must be always progressive and never retrogressive. 'The good old days', 'the good old times', has been the cry of conservatives of every age while they try to stem the irresistible tide of reform.

[184] The Brotherton Library, Leeds, Price papers, MS 100(75).
[185] In the manuscript the word 'paper' is deleted and replaced by 'article', thereby indicating that Price had considered the paper worthy of publication.

One of the main social-political issues of the period was Henry George's scheme for the equal distribution of land revenue, which was to be implemented by taxation—a scheme which gave rise to a variety of radical schemes calling for forms of land nationalization. Marshall spoke out against Henry George's theory in a series of three lectures delivered at Bristol during February and early March 1883.[186] He concentrated on proving that the increase in wealth had not caused an increase in want, and that the reasons for the slow rate at which want had been diminishing, compared with the rate at which wealth had been increasing, should be sought outside the existing system of land ownership. Marshall emphatically defended free competition, arguing that it was a prerequisite of progress, once society learnt how to control it. Whenever free competition had been shown to cause harm it was due to a lack of understanding of its working, resulting in lack of adequate control.

Marshall did not suggest any considerable changes in the existing system of land ownership except for some minor adjustments. In passing he noted the beneficial psychological effect on the agricultural labourer of the ownership of even the smallest plot of land. (In a later debate in the *Western Daily Press* with A. R. Wallace, he argued that there was no reason why the old custom among peasantry of renting 2 or 3 acres of land could not be revived within the existing system.) He concentrated on the more general analysis of the wages system on the basis of which he suggested that the overall solution for poverty was 'to increase the competition of capital and of the upper classes of industry for the aid of the lower classes'. This could be done if the number of skilled and better-paid workers could be increased at the expense of the number of unskilled labourers. Production would rise as would the demand for unskilled labour, now relatively undersupplied, which would allow for a rise in wages. As practical and immediate measures Marshall suggested advancing the age of working-class marriage, emigration of labour, abolition of child labour, cheap general and technical state education, working-class active sup-

---

[186] The lectures were given on the evenings of 19 and 26 Feb. and 5 Mar. 1883, and are reprinted in George J. Stigler, 'Alfred Marshall's Lectures on Progress and Poverty'. in the *Journal of Law and Economics*, April 1969.

pression of 'lazy and vicious paupers', improved inspection of factory working conditions and sanitation, better education of the working classes in the principles of production, and finally the encouragement in society in general of the development of a 'higher sense of duty'.

In his 'Progress and Poverty' lectures earlier in 1883, Toynbee had dealt with the existing land-ownership system and suggested measures that could and should be adopted to improve it. Waste lands should be placed in the hands of a village commune or the country board in order to prevent further enclosures; more land should be made available for renting, to allow a widespread experimentation in peasant proprietorship; and it should be made possible for every labourer to buy his own house with a small plot.[187] At the same time he professed doubts as to the advisability and feasibility of encouraging peasant proprietorship by allowing free trade in land. Such a move without some careful experimentation was too hasty: 'It is quite clear that by putting the labourer on the land you may simply involve him in ruin. You have to wait, and this is what I especially want to impress upon you, you have to wait to deal with this thing until the economic conditions are more settled.'[188]

Price, then still an undergraduate, had no such doubts. By 1884 he had combined Marshall's unwavering faith in free competition with a conern for more immediate measures to be taken regarding the land system. In his concern for action he may have gone beyond Marshall's suggestions in 'Progress and Poverty' but, while preserving Marshall's reasoning, his approach was noticeably different from Toynbee's.

Following a speech delivered by John Bright in Birmingham, on 2 February 1884 Price wrote to the *Daily News* supporting free trade in land as the best means for ensuring greater dispersal of land ownership:[189]

At present our agrarian constitution is prejudicial to the increase of small purchases, and . . . therefore no conclusive inference can be drawn as to the action of economic forces, but . . . so far as any argument can be urged, they

---

[187] Toynbee, *Progress and Poverty*, p. 48.
[188] Ibid., p. 47.
[189] Leeds, Price papers, MS 106(77).

point to a greater dispersion rather than an increased concentration of landed property as the future effects of Free Trade in Land.

The theme was developed by Price in some essays,[190] including his entry for the 1886 Cobden Prize, which demonstrated the increasing influence of Marshall's thinking on his work. In them Price incorporated most of the main points made by Marshall in the 'Progress and Poverty' lectures, which may have been further elaborated in Marshall's lectures at Balliol, as well as the methodological position presented in Marshall's Cambridge inaugural lecture.[191] Ever eager to defend the reputation of the 'old' economists, Marshall argued that 'Mr. George in his books had not in any single case really understood the author whom he had undertaken to criticise.'[192] Price extended the argument to socialism in general which he claimed was based as a whole on a misinterpretation of the orthodox theories — a generalization Marshall had avoided in his 'Progress and Poverty' lectures. More specifically 'the special attack upon landed property which is the chief feature of English Socialism is founded on exaggerated interpretation of Ricardo's theory of rent' and 'the special attack upon capital, which is the chief feature of Continental Socialism, is based upon a perversion of Ricardo's theory of value.' Socialism, then, could be proved false if one established its misinterpretation of otherwise basically sound theories.

Price chose to refer to socialism as a whole as a negative and destructive movement. He acknowledged the use of the term by non-revolutionaries who wished to promote immediate practical reforms through state intervention or independent of it. But these were exceptional private cases. Contemporary socialism, according to Price, was synonymous with revolutionary socialism, a creed which was united solely by its call for nihilism and which lacked a positive unifying vision of an alternative system. Price tried to show that 'tried at the bar of

---

[190] Ibid. (78).
[191] A. Marshall, 'The Present Position of Economics', in A. C. Pigon (ed.), *Memorials of Alfred Marshall* (London, 1925). For Marshall's views on the subject see pp. 130 ff.
[192] In Stigler, 'Alfred Marshall's Lectures on Progress and Poverty'. The point was made by Marshall during the discussion following Henry George's address at the Clarendon Hotel, Oxford, on 14 Mar. 1884.

Political Economy, to which it ostentatiously appeals, the damning verdict alone can be given that the criticism and proposals alike of contemporary socialism are conspicuous at once for their vaunting promise and their sorry performance.'

In his essays Price incorporated Marshall's attempt in the 'Present Position' to sidestep the issue of historical relativism and, like Marshall, he saw no contradiction between historical relativism and the validity he claimed for the misused orthodox theories of value and rent. Marshall's concession to the arguments of historical relativism was made in order to demonstrate that the acceptance of the notion of constant change did not necessarily rule out all notions of universalism which, in the case of economics, applied to its methodology. Price faithfully repeated Marshall's argument. As in the biological sciences the subject matter of economics was in a constant flux.

The laws of physical and still more of moral and political philosophy are not laws in the imperative sense, imposed by nature upon phenomena. But they are really the way in which we represent facts to ourselves and reduce the world of sense into an intelligible world of knowledge. If then facts be altered the law which is the representative of facts must be altered also.

However, the method by which the laws were derived from facts remained basically unaltered, being continuously improved and refined: 'It follows that it is erroneous to draw the conclusion, as some people have done, that, with the modification or even overthrow of particular practical dogmas of particular economists, is involved the rejection of economic method and economic science.'

In the same essay Price had argued that Ricardo's theories may prove inapplicable with the changing circumstances; that in the case of material progress circumstances had indeed changed over the past thirty years; that, nevertheless his theories were still basically sound when slightly modified, so that if socialist theory could be shown to be a misinterpretation of them, socialist theory was therefore invalid; and finally that even if Ricardo's theories were disproved, that would have no bearing on the status of the scientific methodology of economics. Economic theory was still considered by Price to be the product of Baconian inductivism.

As for state intervention, Price was as cautious as most of his fellow Oxford economists. Since in his view the existing structure of society was basically sound and since the fruits of scientifically monitored free competition were just beginning to be reaped, the burden of proof was on the advocates of specific acts of state intervention. As a principle, state action was not rejected.

Price showed at the time little, if any, inclination towards independent work on theory. Instead, and more in keeping with the general trend in research of his Oxford contemporaries, he concentrated on current issues, seeking practical and prescriptive conclusions. Practical suggestions for immediate action were commonly held to be one of the main purposes of the studying and teaching of economics, and at first Price continued to follow Marshall's lead. In his first independent Extension course at Newcastle upon Tyne, as the first Toynbee Trust lecturer, Price based his lectures, on the whole, on an exposition of Marshallian theory. Thus in lecture eight on 'The Wages Question',[192] after explaining the theory of wages on Marshallian lines, he suggested possible forms of working-class action: an increase in working men's savings as a means to improve their bargaining position in industrial disputes, which would at the same time contribute to capital investment and create more wealth; the education of working men so that they might understand their true interests and use their knowledge to advantage; and the building up of the working man's moral character which would manifest itself in advancing the average age of marriage. Price also expressed support of protective legislation which would regulate working conditions. He emphatically advised the working classes to cultivate public opinion which, he argued, could be 'far more powerful than law' and 'may work wonders . . . in changing human nature'.

While Price was teaching this course on the 'Division of Wealth', he was to embark, as the terms of the lectureship stipulated, on his first project of independent field research. Coming up to Newcastle he had no clear idea as to which subject he should concentrate on, and decision was further delayed by the work required in the preparation of the course and then by the unexpectedly large number of weekly essays. At first

---

[192] Leeds, Price papers, MS 106(17).

Price had considered working on two subjects—industrial arbitration and the migration of labour.[193] His final decision to concentrate on industrial arbitration may have been influenced by Robert Spence Watson, one of the Toynbee Trustees, a local expert on conciliation, and one of the main promotors of Extension teaching in Newcastle. In any event, Spence Watson was one of Price's main sources on the workings of arbitration[194] and Price seems to have adopted most of his conclusions.[195] In his work Price laid emphasis on the positive role of trade unions in promoting industrial peace and, appropriately, when he lectured on his findings in Oxford he chose to call his lecture 'The Trades Union alternative to strikes; an account of the methods employed in the arrangement of wages in the Iron and Coal Trades of the North'.[196]

While working on industrial peace Price sought a theoretical framework and turned from Marshall to Jevons's *The State in Relation to Labour* (London 1882), which in the final report to the Trust[197] is quoted as one of his main authorities. Price shared Jevons's basic philosophical premiss concerning state action. Assuming the general validity of the principle of free competition, each case of suggested state action should be examined separately and judged on its merits. The examination in each case would be based on accumulated experience and wherever possible on controlled experimentation. In dealing with such issues Jevons admitted that pure deductive theory of the type he himself had developed had little bearing on the work of the legislator. Similarly, although in his conclusions Price claimed that he had remained faithful to Marshall's synthesis of deductive and inductive reasoning, the course he actually seems to have followed made little use of deductive theory.[198]

Jevons advised extreme caution in adopting new reform

---

[193] Gell family papers, L. L. Price to A. H. D. Acland, 22 May 1886.
[194] Price, 'Miscellaneous Reminiscences', ch. 2.
[195] For Spence Watson's experience in the matter see Percy Corder, *The Life of Robert Spence Watson* (London, 1914).
[196] Gell family papers, L. L. Price to A. H. D. Acland, 22 May 1886.
[197] L. L. Price, *Industrial Peace; its Advantages, Methods, and Difficulties* (London, 1887).
[198] Cf. ibid., pp. 127 and 54. That little use was made of deductive theory was also the understanding of Ashley and Cannan when discussing the point in the *Oxford Magazine*. See pp. 162 ff.

schemes. The reformer, he warned, must be careful not to overlook the good in an existing institution or form of economic activity which he might wish to replace: 'We may be obliged to bear with evil for a time that we may avoid a worse evil, or that we may not extinguish the beginning of good. In the end we shall not be disappointed if our efforts are really directed towards that good of the people which was long ago pronounced to be the highest law.'[199]

One such case was that of the trade unions. Jevons described the faults he found in the principle of trade unionism, thereby indicating that one could not expect trade unions to solve all the problems of society: 'Each trade which maintains a strict union is, in fact, striving to secure an unfair share of the public expenditure . . . it is quite impossible for trades unions in general to effect any permanent increase of wages. . . . success in maintaining exclusive monopolies leads to great loss and injury to the community in general.'[200]

On the other hand, combination laws were clearly a greater evil and any attempt to do away with trade unions would also abrogate the benefits resulting from their action, benefits which would survive the eventual gradual disintegration of the unions, if not in fact cause their disappearance:

> The existing great trade societies only need to be let alone and they will probably degenerate from their original trade purposes. But inasmuch as those trade purposes were against the public good, the process of degeneration will probably bring them more nearly into consonance with public interests . . . . The more extensive the federation of trades which . . . meet in peaceful conference, the more wide and generous must of necessity become their views. Enjoying all the rights and performing all the duties of the English citizen, the trades unionist will before long cease his exclusive strife against his true ally, his wealthy employer.[201]

It was this effect of trade unions on the workers they represented, as well as on their representatives, that Price considered to be the most important contribution of trade unionism to the promotion of industrial peace.[202]

Jevons found that the form in which wage negotiations were

---

[199] W. Stanley Jevons, *The State in Relation to Labour* (London, 1882), p. 166.
[200] Ibid., p. 106.
[201] Ibid., p. 126.
[202] Price, *Industrial Peace*, p. 16.

conducted meant as much as, if not more than, the actual issues at hand. Once a dispute deteriorated into a strike it stopped being a question of economics and became an issue of class antagonism. Therefore all forms of arbitration and conciliation were of considerable benefit to society in that they helped to bring together the two sides, allowing the development of a measure of mutual trust. Arbitration and sliding scales, imperfect means as they were, were instrumental in promoting 'a sounder method of partnership and participation in profits which a future generation will certainly enjoy'.[203]

Price was less certain about the future form of industrial organization. Instead he chose to concentrate on the means for promoting industrial peace without committing himself to any definite vision of the future industrial system. At the same time he felt certain that whatever the future system may be, industrial peace was an essential precondition:

It is the promise of the future which is the basis at once of the hopefulness of arbitration and the despair of industrial conflict. For when once the opposing parties have met on equal footing and have learnt to rely for the maintenance of their claims upon argument rather than force they have taken the first and most difficult step upon the path which conducts naturally to conciliation—to mutual concession instead of contentious argument.[204]

Price's approach to the methods by which industrial peace was to be achieved was pluralistic and carefully optimistic. He seems to have discarded the certainty of free competition as the main course of progress without replacing it with an alternative vision. Similarly he saw no single superior means for dealing with industrial strife, although, like Spence-Watson, he felt that where possible sliding scales were probably the best method of wage settlement. Yet, having argued that industrial peace was a distinct possibility, that it was the way to progress, and that trade unions had a positive contribution in promoting industrial peace, Price developed a certain commitment to his view on how society was moving towards a better future. As a result, over the next few years he found it necessary to explain various developments that seemed to run contrary to his main argument. He found that one of the chief conditions for

---

[203] Jevons, *The State in Relation to Labour*, p. 158.
[204] Price, *Industrial Peace*, p. 72.

establishing any form of regular wage settlement was stability of prices.[205] This eventually led Price to consider more closely the issue of fluctuations in prices from the viewpoint of bimetallism. This interest was an extension of his work on industrial peace, since bimetallism would hopefully result in stabilizing the currency. This in turn would stabilize prices, thereby creating the necessary condition for industrial peace.

The influence of Jevons's views on practical forms of reform and state action is also evident in the early work of Hubert Llewellyn Smith. Ll. Smith's knowledge of economics developed mainly through his own reading of contemporary works, and at least in the case of his reading for the Adam Smith Club debates, texts were chosen according to the subject to be debated. In other words, his reading was more oriented towards individual issues than a systematic attempt to deal with economic theory in general, which might have been the case if he had had to read political economy for Schools. As a result he never developed much of an interest in pure theory and seems to have been content to accept first the authority of Jevons and later that of Charles Booth on theoretical issues, while he himself was much more interested in actual field work.

The subject set for the Cobden prize essay in 1886 was 'Political Economy and Socialism: What is the teaching of Political Economy as to the effects of Private Property and Free Exchange on the one hand, and of State Property and Regulated Contracts on the other hand, on the Production and Distribution of Wealth?' Following Jevons's advice as to how issues of state action should be dealt with, Ll.Smith stated:

> As it is hopeless to expect to be able to lay down any single rule of universal validity, it will be best in our examination of the various theories that have been propounded to follow roughly the order of their historical development. It will afterwards be necessary to consider the application of these theories to modern industrial legislation, and to various proposals for measures of social reform.'[206]

Elsewhere he pointed out that whereas the legislative experiments suggested by Jevons were, perhaps unfortunately, rare,

---

[205] e.g. in L. L. Price, 'The Position and Prospects of Industrial Conciliation', read before the Royal Statistical Society in May 1890 and printed in the *Journal of the Royal Statistical Society*, September 1890.

[206] H. Ll. Smith, *Economic Aspects of State Socialism* (Oxford, 1887), p. 30.

an alternative source of information could be found in history: 'History, rightly understood, supplies us with a series of such experiments, from whose immediate and remote effects we can often gather much valuable information as to the probable success or failure of schemes of state interference.'[207]

Ll. Smith had also adopted the historical-relativistic approach to theory without Price's qualifications. Theories were not of universal validity and any attempt to construct them as such was an 'attempt to rear a permanent structure on a continually shifting basis'.[208] More specifically Ricardo's theories were 'drawn from observations extending over but a limited range of time, and influenced by an abnormal set of circumstances, they have progressively become less adequate as an explanation as times and circumstances have changed.'[209] But here Ll. Smith added an argument that placed him on this issue midway between Ashley and Cannan on the one hand and Price on the other. He found, in agreement with Price, that Lassale, Engels, and Marx had all misinterpreted Ricardo. However, since Ricardo himself was outdated, their misinterpretation did not automatically render their theories invalid. Socialist theories, therefore, required separate consideration: their value could not be determined solely by the discussion of the value of Ricardo's work. In later years this position would lead Ll. Smith, when the issue arose, not to consider it essential to disprove Ricardo in order to disprove revolutionary socialism. These were two different problems and Ll. Smith unquestionably awarded the second one a higher priority.

After dealing with a number of possible directions that state action might take, Ll. Smith summed up his essay in a Jevonian vein:

> Our conclusion have indeed been more negative than positive. We have seen the impossibility of enunciating a universal law which shall determine the limits of beneficial interference with private property and private contract, and the few principles we have been able to lay down are rather of the nature of the finger posts pointing out directions in which difficulties and dangers are likely to be encountered and indicating the general aims which the legislator

---

[207] Ibid., pp. 3-4.
[208] Ibid., pp. 2-3.
[209] Ibid., p. 25.

should keep before his mind, than ready made laws dispensing with detailed examination of every particular case.²¹⁰

A year later, on the basis of some limited experience of dealing with more specific issues, Ll. Smith offered the members of the Oxford Economic Society²¹¹ three main guidelines for state action in industrial matters:

1. It must aim at promoting a state of things which the individuals interfered with would spontaneously aim at and attain themselves if only they recognised their own ultimate as well as immediate interests in their widest sense and provided the obstacles which now artificially impede freedom of movement and equal competition were absent. It must tend to promote the real power of the labourer to attain his real economic advantage, it must help him to help himself.
2. It must not be based on a false estimate of human nature.
3. It must not diminish self reliance.

Ll. Smith may have adopted Jevons's theoretical guidelines for dealing with issues of state action, but the ideology which motivated him in his choice of vocation and field of enquiry was clearly Oxonian. His conviction was expressed in his paper to the OES.

We deny the right of any man to do what he likes with his own, *we* demand that he shall so use it as to fulfil his duty to Society in which he is placed. And *we* do not despair of gradually forming a public opinion which shall regard not as an ornament but as a blot on society the man who uses his wealth be it great or be it small regardless of the interests of the Society in which he lives [my italics].

This faith in the power of public opinion, which he shared with Price, was not an idle notion. Ll. Smith had realized, possibly through his experience of working for temperance,²¹² of the use of public pressure and the sense of shame stimulated at public meetings to bring people to sign the pledge, the power of the public to induce people to change their views and actions through shame. When working in the East End he made good use of this knowledge to raise public opinion in favour of the Bryant & May strike and later the Dockers' strike.

---

²¹⁰ Ibid., p. 119.
²¹¹ H. Ll. Smith, 'Shop Hours Regulation', read to the Oxford Economic Society of 3 May 1887, MS in the Ll. Smith family papers.
²¹² Ll. Smith family papers, H. Ll. Smith to his mother, 12 Sept. 1887.

Like Toynbee, Ashley, and Cannan Ll. Smith was sympathetic to the cause of socialism. He accepted the economic evils it set out to remedy as a just and valid cause for action but found that the means it advocated were inadequate, based as they were on a misunderstanding of the structure of the economic system. Nevertheless, in an address to working men at Bradford in 1887,[213] he clearly stated his preferences: 'If there be no outlook I am bound to say I would rather be wrong with Karl Marx than right with David Ricardo.'

Consequently, Ll. Smith found it necessary to define his own brand of socialism, which he did in his paper to the OES:[214]

> The breaking down of the barriers of class exclusiveness, the development of the spirit of class union and social sympathy, the formation of a sound and healthy public opinion which shall make it impossible for a self respecting man to live entirely to himself, the simplification of the lives of the rich, the elevation of the lives of the poor, the bringing close to every man the means of contact with all great subjects, in a word the education and moralisation of society from top to bottom—surely this is a socialism of a far more searching and radical kind than that which often passes under its name. You would redistribute, we would transform, it is the difference between pounding a thing in a pestle and dissolving it with a chemical. And we can begin at once, now and here.

In his Cobden Prize essay, Ll. Smith stated that the major concern of modern society was the better distribution of wealth, a change which to his way of thinking would have to be the outcome of some 'chemical' changes in society and could not be effected merely be legislation. By way of some preliminary suggestion as to how this change might be practically effected, he pointed out that better distribution was 'promoted by any change which tends to break down monopolies, nominal or disguised, by anything which increases the mobility of labour or which raises the intelligence of the working classes.'[215] These two positive suggestions were adopted by Ll. Smith himself as the two main issues on which he was to concentrate over the next few years — the study of the mobility of labour and the education of the working classes through the Extension movement and technical education.

---

[213] Ll. Smith family papers, H. Ll. Smith, 'Socialism', MS.
[214] Ll. Smith, 'Shop Hours Regulation'.
[215] Ll. Smith, *State Socialism*, p. 45.

The theoretical significance of the study of the mobility of labour is partly to be found in Ll. Smith's analysis of Ricardo's theories in his Extension course on the 'Makers of Political Economy' which, like Price's course delivered at Newcastle, was a Toynbee Trust project aimed at combining lecturing with field research. In dealing with Ricardo,[216] Ll. Smith elaborated on the historical-relativistic approach suggested in his Cobden Prize essay. Ricardo should be studied in relation to the historical circumstances in which he worked. The logical structure of his theory of rent was quite sound and with some modification it could be valid if the presuppositions could be shown to exist. Yet his overall evaluation of Ricardo's position in the history of economic theory was considerably harsher, using idioms reminiscent of Jevons:[217]

> The science has been shunted from the groove of fact on to the groove of theory. The man who would advance it had not gone with Adam Smith to France, or with Matthews on his tour round Europe collecting, arranging, and sifting facts about industry and social science, but could sit in a comfortable chair before a roaring fire and if he did not go to sleep could spin a theory in his brain of the action and reaction of the complicated parts of the Social Mechanism. It's a great change—Political Economy has become an abstract science.
> And this change—all that is meant and involved by the gap that separates the work of Mill from the work of Adam Smith is due to one remarkable man—and that man is David Ricardo.

Here, then, was another major objection to Ricardo — his methodology. His whole work was based on completely hypothetical premisses. His laws of the equality of wages, profits, interest, and his theory of value were based on the premiss of the unhindered mobility of labour and capital. The issue, as far as Ll. Smith was concerned, was not whether the theory was logically sound. To his mind it was obvious that labour did not enjoy complete freedom of mobility and, as he had stated in his Cobden Prize essay, increased mobility led to a better distribution of wealth. The real issue then was to find the true premisses on which one could construct a theory that would

---

[216] Unfortunately the full course has not been preserved. The one surviving lecture is on Ricardo: MS in the Ll. Smith family papers. It is possible that Ll. Smith himself considered it the only lecture of the course worth preserving.

[217] Inappropriately perhaps, since he was discussing methodology rather than the validity of specific theories.

reflect reality. Mobility of labour had to be studied in detail in order to guide the politician's hand in augmenting its freedom.

Like Price before him, Ll. Smith was unsure, when he was appointed the second Toynbee Trust lecturer, on what subject he was going to concentrate.[218] After the course in Bradford had begun, Ll. Smith started gathering general information on industrial conditions and the state of some of the local trades with the aid of the Bradford and District Trades Council.[219] However, the popularity of the course, which forced him to add on extra classes and examine an unexpectedly large number of weekly essays, meant that the research would have to wait till the end of the course. By then Ll. Smith had decided to concentrate on the mobility of labour between trades, based mainly on material collected from local silk mills.[220] He had been given advice by Giffen and by the Secretary of the London Charity Organisation Society from whom he may have learnt of Booth's project in the East End. In any event, he obtained permission from the Trust to extend his study and in the following year he moved to the East End as a Toynbee Hall resident where he joined Booth's team of researchers examining the migration of labour into London.

As he himself probably anticipated, his study revealed that 'there is no rest, no absolute equilibrium in the economic world — all is a perpetual state of flux and change',[221] so that apart from the conviction that progress meant increased mobility, each trade in each type of locality at any given time had to be examined separately in order to furnish an accurate picture of what should and what could be done.

---

[218] Ll. Smith family papers, H. Ll. Smith to his mother from Bradford, n.d.

[219] Ll. Smith family papers, H. Ll. Smith to his mother from Bradford (n.d. but after his second lecture) and a circular of the Bradford and District Trades Council dated 12 Nov. 1887.

[220] H. Ll. Smith, *Modern Changes in the Mobility of Labour; Especially between trade and trade* (London, 1890).

[221] Ibid., p. 20.

2
THE EXTENSION MOVEMENT AND OXFORD'S ECONOMISTS

Oxford in the mid-1880s was a difficult place in which to attempt the beginning of an academic career, especially in political economy, which was not a subject greatly in demand by the Oxford colleges. They rarely had need of a full-time tutor in that subject. Instruction in it was usually the supplementary task of a college tutor in history or classics, in the same way that the political economy paper for the Honours School of Modern History was of a supplementary nature. The subject was taught with a strong emphasis on orthodox theory, the most commonly used textbooks being Mill's *Principles* and Adam Smith's *Wealth of Nations*.[1] College tutors did not hesitate to teach a subject in which they had no training other than, at best, some reading and an interest in practical and political issues, nor is there any evidence that they felt unequal to the task. A rather exaggerated example can be found in a description of one of Jowett's lectures in political economy when he was still a Balliol tutor. Jowett's lectures, we are told,

> consisted of readings out of Wilhelm Meister and Carlyle and Ruskin and others of a similar kind. They were interesting but it was difficult to see where the Political Economy came in. He also invited questions and when someone asked him what was the relation between supply and demand he replied in his gentle staccato voice, 'Well, you know the world is a very large place.'[2]

---

[1] See in the *Oxford University Gazette* the lists of lectures given in political economy by Professor Bonamy Price. Whenever a textbook is used it is either a work of J. S. Mill or of Adam Smith. However, some of his courses dealt with special subjects such as 'Currency and Banking', 'Free Trade and Fair Trade' (21 Jan. 1881, 20 Jan. 1882), 'Land' (14 June 1881, 5 June 1883), and 'The Relation of Political Economy to Socialism' (5 June 1883). An example can be found in the case of Strachan-Davidson of Balliol who taught political economy there and, in 1886, helped H. Ll. Smith to revise his Cobden Prize essay: J. W. Mackail, *James Leigh Strachan Davidson* (London, 1925).

[2] Sir Henry Studdy Theobald, *Remembrance of Things Past* (Oxford, 1935), p. 40. Theobald matriculated in the Michaelmas Term of 1866. (Jowett was elected Master in 1870.) One suspects that the description is something of an unfair caricature, considering the care that Jowett took with his lecture on political economy in Aristotle, as can be seen from his notes in the Jowett Papers, Balliol College Library, Oxford.

Despite possible exaggeration, this is the kind of impression left by some of the college lecturers in political economy. By the mid-1880s the inspiring lectures of Arnold Toynbee and the competence of Marshall were things of the past, and the teaching of economics had settled into a rut.

To the comparatively unimportant status of political economy in Oxford and the lack of interest in trying new approaches to its study must be added the general dearth in Fellowships during the years of the Government Committee[3] and the effects of the agricultural depression on college revenues.[4] All these factors combined to create a situation in which most colleges considered the position of a college tutor solely for political economy as unnecessary academically and impossible financially.

Following the growing popularity of the extension work at Cambridge, an Oxford Standing Committee of Delegates of Local Examination was formed on 16 June 1878, to initiate similar work at Oxford. The Committee met for the first time on 13 July 1878, chaired by T. H. Green, with Thorold Rogers as one of its members, and A. H. D. Acland its secretary.[5] Acland and the Committee seem to have been under the impression that all they needed to do in the way of organization was to sit back and wait for requests for lecturers from the localities.[6] Whether this was the case or not, the lack of spontaneous demand made it clear that demand had first to be created and that the promoters of extension work would have to convince its potential customers of the value of adult education. Rather than approach various localities separately, Acland decided to try to reach a much larger public which was already in association—the members of the co-operative movement.

---

[3] See Lewis R. Farnell, *An Oxonian Looks Back* (London, 1934), p. 70. E. A. Freeman, 'Oxford After Forty Years', in the *Contemporary Reveiw* 1887, pp. 609-23, 814-30.

[4] An analysis of the depression based on the falls in revenue to Oriel College may be found in L. L. Price, 'The Recent Depression in Agriculture, as shown in the accounts of an Oxford College 1876-1890', in the *Journal of the Royal Statistical Society*, March 1892.

[5] Rewley House, Oxford, Department of External Studies, Extension Archives, Minutes of Meetings of the Committee for University Extension.

[6] Stuart Marriott, 'Dr. Welch on "Oxford and University Extension", a critical Note', in *Studies in Adult Education*, April 1979.

The choice of the co-operative movement was more than a matter of expediency. If progress took the form of corporate action it was only natural to approach the sector of the working class that had already taken a significant step towards the future form of social organization. Co-operators were not just a potential public, they were the vanguard of a new society. Furthermore, most co-operative societies had an education fund of up to 2.5 per cent of their net annual profits. In most cases, having already used the money to create reading rooms, libraries, etc., the societies were at a loss as to what should be done with the fund.

Acland first made contact with the Oxford Co-operative and Industrial Society in 1878. He was a speaker at its District Conference on 7 January 1878 and was instrumental in influencing the District Committee to recommend the start of an educational fund. He became an active supporter of local co-operatism, representing the Society at the Manchester Congress, but it was not until 1880 that he managed to persuade the Oxford Society to agree to a series of lectures given by members of the University.[7]

Acland aimed at the gradual creation of a demand for such lectures all through the Southern Sector of the co-operative movement and eventually all through England. In this he was supported by the Council of the Guild of Co-operators which, formed by the Southern Sector, aimed at propagating the ideals of co-operation among the general public.[8] The Guild's activity within the movement included the promotion of internal education by the foundation of circulating library boxes, each containing some thirty volumes on various subjects considered to be of value to the co-operators, and by supporting schemes for technical education as well as classes on historical and economic subjects.

To effect the launching of the Extension courses on a large scale, in 1882 the annual Co-operative Congress was brought to Oxford. The delegates were to be received and entertained by a volunteer committee of senior and junior members of the

---

[7] *Oxford Co-operative and Industrial Society Ltd. An Historical Sketch From 1872 to 1909* (Manchester, 1909), pp. 42–5.

[8] *Guide to the Co-operative Congress of 1882* (Oxford, 1882), p. 184. A member of the Guild's Council in 1882 was H. V. Toynbee, brother of Arnold.

University, including some of Oxford's most active Liberals. These included J. Percival, W. R. Anson (Warden of All Souls), A. H. D. Acland, L. R. Phelps, R. L. Nettleship, Arnold Toynbee, A. L. Smith, T. H. Warren, A. Sidgwick, A. Robinson, D. G. Ritchie, Henry Scott Holland, and A. T. Lyttelton.[9] Junior members included Bolton King and M. E. Sadler, both members of Acland's Inner Circle.

In his address to the Congress, Acland was eager to make it clear that the aim of the members of the reception committee—the 'joining in the bonds of friendship of the University people with our fellow citizens and the members of our own co-operative society'—was free of any condescension: 'We do not stand aloof from your movement, but we stand outside in admiration. We . . . look up at you and hold out our hands in admiration and sympathy.'[10] Their hope was to forge an alliance with what might be the beginning of the movement that would change society: 'a platform, a basis, a foundation upon which any number of hopeful movements and any amount of hopeful progress may be raised.'[11]

In the University's main contribution to the proceedings of the Congress, Arnold Toynbee laid down a possible framework of co-operation between the movement and Oxford. In his paper 'The Education of Co-operators', Toynbee expressed his view of the ideological significance of the movement in the eyes of the University. This was done by a comparison with trade unionism:

Trades Unions which accept the facts of the present industrial system, and are engaged in a hand-to-hand fight with capitalists, have not time to indulge in dreams that are natural to bodies of men whose aim is the radical transformation of the entire conditions of industrial life. For we know that, however seemingly immersed in the petty business of the shop co-operators may be, their real aim and their real determination is to put an end to competition and the division of men into capitalists and labourers.[12]

In Toynbee's view the nature and goals of co-operation necessitated a concentrated effort towards the education of the

---

[9] Holland and Lyttelton were to become members of the *Lux Mundi* group.
[10] *The Fourteenth Annual Co-operative Congress of 1882* (Manchester, 1882), p. 24.
[11] Ibid., p. 23.
[12] A. Toynbee, 'The Education of Co-operators', pp. 59–61. Reprinted in A. Toynbee, *The Industrial Revolution* new edn., London 1908).

movement's members as citizens — 'the relation in which he stands to other individual citizens and to the community as a whole'[13] — since, it was hoped, the movement would eventually become a national one.

Toynbee outlined three main subjects which would form the basis of the co-operators' education: politics, industry, and sanitation, the latter being a technical subject aimed at disease prevention. The teaching of politics and industry was to follow three main lines of approach — analysis of the current state of the subject, the history of the existing system, and the history of the relevant theories. Instruction on these lines would teach the individual co-operator his 'duties to his fellow men, and in what way union with them was possible',[14] leading to the reconstruction of the industrial system through the union of capital and labour. Teachers would be provided from both the universities and the societies themselves and a system could be set up whereby lecturers appointed by a central board would be made responsible for teaching within a given district.

Toynbee had realized that a major obstacle was the co-operators themselves. Since they were interested primarily in their dividends, it would be difficult to make them see beyond schemes for immediate profit. For that purpose the movement wanted the regeneration of enthusiasm, which 'can only be kindled by two things: an ideal which takes the imagination by storm and a definite intelligible plan for carrying out that ideal into practice.'[15]

The delegates to the Congress took the opportunity to express their concern over the general air of apathy among co-operators. But their concern was not founded on an abstract notion of co-operatives as the model and vanguard of a new industrial order. They were mainly worried by the reluctance of successful distributive societies to invest their profits in more advanced (i.e. productive) forms of co-operation. Their hope was that courses in the principles of co-operation would lead to a more widespread readiness of the rank and file to develop new co-operative enterprises. This view was expressed by Benjamin Jones in a paper which followed Toynbee's rather

[13] Ibid., p. 243.
[14] Ibid., p. 245.
[15] Ibid., p. 248.

abstract discourse. It was Jones's view that the future of the movement was in jeopardy unless co-operators 'accumulate capital to make them independent of masters, become sufficiently well educated in co-operative principles to enable them to successfully combine for self employment, and acquire a knowledge of sundry economic truths closely concerning their prosperity.'[16] This was essential, since 'it is an admitted fact that the wages of the workers who have no capital have always a tendency to dwindle down to the smallest sum necessary to keep workmen alive.'[17] Acceptance of this orthodox theory of wages meant that in the co-operators' view the future of the movement could be ensured only if societies used their profits to replace the capitalist within the existing system by fulfilling his function. It was a vision of increased self-sufficiency rather than a union between labour and capital.

It was Jones's opinion that instruction in the history of co-operation, the theory of credit, and the theory of productive co-operation would lead co-operators to invest their profits in productive co-operation. He envisaged the job being done by volunteer teachers, members of co-operative societies. The first task was to train a group of such teachers who would be the nucleus of an independent, internal education system.

Whereas few of the delegates understood Toynbee's arguments, they all shared Jones's concern for the investment of profits. It was the view of one delegate that 'Both papers [Toynbee's and Jones's] were excellent, and that Mr. Jones was practical.'[18] This seems to have been appreciated by Acland. Using his official position as a delegate, he managed to save Toynbee's scheme from being completely ignored, suggesting that Toynbee and some other university friends of the movement should be asked to form a small committee under the auspices of the Central Board aimed at producing papers on political economy and related subjects for the use of co-operative teachers.[19] To this Toynbee added the suggestion that the Central Board should go a step further and draw up a detailed education scheme, with the additional possibility of us-

---

[16] *Fourteenth Annual Congress*, p. 62.
[17] Ibid., p. 61.
[18] Ibid., p. 70.
[19] Ibid.

ing university men as teachers. Following the debate Acland's suggestion was adopted as a resolution, as was a suggestion that the Central Board should draw up a 'report on the whole question of education' which would be used as guide lines for the various sections.

By 1883 little had been done in the way of an overall scheme. However, co-operation between Acland and Jones in the Southern Section resulted in an experimental training class for teachers and a draft syllabus submitted to the Fifteenth Congress.[20] The committee recommended by Acland, including himself, Toynbee, and A. Sidgwick, was set up by the Southern Section as a consultative body on educational matters, to work with Benjamin Jones in promoting co-operative teachers' training classes.

The partnership between Jones and the Oxford men was clearly an uneasy one. The draft syllabus he drew up for the teacher-training classes allowed only one lesson out of fourteen for the subject of 'The Co-operator as a Citizen; his Duties and his attitude towards the Movements of his Time'. It seems that Jones was worried that the Oxford men might try to take over co-operative education and that he himself would be replaced by an Oxford man in the teachers' training scheme.[21] During the 1883 Congress Acland pointed out: 'The co-operative movement as being so closely watched by all the economists of the kingdom that if any of these were asked to prepare such a work or statement of facts [to be used as co-operative education textbooks], they would gladly help them and consider it an honour to do so.'[22] To this Jones resentfully replied:

> They were not going to do the bidding of university dons, but think for themselves, develop their own faculties, and instruct their members and children in a thorough knowledge of the principles of co-operation. They must not overshoot the mark in aiming at university. The kernel of the system must be education in co-operation.[23]

To prevent a confrontation, while preserving the Oxford involvement, Acland suggested a short course of about three lec-

---

[20] *Fifteenth Annual Congress 1883* (Manchester, 1883), pp. 20-3.
[21] Ibid., p. 21.
[22] Ibid., p. 40.
[23] Ibid.

tures by university men 'on topics bearing on the duties of co-operators as men and as citizens upon which . . . it is more incumbent for them to dwell in proportion to the greater powers of fulfilling them arising from the higher position which co-operation gives them'.[24] This was accepted: it would allow the two concepts of co-operative education to develop separately.

Acland had no wish to confront Jones on the issue. As secretary of the educational committee of the United Board (set up in 1883) he submitted a report to the 1884 Congress considering the general state of co-operative education. One of its conclusions was that 'co-operators must not look to outside persons for the chief educational work that is to be done'.[25] At the same time the short courses he had begun with Toynbee during the winter of 1882 were continued. However, demand was still limited and by 1885 Acland could report no more than two twelve-lecture courses, the first of their kind, given to societies at Bolton and Manchester.[26] It became clear that although co-operative lecturing had been established as a sphere of Oxford Extension lecturing it was still far from providing the framework of a national system. Even if co-operative education on the lines suggested by Jones were to develop into a system covering all the societies in England, Extension work within the movement would remain limited. If the Extension was to reach a wide public, it had to adopt a different organizational approach.

For the short co-operative courses Acland recruited a number of young graduates, one of whom was M. E. Sadler.[27] After graduation, Sadler's search for a job was influenced by two major considerations: his wish to marry and his intention of finding a job that would coincide with his social ideology and active interest in political economy. He would not read for the Bar. He turned down an offer of a headmastership of an unendowed school and an offer made through D. S. MacColl of a professorship at the Muslim College, Aligarh, India, not

---

[24] Ibid., p. 17.
[25] The *Sixteenth Annual Co-operative Congress 1884* (Manchester, 1884), p. 9.
[26] *Seventeenth Annual Congress 1885* (Manchester, 1885), p. 21.
[27] Sadleir, *Michael Ernest Sadler*, p. 62.

wishing to take his wife 'to a place in which no one could live'. He failed to obtain a Fellowship at All Souls and because of his wish to marry could not obtain one at Merton. There were some other, more enticing possibilities, a lectureship in political economy mentioned by Phelps[28] and a combined lectureship at Trinity College (Oxford) and University College, Bristol, suggested by Dr Percival, but nothing came of either of them.

While still searching for a job, Sadler became gradually more and more involved in co-operative teaching. During 1884 Acland had managed to secure Sadler's appointment as Deputy Steward at Christ Church and was contemplating a joint secretaryship, with himself, of the Extension.[29] However, having decided by the beginning of 1885 to stand for Parliament, Acland managed to secure for Sadler the secretaryship he had just vacated. Thus on 30 April 1885 Sadler was elected Secretary of the University Extension Lectures Sub-Committee.[30]

Sadler's secretaryship saw the introduction of an entirely different form of Oxford Extension organization. Instead of aiming exclusively at an existing organization, it set out, following the earlier example of Cambridge, to stimulate the creation of local committees for the specific purpose of arranging Extension teaching. These would combine with co-operative societies and working men's clubs to create a non-centralized market for Extension lecturing in which demand would be dictated by local wants as assessed by local bodies. Each local organization would usually set up an *ad hoc* fund to finance a course of lectures given by a lecturer whose name they found on the list published and circulated by the Extension Committee. Thus it was not the lecturer but the local organization that decided on the topic and length of the course, according to the funds available and what was considered to be the intellectual interests of the community catered for, from which funds were sought to cover the expenses.

Sadler introduced some innovations in the method of exter-

---

[28] The exact details of Phelps' idea are unknown. See letter from Sadler to Phelps, 24 Feb. 1885 in the Phelps papers, Oriel College, Oxford.
[29] Sadleir, *Michael Ernest Sadler*, p. 69.
[30] In 1892 it became the Delegacy.

nal lecturing, some of which resulted in a rise in popularity and demand for Oxford lecturers:

(a) Short courses of six lectures were added to the usual option of ten- and twelve-lecture courses. This, one of Sadler's most important changes, probably derived from experience gained from co-operative lecturing, gave new centres the option of comparatively low-priced courses with which to begin their work. It was generally assumed by the Committee and some of the local centres that short courses would create an interest that would lead to a demand for longer ones. The short courses became a unique feature of Oxford Extension lecturing and a source of friction with other Extension organizations.

(b) Travelling libraries were sent out, for the duration of a course, to each centre. The library contained all the books recommended by the lecturer for the use of students who might wish to follow up the subject of the lectures, write papers, or take the course's final examination.

(c) Every lecturer produced a syllabus of his course which included an outline of the subject, books recommended, and questions for independent work by the student. The fees paid by the local organization to the University covered a travelling library and sixty syllabuses.

(d) Classes for more detailed treatment of the lecture's subjects were held after lectures, whereas the Cambridge method placed the class before the lecture. It was assumed that the change would allow members of the public who were interested in a specific point or subject raised in a lecture to pursue the matter in the class immediately following the lecture. The Oxford class was not necessarily a regular group and the numbers of those attending classes varied according to the interest stimulated by the lecture. The arrangement was also found convenient when it came to fitting the lectures into the working man's day. The public did not have to wait for the class to end for the lecture to begin, and only those actively interested in the subject had to stay up late.

(e) Until 1890 certificates were awarded to every student who sent in at least three-quarters of the weekly papers assigned and sat the final examination successfully, including students attending courses of six lectures. The standards demanded by the examiners—Oxford dons other than the lecturers — were a pass degree standard for the pass certificates and an honours standard for certificates of distinction, with a prize given to the best examinee. By 1890 it was agreed that in the case of the six-lecture courses the certificate would be replaced by the list of students who passed the examination; however, two short courses on related subjects would be considered as one long course entitling a student to a certificate.

It was hoped that the more promising students would eventually come up to Oxford as students, in which case the certificates would be used as the criteria for acceptance and would possibly be recognized as part of the studies required for taking a degree and thus serve to shorten the period of residence. However, no serious movement of Extension students developed in this direction.

The fees for 1889[31] are given in Table 1 with a comparison of Cambridge fees. The figures were slightly lower for previous years.

Table 1

	Oxford			Cambridge		
	Lecturers' fees	University fees	Total	Lecturers' fees	University fees	Total
	£.s.d.	£.s.d.	£.s.d.	£.s.d.	£.s.d.	£.s.d.
6 lectures	18. 0.0.	6.12.0.	24.12.0.			
12 lectures	36. 0.0.	6.12.0.	42.12.0.	40. 0.0.	7. 0.0.	47. 0.0.
2 × 12 lectures (evening and afternoon)	60. 0.0.	11. 4.0.	71. 4.0.	60. 0.0.	9.10.0.	69. 0.0.

The Cambridge lectures did not include short courses, nor did their fees include syllabuses; a special additional fee was demanded for the examination. The Oxford fees included, besides the library and syllabuses, examination fees and a prize. The lecturers' fees excluded transport expenses (second class rail), advertisements, local expenses, and room and board, usually provided by members of the local committee.

[31] Extension Archive, Extension Committee Minutes, 30 May 1889.

The fees applied to regular lecturers. Senior lecturers at Oxford received £48 for a twelve-lecture course and £72 for a double twelve-lecture course. A list of lecturers and subjects was printed and distributed by the Extension Committee, the courses being given during autumn, winter, and early spring. A popular lecturer, by acccepting as many invitations as he could, could give a large number of lectures during a few months and earn enough to form a very substantial part of an adequate annual income. But the work was hard and the lecturers depended on arousing the interest of the local committees, and although Sadler and the Committee launched various schemes to supplement the lectuerers' fees it usually remained a rather undependable source of income. Lecturers tended to seek supplementary sources, and eventually to replace Extension work with a more secure job.

The Extension had a potential with a special appeal for Oxford's young economists. It offered the chance to teach political economy and economic history as well as offering the challenge of realizing Toynbee's impassioned promise to England's working class. Through the Extension young Oxford idealists could dedicate themselves to the education and betterment of the working classes on a grander and more ambitious scale than through the co-operative classes or Toynbee Hall. When one considers the widespread involvement in the East End settlements of the younger Oxford economists—undergraduates and young graduates—and their problem of finding a career that would be more than just a means of livelihood, the appeal of the Extension becomes apparent.

The career option offered by the Extension was described by Sadler in the Secretary's annual report for the year 1886–7.[32]

> The greater part of the lecturing staff will always be composed of young Graduates who are glad to have a University Extension engagement for a year or two after taking their degrees, partly because of the practical experience in teaching which they gain from it, and partly because it gives them in each year twenty eight weeks of unbroken vacation in which they can continue their studies more uninterruptedly than would be possible in almost any other remunerated occupation.

---

[32] *Oxford University Extension Lectures. Annual Report for the year 1886–1887* (Oxford, 1887).

The fact was, Sadler added, that already 'University Extension lecturing has... provided for younger graduates an entirely new means of earning a livelihood during the first few years after taking their degrees.'

Besides affording a temporary and useful phase in the career of the young graduate there was the hope that eventually the Extension would become a recognized and integral part of the University, and its young lecturers, instead of being dependent on the interest and goodwill of local committees, would become university or college lecturers and thus obtain financial security as well as academic status. Such a status would give Extension lecturers a durable and formal position within the University, with teaching responsibilities outside it. Thus there was a certain element of wishful thinking when Sadler argued that 'the Lecturers appointed by the Delegates form in fact the staff of an itinerant University College established through the co-operation of more than fifty towns.'

The practical implementation of Sadler's vision would have been the establishment, in towns too small for a university college, of local centres housed in a building containing all the elementary facilities necessary for carrying out educational work, such as a lecture room, classroom, and library. Each centre would have attached, and in temporary residence, one or two lecturers who would use the centre as a base for lecturing throughout the district and who, as residents, would also be available for the instruction and supervision of those who wished to pursue their studies beyond the passive attendance of lectures. The lecturer would not wear himself out by continuous travel from one town to another, thus cutting expenses and establishing better and more fruitful contact with the local population. The Delegates went so far as to distribute among the local committees a general floor plan of an artist's concept of an ideal local centre.

The idea of small Extension centres independent of the new provincial university colleges was an application of the Toynbee Hall principle enhanced by the experience gained through the Toynbee Trust Lectures.[33] Towards the end of 1885 the Executive Committee of the Toynbee Trust

[33] Extension Archives, Minutes of the Meetings of the Committee for University Extension, 12 Dec. 1885. 24 June 1886.

approached the Extension Committee with a proposal to appoint L. L. Price as the first Toynbee Trust Lecturer.[34] The Trust's Committee had decided at a meeting on 21 March 1884[35] that its first lectures would be held at Newcastle upon Tyne where they would be organized by R. Spence Watson. Yet neither Price nor the Oxford Extension was its first choice. A subcommittee was appointed consisting of Sidgwick, Foxwell, and Milner (to whom Acland was added in May 1884), with the responsibility of choosing a lecturer. Although Spence Watson was able to inform the Committee later the same year of the completion of the necessary arrangements at Newcastle, the subcommittee found itself unable to recommend an appointment. Its first attempts were to engage a Cambridge man. Sedley Taylor was suggested,[36] but was unable to accept. In June 1884[37] it was agreed that R. D. Roberts should be approached, with a view to the Cambridge Syndicate providing a lecturer, but apparently the Syndicate failed to satisfy the Trust's requirements. It was only the reorganization of the Oxford Extension and the appointment of Sadler to the secretaryship that led the Trust to turn to Oxford.

The Trust suggested that Price, who was probably recommended to the subcommittee by Marshall,[38] should give two full twelve-lecture Extension courses on political economy at Newcastle, where he would reside for their duration and conduct research into local social and economic conditions.[39] In this instance the Trust, through Spence-Watson, was able to provide for the local organization. It would cover Price's expenses and those of the Extension, as well as the cost of printing the lecturer's report to the Trust on his research. The Extension would provide the services that usually accompanied its courses — syllabuses, travelling libraries, examiners, etc. The continuation of this co-operation between the Trust, which covered all expenses, and the Oxford Extension, which provided the organization and suitable lecturers, initiated an

---

[34] Minutes, 12 Dec. 1885.
[35] GLC Record Office A/Toy/1, 21 Mar. 1884.
[36] Ibid., 25 June 1884.
[37] Ibid., 27 June 1885.
[38] Marshall became a Trustee in 1887, replacing H. Sidgwick.
[39] *Oxford University Extension Lectures Annual Report . . . 1886-7.*

Extension experiment in courses delivered by temporarily resident lecturers. In addition, the Trust furnished its lecturers with a venue for their first academic publications as well as an opportunity, arranged by the Trustees, to present their findings in papers read to the Statistical Society or to Section F of the British Association for the Advancement of Science.

L. L. Price gave two coinciding courses of twelve lectures, each in Newcastle upon Tyne, during the period 17 February–5 May 1886. His reports to the Extension Committee and the Toynbee Trust were enthusiastic and he did his best to promote the teaching of political economy to working-class audiences, as well as to justify the Trust's initiative. In his report to the Trustees he wrote: 'I need hardly say how interesting to myself and encouraging has been my first experience at teaching those who have been eager to learn and in removing so far as I have been able a prejudice felt (and perhaps not unnaturally felt in the light of the history of the past) against Political Economy.'[40]

In his report to the Extension Committee Price enclosed, in support of his own impressions, reports of some of his students' comments, in addition to the general information on attendance in lectures and classes, the number of weekly papers, and the number of students who sat the final examination.[41] After the last lecture of one of the courses the vote of thanks was seconded by a student who declared that 'he had thought Political Economy was very dry and not used at all. . . but during the three months that the lectures had been going on there was not a day on which he had not read some Political Economy.' Another student wrote to Price confessing that 'As a working man previously knowing nothing about Political Economics (rather with a prejudice against it) I think these lectures have accomplished their end in my case and I do not stand alone'; he added that it was his intention to pursue his

---

[40] Gell family papers, L. L. Price to Acland, 22 May 1886.
[41] Extension Archives, Oxford University Lectures and Examiners Reports 1886–1887. See also Minutes, 11 Mar. 1886, in which Price's lectures are described by the local secretary as an overall success. The Secretary's estimate of attendance is somewhat higher than that of Price. He points out that 'the right sort of men have come from long distances at great inconvenience.' The distance factor was a fairly popular theme in early reports.

studies in the subject. Price found the general standard of work produced by his students high; the answers to the weekly papers were usually 'clear and pointed' and the use made of the travelling library books intelligent and assiduous.

The same combination of Extension lecturing in political economy and field research was repeated by Price in Cornwall during the autumn of 1886 and the winter of 1887. The results were produced in a paper for the Royal Statistical Society.[42] The Trust's next project was H. Ll. Smith's courses in Bradford and Halifax during autumn 1887,[43] where again the reports were enthusiastic. The average attendance at each lecture in Bradford was 350-400, rising to 500 during the last lecture of the course. Because of the size of the classes (which averaged seventy-seven students) those who wished for more detailed discussion of the matters raised during the lecture and the class stayed after class for an additional session. H. Ll. Smith found it necessary to set aside twenty minutes before each lecture for special instruction for students wishing to write weekly papers. A group of students, finding the time allocated for more detailed study insufficient, met unofficially every week for meetings during which they went over the subject of the lectures with the aid of notes taken during the lectures. H. Ll. Smith was told, and in turn informed the Extension Committee, that some of the students were resolved to pursue systematic studies of political economy through the formation of 'The Bradford Economic and Statistical Society' at which papers would be read and relevant issues discussed. 'I think', Ll. Smith concluded his report, 'that no more satisfactory outcome of such lectures is possible.'

Ll. Smith, like Price before him, found much pleasing evidence of a change in attitude towards the study of political economy which had previously been considered 'dry'. He pointed out that whereas working men had argued before the course that what was needed was not a course in political economy but one on party politics, they now wished for a continuation of educational, in preference to political, lectures.

Despite his popularity as a lecturer, Ll. Smith was still

---

[42] L. L. Price, 'West Barbary or Notes on the System of Work and Wages in the Cornish Mines', *Journal of the Royal Statistical Society*, September 1888.

[43] Extension Archives, Reports 1887-8.

uncertain of the career he wished to pursue. While at Bradford, he heard of a vacancy in the Treasury and decided that if it were to be filled by competition he would stand as a candidate.[44] He was also invited by Acland to spend a week with him in Caernarvon following the completion of his Toynbee Trust courses, to help with work on pamphlets for the National Association for the Promotion of Technical Education of which Acland was now chairman.[45] However, nothing came of the Treasury appointment and the delay in gathering material for his research resulted in Ll. Smith's putting off his stay with Acland until after Christmas.

Still on the lookout for employment, he was offered by Dr Percival, by then Headmaster of Rugby, the job of temporary mathematics master for the spring term of 1888. On the way back from his talk with Percival, Ll. Smith stopped at Oxford, dined with Price, and had a long talk with Sadler. The Extension Committee had begun toying with the idea of a summer meeting and Sadler offered Ll. Smith the job of assistant secretary for the summer, to be followed by further Extension lecturing during the winter. But Ll. Smith was still unable to make up his mind.[46]

The issue was settled on 12 February 1888 when Ll. Smith was visited at Rugby by Acland and Sadler (both ex-Rugby men). Acland informed him that the Technical Association had elected him assistant secretary, although it was not certain how permanent the post would be since the Association's work was still in its early stages. Ll. Smith consulted Percival and Sir Henry Roscoe — Acland's co-chairman of the Association — and on the basis of their advice decided to take the job which, Roscoe assured him, would bring him 'into contact with men worth knowing'.[47] He would finish the term at Rugby, join Sadler and Bolton King on a Toynbee Hall trip to Italy, and then enter Toynbee Hall as a resident, combining continued research, work for the Association, and occasional Extension lecturing.

Thus Ll. Smith began a gradual move away from the Oxford

---

[44] Ll. Smith family papers, Ll. Smith to his mother, *c.* Oct. 1887.
[45] The same, *c.* Oct.-Nov. 1887.
[46] The same, *c.* Nov.-Dec. 1887.
[47] The same, 19 Feb. 1888.

circle, a move which was neither drastic nor final. He continued to give Extension courses, including an advanced course given during autumn 1888 to some of his Toynbee Trust students in Bradford. At the same time he became more actively absorbed in the East End. Eventually, during the spring of 1889, he left Toynbee Hall with some friends for a house in Beaumont Square.[48] In the summer he was nominated as Assistant General Secretary of the British Association for the Advancement of Science, but because of internal Association politics he was forced to withdraw his candidacy.[49] Nevertheless this had demonstrated his growing involvement in various national organizations and activities centred in London. These, combined with his work with Booth, were to pave the way to his appointment by the end of 1892 to the newly created Labour Department of the Board of Trade.

Despite the enthusiasm of the young lecturers (the Toynbee Lectures were their first Extension engagements for Price and Ll. Smith) and of the newly organized Extension, the euphoria gradually dissipated. The Toynbee Trust sponsored one more Extension lectureship—Hewins's two twelve-lecture courses in the autumn of 1889. In the autumn of 1887 it had provided for its only Cambridge Syndicate lectureship—a series of lectures delivered by W. R. Sorley, Fellow of Trinity College, Cambridge, who resided at Middlesborough for fifteen weeks, during which he conducted research on mining royalties.[50] But despite repeated efforts, the Trustees chose not to engage any other lecturers. A number of young Cambridge men were suggested, including Ernest Aves and Stanley Mordant Leathes, but either they were found unsuitable or the projects they suggested 'though meritorious did not appear of distinctive character and of special value'.[51] It was also evident that the Cambridge Syndicate seemed unable to adapt itself to the

---

[48] The same, 1 Apr. 1889; Arthur P. Laurie, *Pictures and Politics; A Book of Reminiscences* (London, 1934), p. 73.

[49] Ll. Smith family papers, Ll. Smith to his mother, 17 Sept. 1889, 10 Oct. 1889, 9 Dec. 1889, *c.* end of Dec. 1889, *Report of the Fifty Ninth Meeting of the British Association for the Advancement of Science held at Newcastle upon Tyne in September 1889* (London, 1890), p. lxxv.

[50] W. R. Sorley, *Mining Royalties and their Effect on the Iron and Coal Trade* (London, 1859) p. vi.

[51] GLC A/Toy./1, 18 June 1888.

Trust's requirements, whereas the Oxford Extension ran out of suitable lecturers for the Trust. The Toynbee Trust was eventually incorporated in Toynbee Hall and the experiment in temporarily resident lecturers was discontinued. Thus, nothing came of the Extension's hopes for the establishment of local Extension colleges with resident lecturers. Instead, the emerging university colleges in the provincial industrial centres competed for the education work within their vicinity and soon came to resent the continued Extension activity which was regarded as an encroachment on their status as local centres of advanced studies.

To understand the contrast between the ideals behind the new surge in Extension activity from 1885 and the reality of the environment with which the actual work was confronted, one must examine the basic concepts with which the Extension and its supporters set out to change the state of British adult education. These concepts were Oxford's assessment of the needs of the nation as a whole and the solutions deemed desirable and feasible. The analysis of the problems and the needs of the nation were usually set in concepts derived from the philosophical framework of Oxford Idealism, as indeed being the basic assumption involved in considering problems and duties on a national scale. These problems and their solutions were one of the forms taken by the practical implementation of Oxford Idealism in a field considered to be of primary importance — the education of the citizen.

Most of the underlying ideals of the Extension can conveniently be found in the report of a conference of representatives of the local committees which took place in Oxford during April 1887.[52] One of the general concepts which recurs as an underlying theme in all types of Oxford Extension work, as well as the East End settlements, was the fear of the widening gulf between the 'two nations', a gulf which might lead through mistrust and ignorance to an outright class war. This fear of the disintegration of society into the chaos of class war was a major theme in Toynbee's lectures to the working classes

---

[52] *Oxford University Extension Lectures. Report of a Conference of Representatives of the Local Committees. Oxford, April 20–21 1887* (Clarendon Press, 1887). Members of the Oxford Economic Society who were present were Campion, Phelps, Sadler, L. L. Price, and Ll. Smith.

and it was carried on by both young and old Oxford radicals. The sentiment was stated in the conference by Jowett who argued that Extension work 'brings into close contact the educated men and the artisan . . . it makes them know one another better, and so they come to entertain much more friendly feelings towards one another'.[53] The Marquis of Ripon presented the same argument, but with reference to the universities and the nation. The Extension, he claimed, would become a permanent institute 'bringing together with it in closer intercourse those ancient Universities, and the people of this country in every part of the land and every class which is found within our varied community.'[54] Through this 'closer intercourse' the gap would gradually close and the pre-Extension antagonism and suspicion the working classes harboured against the universities would slowly disappear.

It was believed that the gap could be closed mainly through the elevation of the working classes by allowing them a share of the benefits of higher education. It would be the nation's next great step forward after ensuring elementary education to all. The participants in the conference believed that pressure for higher education originated from the 'ranks' below. It was nothing less than a national service to provide this need, but eventually state support would be essential.[55] The Oxford Extension regarded itself at this stage as the vanguard of a centralized national effort which, it was only reasonable to assume, would soon materialize. Statesmen such as Chamberlain, Morley, or Mundella, Jowett argued,[56] 'who represent the statesmen of the future, and who are likely to exercise a great influence on public affairs, are in favour of giving the greatest facilities for education and the utmost extension to it.'

Throughout the conference, and indeed throughout the whole period, the Extension was frequently referred to as a Movement, missionary by nature. Lecturers did not join the Movement for the mere purpose of pointing out to the working class the way to material progress — indeed it is difficult to imagine the direct material benefits derived from lectures in

---

[53] *Oxford University Extension Lectures. Report of a Conference* . . ., p. 90.
[54] Ibid., p. 41.
[55] Ibid. (the Bishop of London), p. 44.
[56] Ibid., p. 98.

English literature or Italian art. The objective was moral improvement, and whenever material progress was discussed it was but the means for the same objective. Price described the Extension work a few years later as of a missionary nature 'not merely in the sense of diffusing a taste for intellectual culture but also in that of relieving the monotony and elevating the tone of material pursuits, by nurturing an enthusiasm for moral ideal'.[57] The missionary zeal was a special feature of the Oxford Extension. One might even regard it as a feature of the Oxford spirit. During the conference Roberts, the Secretary of the Cambridge University Syndicate for Local Lectures, pointed out that although during the early stages of the work the missionary strand was dominant, at present it was not enough. The work should be systematized beyond the confidence that zeal alone could carry it off.[58] But even if the argument was practically valid, Oxford refused to drop the missionary spirit. The Revd. Hudson-Shaw, one of the Extension's most popular lecturers, turned down the attempt to replace the spirit with utility. 'If it is not a missionary movement,' he stated, 'there are a good many of us who do not want to have anything to do with it.'[59]

Many of the young graduates who became members of the Oxford Economic Society joined the Extension at roughly the same time. Price joined by virtue of becoming a Toynbee Trust lecturer.[60] Ll. Smith was added after a trial course during the spring of 1887,[61] as was F. S. Marvin. Hewins applied during February 1888 and was added to the list in June.[62] P. F. Willert lectured during the summer meeting of 1888, in which the list of lecturers included Price, Hewins, Ll. Smith, and Thorold Rogers.[63] D. J. Medley applied to become a lecturer during January 1888 and later that year was appointed examiner (he was added to the list in March 1885).[64] O. M.

[57] L. L. Price, review of the Revd. W. Cunningham's, *The Use and Abuse of Money* (London, 1891), in the *International Journal of Ethics*, October 1892.
[58] *Report of . . . Conference*, p. 87.
[59] Ibid., p. 74.
[60] Minutes, 12 Dec. 1885.
[61] Ibid., 27 Jan. 15 June 1887.
[62] Ibid., 23 Feb. 14 June 1888.
[63] *Summer Meeting of University Extension Students and Others in Oxford, August 1888* (Oxford, 1888).
[64] Minutes, 20 Oct. 1888.

Edwards, Campion, and Robert Ewing were on the list of Home Reading Circles Leaders by the end of 1888. L. R. Phelps gave a course on 'Making and Sharing of Wealth' in Oxford towards the end of 1888 and was a regular examiner from early 1889.[65] Only Price, Ll. Smith, and Hewins were in popular demand. The rest helped in the Extension work whenever they were asked to. For the non-regular lecturers Extension work was no more than a supplementary source of income. Nevertheless, they were all interested in the Movement and were quite willing to join in its work.

The only young Oxford economists who were not active in Extension lecturing were Cannan and Ashley. Cannan did approach the Extension Committee during January 1887,[66] but his health may have dictated conditions unacceptable to the Committee and nothing further was heard of the matter. In any event Cannan's private income enabled him, unlike most of his fellow members of the Oxford Economic Society, to remain in residence in Oxford without worrying too much about earning a living. Ashley gave an Extension course for the Cambridge Syndicate at Southport[67] during Michaelmas 1883, but was disappointed by the small number of working men who attended and did not continue lecturing in the Extension. After 1885 his Fellowship prevented him from any active participation in the Extension's work, as was the case with L. T. Hobhouse and Sidney Ball, though Hobhouse and Ashley appear on the list of the Oxford Committee which organized the first summer meeting of 1888. The other names on the list include Campion, Phelps, Price, Sadler, and Hewins—a total of seven members of the Oxford Economic Society.[68]

The young economists were not the only ones to lecture on political economy or economic history. Since the basic attitude in Oxford towards the subject was carried over to the Extension, lecturers in modern history gave occasional courses in political economics. However, by the late 1880s Price, Ll.

---

[65] Reports, 1888-9.
[66] Minutes, 27 Jan. 1887. The following appears beside Cannan's name: 'further inquiries to be made as Mr. Cannan wishes'.
[67] Ann Ashley, *William James Ashley*, and Cambridge University Archives BEMS 22/1, Annual Report Local Lectures. Because of the limited range of Oxford Extension activities before 1885, lecturing for the Cambridge Syndicate was not uncommon.
[68] *Summer Meeting . . . August 1888.*

Smith, and Hewins (joined by J. A. Hobson in 1891) were the only regular lecturers on the subject and in any event were the only ones to give advanced courses, whether at the local centres, as Home Reading Circles' leaders or during the summer conferences.

Towards the end of February 1888 Hudson-Shaw's wife Edith died and he was forced to discontinue courses. He had already begun one on 'Irish History' for the Co-operative Society in Doncaster, where the Committee had hoped that the course would be followed by the establishment of a permanent Extension centre. Sadler turned to Hewins and asked him to take over Hudson-Shaw's courses on 'Social Reformers', 'English History', and 'Irish History'. Thus, half a year after obtaining his degree in mathematics and without having been required to give a trial course, Hewins became an Extension lecturer.[69] In March 1888, while the courses taken over from Hudson-Shaw were still in progress, the Extension Committee decided to embark on a Home Reading scheme combined with a summer conference. Both projects were to enable promising students to pursue their studies in a systematic manner, through personal instruction by mail and in contact with a small group of fellow students. The summer conference was to allow an annual period of intensive studies at Oxford which would, in addition, serve to tighten the ties between the Extension students and Oxford and her dons. The intention was to use the first summer meeting to launch the Home Reading scheme. A committee set up for the Home Reading project authorized Sadler[70] to recommend the appointment of a suitable person as the secretary for the summer conference (at a fee of 20 guineas). Work on the conference was to begin by the end of May. The Secretary appointed for the summer might be asked to continue his job and organize the winter activity of the Home Reading Circles. Sadler recommended Hewins,[71] who began work at the end of May and was added to the list of lecturers during the following month. By then he had already gained some experience in lecturing and had the beginning of a

---

[69] W. A. S. Hewins, *The Apologia of an Imperialist*, p. 19. Hewins papers 41/1604, 41/162-3, Sadler to Hewins, 27 and 28 Feb. 1888.
[70] Minutes, 7 Mar. 1888.
[71] Hewins papers, 41/168-9, 41/170-1. Sadler to Hewins, 26 and 27 Mar. 1888.

reputation, which was essential in order to secure further invitations.

To the economists, and to most of the Extension lecturers, Extension teaching was a vocation which demanded constant sacrifice. 'The Life of an earnest University Extension Lecturer must be one of self denial and devotion.'[72] It was extremely difficult to make ends meet on a lecturer's pay, yet Price and Ll. Smith, after securing an adequate source of income, continued for a couple of years to give Extension courses although they did not need the money.

Hewins's case was somewhat different. Despite the success of his summer meetings and his popularity as a lecturer, he did not regard his income as sufficient to allow him to marry. An attempt was made to secure a more steady and remunerative post—as Bursar of St. John's College, Oxford—which would allow him to continue his lecturing as Price had done. But the attempt failed,[73] and financial uncertainty remained with him for some years to come. With Charles Firth's support he tried to induce first Pembroke College and then the Board of Modern History to employ him as a paid lecturer[74] in economic history, but to no avail. Without a change in the academic status of the subject in the curriculum, such an appointment was regarded as superfluous. Nevertheless, despite constantly having to supplement his income by taking private pupils, it was not till 1891 that Hewins began to seek employment away from Oxford. In 1889 he turned down an offer to organize a centre for economic studies at Toynbee Hall.[75] During 1891 he unsuccessfully applied for the post of Secretary to the Publishing Department of the National Liberal Foundation,[76] and for the Tooke Professorship, vacated by F. Y. Edgeworth and eventually filled by the Revd. William Cunningham

Price's and Ll. Smith's lecturing came to an end at the same time as Hewins was searching for jobs outside Oxford. The

---

[72] Minutes, circular, 29 Aug. 1889, on the theme of 'sacrifice'; see also Hudson-Shaw's comments in *Report of Conference*.

[73] Hewins papers, 41/217, 41/223, 41/227, 41/229, 41/233, 41/234, 41/239. Hewins's referees included J. Percival, J. E. Thorold Rogers, Frederic Harrison, the Master of Pembroke, and the Bishop of Ripon.

[74] Phelps papers, C. H. Firth to Phelps, 13 Nov. 1894.

[75] Hewins papers, 42/15-17, Barnett to Hewins, 21 June 1889.

[76] Ibid. 43/45-49, c.mid March 1891.

young economists who joined the Extension Movement added to the general ideology of the Movement their particular faith in the use of political economy to educate and elevate the working class. They felt certain that if the working man were given the correct knowledge as to the reasons for his condition and instructed in the means for changing it, he would come to realize the fallacy of revolutionary socialism and adopt the right and best form of progress—gradual reform. Progress was to be both material and moral, achieved by maintaining overall social harmony during gradual change. Pointing the way would in itself prove that class warfare was not an inevitable outcome of social and material differences, since it was the so-called 'enemy' who was volunteering the information. The fruits of their knowledge and research would be given in true faith and they expected the working men of England to be quick to realize it. One anticipated observation was that the working men would be interested primarily in the practical applications of political economy, an anticipation which reflected the economists' concept of their subject and its use. It was not merely a successful speculation. During the conference held in 1887 a Mr. A. Greenwood of the Hebden Bridge Manufacturing Co-operative Society pointed out that his reason for inviting a lecturer to give a course in industrial history was 'in order to guide working men into the way of acquiring knowledge conducive to their welfare. We thought it would bring us together and make us each think more particularly and directly of the causes which affect our position and the purpose which we are trying to carry out co-operatively.'[77]

It was also hoped that contact with the working men and subsequent experience would have a salutary effect on the economists' work and that the process of learning would work both ways.[78] Experience did show that in some cases the exchange of historical and theoretical knowledge with practical experience proved extremely fruitful. An example may be found in Ll. Smith's report on a course he gave at Ancoats, Manchester, on 'Wealth and Industry' during late 1885.[79] The class after the lecture always took the form of a discussion 'from

[77] *Report . . . April 1887*, p. 72.
[78] Ibid., p. 96.
[79] Reports, 1887–8.

which I myself learnt much, as those who took part almost always brought knowledge of practical detail to bear on the points raised. I have never had an audience with whom it was such a pleasure to discuss Economic problems.'

A different result of the Extension lecturing was another kind of gap being bridged within the communities themselves. Where local centres were successful they brought together working men with their middle-class neighbours, including a large proportion of women. When the phenomenon was observed it was hoped that local centres would serve to improve community relations.[80]

As experience accumulated, lecturers began to realize that their original expectations of the actual work at times fell short of reality. It was still true that the practical implications of political economy were found to be of great interest to working-class audiences and that, according to the lecturers, many changed their attitude towards the subject as a result of the courses.[81] However, these implications were given in the form of conclusions derived from a longer discussion of political economic theory or historical development, for both of which working men had little patience or inclination, whereas the economists at that time did not conceive of any other valid way of presenting the case at hand. No short cuts should be made in the scientific argument or, as Ll. Smith pointed out towards the end of 1888, 'Perhaps the greatest danger which a lecturer on Economics notices, lies in the tendency of a popular audience to demand a degree of clearness and simplicity in Economic expositions which sometimes scientific accuracy does not admit of. They find a difficulty in looking at such questions from a "historic point of view".'[82] Hewins, reporting on the same problem about a year later, realized what was expected of the 'practical lecturer':

Working class centres, at any rate when they are just starting, should not be advised to take a special subject like Economic History. The English workman is a politician first and a working man afterwards. Subjects dealing

---

[80] e.g. Sadler's report in the *Annual Report . . . 1886–7*.
[81] e.g. the reports of Price and Phelps on the course given by Price at Godalming, 23 Oct. 1888–12 Mar. 1889, in Reports, 1888–9.
[82] From a report on a course given at Bradford on 'Makers of Political Economy', Reports 1888–9.

with political and general history are far more efficient in rousing his enthusiasm and encouraging him to read. . . . the difficulties in the way of an ordinary working many in the study of Economic History are at present inseparable.[83]

This explanation clarified for Hewins his earlier perplexity over the lack of sufficient interest on the part of working men in subjects that theoretically should have been popular since they concerned them directly.[84] Two solutions were possible: the first — presenting the same conclusions within a political argument — was not at that time acceptable to any of the economists; the second — which was adopted by most of the Extension lecturers — was the investment of greater effort in systematic studies. However, while in most subjects systematization led to a series of courses on related topics, the systematic study of political economy could mean only longer courses and advanced follow-up courses at the same centres.

Some advanced courses were occasionally requested but they were but a drop in the ocean, despite constant recommendations for such courses in the lecturers' and examiners' reports to the local committees. What must have been especially frustrating to the lecturing economists was the comparison with some other lecturers and subjects. Not one of them came near Hudson-Shaw's achievement at the Oldham Co-operative. In 1891 he could report of lectures at Oldham during four consecutive years to crowds reaching 500 and classes of 100 or 200 men.[85]

The Home Reading Circles scheme falls within the category of attempts at systematization. In addition it was to provide the lecturer with additional employment.[86] It was assumed that the summer conference would bring together the lecturers and the Extension's more promising and serious students for a period during which the scheme would be launched, with the aid of special introductory lectures to the various subjects offered within the scheme. Accordingly special syllabuses for indepen-

---

[83] Reports, vol. 5. The course was given during early 1890.
[84] Reports, 1888–9. Report of Hewins on his course, 'History of the English Labourer', given in Huddersfield, 27 Sept.–13 Dec. 1889.
[85] 'An Ideal Working Men's Centre', in the *Oxford University Extension Gazette*, 10 Aug. 1891.
[86] Extension Archives, Misc. Files, letter from Sadler, 18 Aug. 1888.

dent work were prepared (including one compiled by Ashley for an advanced course in economics). The scheme seemed ideal at the time and there were few, if any, doubts expressed as to its chances of success. Dr Percival, who was the chairman of the Home Reading Circles Committee,[87] saw in the scheme the nucleus of a national organization independent of the Extension. Over the demand for separate organization Percival found himself in opposition to Sadler who was supported by Hudson-Shaw and Hewins (despite the fact that if his demand had been accepted, Hewins would have been appointed secretary of the new organization). Eventually the Home Reading Circles remained part of the Extension Movement as a supplementary scheme. The circles were established, with a large number of Oxford Economic Society members as leaders, including some lecturers in the Extension;[88] but they never reached the proportions that Percival seems to have expected. The annual report for 1889 could report the establishment of only thirty circles; they became a supplementary aid to regular courses and not a substitute.[89] It was argued that the relative failure was due to the lack of direct contact with the lecturer[90] and that the circles therefore could not replace lectures and classes.

One result of the circles scheme was the turning of the summer meeting into an annual event. The first three summer meetings were all organized by Hewins, who was repeatedly appointed secretary for the purpose. In the meetings a large contingent of the Oxford Economic Society's members took an active part as lecturers in English history and political economy. However, after the 1890 meeting the Extension Committee decided not to appoint a special secretary for the summer meeting, and although Hewins was appointed as assistant secretary to Sadler for the 1891 meeting, neither he nor any other member of the Economic Society (except Sadler) took

---

[87] The other members were Sadler, Acland, Rewley, Sargant, King, and probably Hudson-Shaw. See Minutes, 7 Mar. 1888. For the dispute between Percival and Sadler, see Sadleir, *M. E. Sadler*, pp. 102–3.

[88] O. M. Edwards and D. J. Medley directed circles in English history; Ewing in logic; Price, Hewins, and Campion in political economy. See Minutes, 15 Nov. 1888.

[89] Extension Archives, circular Home Reading Circles 1890.

[90] H. J. Mackinder and M. E. Sadler, *University Extension, Past, Present and Future* (London, 1891), p. 75.

an active part in the summer meetings' lectures in 1891, or in any of the following years.

It was realized eventually that systematic work would, at best, be pursued by not more than a small minority of Extension students. The contact of most of the students with higher education, and with Oxford itself, did not result in their wanting to become professional students, nor were they in a position that would technically enable them to pursue any kind of university studies even for a short period. Their aim was limited, but still of major importance: 'by self culture to widen and deepen their ideals of life'.[91] The Extension would continue to provide an opportunity for the small number of specially gifted students who would still seek contact with higher education. But the realization that systematic studies were not the goal of most students rendered the certificates useless except to provide the student with some sense of achievement.

The realization had an obvious effect upon the teaching of political economy and economic history in the Extension. The full benefits of the study of political economy and economic history could not be derived without systematization. If systematization was unattainable within the Extension, and if one still believed in the feasibility of showing the working class the way to progress through political economy, then the Extension was the wrong place for it.

Attendance at political economy lectures, and their popularity, led to a similar conclusion. Lectures on the subject did not prove nearly as popular as had been hoped. Compared with the overall rate of increase in number and length of courses, political economy had long since lost its position of relative popularity during the mid-1880s when few courses were offered.

The overall figures of growth are given in Table 2:[92]

---

[91] Ibid., p. 73. See also Hudson-Shaw in the *Oxford University Extension Gazette*, July 1892.
[92] *Gazette*, August 1891.

Table 2

	1885–6	1886–7	1887–8	1888–9	1889–90	1890–1
Courses delivered	27	67	82	109	148	192
Lecture centres	22	50	52	82	109	146
Students	c. 3,000	9,908	13,036	14,351	17,904	20,248
Average number of weeks in each course	c. 7	7½	8½	9¾	10	12½

The general trend of growth continued. In political economy and economic history the trend is reversed. The numbers of courses given are eleven in 1886–7, four in 1887–8 (plus five on 'Social Reformers'), eight in 1888–9, ten in 1889–90, and five in 1890–1, with the number continuing through the next few years to fluctuate around five. Nor is there a noticeable increase in length of courses. Hewins, for instance, from autumn 1890 until autumn 1895 gave nineteen courses of which one was a twelve-lecture course given in co-operation with J.A. Hobson. All the rest were six-lecture courses.

But the major problem that plagued the Movement as a whole was the low attendance of working men despite the overall growth in the number of students. Various explanations were offered: Sadler argued that it was because courses were not given in sequence (a variation on the systematization issue, this time with the argument that sequence could prove successful, but it would have to be subsidized), and because of the loss of the best lecturers through the uncertainty of income.[93] An article in the *Gazette* of March 1893[94] blamed the high price of the courses. It argued that the worker would not attend a course unless he paid, but that the fee would have to be within his means. Another reason was the resentment of the middle-class condescension to the working class frequently shown by those who took over the organization of the local centres.[95] In

---

[93] Mackinder and Sadler, *University Extension*, p. 97.
[94] *Gazette*, Mar. 1893. The article was by R. A. Gregory.
[95] A similar observation can be found in Hewins's report on a course given at Rochdale in 1894.

some cases the impression created within the working class by this attitude was that the lectures were meant solely for those who already had some education. In other cases the organizers were blamed because the lectures started at an early hour inconvenient for the workers. No fault was found with the courses or with the lecturers, nothing was inherently wrong in the method, nor was the ideology unrealistic.[96] The problem was conceived of as basically one of finance and local organization. By 1891, following the state aid given to technical education, the Extension developed a new programme of county council courses mostly on chemistry and agriculture, with subjects such as 'Management of Stock', 'Laws of Health', 'Soils and Crops', 'Crop Diseases', etc.[97] Yet it was only one part of the desired education of the citizen, since no state aid was given to the teaching of history, literature, or political economy, which were considered by the Extension Movement to be at least as important as technical education. It was not until the spring of 1892 that, in accordance with the Technical Instruction Act of 1889, the Science and Art Department induced Parliament to add political economy to the category of technical instruction for the county of Nottingham on the basis of the county council's request.

The battle for state aid and the hope of an eventual centralized national scheme for higher education dates in the history of Oxford Extension as far back as the battle for university endowment. By 1890 no decision had been reached on these issues.[98] In the case of state aid every conceivable scheme was suggested, from financing local centres to subsidizing the Movement through the Extension Committee. It was further argued that not only was support of technical instruction alone insufficient, it was actually dangerous 'by stereotyping present methods instead of leaving the power of rapid and intelligent adaptation to our ever changing conditions'.[99] There was also an attempt to show the benefits of the Extension to the Univer-

---

[96] It was not till some years later that it was admitted that working men after a hard day's work were not interested in economics, preferring a lighter subject.
[97] See *Oxford University Extension Lecturers' and Examiners' Reports. County Council Courses*, Autumn 1891, vol. 11, Spring 1892, vol. 12.
[98] At Cambridge the issue of state aid was raised as early as 1882.
[99] Mackinder and Sadler, *University Extension*, p. 57.

sity and the colleges. It was argued that they should support the Extension financially since the colleges had found in the Movement a means of employing their young graduates, while the University would find that the Extension had been creating a potential political backing for it in the Parliamentary Commissions of the future, through changing the attitude of at least part of the population towards the University from hostility to affection.[100] More money, either from the State or from the University, would allow centres to organize courses in sequence[101] and attract more working men with the lower fees. The Extension Committee could offer senior lecturers a higher salary and thus maintain a staff of experienced lecturers. Junior lecturers would be attracted once the promise of a secure income was added to the rest of the Movement's attractions for the young graduate.[102] External finance might help to break the hold of the middle class on the local centres by destroying their monopoly over local funds for financing courses. But although financial aid was expected to solve most of the Extension's problems, by 1890 a solution on these lines was not yet in sight.

Around 1890 there was a decline in the activity of Oxford's economists in the Extension. Despite the Extension Committee's appointment, during 1890, of H. Ll. Smith and L. L. Price as staff lecturers (which meant higher fees for their lectures), their careers took a direction away from Extension work. Ll. Smith's last Extension lectures were given during autumn 1890. Price gave no lectures in the Extension after the autumn of 1890, with the exception of a course during autumn 1892 and one during spring 1893, although he remained on the list of lecturers until 1900 when he resigned. (He did, however, contribute to the Movement by looking into co-operative educational work.[103]) Hewins remained the only Oxford economist active in the Movement during the early 1890s, up to his appointment as Director of the London School of Economics. When he did leave, it was because of the promise

---

[100] Ibid., p. 116.
[101] Ibid., pp. 119-20.
[102] For what were considered as the other attractions, see 'Open letters on open questions', in the *Gazette*, March 1891, p. 79.
[103] Extension Archives, early papers, mjsc.123, Price to Marriott.

of the new School as an institute of higher education that would use Extension methods and ideas to succeed where the Extension failed.

Oxford was by no means the first university to introduce Extension lectures. Yet its different methods and uncompromising zeal caused almost constant friction with the other main Extension bodies active during the eighties — the Cambridge Syndicate, the London Society, and Victoria University, the representative of the interests of the northern university colleges. Confrontations were mainly due to the status of the six-lecture courses[104] (at first given the same status at Oxford as the longer courses, with the awarding of certificates) and to Oxford's 'free market' policy concerning the geographical range of its activity. The Oxford Committee felt that local centres had the right to unimpeded free choice of courses, from whichever Extension body available. None of the bodies had a geographical monopoly over particular centres or districts. Matters were considerably worsened by the uncompromising posture of the Oxford Committee. Theirs was a national mission which must not be compromised in order to mollify other Extension bodies.

These differences between Oxford and the other Extension bodies on matters of adult education reflect a much more fundamental ideological difference. Furthermore, the Oxford Extension was an institutional expression of an ideology shared by a group larger than the small number of active lecturers. Hence, the fundamental ideological attitudes underlying the differences on adult education should also be regarded as the ideological background of the debate on the nature of the study of economics. And these beliefs initially led to confrontations. The practical implementation of the ideology of the new liberalism[105] was based on a strong sense of the individual's duty towards society and the individual's power to influence the course of progress. The vision of a desirable and attainable future state of society was not enough. It was the liberals' duty,

---

[104] The Cambridge Syndicate complained about the six-lecture courses as early as autumn 1886. Cambridge University Archives, Syndicate Minutes 1/3, 16 November 1886.

[105] For a detailed account of the new liberalism see Michael Freeden, *The New Liberalism; An Ideology of Social Reform* (Oxford, 1978).

and within their power, to introduce their vision to the nation. As a national university, Oxford had a responsibility towards the whole nation and its mission was of national importance. Compromise on either the means or the ends was virtually unthinkable since, like the economists a few years later, they regarded their work as being in the service of the community rather than as the pursuit of an abstract truth.

The differences between Oxford and Cambridge on the means and aims of adult education were not primarily caused by the operation of two competing organizations within one market. Since the differences were ideological and therefore much more fundamental than differences caused by market competition, they could not be resolved by means of discussion or persuasion. Cambridge did not possess a comparable evangelical creed, and Oxford's faith in its mission was not entirely rational. At Cambridge there was a stronger emphasis on the pursuit of knowledge for its own sake, or alternatively on limited training for a certain practical well-defined purpose (e.g. women's education for their role as teachers). If an adult sought higher education, for whatever purpose, he was to be brought into the university system. At Oxford it was felt that the University must seek out its public and first convince it of the value of higher education. In order to bring about a change in the national attitude towards education all means were justifiable. Their adequacy could be judged only on the basis of results, rather than on their compliance with a certain organizational concept. Thus, Oxford dropped the short-course certificate not so much because of external pressure but from the realization that it was not serving any practical purpose. Significantly, the short courses themselves were continued and it was decided that if a student pursued a systematic course of study, two short courses would count as one long one, and would entitle him to a certificate.[106]

The first confrontation with the Cambridge Syndicate dates from early 1889. The Committee received an invitation from the Halifax centre (originally operated by the Cambridge Syndicate) for D. S. McColl to deliver a course of six lectures on English painters. To prevent unnecessary squabbles, a pro-

---

[106] Minutes, circular 'Certificates on Short Courses', 10 Feb. 1890.

cedure was adopted whereby in such cases Cambridge was notified of the invitation and asked, as a matter of routine, for its approval. This time the answer from the Cambridge Syndicate was slow to arrive and since the invitation was for a course beginning shortly, another letter was sent to the Syndicate asking for an urgent answer. On 26 January Professor Browne of the Cambridge Syndicate telegraphed back: 'If the course is of eleven or twelve lectures it will not embarrass our work, if it is a short course, it will.' The objection was not that Halifax had originally been a Cambridge centre, but to the length of the course. In other words, the Syndicate chose to make an issue out of its objection to Oxford's extremely popular short courses. In its reply the Oxford Committee pointed out that the Halifax centre did not require an examination at the end of the course and therefore no certificates would be given, so that if Cambridge had no plans for a simultaneous course in Halifax the course would be given as planned. Browne telegraphed back repeating his previous message: 'If the course etc.' The course was eventually given through a direct arrangement between McColl and the Halifax centre, with the Extension Committee's tacit approval.

The Oxford Committee and the Cambridge Syndicate did not budge from their positions and in this instance the Oxford Committee decided to pursue the issue and assert it as a principle. The Extension Committee circulated a questionnaire amongst centres and lecturers asking for their opinion on courses shorter than twelve lectures, and on allowing examinations at their end. The consensus was that any different policy was 'an impediment to the continuance and development of University Extension Work'.[107]

On the basis of the answers, and in order to establish the principle, the Extension Committee put forward a resolution on 2 February 1889:

That the Committee is of the opinion that in the interest of Education the Local Committee should be left free to make such arrangements for Lectures

---

[107] On the matter of the short courses nineteen lecturers were in favour, one against. On the matter of examinations fifteen lecturers were in favour, three against, and two doubtful.

as are most convenient to the Centres without reference to their previous relations to either University, but that while the Local Committees are left free, it is hoped that the Delegacy and Syndicate may maintain their present friendly relations and exchange information about their respective arrangments.

It was an unequivocal declaration in favour of the principle of 'free trade', with the conviction that the local centres would prove the point by sustaining a demand for the short courses. Results did indeed prove the Committee to be right. The trend of constant increase in the average length of courses strengthened the Committee's hands, proving that popular short courses led to longer ones, creating a demand in places where it might not otherwise have existed.

Following the Committee's resolution the issue was broached once again during the summer meeting of 1889 at which Dr Roberts, Assistant Secretary of the Cambridge Syndicate and Secretary of the London Society, was present. In discussion[108] of the value of short courses a number of fundamental differences emerged between the Cambridge and London position on the one hand and the Oxford position on the other. Roberts argued that Extension work should conform as much as possible to the standards and form of university teaching, i.e. each term's work should be considered as one unit. A term in Extension work meant a ten- to twelve-lecture course. Therefore, to award a certificate at the end of a six-lecture course made a mockery of the certificates and undermined the efforts being made to obtain official recognition of the certificate as a record of academic achievement — e.g. for elementary-school teachers by school boards. Short courses, in his view, should be used as no more than introductory courses to stimulate demand for the longer ones.

At that time the Oxford Extension still entertained hopes that a significant number of its students could eventually be encouraged to become full-time students. Its main concern was not the training of certain professions, such as school teachers, but the education of the nation. The main targets were small towns and working-class centres. In reaching these M. E. Sadler, who as the Extension's secretary presented its official policy, argued that Oxford had a better record than

[108] The discussion is reported in the *Oxford Times*, 17 Aug. 1889.

Cambridge. What mattered was the basic approach, not the length of courses. If a small centre kept asking for short courses, thereby familiarizing students with a systematic approach to any subject, the length of the course was of relatively little consequence. It was far more important to ensure the continuation of educational activity in small centres through the use of short courses than to force on the Extension system a non-realistic academic structure. Oxford was not aiming at an approximation of a university term's work, but at the stimulation of continuous study all the year round. Working men, it was hoped, would be encouraged to adopt regular study as part of their way of life, rather than content themselves with occasional bursts of study.

A second confrontation, this time with the London Society, occurred when the Secretary of the Oxford Committee received a request from a Miss Williamson—the Principal of Princess Helena College, Ealing — for a course of six lectures on Shakespeare. As in the instance of Halifax, Sadler wrote to the London Society informing them of the invitation, although there was no previously established centre at Ealing. In reply Roberts, for the London Society, asked Sadler to refrain from any further action on the matter until Lord Goschen, the President of the Society, could be brought in to deal with it. In reply to a similar letter sent by Roberts, Miss Williamson informed the London Society that in any case she would rather have her school affiliated to Oxford than to the London Society.

The main issue raised by the London Society was that the Oxford Extension had no right to operate within the metropolitan area. On this matter London had the support of Professor Stuart, Chairman of the University Joint Board set up originally to co-ordinate Extension lecturing between Oxford, Cambridge, and London. However, the Committee, including those of its members who were Oxford's representatives on the Joint Board, supported Sadler, arguing that there was no clause committing Oxford to keeping its activities outside the metropolitan area. None of the other organizations seemed to conform to such a principle, since Cambridge had courses at Sydenham down to April 1881, and London was active outside the metropolitan area, e.g. in Basingstoke. The Oxford Committee re-stated the 'free market' principle, pointing out that the London Society, being able to offer cheaper courses, enjoyed a competitively advantageous position within the metropolitan area. All local centres should be given complete freedom of choice, while the responsibility of the Joint Committee was to prevent the overlapping of courses.

The London Society failed to come up with a decree to prove its contention. A resolution on the lines of the Halifax resolution was passed in the Committee on 16 May 1889 and sent to Roberts two days later.

The matter was set aside until the end of the year, when it was raised again in a letter from Lord Goschen to Oxford's Vice-Chancellor and relayed by the latter to the Committee. Goschen argued that on principle the London Society alone should handle Extension courses in the metropolitan area, although that in itself should make little difference to Oxford and Cambridge lecturers, since by being Extension lecturers they belonged *ipso facto* to the London Society. On this point Goschen either ignored or misinterpreted the principle of free competition stated by Oxford, arguing that the lecturers would not lose their chances at lecturing within the metropolitan area, a point which was not the main bone of contention. Goschen further maintained that the intervention of an external organization in the educational work executed within the metropolitan area would obstruct the London Society in its effort to link permanently the various educational institutions within the area, and thus 'would act as a disintegrating force with no compensating advantage'. In any event, he added, the Society was really competing from a disadvantageous position since, unlike Oxford, it did not offer any certificates for courses shorter than ten lectures.

The reply was drafted by J. Magrath, the Provost of Queen's, and J. F. Bright, the Master of University College, and brought before the Committee for approval. It was pointed out that the matter of certificates had already been dealt with by the Committee independently of the disagreement with the London Society, and it was decided that although lists of successful examinees would replace certificates for short courses, the short courses would remain. As for the geographical limits on Oxford Extension activity, it was moved that:

(a) The Delegacy[109] (through its standing Committee) 'would consider the restriction of its activity to a limited area as an unjustifiable restraint upon the freedom of the centres and of itself', especially since the limits were not reciprocal, considering the London Society's activity outside the metropolitan area.

(b) Competition was advantageous and would serve as an incentive to both the lecturers and the organizations behind them, whereas monopoly would breed inefficiency.

(c) The competition, in any event, would not be completely free, since the London Society charged lower fees for its courses.

The Committee argued that contrary to Goschen's allegation, experience proved that the Oxford Extension's work had no disintegrative effect on attempts at centralization, but out of goodwill they would refrain for a while from any action that might obstruct centralization. With the resolution the matter rested.[110]

These were not isolated cases and, since Oxford refused to modify its position, similar clashes were inevitable. Later in 1890 disagreement occurred between Oxford and the Victoria University concerning Oxford Extension activities in the neighbourhoods of Manchester, Liverpool, and Leeds, which the Victoria University considered its own exclusive area of responsibility.[111] As in the previous instances, the Committee rejected an appeal from the Victoria University to limit its activities geographically, by stressing the dangers of monopoly and the principles of complete freedom of choice for local centres.

---

[109] The delegates of Local Examinations were at the time: the Revd. J. R. Magrath, DD, Provost of Queen's College, the Revd. J. F. Bright, DD, Master of University College, the Revd. W. W. Jackson, MA, Rector of Exeter College, the Revd. H. B. George, MA, Fellow and Tutor of New College, A. Robinson, MA, Fellow and Bursar of New College, A H. D. Acland, MA, Christ Church, and Honorary Fellow of Balliol, E. B. Poulton MA, FRS, Keble and Jesus College, H. F. Pelham, MA, Fellow and Tutor of Exeter College, Camden Professor of Ancient History, the Revd. W. Lock, MA, Fellow of Magdalen College, Tutor of Keble College, A. Sidgwick, MA, Fellow and Tutor of Corpus Christi College.
[110] Minutes, 20 Feb. 1890, 13 Mar. 1890.
[111] Minutes, 15 May 1890.

3
THE EXTENSION AND ECONOMIC THOUGHT—
THE ECONOMISTS' COURSES

The correlation between the general ideals of the Oxford Extension Movement and the particular ideals of the Oxford economists concerning their image of the economist's place in society and the social and moral significance of their work meant that the economists' involvement in Extension work stemmed not solely from practical necessity, but from a strong sense of identification with the Movement's ideals as well. Accordingly, the work done by the economists working in the Extension reflects not only a sequel to their early professional development but also the nature the reality of their Extension work. Their courses were not merely a repetition of what they had learnt or of their researches, adapted to the needs of the institution they worked for, but were primarily an adaptation of their work to the aims of an educational movement with which they identified. The period of Extension lecturing in their professional development was an active one in terms of research and the impact of their Extension experience on the development of their ideas. This description of their Extension work would not be complete without a discussion of the changing contents of their courses, since what they taught was closely linked to the more technical aspects of the development of their careers. As each lecturer wrote the syllabuses for his own courses, the syllabuses written by the economists, combined with some of their other writings during the period, and the occasional single lecture, allow a fairly detailed description of the contents of their Extension work. The courses, not being aimed at an audience of fellow economists, rarely contained a full exposition of research results or any novel theoretical developments, so that in themselves they are an insufficient source. Nevertheless, the results of independent work were usually incorporated into the syllabuses in one way or another.

The economists maintained that once the full theoretical apparatus had been used to reach a certain conclusion it need not be used in its entirety to explain the conclusion to the public. In other words, the conclusion derived didactically from a modified theoretical explanation in the courses was identical with the conclusion explained by the use of a much more elaborate argument in a professional publication. Simplification of the process was not necessarily considered a concession. The economists shared the belief that simplified economic arguments were not in all cases distorted arguments. To think otherwise — that an economic argument could not be transmitted in a valid and yet clear form to the general public and specifically to the working class — would have been self-defeating.

The structure of the syllabuses dealing in theory was fairly uniform: a few lectures on elementary theory, usually including the use of historical developments, leading in the final lectures to conclusions of practical and relevant application. If the problem was considered too complex for simplification, or if it was felt that it could not be adequately explained within the confinements of a short course, the scope of the subject would be narrowed so that the argument, even if limited, could be made as comprehensible as possible. No attempts were made to gloss over unavoidable complexities, as may be judged from the syllabuses for the advanced courses. The simple theoretical argument and an elementary historical description were meant to enlighten the worker in the right way to progresss and to give him the tools for a critical analysis of false social theories as well. It was hoped that once the worker realized the usefulness of political economy he would develop his capacity for economic analysis through more systematic studies and would learn to trust his newly acquired skill in preference to vague and pretentious schemes derived from false theories. Bearing this attitude in mind, one realizes the extent of frustration caused by the Extension's failure to systematize the study of political economy. The loss was not to the working man alone, but to society as a whole, since the education offered by political economy was deemed vital to the harmonious progress of society. For how could the working classes realize the fallacy of radical socialism which endangered that progress without acquiring the critical faculty offered by the study of political economy?

The first of the young economists to lecture in the Extension were Sadler and Price, both before the Oxford Economic Society was founded. Price's second Extension course—'Great English Economists: Their Life and Teaching'[1] formed the basis of his book, *A Short History of Political Economy in England*, first published in February 1891.[2] The course reflected the trend in Price's early work towards the historical relativism commonly held at Oxford and the beginning of his interest in bimetallism.

The link in Price's reasoning between the disappointing developments in industrial conciliation and bimetallism is evident in his lecture on Jevons, in which he stated that the importance of Jevon's work on prices was that 'it (a) explains the history of the *past*, and (b) shows the causes of irregularity of employment in the *present*', and that irregularity of employment as well as unstable prices seriously hindered industrial peace. Price's argument also reveals the extent to which he had adopted the historian's view regarding the value of history. Elsewhere, in discussing Arnold Toynbee's life and work, he pointed out that 'Political Economy is said by some to be *neutral* in the matter of social reform . . . this view is often *exaggerated*. Theory and practice are closely connected. The best theorist is the most practical man . . . This may be illustrated by the *historical* method . . . Theory is necessary but facts are important.'

In arguing that each theory should be examined in the light of the circumstances in which it was formed, Price came close to accepting a relativistic view similar to Cannan's. In his view the historical method prevented one from condemning too severely the mistaken theories of the past, from attaching too much value to the theories of the present, and from predicting the future too hastily, on the basis of contemporary theories likely to become outdated. He used past theories in his course as introductions to contemporary theories. The work of the 'old' economists was compared with present-day reality as analysed by 'new' theory. Thus, when Price referred to 'history' he meant primarily the use of historical circumstances

[1] Oxford Extension Archives, Extension Syllabuses, L. L. Price, *Great English Economists* (Oxford, 1888).
[2] By 1931 the book had gone through fifteen editions.

to explain the development of a theory. Accordingly, the validity of theories was determined on the basis of their application to changing circumstances. Price stopped short of extending his historical approach to the study of theory as a historical agent worthy of attention regardless of its present-day validity, an approach evident in the syllabuses of Ashley, Hewins, Campion, and Ll. Smith.[3] Nor does Price seem to have adopted the more extreme relativistic argument according to which all past theories were, virtually by definition, inapplicable in any set of circumstances different, in either space or time, from the one in which it was formed.

The historian's view of the study of theory was stated in general terms in Ashley's syllabus:[4] 'The student should aim, above everything else, at bringing theories into relation to the actual conditions of the period at which they arose, at tracing the influence of changing facts upon theories and of changing theories upon facts.' The approach was demonstrated in Hewins's discussion of mercantilism in a course which formed the nucleus of his book, *English Trade and Finance* (London, 1892):

> We cannot understand the conditions of Europe during the seventeenth and eighteenth centuries without allowing for the influence of Mecantilism in determining the commercial policy of the time. It is therefore important to know what the theory was, what circumstances were favourable to its rise and growth, and how the general belief in it reacted on the history of the period during which it prevailed.[5]

By 'circumstances' Hewins, like Ashley, felt that the theorist's biography was not enough. Nothing less than a detailed account of 'what was going on at the time in the world of ordinary people' would do.

Despite some differences in the application of the historical method, the syllabuses reflect a general consensus on the nature of progress and the means for ensuring its continuity. Price, Ll. Smith, and Hewins saw the future in terms of an in-

---

[3] Extension Syllabuses: W. J. Ashley, *Home Reading in Economics* (Oxford, 1889); W. A. S. Hewins, *Economic History — Chiefly in the Seventeenth Century* (Oxford, 1889); W. J. H. Campion, *The Growth of Economic Theory* (Oxford, n.d.); and H. Ll. Smith, *Makers of Political Economy* (Oxford, 1888).
[4] Extension Syllabuses: Ashley, *Home Reading in Economics*.
[5] Extension Syllabuses: Hewins, *Economic History*.

crease in working-class self-help through corporate action, namely trade unions, co-operatives, and friendly societies within a system of free trade and free competition. This view was stated in Hewins's courses as boldly and confidently as in the earlier pronouncements of Price and Ll. Smith. Hewins's syllabuses revealed traces of the Toynbee spirit with their emphasis on the spiritual aspects of progress. Thus, in his treatment of the division of labour he argued that the increase it caused in mutual dependence spread from economic to social relations. An advanced state of industry therefore forced individuals to look beyond their own narrow interests and promoted various forms of association 'which should be the basis of all economic effort'.[6] A difference in perspective could change the whole attitude towards industrialization: 'Bring the fact of spiritual oneness of society to bear on the principle of the division of labour and every process which is gone through in the various walks of life becomes clothed with the beauty of an act of worship.'[7] Hewins described economics as a practical guide demonstrating the way in which the present had been shaped and indicating the lines on which society would evolve in the future. The study of economics was not only desirable 'but necessary for everyone who wished to discharge a citizen's duties'.

Like Toynbee, Hewins regarded co-operative production as the vanguard of a new social and economic order. In his view trade unions and distributive co-operation were basically trying to improve working-class conditions within the existing order.

The success of Distributive Co-operation is a good basis for and inevitably leads to the consideration of Co-operative Production [which aimed at changing the system].

The progress of the movement [of productive co-operation] so far, to some extent justifies the adverse criticism or qualified approval of economists. There has, however, been sufficient success to create confidence in the future, and to encourage a more extended development.[8]

---

[6] Extension Syllabuses: W. A. S. Hewins, *The English Labourer Past and Present* (Oxford, 1888).
[7] Hewins papers, Box 142, W. A. S. Hewins, 'The Practical Value of Economics', delivered at the Wolverhampton Free Library, December 1887.
[8] Extension Syllabuses: Hewins, *The English Labourer*.

Free trade was an integral part of Hewins's vision of progress and accordingly an issue emphasized in his course. In his application for the Tooke Professorship in 1891 he used as one of his testimonials, attesting his teaching ability, a letter from one of his Extension pupils, L. Brown, who wrote: 'I had been a Fair Trader but very much against my inclination and with many lookings back, your teaching compelled me to become a believer in Free Trade for you did not leave the Fair Traders a leg to stand upon.'[9]

The condemnation of monopolies and the advocacy of free trade were the main themes of Hewins's first book, *English Trade and Finance*. His blend of economic beliefs and a pronounced political bias were described by Ashley in his review of the book:

> If one might venture to dissect Mr. Hewins's mind rather than grab at the facts for one's self—of course a wrong proceedings—one might possibly find the explanation of some of his severe utterances concerning the [seventeenth-century merchant] companies in two characteristics. The first of these is perhaps a certain political bias which makes him sympathize with the opposition to the first two Stuarts; and the second is a remnant of—dare one say?—Manchesterism.[10]

Hewins's 'Manchesterism' was equally noticeable in his first published article 'The National Debt',[11] in which he dealt solely with national finance and wealth, without any reference to working-class issues. In it he revealed a minimalist position regarding state action. His main argument in favour of reducing the National Debt stated:

> England, financially is immensely strong, the only European nation that succeeds in balancing revenue and expenditure. But this forms no reason for refusing to take definite measures for the reduction of the Debt and so shifting the responsibility on to a future generation, which may be less fitted to bear it than our own. The nation as a whole, must look well into the finances, and put a curb upon the growing expenditure in all branches of the public services.[12]

---

[9] Hewins papers 43/68–9, G. Brown to Hewins, 13 Apr. 1891.

[10] W. J. Ashley, review of W. A. S. Hewins, *English Trade and Finance*, in the *Political Science Quarterly*, viii (1893), 546.

[11] W. A. S. Hewins, 'The National Debt. Its origin, growth, and the methods which have been adopted from time to time for its reduction', in the *Co-operative Wholesale Annual 1889*, pp. 227–65.

[12] Ibid., p. 265.

By implication, if the reduction of the National Debt were given immediate national priority, then the material progress of the working classes would best be carried out by self-help, aided by careful state legislation, rather than by an extension of state industrial or commercial undertakings which would require, at least in the short term, an increase in state expenditure. If self-help eventually proved insufficient to ensure progress and state intervention was required, an additional sourse of national income would have to be found.

Hewins's political views were clearly revealed in the article in his frequent praise of Gladstone. Gladstone was compared a number of times to William Pitt and his first Budget speech was lauded as 'a marvellous example, not only of his oratorical power, but of that faculty of lighting up financial detail with enthusiasm which is the unmistakable stamp of genius.'[13] In comparison, G. J. Goschen's reduction of income tax in 1887 by one penny was condemned as hindering the reduction of the National Debt in favour of a relatively insignificant, though popular, measure.[14]

In the light of his interpretation of English history as a process of constant progress, Hewins took Toynbee's argument a step further back in time by demonstrating that the industrial revolution did not cause a total break in the previous march of progress. It did not destroy an idyllic community and, although industrialization intensified the effects of certain evils, the same evils had been present in the pre-industrial order. The increased capacity of these evils to cause mischief had led to efforts to rectify them through reform. In particular, Hewins found that the big merchant companies were not primarily responsible for England's wealth; therefore their disintegration — which otherwise might be viewed as contrary to the principle of association and therefore regressive — was in fact a progressive development.[15] Monopolies prevented equality in trading and competition and were not to be confused with combinations which to a large extent were made possible by industrialization. The development of working men's combina-

---

[13] Ibid., p. 244.
[14] Ibid., p. 247.
[15] Hewins's view on the industrial revolution is also stated in his syllabus, *The English Labourer*.

tions confronting their employers restored a measure of equality to the labour market. 'Combination does not supersede competition, but makes it more equal, less wasteful, and therefore eventually more beneficial.'[16]

Whereas Price's syllabuses reflect his conforming with the historical relativism of his Oxford contemporaries, Ll. Smith's syllabuses on the nature of the study of economics bear evidence of an opposite trend in the development of his ideas. In 1888[17] he described the position of the modern school as 'a general return to facts and history, a general rigorous examination of the foundations of economics, and rigorous comparison of its conclusions with facts, a cautious statement of theory, a laborious examination of real sources of information.' In his view methodology should not concern the beginner nor, for that matter, the advanced scholar. 'The problems it deals with are no longer in air.'[18] He regarded the controversy between induction and deduction as settled. Methodology seemed to him to be a relatively straightforward issue and accordingly was not given too much attention in his work.

Nevertheless when dealing with the scientific status of socialism Ll. Smith stated:

Political Economy deals with facts and fictions; it explains, it infers, it asserts, it denies, but it does not command or forbid. It deals with such words as 'can', 'cannot', 'will', 'will not', but the word 'ought' does not occur in its vocabulary. Socialism emphatically is concerned with the word 'ought'. It is a theory of social duties founded on a theory of social right.[19]

The position in favour of separating science from policy was further elaborated in the summer courses given by Ll. Smith in 1889:

The Political Economist does not profess to approve or disapprove of the things which he describes. He is in the position of an investigator, not a judge. No doubt Political Economy is a great *aid* to the formation of judge-

---

[16] Cf. Extension Summer Meeting Syllabuses: M. E. Sadler, *The Economic Force of Combination, as illustrated by the history of Merchant Guilds, Craft Guilds, Trades Unions, Syndicates, and Distributive Co-operation* (Oxford, 1889). On combinations see also Extension Syllabuses; H. Ll. Smith, *Problems of Wealth and Industry* (Oxford, n.d.); L. L. Price, *English Industry and Commerce 1800–1850* (Oxford n.d.).
[17] H. Ll. Smith, *The Books of Political Economy* (London *c.*1888), p. 148.
[18] Ibid., p. 152.
[19] Ll. Smith, *The Books of Political Economy*, p. 147.

ment, but many other considerations of equity, political expediency, etc. must be taken into account before a judgement can be pronounced.[20]

This position was contrary to the view commonly held within the Extension and expressed by Sadler during the same summer meeting: 'We should . . . look to Political Economy, not merely for a statement of what is the present form of industrial society, but also for some indication of what that form *ought* to be; to prescribe as well as to describe; to furnish us both with a science of wealth and with an art of its social production and distribution.'[21]

Although in substance Ll. Smith's position is similar to Marshall's argument in favour of preserving the scientist's neutrality, it is evident that Cambridge was not the source of his new view on the matter. It is significant that, unlike Marshall, he continued to use the term 'political economy' rather than 'economics' and he obviously did not consider 'political economy' necessarily to denote the art as well as the science. Nor did he consider that this position affected his personal involvement in the support of various social causes: support which he justified by the use of economic reasoning.

After his move to London, Ll. Smith became an active supporter of the new unionism. He helped to arouse public opinion in support of the Bryant & May girls' strike and the busmen of the General Omnibus Company, and later to organize and publicize the Dockers' strike. The latter had served to demonstrate the cause of new unionism. In 1889 Ll. Smith published with Vaughan Nash an account of the strike[22] which used it as proof of the value of unskilled workers' combinations. After the book's publication Ll. Smith continued to work in the cause of new unionism: he lectured on the Dockers' strike[23] and joined Sadler and Hobhouse in a renewed effort to

---

[20] Extension Home Reading Syllabuses: H. Ll. Smith, *Elementary Course in Reading in Political Economy* (Oxford, 1889).

[21] M. E. Sadler, *Three Lectures on the Beginnings of Modern Socialism* (Oxford, 1889), p. 5. See also id. 'Arbitrary Reconstructions and Laissez Faire' in *Co-operative Life* (London, 1889), p. 7

[22] H. Ll. Smith and V. Nash, *The Story of the Dockers' Strike* (London, 1889).

[23] Ll. Smith papers, Ll. Smith to his mother, letters at about the end of 1889.

organize farm labourers in the vicinity of Oxford in the National Agriculture Labour Union.[24]

As for the subject matter of economic investigation, Ll. Smith stated in a lecture given during the summer meeting of 1890 that 'Political Economy is usually defined as the Science of Wealth. Much, however, of the interest taken in it at the present time is an interest in the question of Poverty — or the absence of wealth. This is shown by the much greater attention paid by the public to the Economics of Labour than to the Economics of Trade and Finance.'[25] The lecture was part of a course on urban poverty, followed by a course on methods of social investigation. The source of Ll. Smith's modified views on methodology, the scientist's neutrality, and the focus of economic investigation is revealed in a letter he wrote to his sister between lectures: 'I have now given two out of my three final lectures — subject "Methods of Social Inquiry" (i.e. Booth's methods, etc.etc.etc. — a sequel to my lectures on Town Poverty). I have nothing written except the printed syllabus and a note or two and simply chat with no attempt at form, and no attempt at making the subject easy.'[26] In other words, Ll. Smith had been generalizing from his current work with Charles Booth. While resident at Toynbee Hall and working on the London aspect of his research on labour demography, he joined Booth's *Life and Labour* project by first helping with the Poverty Map and then becoming one of Booth's assistants.[27] He seemed to have adopted unquestioningly Booth's views on the nature and method of the study of

---

[24] Viscount Samuel, *Memoirs* (London, 1945), p. 14; J. A. Hobson and M. Ginsberg, *L. T. Hobhouse, His Life and Work* (London, 1931), p. 29. See Pamela Horn, 'Agricultural Trade Unionism in Oxfordshire', in J. P. D. Dunbabin, *Rural Discontent in Nineteenth Century England* (London, 1971), pp. 121–2. By January 1891 the effort had switched from the National Agriculture Labour Union to the Dock, Wharf, Riverside and General Workers Union which, as the Dockers' Union, became the pioneer in an effort to organize unskilled labour. The effort was finally abandoned in 1892.

[25] Extension Summer Meetings Syllabuses: H. Ll. Smith, *Some Problems of Town Poverty* (Oxford, 1890).

[26] Ll. Smith papers, Ll. Smith to his sister, 15 Sept. 1890.

[27] Clara E. Collet, 'Charles Booth, the Denison Club and H. Llewellyn Smith', in the *Journal of the Royal Statistical Society*, vol. cviii (1945), 482–5. On the circumstances of Ll. Smith's meeting Booth, see T. S. and M. B. Timey, *Charles Booth, Social Scientist* (OUP, 1960), p. 101 n, and Belinda Norman-Butler, *Victorian Aspirations. The Life and Labour of Charles and Mary Booth* (London, 1972), p. 94.

economics while continuing with his own work and political activity. Accordingly, it is possible to find in Booth's work of that period, passages that correspond closely to Ll. Smith's statements quoted above. For instance, Ll. Smith's statement on the prescription of remedies for social evils may be compared with Booth's comments on his work in *Life and Labour*:

> The facts as given have been gathered and stated with no bias nor distorting aim, and with no foregone conclusions. . . . If the facts thus stated are of use in helping social reformers to find remedies for the evils which exist, or do anything to prevent the adoption of false remedies, my purpose is answered. It was not my intention to bring forward any suggestions of my own, and with regard to the disadvantages under which the poor labour and the evils of poverty, there is a great sense of helplessness . . . a better stating of the problems involved is the first step. . . . In this direction must be sought the utility of my attempt.[28]

Similar examples may be given of the emphasis on the study of poverty, the use of technical hypotheses, the minor importance of deductive political economy, and the major importance of observed and quantifiable facts.[29] The same direction was indicated for a possible solution by means of a limited system of state interference in what Booth called 'Limited Socialism'.

The change in Ll. Smith's career and research explains why he did not become active in the *Economic Review* and why he was almost as inactive in the *Economic Journal*. Accordingly, he did not take a strong position on the relevance of past theories and did not publicly participate in the controversy concerning methodology that was to develop.

The books most commonly recommended by the Oxford economists in their courses were those of Marshall and Walker. The student was warned away from James Mill, McCulloch, and Senior and cautioned on the use of J. S. Mill. As an example of theorists on socialism, Henry George was most commonly mentioned, although Marx's name makes its first appearances. In economic history the most commonly used books were those of Toynbee and Thorold Rogers.

Mutual recommendation was quite common and the early works of W. J. Ashley, H. Ll. Smith, L. L. Price, and even

---

[28] Charles Booth (ed.), *Life and Labour of the People of London*, vol. 1 (London, 1892), pp. 4, 6.
[29] Ibid., pp. 165, 178.

M. E. Sadler's lectures on the *Beginnings of Socialism* were often mentioned. The only exception is Cannan's *Elements* whose arguments were considered (at least by Price[30]) to be too advanced in theory to be of any use for Extension courses and which could not compete with the works of Marshall or Walker in economic theory.

The Extension courses form a link between the primary professional positions held by the Oxford economists and those maintained during the general debates and the formation of professional alliances during the early 1890s. The developments of the nineties have their biographical and intellectual sides. It would therefore be impossible to try to describe or to analyse them without describing the two sides of the Extension work which led, on both accounts, to these developments. The contents of the early courses may be considered a common point of departure. The differences that emerged with time were due to individual professional developments. The extent of the deviations from the basic ideas held in common was limited and much of the common ground remained undisputed. Generally speaking, the disappointment caused by the reality of Extension work did not change the substance of the courses. It did not lead to doubt of the value of an education in political economy or the contents of its teaching as the political economists understood it. However, they did realize that a different form of popular education, or perhaps an equally important sphere of work, would have to replace the Extension in order to harness their knowledge of political economy to the movement towards progress.

---

[30] L. L. Price's review of Cannan's *Elementary Political*, in the *Oxford Magazine*, 23 January 1889.

4
THE DEBATE ON THE STUDY OF ECONOMICS— INITIAL MOVES

During the early 1880s the reputation of the study of political economy reached an unprecedented nadir. Within the scientific community it came under attack from the Comtists, and closer to home from the historical economists. At the same time the economists' work was held in unusually low esteem by various sections of the general public. Except for the historical economists' criticism, which in its extreme form dominated debates on the nature of the study during the 1870s, practically all forms of criticism and manifestation of dislike of the science of economics were voiced during the Industrial Remuneration Conference held in London from 28 to 30 January 1885.[1] William Cunningham, who had been a member of the Conference's Committee on behalf of the Royal Statistical Society, concluded in his report to the meeting of Section F in September the same year that 'The discussions at the Conference . . . showed that economic science was little appreciated, and much remained to be done before the public could be convinced that there is such a science, or cultivated men could be found to agree as to its nature'.[2] From a multitude of quarters it was argued that the so-called science and its propagators were incompetent to deal with the economic problems of the period, which the Conference was meant to explore.

The Comtist Positivist Society, represented by Professor E. S. Beesly, one of the founders of the Democratic Federation in 1881, argued:

Hitherto many of the most accredited economic doctrines, though worked out with irreproachable logic, have started from the unsound assumption that the laws of the production of wealth could be studied usefully apart from

---

[1] *Industrial Remuneration Conference, 28–30 Jan. 1885* (London, 1885).
[2] *Reports of the British Association for the Advancement of Science—Aberdeen 1885.* W. Cunningham, 'On the Industrial Remuneration Conference'.

sociology as a whole. The consequence has been that public opinion, instead of being enlightened by such speculation, has been disastrously led astray.[3]

The Positivists' argument concluded that the study of the economic activity of man within society should be absorbed by sociology — the overall study of society. This was considered one of the major threats to the position of economics within the scientific community. It was accordingly dealt with at length when the economists, later that year, moved to the counter-attack.

The rest of the criticism presented by representatives of various sectors of the general public covered an impressive spectrum. The Fair Traders, represented by W. J. Harris, MP, described English teachers of political economy as irresponsible doctrinaires. In a debate with Morley, Harris presented the common view on the laws of political economy by relating that 'A gentleman in the body of the hall had reproached him for undervaluing the laws of political economy, and had asked him "why he did not value this as much as the laws of gravitation". His reply to that was that the laws of gravitation were created by the Almighty, but the laws of political economy only emanated from man'.[4] This confused usage of the meanings of 'law' was overlooked by the crowd, which applauded his astuteness.

Stephen Harding of the Bedminster Union argued: 'We have been too long under the domination of mere theorists; if we are to have a return of prosperity, we must come back to the first principles of common sense'.[5] Edward W. Greening of the Labour Association denounced the advocacy of free trade and free competition by political economists as fallacious. 'Unrestricted competition', he claimed, 'is acknowledged to produce many evils, social and commercial.'[6]

Professor (Emeritus) F. W. Newman, of the Land Nationalisation Society, claimed that the political economists who 'trumpeted' in the superiority of large farms, had refused to consider the success of small farm holdings in France, Belgium,

---

[3] Beesly, 'The Education of Public Opinion', in the *Industrial Remuneration Conference*, p. 220.
[4] Ibid., pp. 226, 249.
[5] Ibid., p. 236.
[6] Ibid., p. 304.

and the Channel Islands.[7] Finally, George Bernard Shaw, representing the Fabian Society, pronounced political economy to be ethically wrong, though logically valid, since by dealing primarily with abstract concepts instead of analysing economic relations on the individual's level it 'obscures the ethical aspect of the case by concealing the immoral relation between the worker and the employer who exploits his labour.'[8] A fine example of Shaw's Marxist, pre-Jevonian period.

The rejection of economics as invalid and immoral by those who represented the various, and generally radical, solutions to the problem of maldistribution of wealth, signified an ominous trend. If the whole discipline of enquiry was rejected like this, how could its findings be used to convince the more radical elements in society to accept more moderate solutions? The position of authority endangered by this type of total rejection had been presented by Charles Dilke, the Conference's president, in his opening remarks. He argued that the strong link between the study of political economy and morality enabled the economist to go beyond the analysis of the problem of industrial remuneration and its causes to state 'what aid we may expect from society, from the State, and what we must expect from ourselves as individuals.' Furthermore, the economist, in dealing with the solutions, goes beyond technical measures and appeals 'for aid to the cultivation of habits of self control, of foresight, to the development of the intelligence and of the moral nature'.[9]

Dilke's description of the economists' work was not contested by the economists present.[10] It was supported by Marshall's own paper to the Conference, in which he presented his vision of an ideal society which would combine moral and economic principles in perfect harmony:

I hold that the ultimate good for all endeavour is a state of things in which there shall be no rights but only duties; where everyone shall work for the public weal with all his might, expecting no further reward than that he is in common with his neighbours, shall have whatever is necessary to enable him

---

[7] Ibid., p. 394.
[8] Ibid., p. 401.
[9] *Industrial Remuneration Conference*, p. 2.
[10] These included H. S. Foxwell and R. Giffen as officials, and Marshall and J. S. Nicholson, who were invited to present papers.

to work well, and to lead a refined and intellectual life, brightened by pleasures that have in them no taint of waste or extravagence.[11]

Dilke's blend of moral and economic reasoning was obvious in Marshall's practical recommendations. He warned against the careless and overzealous promotion of state invervention on the grounds that 'whatever tends to bring money into politics leads to great loss to all, particularly to the working classes.' He condemned 'the vagaries of fashion' and reckless speculation against which education should be directed so that it may 'encourage the growth of moral feeling against gambling.' He saw in education the chief remedy for low wages and argued that human progress towards a more noble life was dependent on the development of a better physical and moral environment.

The Conference took place some weeks after Marshall had been assured of his election to the Cambridge professorship vacated by Fawcett's death on 6 November 1884. In his paper to the Conference, he referred to the need for more work in economic science and 'a wider diffusion of the very little that is already known'. It is probable that the torrent of criticism and suspicion hurled at political economy during the Conference, coupled with the authority of his new position, prodded Marshall at this point in his career into embarking on a major effort to re-establish the position of economics as a recognized and respected science, an effort which in various ways would occupy him in subsequent years. This effort had two forms of expression: institutional and theoretical, the latter including the ideology or meta-theory concerning the nature of the study of theoretical work, which would be accepted as the basic consensus lying, according to the Comtist definition, at the foundation of all valid scientific disciplines. The institutional effort, at the national level, culminated in the foundation of the British Economic Association and the publication of the *Economic Journal*. Efforts to establish a new theoretical core included the publication of Marshall's *Principles* as well as similar attempts at synthesizing a consensus on the part of J. N. Keynes, J. S. Nicholson, and others. The resulting controversy of the early 1890s was to place the school of thought to which the young Oxford economists belonged apart from the main-

[11] *Industrial Remuneration Conference.*

stream of Marshallian economics. It is with this ideological controversy that the rest of this study is mainly concerned.

Marshall's inaugural lecture[12] gave him the opportunity for a comprehensive statement on the nature of the study of economics. The lecture was not directed at the general public, but rather at the scientific community in general, and Cambridge in particular. It was mainly concerned with answering criticism from two important quarters—the Comtists and the historical economists. A central theme used to counter criticism from within the scientific community and to establish a positive position dealt with the status of the works of the 'older economists' later to be commonly referred to as the 'classical economists'. Since their authority was the main target of the critics, the issue had to be dealt with if an undisputed scientific basis for the study of economics was to be established. On the one hand their work was rejected as invalid, while on the other the Comtist definition of science stressed the importance of continuity. Marshall chose to sidestep the issue and avoid confrontation by arguing that the main importance of the work done by economists since Adam Smith has lain in the development of a method of enquiry—an 'organon' of universal applicability. This method—'an engine for the discovery of concrete truth'—was comparable in its validity to the theory of mechanics in physics. It demonstrated how to deal with the human motives that were measurable. This did not mean that it claimed to cover the totality of human activity. By concentrating on method, Marshall demonstrated continuity without confronting the issue of validity. Indeed, he pointed out that conclusions reached at different periods by use of the method could not be universally valid since reality was not static. In keeping with the change of perspective in scientific enquiry which resulted from the theory of evolution, Marshall maintained that neither man nor society were a constant quantity. Economic factors were therefore subject to constant change. However, the tools used to analyse these factors were not subject to these changes. The attack on the validity of 'old' dogmas might be justified, but it did not affect the scientific status of economics, since the attributes of 'universality'

[12] A. Marshall, 'The Present Position of Economics', reprinted in A. C. Pigou (ed.), *Memorials of Alfred Marshall* (London, 1925), pp. 152–74.

and 'continuity' were attached not to dogmas, but to method. Carrying the attack over to the Comtist camp, Marshall argued that there were no grounds for an attack on economic method. Sociology was in an inferior position, lacking a consensus on method and unable to suggest an alternative. Both fields of enquiry could in fact rely on no more than common sense, in the use of which sociologists had no advantage over economists.

The historical economists, on the other hand, had challenged the use of abstract deductive reasoning. Against them a different argument was employed. Marshall argued that the historical economists used the very method they condemned: 'They do not in any way help us to dispense with the use of the economic organon, but rather make use of its aid at every step'. Bare facts were meaningless unless a deductive theory, commonly accepted, was used to interpret them. Without such an interpretative theory, different, if not opposite, conclusions might be reached. As for the advantage claimed by the historical economists for their form of investigation into current issues, Marshall argued that the works of that school 'do not throw a direct light on particular economic problems of our age', since 'history does not repeat itself' and 'the past can never throw a simple and direct light on the future.'

Another major criticism raised against economics was that of the applicability of its doctrines. One of the criteria in the Comtist definition of a science, besides continuity of theory and consensus, was its ability to predict. It had been widely argued that the teachings of economics simply did not apply to the present and could not be used to predict future developments. Again Marshall sidestepped the issue. He pointed out that economic theory dealt with a multiplicity of subjects, only a few of which could be used in practical analysis. In this respect he accepted the criticism against the 'older economists' since their choice of subjects served to create this common fault. This, Marshall argued, had been rectified by modern economists in their work on subjects that had practical implications. What was needed for further rectification was 'an organon stronger and more complete, more able to analyse and help in the solution of the economic problems of the age'. On this issue Marshall was in a delicate situation: while there was the obvious need to disprove the popular scientific criticism against economics, overemphasis on the issue of practicability might have led him to clash with Henry Sidgwick, who strongly advocated a neutral objective position for all sciences including economics.[13] Accordingly, Marshall was careful to qualify his comments on practicability. The economist should not become directly involved in the actual debates over positive measures. His role was one of a consultant whose contribution would be mainly negative, revealing the flaws and fallacies in suggested schemes. The economist as such 'cannot say which is the best course to pursue' and if he did voice an opinion he could only do so as a private citizen.

In this instance, Marshall had taken his previously held position a step closer to Sidgwick's. In the past[14] he had argued that the economist as such could not pass moral judgement on economic actions, but up to and including the Industrial Remuneration Conference he did not hesitate to voice an expert opinion in favour of practical, immediate, and, at times, morally charged solutions for current problems. It seems likely that the change was due not so much to conviction as to expediency. It was significantly not emphasizd in the address as a whole, which ended by pointing out the necessity of training students so that they might forward the enquiry into 'how far is it possible to remedy the economic evils of the present day'. This implied a role more active than negative criticism. In any event, at least one person, H. S. Foxwell, did not attach much significance to Marshall's few utterances in favour of complete neutrality and claimed, in a lecture later the same year, to be in agreement with Marshall's 'Present Positon' when he said, 'No study is more *inspired by a practical object* than Economics. Its end is pre-eminently Action.'[15]

Despite the need to tread cautiously on the question of practicality, Marshall made it clear that the economist's method of investigation did enable him to predict. Economics thus qualified as a science according to the Comtist definition. This was made possible by the description of the economic activities

---

[13] e.g. H. Sidgwick, *The Principles of Political Economy* (London, 1883), pp. 27, 32–3.
[14] L. Royden Harrison, 'Two Early Articles by Alfred Marshall', *Economic Journal*, 1963, pp. 422–30.
[15] H. S. Foxwell, 'What is Political Economy?', given on 5 Oct. 1885, in the City of London College, in the *Eagle*, No. 79, p. 75.

of society in terms of 'a slow equilibrium of measurable motives' where the rate of change over the years was relatively slow. Although it might be argued that in the long run current analysis could not be used for predictions (as Marshall argued in the case of the 'older' economists' doctrines), this was not the case in short-range predictions. Its range of predictions was demonstrated in questions such as 'what kind of effects to expect from each cause and how these effects are likely to combine with one another'.

Marshall's statement came under attack first from the 'guardians' of the 'old' doctrines. A lengthy article in *The Times*[16] insisted 'not only that Adam Smith, Ricardo and Malthus pursued the right methods of inquiry, but also that the bulk of their results and teaching remains true.' No changes were required in the study of the subject. 'We go back over the labours of those who built up Political Economy and are convinced again of its strength.' The reaction to the works of the 'older economicsts', the writer maintained, was primarily due to a shift in political power causing a change in the public's attitude towards philanthropy into a position more in keeping with the feelings of the newly enfranchised working classes. The public wanted quicker reform and immediate results in terms of material improvement. The 'older economists', although on the whole pessimistic of such improvements, based their observations on the knowledge that no material improvement was possible without prior moral improvement.

Marshall's answer demonstrated a basic difference in beliefs concerning material progress between himself, as representative of his generation, and an older attitude represented in *The Times's* article. Marshall admitted to a direct link between moral and material improvement but at the same time argued that material improvement could precede and lead to moral improvement, thus creating a continuously rising spiral which he regarded as the dynamic motion of progress in which one type of improvement leads to the other. In his answer to the criticism he concentrated on the results of increasing workers' wages. In the view of the 'older economists', as summarized by

---

[16] *The Times*, 30 May 1885. Marshall's answer, dated 30 May, was printed on 2 June 1885. Both items bear the title of Marshall's inaugural lecture. Compare the criticism with Lord Bramwell's address in the Bath meeting of Section F in 1888.

Marshall, a causal chain in which higher wages bring about a drop in the interest paid on capital and in the earnings of the 'higher ranks of industry', causes a diminution in the demand for labour and results in wages dropping to their previous level. Marshall argued that the first result of the causal chain was not the only possible one. 'If it be true', he maintained, 'that poverty is the chief cause of weakness, and that a rise in wages is likely to increase strength, there is room for hope that the higher waged labour will not be dear labour.'[17] Higher wages were just as likely to lead both to higher efficiency and to an improvement in the moral and mental strength of the worker. Thus the causal chain would not necessarily end in a drop in wages but rather, through the improvement in the efficiency and social morality of the labourer, to a permanently high rate of wages. It should be noted at this point that faith in this form progress was shared by most, if not all, of Marshall's contemporary economists and in the ensuing debate was never brought into question.

When he came to evaluate the work of the 'older economists', Marshall chose a position halfway between complete rejection and the unqualified approval of *The Times*'s article:

> I hold that most of their results were, so far as they went, true when they were written, and that many of them are true now . . . It is the universality and not the truth of their results that I rank so far below that of their organon. I wanted to argue that, whether their doctrines are true or not, no good work can be done without the aid of analysis and methods of reasoning which have been slowly wrought out by their great genius.

It was obvious that under the circumstances Marshall preferred to emphasize the positive value of the 'older' economists' method, rather than to elaborate on which of their theories he accepted and which he rejected. Any such attempt would inevitably have involved him in a debate which could be detrimental to the establishment of a consensus within the science.

Another detailed statement along similar lines, with probably similar aims in mind, came from Sidgwick in his presidential address to Section F at the Aberdeen meeting of

---

[17] A similar argument may be found in classical economics. See A. W. Coats, 'The Classical Economists and the Labourer', in A. W. Coats (ed.), *The Classical Economists and Economic Policy* (London, 1971), p. 161.

the British Association on 10 September 1885: 'The Scope and Method of Economic Science'. Sidgwick addressed himself to many of the problems tackled by Marshall, including some of the current debates on practical measures which had been stated at the Remuneration of Industry Conference. He declared that state intervention was sometimes inevitable but always had to be considered as the exception to the rule of non-intervention. Fair trade he rejected off-hand as dangerous, clumsy, and costly. But in considering both issues, he employed none of the moral arguments used by Marshall at the conference. Indeed, Sidgwick laid special emphasis on the separation of moral issues from the investigation of economic problems as carried out by the economist: 'The English Economist, in giving an explanation of the manner in which prices, wages, profits, etc. are determined, is not attempting to justify the result'. Social justice was a matter for the politician and it was the politician's task to approach the economist with a scheme based on his concept of justice and to ask him to consider its economic aspects. Otherwise, 'it is not with such far reaching proposals of change that the English economist is mainly concerned; his primary business is to ascertain the causes which determine actual prices of products and services.' It may be understood that once given a scheme to analyse, or an existing system to investigate, the economist need bother himself only with understanding the way it works, without considering its moral aspects, a point already made by Sidgwick in his *Principle of Political Economy*.[18]

The clear dichotomy between morals and economics is demonstrated in Sidgwick's *Principles* when he deals with the results of higher wages, the same problem Marshall discussed in his article in *The Times*. Sidgwick argued:

(a) It is no doubt true . . . that any increase in the wages of hired labour not accompanied by an equal increase in its productiveness has some tendency to cause a reaction and subsequent inevitable reduction in the remuneration of such labour.[19]
(b) On the whole there was no adequate reason to assume that higher wages as a rule increase efficiency.[20]

[18] Sidgwick, *The Principles of Political Economy*, p. 500.
[19] Ibid., p. 364.
[20] Ibid., p. 327.

[But]
(c) It was clearly the case when the wages raised were of 'Labour scantily provided with the means of maintaining physical health and vigour.'[21]

One must bear in mind that beyond differences of opinion concerning the likelihood of increased wages increasing production and whether or not the economist should consider the moral benefits of higher wages, Sidgwick was in an easier position than Marshall, being less exposed to external criticism on the issue of morals and enjoying a position of irrefutable authority. The only quarter from which the moral issue was raised, as far as Sidgwick was concerned, was that of the German historical school,[22] and the counter-arguments he employed in his presidential address were very much in keeping with the arguments he had already stated in the *Principles*: (a) The economist did not condone existing practices but merely studied them. Therefore, he did not disallow the possibility that self-interest, which the German school claimed the English economists condoned, might be curbed. (b) The economist did not consider self-interest the only motive to be considered in the study of distribution. However (c) it was the predominant one and no other school had shown otherwise.

As for method, Sidgwick rejected the extreme claims of both the historians and deductivists. The historical method was of some limited use, in 'accurately ascertaining particular facts when we are inquiring into the particular causes of particular values, or of the shares of particular economic classes at any given place and time.' Beyond that, too much had been made by the historical economists of their contribution to theory from the study of the stages in the development of industrial society. Like Marshall, he considered the constants to be generally of greater importance than the variables in the economic activity of societies. In ascertaining these constants they were indebted to the works of their 'most eminent predecessors'.

The other major camp of critics Sidgwick dealt with was the Comtists. He argued that had they established a method of enquiry and a system of laws through which 'we could accurately forecast the main features of the future state with which our

---

[21] Ibid.
[22] Hence his use of the term 'English economists'.

present social world is pregnant', their claim as to the absorption of economics by sociology would have been indisputable. The criteria set down by Comte for the definition of a science were not as yet provided by sociology. It lacked any concensus or sense of continuity, and it was devoid of the power of prediction since in that respect it was, at best, a conglomeration of personally held utopias. It is significant that in answering the Comtists both Marshall and Sidgwick accepted their definition of a science, using it to disprove the Comtists' claims and to establish their own claim for the scientific status of economics.

Marshall and Sidgwick did not see eye to eye on all issues, including some of the questions concerning the nature of the study of economics. Indeed, Marshall considered Sidgwick to be something of an amateur.[23] Sidgwick clearly did not share Marshall's concern for the immediate need within society for well-trained economists. In his *Principles*[24] he emphasized the importance of a purely scientific, i.e. disinterested, pursuit of knowledge. However, his position at Cambridge discouraged any confrontation on these as well as on institutional issues such as the Economics Tripos to which Sidgwick was opposed.[25] Instead, Marshall sought the common ground, minimizing their differences in order to promote the status of economics at Cambridge and in the country as a whole.

These general statements did not, at first, provoke a debate within the economists' community. Since plans for the establishment of the institutional basis of the science were as yet at an early stage, the statements represented at best the academic authority of the economist as invested in his chair and backed by his professional reputation. Since the main issue at stake was to refute the criticisms hurled at economics, statements of a general nature were not yet mutually critical. Nevertheless, the ground for later controversy was laid.

Two other economists, who were at the time close to Marshall, also came out during the same year with general

---

[23] For their relationship, see J. K. Whitaker, *The Early Economic Writings of Alfred Marshall 1867–1890.* (London, 1975).

[24] Sidgwick, *Principles*, p. 466.

[25] At that time papers in political economy were part of the Moral Philosophy Tripos and the Special Examination in Moral Sciences for the ordinary BA Degree. One paper on political economy and economic history was set in the Historical Tripos.

statements: J. S. Nicholson and H. S. Foxwell. Both could claim that (owing to the nature of Marshall's synthesis) they were in line with his views. However, their choice of emphasis placed them in a diametrically opposed position. In 'A Plea for Orthodox Political Economy',[26] Nicholson dealt mainly with the external criticism from various radical reformers by adopting a position similar to Sidgwick's. He did not even refer to the criticisms from within the scientific community. Indeed, in a later statement[27] he professed to be deeply impressed by the results obtained through the use of the historical method by Thorold Rogers and Cliffe Leslie. (He had previously[28] pointed out the mutual benefit derived from one method making use of the findings of the other.) Nicholson concentrated on two arguments: the complete detachment of the economist from current debates and the validity of the classical dogmas of free competition and non-intervention. The first point seems to have been mainly motivated by concern for the professional status of the economist. Whenever an English economist had 'laid down the law on practical points like one in authority, and not as a scribe,' he argued, 'he has lost in reputation and his science has lost in precision.' As for the second point, he argued in favour of the retention of the principles of *laissez-faire*, the abandonment of which would be retrogressive. It was a sound principle, whose value to the welfare of society had been amply proven. Nor did it clash with any social moral issue. 'As a general rule, natural liberty is not found to be opposed to the moral sense of the community; and when the two are harmonious interference on the part of the Government is often injurious and generally unnecessary . . . it has been plausibly maintained that self interest had done more than charity for civilization.' Harmony could be enhanced by the introduction of new principles and by the conservation of the old ones: 'surely the time has not yet come for the abandonment of the teaching of Adam Smith in exchange for the froth of Mr. George or the confused ideals of the German Professors.'

---

[26] J. S. Nicholson, 'A Plea for Orthodox Political Economy', in the *National Review*, December 1885.

[27] Id. Preface to the second edition of *The Effects of Machinery on Wages* (London, 1892).

[28] Id. *Political Economy as a Branch of Education* (Edinburgh, 1881), p. 24.

At the other end of the spectrum one finds the statements of H. S. Foxwell, who had been close to Marshall in his professional views and as a personal friend. During the late 1880s he shared Marshall's vision of the organizational establishment of economics and worked wholeheartedly towards realizing it. His concept of the study of economics laid stress on its practical implications. In this he was in line with Marshall. One need only compare his 'Irregularity of Employment and Fluctuations of Prices', an address delivered during a course of lectures in the summer of 1886 on 'Various aspects of the Labour Problem'[29] and Marshall's suggestions at the Remuneration Conference. Both were put forward in similar circumstances, in addresses to the general public consisting mostly of interested parties eager to forward radical solutions. Like those of Marshall, Foxwell's suggestions mixed moral with economic consideration. He dealt with gambling and uncertain employment, condemned state intervention and radical solutions to social evils, and praised productive co-operatives, profit-sharing schemes, sliding scales, conciliation boards, and the cultivation of an educated public opinion.

However, Foxwell's social vision went beyond that of Marshall. Having accepted the principle of a vertical harmony of interests within society, he envisaged a guild revival: 'new trade associations should unite . . . men and masters of a trade equally for the common purposes of that trade.' These associations would function as complete social units combining technical education, regulation of apprenticeship, bureaus of statistics, trade journals and labour bureaus for each trade, funds for accidents, and saving schemes which would include retirement schemes. The future was in productive co-operatives.[30] 'The English working class will not be slow to recognise the solidarity of interest of the working classes of the civilised nations; nor to see the implied consequence, that they cannot adequately raise their own position without in some degree raising that of others . . . all men could unite in a foreign enterprise of this land.' In such a transformation the

---

[29] *The Claims of Labour* (Edinburgh, 1886).
[30] Compare with A. Toynbee, 'The Education of Co-operators', in his *Lectures on the Industrial Revolution of the Eighteenth Century in England* (London, 1894).

old doctrines of *laissez-faire*, defined as 'fatalistic, crude, antisocial', would have to be abandoned.

In 'Irregularity of Employment' and in 'What is Political Economy'[31] — an introductory lecture given at the City of London College on 5 October, 1885 — Foxwell quoted Marshall as an authority for some of his points; yet in the same lectures the differences between his position and that of Marshall, which he may have considered merely differences in degree, came close to differences in principle. While Marshall was careful in his criticism of the 'old economists', Foxwell argued: 'If Economics is in popular estimation a "dismal" and "brutal" study, most of our thanks are due to Ricardo'; and he stated that the Malthusian practical conclusions regarding population 'have probably been the most serious of all mistakes they have made.' While Marshall preferred the term 'economists' to 'political economy', for its scientific neutrality, Foxwell declared that 'Politics and Economics should be hand and glove [sic] with each other.' Marshall had argued for the separation of moral from economic issues while qualifying his position on the involvement of economists in current debates, whereas Foxwell chose to compare economics to medicine in its work for greater happiness and its clearly prescriptive nature. Nevertheless, since Foxwell's words were addressed not to fellow economists but to the general public, his differences with Marshall did not assume the form of a controversy nor would they for some years to come.

Just as many of the ideas contained in the general statements of Marshall and Sidgwick may be found in their earlier works, the need for an organizational basis for economics as a scientific discipline was felt by some economists before 1885. According to Foxwell,[32] he himself raised the issue during the 1883 meeting of Section F with its president at the time—Sir R. Inglis Palgrave. Explaining the course of events following his suggestions, he wrote in 1890:

> In the winter of the same year [1883], at his [Palgrave's] request, I drafted a scheme for an Association to publish a Journal, to edit a Dictionary, and to undertake reprints and translation. I wrote some 15 4to pp. outlining the pro-

---

[31] Foxwell, 'What is Political Economy'.
[32] Phelps papers, Foxwell to Phelps, 29 Oct. 1890.

posals. What has become of these I do not know. I did not wish at that stage to say much about the Review until we could see our way to the Association. That would explain my not definitely canvassing Oxford men. But Gonner took up the proposal for a review warmly.

But it was not until 1885 that the effort assumed a more definite form towards the creation of a theoretical consensus and its embodiment in an association, a periodical, etc. As the organizational position of economics was slowly realized and the hold of Marshallian economics over it consolidated, the debate as to the nature of economics emerged and intensified so that by the early 1890s lines on both issues became clearly drawn.

Economists were at that time, greatly dissatisfied with the position of economics within the Statistical Society. It was felt that too few papers in economics were read during its meetings and consequently too few were published in the Society's *Journal*. Section F, too, was found wanting, since it met only once a year and was little more than a forum for debate which did little to stimulate further research. Neither association could be considered conducive to the establishment of economics on the lines drawn by Marshall and Sidgwick. During October 1885 Foxwell complained in a letter to Inglis-Palgrave:[33] 'the [Statistical] Society seems to interest itself less and less in general Economic science; it even chafes at having to suffer papers on the theory of statistics itself.' To correct the disproportion in the subjects of the Society's papers, one of the first attempts at organization was to change the Society, with the possibility of publishing a monthly professional journal through it.

English economists were not unique in their wish to have a periodical which would serve to establish the boundaries of professional research while offering a venue for the publication of current work and for communication within the professional community. The same problem had confronted economists elsewhere, as well as English scholars in other fields such as history. Discontent with the annual publication of the Transac-

---

[33] Palgrave family papers, Foxwell to Inglis Palgrave, 28 Oct. 1885. Most of the relevant material in these papers has been dealt with by A. W. Coats, 'Sociological Aspects of British Economic Thought', in the *Journal of Political Economy*, 75 (1967), 706–29.

tions of the Royal Historical Society[34] led to the publication of the *English Historical Review*, the first number of which appeared in January 1886. Since academics in both fields were confronted with somewhat similar problems, they came up with very similar solutions, including attempts to define a central core of research on which there might be general consensus. The periodical would be open to all views, it would be completely objective and would avoid involvement in polemics on present-day issues.[35] During the period 1886–91 economists such as William Cunningham, E. C. K. Gonner, J. S. Nicholson, and L. R. Phelps published essays and reviews in the *EHR*. The benefits derived from the availability of such a platform for the expression of professional views were not lost on them. In 1889 Gonner wrote to Giffen:[36]

> I was writing to Prof. Foxwell the other day or so about the matter of an economic review and I thought that I might perhaps write to you as well. It is, I know, quite needless to say anything as to the importance of such a work being undertaken, but do you not think that some effort might be made in the direction of getting such a Review *speedily* organised. It does make study in England rather hopeless so far as progress and influence go where everyone is engaged in working in isolation. The difference caused by the History Review in the history world has of course been very great, and I imagine that a similar if not a greater difference would be caused by the establishment of an Economic Review in the Economic world in England.

Thus, although during the same period professional periodicals in economics made their appearance outside Britain with contributions by English economists, the problem was not confined to economists, nor was the solution modelled exclusively on foreign economics periodicals.

During 1885 Marshall suggested the changing of the Statistical Society into a Society for Economic Science and Statistics which would take up the publication of a monthly economic review.[37] Economic statistical enquiries would be separated from the non-economic. Foxwell argued that a society dedicated solely to statistics was absurd, since facts were

---

[34] Of which William Cunningham was member of Council as well as member of the Cambridge Branch Committee.
[35] 'Prefatory Note', in the *English Historical Review*, No. 1, January 1886, ed. the Revd. Mandell Creighton.
[36] LSE, Giffen papers, Gonner to Giffen, 18 June 1889.
[37] Palgrave family papers, Foxwell to Inglis Palgrave, 28 Oct. and 25 Nov. 1885.

meaningless without their interpretation by *a priori* deductive reasoning. The economists seem to have aimed at the absorption of statistics into the respective fields of investigation which dealt with data gathered, fields which would provide the data with interpreting theories. Furthermore, Foxwell found fault with the Society's membership; it consisted mainly of civil servants and of too many business men who used their membership as a trade advertisement. It had become too cliquey, too conservative, and too dull—a non-scientific society and, even worse, a society of amateurs.

Needless to say, these views were not shared by the majority of the Society's members who were quite happy with the *status quo*. During November 1885 an abortive proposal was put forward by Mr Hyde Clarke, a member of the Society, that the Society should hold periodical meetings dedicated exclusively to economics. The motion was discussed during a meeting in December and rejected, to Foxwell's disgust:

> I was, I confess, surprised at the temper of the ignorance shown in the discussion. The majority of members seem to make the question personal, though what interests they had in it, it was hard to discover, and I found that the prevailing idea of Political Economy was that it was made up of tables, statistics, and party politics! It was almost hopeless to discuss the question before such an audience.[38]

Since the Statistical Society would have nothing to do with the scheme it became clear that the periodical, which was given top priority, would need an independent society as a sponsor. Plans for another project pointed in the same direction. During 1885 Inglis Palgrave had been sounding opinions on the other two projects suggested by Foxwell—the reprinting of economic texts and the compilation of a dictionary of economics, both of which fitted admirably into Marshall's vision. The reprints would establish the element of continuity within the science,[39] while a dictionary would draw the boundaries of the science as well as contain its core of consensus. On the reprint project, Inglis Palgrave seems to have encountered the problem of sponsorship as well as lack of agreement as to the choice of texts. Foxwell argued that the texts should be printed at Cambridge, since Oxford had lost any claim it might have had

---
[38] Palgrave family papers, Foxwell to Inglis Palgrave, 13 Dec. 1885.
[39] The same, 5 Nov. 1885.

DEBATE ON STUDY OF ECONOMICS—INITIAL MOVES

through the political appointment of Bonamy Price and the untimely death of Arnold Toynbee. Cambridge, on the other hand, had been enjoying a marked revival in the study of economics since Marshall's appointment. As many as six men were lecturing on the subject, which was proving to be increasingly popular.[40] In any event, it was felt that the reprints project too would best be carried out by a new independent association.

More concrete efforts were directed at starting the periodical. The major problem seemed to be to find the right editor, a person whose position in the field would be uncontroversial and whose views were considered comparatively neutral. Furthermore, as long as the exact form of sponsorship remained undecided, he had better be one whose leisure and income would allow him to start the periodical without a full salary.[41] For a time J. N. Keynes seemed to be the obvious choice, to the extent that Foxwell expressed his apprehension that should Keynes be elected to the Oxford Drummond Professorship in 1888 (upon the death of Bonamy Price), the periodical would go with him.[42] The other alternatives were L. L. Price and F. Y. Edgeworth, but they were to be considered only if Keynes turned the position down. Because of the lack of sponsorship, the salary that could be offered was merely £100 per annum,[43] which meant that if no editor could be found to do without a proper salary, the association issue would have to be tackled first. In addition, it was realized during 1887 that the same applied to the reprint scheme,[44] whereas the dictionary fortunately found a commercial sponsor in Macmillan & Co.[45]

The question of the choice of texts for reprinting raised an

[40] The same, 13 Dec. 1885.
[41] The same, 10 Nov. 1885.
[42] Marshall Library, Keynes papers, Foxwell to J. N. Keynes, 15 Mar. 1888.
[43] Ibid., Marshall to J. N. Keynes, 17 Mar. 1888.
[44] Palgrave family papers, J. N. Keynes to Inglis Palgrave, 28 Nov. 1886.
[45] Palgrave family papers, Macmillan & Co. to Inglis Palgrave, 14 June 1888. Not everyone was happy with Inglis Palgrave's editorship. In 1890 Foxwell complained that Inglis Palgrave 'was quite incompetent for the task he undertook and only the very liberal assistance of a number of young men has saved the thing from being ridiculous. As it is, it will be very much less useful than it might have been made if it had been edited by a committee of competent persons.' Phelps papers, Foxwell to Phelps, 29 Oct. 1890.

unanticipated area of major disagreement within the field. No one disputed the principle or the need for an association and a journal, but the actual decision on reprinting raised the whole issue of the attitude towards the work of the 'old economists' and through it to the relationship between economics and morals. These problems had begun to emerge by 1887 in statements from various economists which were meant for 'internal consumption', i.e. for other economists. It is therefore no surprise that the reprint scheme had gradually and imperceptibly been moved aside to prevent a major controversy within the close circle around Marshall before the goals of the organization of economics were achieved.

Just how explosive the issue was can be gauged from Foxwell's article, 'The Economic Movement in England', published in the predominantly theoretical American *Quarterly Journal of Economics* in its issue of October 1887.[46] For the benefit of fellow economists Foxwell set out to describe the revival of economic science in England. He employed the usual arguments to describe its differences from the revolutionary socialism of Marx and Henry George, but he also chose to define the new movement by means of a complete rejection of the 'older economists'. In a description of the 'old' school he wrote:

> In its spirit it was strongly materialistic, sacrificing national welfare to the accumulation of individual wealth. Some of its writers carried capitalism so far as to deplore high wages as a calamity comparable in its effects to a bad harvest. Worst of all, it was distinctly unmoral (a more serious defect than immorality, which provokes a reaction), in as much as it claimed that economic action was subject to a mechanical system of law, of a positive character, independent and superior to any laws of the moral world.

He saw the main difference between the 'old economists' and those of the present day in the former's aloofness: 'With the old school, the worst scandals were calmly referred to "demand and supply", as though such a reference were final. With the new school, if the conditions of the market are such as to lead to injustice or to swell the mass of social wreckage, these conditions must be overhauled, and, as far as may be, rectified.'

The same attitude was sustained in his description of what

---

[46] The article was dated Cambridge, September 1887.

an English association would be like: 'It would aim at the advancement of theory, at the consolidation of economic opinion, at the encouragement of historical research, and at criticism and direction of industrial and economic policy'. Foxwell seems to have been oblivious to Comtist criticism and therefore unconcerned with the question of continuity. Yet in serving the cause of the association, he strove to present contemporary economics as being basically in agreement on the method and treatment of the study, despite what he termed 'superficial and formal' differences. He stressed the unity and complete rejection of the 'old economists' as the main attributes of the 'new ' movement.

Another authoritative general statement from well outside Marshall's zone of influence came from Edward Caird, Professor of Moral Philosophy at Glasgow University, in a lecture given at London during October 1887, entitled 'Political Economy, Old and New',[47] and published in the American *Quarterly Journal of Economics.* On the value of the 'old economists', Caird started from Marshall's position and ended with Foxwell's. He argued that the value of the work of the 'old school' could be dismissed only by those who did not understand it. The results of their work could not be neglected with impunity; 'the future', he stated, 'belongs to those who thoroughly appreciate the achievements of the past.' However, Caird was a relativist of sorts; he regarded theories as the product of a certain frame of mind shaped by current attitudes. The main fault of the 'old' doctrines was their abstract nature. Circumstances had changed and with them the modern economist's sense of social responsibility which 'makes it impossible to isolate the economical problems from the ethical'. It was a significantly different way of dealing with criticism of the 'old' doctrines. It neither entirely approved nor entirely condemned. It merely presented them as an outdated product of an antiquated frame of mind. This concept received further elaboration from Caird's student, William Smart, whose views on the relation between economics and ethics reflected the strong influence of Ruskin.[48] From Glasgow, then, came the

---

[47] Published in the American *Quarterly Journal of Economics*, vol. 3.

[48] In an article appropriately called 'The Old Economy and the New', in the *Fortnightly Review*, August 1891.

first published statements in a new phase in the general debate concerning the nature of economics which was to present the moral-relative view as an alternative to the Marshallian view.

The first direct challenge to Marshall's position came from Cunningham who, in 1889, was described by Ashley as standing 'alone in the breach' against Marshall at Cambridge.[49] Before Marshall's return to Cambridge, Cunningham, as a university lecturer (from 1884) in political economy and economic history, had enjoyed the freedom to teach as he chose. Fawcett, although a member of the History Board, rarely intervened in matters concerning the curriculum, so that Cunningham was free to follow his own concept of economics and teach economic history with occasional references to theoretical concepts as the subject arose in concrete forms in actual history.[50]

In 1884 Cunningham had been a candidate for the chair vacated by Fawcett and had hopes that 'Marshall would have been content to carry on the teaching of analytical economics at Oxford and that he would be left with room to develop a school of empirical political economy at Cambridge.'[51] Not only was he disappointed by Marshall's candidacy and election but, as he was soon to find out, Marshall intended to set a clear policy as to how economics should henceforth be taught. Through the History Board, Marshall forced Cunningham to teach economic theory (i.e. J. S. Mill) for one term out of three, a move Cunningham resented on both personal and professional grounds.

Although isolated within the circles of Cambridge economists, Cunningham's position was not without some strength. He was a member of the Royal Historical Society's Council and was on the Committee of the Society's Cambridge Branch.[52] He had been active in Cambridge extension work, in ecclesiastical politics, and in support of the East End Settlements. According to Foxwell he even contemplated as early as

---

[49] Marshall Library, Ashley to Seligman, 15 Sept. 1889 (copy).
[50] Audrey Cunningham, *William Cunningham; Teacher and Priest* (London, 1950), p. 64.
[51] Ibid.
[52] The other members of the Committee were J. R. Seeley, (chairman), O. Browning (vice-chairman), and G. W. Prothero.

1885 an independent periodical on political economy which Foxwell feared, with considerable justification, would take on 'the colour of a particular school or clique'.[53] In all these activities he acted in alliance with other members of the University so that when it came to his confrontation with Marshall he could depend on some support from quarters other than the economists.

The theoretical and ideological substance of his differences with Marshall may be found in his writings before 1885. These differences included support of increased state intervention;[54] a strong relativist position on economic theories arguing that theories formulated in one period could not be applied to the analysis of another;[55] and the complete rejection of some of the 'older theories', especially those of Malthus whom he singled out in 1883[56] denouncing as occult his population theory, in the light of the facts of English history. The Malthusian population trend had been proved not to be a constant one. There were cases in which the reproductive forces merely perpetuated degradation, occasioned by external conditions otherwise initiated, as well as 'Malthusian' cases in which reproduction had been the direct cause of degradation. In any event, he argued, the reality of a redundant population should not be approached in a purely theoretical manner and condemned as a hopeless evil, but rather should be studied without theoretical bias with the aim of finding and remedying the social disorder that causes it. It would be valid to generalize from this conclusion that Cunningham's fundamental rejection of past theories was mainly based on his regarding their conclusions as an obstructive bias.

In 1888 Cunningham was appointed college lecturer at Trinity College, Cambridge. Having resigned his university lectureship, he was no longer under Marshall's authority. It was Marshall's intention to place all the studies of economics at Cambridge within one discipline — his own. Cunningham's

[53] Palgrave family papers, Foxwell to Inglis Palgrave, 21 Nov. 1885.
[54] W. Cunningham, 'The Progress of Socialism in England', in the *Contemporary Review*, January 1879.
[55] Id. *The Growth of English Industry and Commerce During the Early and Middle Ages* (Cambridge, 1882), pp. 5, 19.
[56] Id. 'On the Statement of the Malthusian Principle', in *Macmillan's Magazine*, December 1883.

main concern, therefore, was to ensure the independence of economic history as an empirical study rather than to suggest a rival, all-encompassing discipline. In 1889 the structure of the Tripos was changed. The Moral Philosophy Tripos were abolished (thus freeing Marshall from Sidgwick's authority) and economic history and political economy were left within the Historical Tripos. Although they were set as two separate papers the power to set the questions was more in the hands of Marshall — as member of the History Board — than of Cunningham who was one of the examiners. This new situation determined the essence and timing of Cunningham's attack on Marshall's 'Present Position' during the meeting of Section F at Newcastle upon Tyne in 1889.

Cunningham's paper was primarily concerned with the Comtist criticisms.[57] However, as a historian he did not concern himself with the Comtist definition of a science or its applicability to economics. His concern, without accepting Comtist criteria, was with the acceptance of economics as a sound and efficient method for the investigation of social phenomena. He did not argue for the exclusiveness of any one approach, but for the necessity of combining sociological and theoretical economic theories. The two disciplines should coexist and co-operate instead of attempting to absorb each other. Turning from the Comtist issue to what was happening within the field of economics, Cunningham applied the same argument to the relationship between historical economics and deductive theory. Marshall, in his opinion, had been trying to do what the Comtists had tried to do. By belittling the contribution of historical economics he aimed at subjecting it to deductive theory. In truth, Cunningham argued, historical economics was more important than Marshall made it out to be.

In the first place, present-day economic theories were of little use in the analysis of the past, since 'the economic facts of the past can only be interpreted in the light of the moral and intellectual conditions of life in the past, not by mere intuitions of an intelligence formed by a nineteenth century education.' The reversal of the argument was equally valid: theories formulated

[57] W. Cunningham, 'The Comtist Criticism of Economic Science', in *Report of the British Association for the Advancement of Science*, 1889, Newcastle upon Tyne.

in the past, such as Ricardo's theory of rent, were applicable only to the period in which they were formed: 'The economic man of each time and place is relative to the economic organism of which he forms a part. Partly by costume, partly through regulation, he will have to do what society around him does'. Therefore only the historian was competent to study the economic reality of the past. By implication, theories of the past could not be used to analyse the present.

Secondly, work in historical research was an invaluable method of training for an economist. 'The simpler transactions of early times afford a field where the beginner can find instruction, not from abstract principles and fancy illustrations, but in the phenomena of actual life'. Here he gave instances of the study of the evils of unproductive consumption, the debasement of coinage, and problems of foreign trade and foreign exchange.

The second argument should be seen in its Cambridge context and in Cunningham's effort to ensure the independence of economic history in the university curriculum. The first argument, on the other hand, came closer to the general issue. As the first direct challenge to Marshall's 'Present Position', it required an answer that would prevent the development of a major controversy which could only harm the cause of unity. Marshall protested that Cunningham had misrepresented his views and that he did not mean to place historical economics in an inferior position, as Cunningham claimed. Cunningham appended Marshall's protest to the printed version of his paper, adding that it did not warrant any change in his words. Although the exchange did not then develop into a full-scale public debate, it was Cunningham's feeling that ever since his 'mutiny' Marshall had been against him.[58]

As long as plans for the association and the periodical were unrealized, the various statements and articles dealing with the nature of the study of economics assumed a predominantly conciliatory air when directed at fellow economists, while presenting an image of competence, unity and confidence to the outside. All were concerned with finding a workable formula which would ensure unity, or rather, prevent one school of thought from subjugating the rest. Since no such claim of

[58] Phelps papers, Cunningham to Phelps, 6 Jan. 1890.

domination was apparent, the various statements, except for the Cunningham-Marshall exchange, were presented in cautious and relaxed tones. The various economists involved stated their studied opinion for the benefit of the consensus for which they hoped, and continued going about their business as before. This wish to avoid confrontation was reflected in the nature of J. N. Keynes's *Scope and Method* and Marshall's *Principles*. However, by the time these books were published, the organizational reality had changed. The British Economic Association had been founded, with Marshall and his supporters in clear control of the Association and its journal, and a rival camp had set itself up in the form of the Oxford-based *Economic Review*. The organizational lines had been drawn between the schools of thought, and the debate assumed a fiercer style of polemic.

5

THE DEBATE—OXFORD VARIANTS

The preoccupation of Marshall and like-minded contemporaries in Cambridge and elsewhere with the promotion of the status of economics, which manifested itself partly in an effort to reach and maintain a consensus, was not shared by Oxford's young economists during the 1880s. They were less concerned with these issues on a national scale, and whenever their work took a general form, such as in Ashley's unfinished *Economic History* or Cannan's *Elementary Political Economy*, they were far from conciliatory.

During the early 1880s, whenever the young Oxford graduates were dealing with the question of the nature of the study of economics, they expressed opinions which roughly covered the whole of the debate as it had been expressed between Cliffe Leslie and Cairnes. W. J. Ashley adopted a position very similar to Cliffe Leslie's, although at the same time he had formed a favourable opinion of some of Ricardo's theories. In a letter to his future wife, written in 1886, proclaiming what he called his 'economic faith', he wrote:

I think that the Socialist analysis of *factory* industry is in the main correct, and it is identical with that of the great founders of abstract Economics—Ricardo and Cairnes. The point was that in much of the factory industry many of the conditions the orthodox theorists pre-supposed are at present being realized and as a consequence the results they reached theoretically are being realized.[1]

This view he incorporated into a more general position in line with Cliffe Leslie's. In a chapter on 'Modern History', written for a guide book on Oxford studies published in 1887,[2] he described the current trend of change in the study of economics in England as he saw it:

---

[1] Anne Ashley, *William James Ashley*, pp. 34–5.
[2] W. J. Ashley, 'Modern History', chapter in A. M. M. Stedman (ed.), *Oxford, Its Life and Schools* (London, 1887).

For the present most investigators of Economic History would agree in thus defending their attitude towards orthodox Economics: they do not deny that the teaching of Ricardo and Mill is a logical construction upon given assumptions, nor that these assumptions are in a large measure true of certain important sides of modern industrial life, but they assert that these assumptions were certainly not all true until very recent times. And therefore, they urge, the so-called 'principles' of Political Economy are at any rate not universally true for all times and places, and in consequence contribute scarcely at all to the understanding of the economic life of the past.

This seems a fairly catholic approach; however, it was because of the limited applicability and practicability of theories that he considered them generally trivial. The main issue, in his view, was applicability. As he pointed out in a short monograph on *The Early History of the English Woollen Industry*, first read as a paper to the Oxford Economic Society in January 1887, 'Where the real divergence [between deductive and historical economists] begins is upon the question what use is to be made of these doctrines.'[3] In his 'economic faith'[4] he prescribed the tasks of the would-be economist as:

(i) the investigation of economic history — no facts are too remote to be without significance for the present, and both Lassalle and Marx have given a great impulse to investigation in this direction, and (ii) the examination of *modern life in the piece*. We can leave to the Cambridge people hair splitting analysis of abstract doctrine.

Thus Ashley's contempt for the 'Cambridge' preoccupation with theory was not due to a total rejection of theory but to its unsuitability for the tasks of the economist. If the point seemed to be vague or mildly stated in 1886, that is not the case with the following passage from the *English Woollen Industry* (1887):

The orthodox economist of today no longer thinks that he is in possession of a body of truths applicable to all times and places; and he is even too anxious to point out that he does not claim to give practical advice. The historian, therefore, will do well to acknowledge that deduction is a defensible method, and to leave the believer in abstract economics to justify his argumentation by its results.[5]

---

[3] W. J. Ashley, *The Early History of the English Woollen Industry* (The American Economic Association, September 1887).

[4] Anne Ashley, *William James Ashley*, p. 35.

[5] Ashley, *English Woollen History*, p. 9.

In other words, deductive theorizing, agreed to be impractical, was a waste of time, contrasted with historical economics: 'If by "truth" is meant such generalizations about the condition of things now and the direction in which they are going, as are of practical value to the politician or philanthropist, then historical inquiry has discovered truth, and will discover yet more.'[6]

Applied to the statements of Marshall, Cunningham, and others, this position is far from conciliatory. Not only does it state that deductive theory is of limited value, it further indicates that for practical purposes deductive theorizing is superfluous. Its limited contribution to knowledge could be produced by historical investigation. On the whole, Ashley's position on the study of economics was akin to Cliffe Leslie's Comtist position. It provided for practicability and prediction and when seen in terms of historical research, there was no doubt as to continuity or a core of consensus. As far as he was concerned, there was no debate concerning the practical value of historical investigations in their alliance with moral considerations. 'It made us discover the good in some cause or movement which yet we may feel it our duty to oppose, may make us see the long past causes of present evils, and the far future results of action now lightly begun; and it may encourage the habit of suspension of judgement till the judgement has sufficient materials to build upon.'[7]

Aligning economics with history would ensure the former's status and the validity of its results—a view reflecting Ashley's academic position as college tutor and lecturer in the well-established School of History. What such a view entails in terms of actual work is demonstrated in Ashley's first major book, *An Introduction to English Economic History and Theory* (London 1888), which provided for the scope of enquiry laid down by Cliffe Leslie,[8] the explanation of the economic behaviour of a society through the study of society as a whole.

---

[6] Ibid., p. 11.

[7] Ashley, 'Modern History'.

[8] For Cliffe Leslie's position, see his *Essays in Political Economy* (London and Dublin, 1888), especially 'On the Philosophical Method of Political Economy', first published in *Hermathena*, vol. 2, 1876, and 'Political Economy and Sociology', first published in the *Fortnightly Review*, 1 Jan. 1879.

At that time Ashley adopted a somewhat Darwinian attitude towards the question of theory versus history. Let each do as he pleased; results would determine which discipline would survive and in the academic reality of contemporary Oxford there could be little doubt as to which that would be.

On 12 May 1886, the *Oxford Magazine* published an unsigned review of J. T. Danson's *The Wealth of Households* (Oxford 1886), written in defence of individualism against socialism. The review summed up its criticism of the book thus:

> Such *bourgeoise* optimism will disgust the 'reformer', nor will Mr. Danson's habit of beginning a subject with a definition approve itself to those who think definitions academic futilities. But the book states clearly the *media axiomata* of the science, with a certain daintiness and freshness of style which contrasts agreeably with the long-drawn sermonizing of Mill, or the Blue-book manner of Fawcett.

The next issue[9] of the magazine published a letter signed by 'An Agitated Enquirer' stating:

> I have . . . the disagreeable task of informing you that neither your review nor the book itself have been well received by those who are making a special study of the subject. I have heard some very strong language, and so far as I know the least offensive epithet hurled at Mr. Danson has been 'McCulloch redivivus'. . . . And I have heard that the able lecturers of the University Extension, who charm while they instruct the populations of the great towns, are accustomed to speak with contempt of Adam Smith, of Ricardo, and even of more recent writers. . . . the excessively able persons who are reading for the School of Modern History report from the lectures which they attend, a contempt for 'an abstract and unhistorical school of thought' which fills me with vague alarm. On all hands, therefore, I gather that there is a new political economy; and further that this new school is largely represented not only in Oxford but by lecturers in the provinces. . . . I should like to appeal . . . to the new school which certainly exists to put forward some statement of their doctrines.

The following week[10] Edwin Cannan, whose brother Charles had been one of the editors of the *Magazine,* tried to comply. He explained that the new political economy had no central textbook since it was mainly concerned with refuting the old doctrines rather than replacing them with a new one, which a central textbook would contain. To demonstrate his meaning,

---
[9] *Oxford Magazine*, 19 May 1886.
[10] Ibid., 26 May 1886.

Cannan took to task the wage-fund theory of which he argued: 'Any one who will take the trouble to think, instead of murmuring the name of Ricardo, can see that the idea of wages existing in a kind of store or reservoir before they are paid is absurd.' He concluded his answer to the 'Agitated Enquirer' by stating: 'Political Economy is not "resting on its old foundations" and I shall remain in my present opinion that "the old Political Economy" in making capital a kind of god which "sets labour in motion" committed an error which vitiated an enormous quantity of economic reasoning.'

There ensued an exchange of letters in which Cannan was criticized by a certain R. J. F., of Cambridge, for following Henry George in his rejection of the wage-fund theory.[11] Cannan replied that his views, which allegedly were held by all Oxford economists under the age of thirty, were supported by similar statements in Marshall's *Economics of Industry* (III vi. 54), and Sidgwick's *Principles* (pp. 318–20) as well as 'everyone who had considered the subject comprehensively'. In no circumstances should it be misinterpreted as support of the 'verbose Ricardian' Henry George. In the course of his answer, he mentioned as orthodox economists Fawcett, Cairnes, McCulloch, Ricardo, and—in a later letter—[12] Mill.

The rest of the exchange is of little interest except for the point raised by R. J. F.[13] that the passage Cannan quoted from Marshall's work seemed in fact to confirm his view less than he supposed. That this was so was clearly brought out during 1888[14] in the American *Quarterly Journal of Economics* in which Marshall, in an answer to Professor S. M. MacVane, stated that he regarded the wage-fund doctrine 'not as false, but as pretentious and misleading'. It was in need of modification and correction, but did not require complete replacement. Perhaps the question of the validity of Ricardo's wage-fund theory was the first instance of disagreement between Cannan and Marshall.

In later years Cannan recalled[15] that his first independent

[11] Ibid., 2 June 1886.
[12] Ibid., 9 and 25 June 1886.
[13] Ibid., 16 June 1886.
[14] A. Marshall, 'Wages and Profits', in the *Quarterly Journal of Economics*, January 1888.
[15] Cannan, *The Economic Outlook*, p. 10.

views on economics were due to his inability, while at Clifton, to accept the J. S. Mill–Fawcett maxim that 'Demand for commodities is not a demand for labour.'[16] The rejection was purely on theoretical grounds and it re-emerged at Oxford when he was reading the required passages from *Wealth of Nations* and Fawcett's *Manual of Political Economy* for the Pass School paper in political economy. However, by then an important element had been added to his previously deductive rejection of their theories. He had adopted the evolutionary concept of history,[17] and with it a relativistic approach to theory. His relativism is reflected in his undergraduate essays on subjects such as 'an absolutely best form of government' and 'the right of the State to interfere with private property',[18] and (after his graduation) in the Lothian Prize Essay of 1885 on the *Duke of Saint Simon*.[19] Relativism led Cannan to confine the applicability of political economy to a very limited point in time. In his unsuccessful attempt at the Cobden Prize Essay in 1886 he wrote: 'Political Economy does not and cannot say now what the effect of a particular form of property will be if it occur in 1986. Political Economy does not tell us beforehand what lines the evolution of society will follow.'[20] Political economy offered answers solely to particular questions concerning particular current events, on the basis of a theoretical analysis. Although Cannan conceived a limited field of enquiry for political economy as such, he agreed with Ashley that the possibility of long-range projections must be sought in disciplines outside theoretical political economy, such as history. Since Cannan lived in comparative isolation from Oxford society in his rooms in St. Giles, under the constant care of his aunt, his concentration on the limited field of theoretical criticism and his narrow approach to the boundaries of political economy did not bring him into conflict with any

---

[16] Cannan specifically referred to the fourth edition of Mrs M. G. Fawcett, *Political Economy for Beginners* (London, 1876), p. 28.
[17] Cannan, *The Economic Outlook*, p. 11.
[18] Both date from 1881. LSE Cannan papers, vol. 895.
[19] E. Cannan, *The Duke of Saint Simon* (Oxford and London, 1885). See p. 150 on judging Saint Simon on the basis of the criteria of his age and not as a contemporary figure.
[20] Cannan, *The Economic Outlook*, p. 13.

academic or other position which might have caused him at that stage to modify his views.

Cannan's first paper to the Oxford Economic Society, read on 1 March 1887,[21] combined the rejection of 'old' theories with a purely theoretical treatment of the definition of wealth. He distinguished between two types of wealth: (1) stock, i.e. material objects, and (2) enjoyed income, i.e. non-material objects. This definition of the second type of wealth he considered to be in direct conflict 'with all the economists with whose works I am acquainted', and yet to his surprise he noticed while reading the paper to the Society that 'this is just the part of the paper to which no one offered any objections!'. His avowed rejection of past and contemporary theoretical definitions of wealth, capital, productive and non-productive labour, the wage-fund theory, etc., assumed a form that was to become characteristic of his work. Describing his exchange with Cannan in the *Oxford Magazine* in 1888, Ashley remarked that Cannan at the time 'believed in deduction but thought everything anybody has done in that way obvious bosh'.[22] Gilbert Cannan described his cousin's professional attitude, rather caustically, as regarding 'all men inferior editions of himself. . . . It was inconceivable to him that any other man could know as much about his subject as himself.'[23]

In his paper on Wealth Cannan pointed out absurdities in Marshall, an 'entire lack of originality in Mill',[24] errors in Walker, and 'the vain imaginations of the Ricardian economics'. He had by then reconsidered Marshall's wage–capital theory which he declared to be a vaguer form of the wage-fund theory. One authority he did accept was that of Toynbee — on Ricardo's wage-fund doctrine. He was quite

---

[21] The paper has survived in two versions and with three titles. The original draft, preserved in Balliol College Library, is called 'The Capital of a Community'. It was presented to the Oxford Economic Society as 'The Economic Conception of Wealth' and was advertised by the Society under that title. Later it was prepared for publication (although never published) as 'The Two Wealths'—LSE Cannan papers, vol. 899. Quotations are from the original draft.

[22] Marshall Library, W. J. Ashley to Seligman, 19 Sept. 1889 (copy).

[23] Gilbert Cannan, *Little Brother*, p. 15.

[24] Criticism of Mill was becoming something of a family trait. Price wrote of Edwin's brother Charles's treatment of Mill's *Logic* at around the same period that 'he was wont to assign classes generally low to particular chapters or statements'. Trinity College, Price, 'Trinity College, Oxford 1881–1885'.

content to accept Toynbee's description of the doctrine and saw no need to modify it. His overall tone is well represented in his opening comment on the wage–capital theory: 'I have said nothing about Wage–Capital or remunerating capital as Prof. Marshall calls it simply because no such thing exists or be supposed to exist without the utmost confusion of mind.'

While rejecting the past treatment of wealth, Cannan tried to offer an alternative in his *Elementary Political Economy* (Oxford, 1888), based on his unsuccessful Cobden Prize essay. It was a curious exercise in that it avoided the employment of the word 'capital'. A puzzled biographer commented: 'It is not clear what advantage he saw in ignoring the word. His disapproval of the emphasis laid by the Ricardian school upon the importance of capital as an economic factor might have been shown in a better way, and he had no imitators in this experiment.'[25] At Oxford it was something of a cry in the wilderness. Amongst his contemporaries there was little, if any, interest in the reconstruction of a theoretical edifice, and therefore little demand for this type of work. To its reviewers it was the cause of some confusion and evoked various mixed appraisals. In the *Scotsman*[26] it was praised for its 'clear explanations and illustrations of the theories generally accepted by orthodox economists', while the *National Reformer*'s[27] reviewer condemned it as a 'discreditable work, the whole object of which seems to be to cloud and confuse economic issues'. Some reviewers[28] found it an 'excellent and practical little handbook'. Others[29] argued that 'so long as the old definitions and distinctions are adhered to in the standard text-books it is doubtful whether Mr. Cannan's work can be recommended to beginners in the study of economics'. The practical reasons for rejecting the work as a basic book for beginners were elaborated by L. L. Price in a review in the *Oxford Magazine*:[30]

[25] 'Professor Cannan, An Orthodox Economist', in *The Times*, 9 Apr. 1935. He may have got the idea from Jevons's criticism of the use of the term 'capital' and his preference for 'capitalisation'. According to one reviewer, Cannan's was the first work to work out Jevons's doctrine of utility—*Guardian*, 17 Apr. 1889.
[26] *Scotsman*, 27 Aug. 1888.
[27] *National Reformer*, 6 Jan. 1889.
[28] *Liverpool Courier*, 20 Apr. 1889; *Glasgow Herald*, 6 Sept. 1888.
[29] *Guardian*, 17 Apr. 1889; *Journal of Education*, 1 Jan. 1889; *Nation*, 11 Oct. 1888.
[30] *Oxford Magazine*, 23 Jan. 1889.

We cannot think that it is wise in an elementary treatise to break almost entirely, as Mr. Cannan does, with the past history of his subject, to introduce a new terminology, and in some cases to depart from an old definition and yet to treat the departure as one which is familiar and well understood. . . . The whole of our quarrel then, with Mr. Cannan, centres about the title of his book. It is too difficult to be elementary . . . he underrates the value . . . of his work by applying this epithet to it.

From his position of financial security and comparative isolation, Cannan could afford the luxury of indulging in the theoretical analysis which led to the publication of *Elementary Political Economy* largely in order to refute theories still current. His contemporaries, most of whom shared his rejection of these theories, were more concerned with the achievement of practical results through the investigation of historical trends and current problems. Yet this difference in choice of specialization does not indicate a different attitude to the question of application. On the basis of his theoretical deliberations, he stated as conclusions policies which Price, Ll. Smith, and Hewins were at the same time preaching to their Extension audiences, such as free trade, balanced state intervention, productive co-operatives, etc. Cannan's interest in current issues was to become obvious a few years later in his analysis of 'Legislation', 'Parliamentary Inquiries', and 'Official Returns' in each issue of the *Economic Review*.

Within the narrow confines of Oxford economics, the 'theory versus history' debate remains basically unchanged, while the need for applicability was generally accepted. This was at a time when elsewhere the same debate seemed to be resolved on the basis of a peaceful co-existence, if not an actual synthesis, while the ground was being laid for new controversies, including one on the question of applicability. The positions of both Ashley and Cannan on the status of the 'old' doctrines suggest that they were not concerned with establishing the scientific status of theoretical economics on the basis of the Comtist definition. They were much more concerned with the role and duty of the economist in society and the value of his work for the community. The contrast between the philosophical and ideological premises of Oxford and those of Cambridge may be described as the contrast between T. H. Green and H. Sidgwick.

The final statement of the early positions of Ashley and Cannan is contained in their exchange in the *Oxford Magazine*. Change during subsequent years came not so much in their views but rather in the organizational developments within economics and the new issues raised in the debate on the nature of economics at the national level. Thus, although both did modify their positions, it was the change in circumstances that placed them on a common front against the new Marshallian central core.

In the exchange in the *Oxford Magazine*, what was to become the core of methodological consensus was represented by L. L. Price. His first book, *Industrial Peace: its Advantages, Methods and Difficulties* (London, 1887)[31]—the results of research conducted by Price in Newcastle upon Tyne when he was the first Toynbee Trust lecturer—was reviewed by Ashley in the *Oxford Magazine*. Like most of his Oxford contemporaries, Price was committed ideologically to a vision of social harmony and mutual class understanding achieved by gradual non-revolutionary means. That a work on arbitration would result in an optimistic conclusion was practically inevitable. The question was, how was such a conclusion reached scientifically? What type of reasoning was employed to prove the feasibility of a harmonious social future? Price relied heavily on historical and current case studies to prove his point. Nevertheless, he was careful to note that 'It would hardly be possible, without the assistance of a preliminary hypothesis to evolve by any purely inductive process . . . a satisfactory theory of value out of such a collection of materials.'[32] In keeping with Marshall's statement, Price thus placed theory before fact-gathering in the process of investigation. Yet, whether he had actually placed theory before fact-gathering in his work was not made clear in the text, and led to the following comment from Ashley in his review of Price's work:[33]

---

[31] Papers based on the research done for the book were read to the Statistical Society on 21 Dec. 1886 and published in its *Journal*, March 1887, and in the Hall at Trinity College, Oxford, on 16 Feb. 1887, to a crowd of college friends and 'specialists'. See the *Oxford Magazine*, 25 Feb. 1887.
[32] Ll. Price, *Industrial Peace* (London, 1887), p. 72.
[33] *Oxford Magazine*, 1 Feb. 1887.

It [the study] is heralded by a Preface by Professor Marshall, who had done more than any one else of late to maintain in England the credit of the old abstract or deductive Political Economy . . . yet this work of his pupil is precisely the outcome of 'common sense' working upon historical and statistical material 'unaided' by economic theory.'

In his review Ashley referred directly to Marshall's position as put forward in the 'Present Position' statement. He brushed aside Marshall's claim to the separation of his views on practical issues from his professional status. While Marshall argued that his opinion (given to the Royal Commission on the Value of Gold and Silver) on state action as regards the standard of value of currency was offered as that of a private citizen, Ashley maintained that 'the public of this country are as little likely to make the distinctions [between Marshall and the "private citizen"] as did the public of the thirteenth century to separate Benedetto Gaetani and Pope Boniface.'

Cannan, naturally, took a different view of the matter, but, like Ashley, he did not consider Price's statement on the formation of theory preceding the collection of data as an accurate description of his work. 'It is clear', he wrote in the next issue of the *Magazine*, 'that the neglect of economic theory, which rejoices the heart of W. J. A. is the one grave defect in Mr. Price's otherwise excellent book.'[34] Furthermore, he criticized Price specifically for not making use of the existing theory of wage adjustments.

Turning to Ashley's general claims, Cannan argued that modern theory, purged of the Ricardian tradition 'has made great progress in the past and it will make still greater progress in the future, after the failure of the efforts of your reviewer [W. J. A.] and others to draw across the scent of red herring of the "new Political Economy" which after all is little more than economic history.' He contested the usefulness of the historical school 'which', he maintained, 'has now been with us for a considerable time', during which it 'has gathered much, selected a little, and generalized none'.

In his reply,[35] Ashley stuck to his position. Theory was not

---

[34] E. C., ' "Industrial Peace", Our Reviewer Reviewed', in the *Oxford Magazine*, 8 Feb. 1888.
[35] W. J. A., ' "Industrial Peace", Our Reviewer Replies', in the *Oxford Magazine*, 7 Mar. 1888.

entirely useless, but unnecessary. It was through the endeavours of the historical school, and of the German one in particular, that 'we are now beginning to understand how present social conditions have come into being and what are their essential characteristics', precisely the type of results Cannan had denied to the historical school. The historical school's approach could just as well be called the realistic or the empirical method and in the study of past or present realities theories were found to be unnecessary since all that was needed was common sense, the kind that links high wages with scarcity of labour. Following this method, the historical school 'hope to arrive at laws of special development, and they expect to obtain from this knowledge a power of dealing with particular problems which those who follow other methods seem scarcely to possess.'

Ashley did not stop at rejection of the use of theory on the grounds of practicability alone. It had been proved in the past to be actually harmful since, at least partly, it shared responsibility for the extremes of modern individualism and socialism. Theory was not only useless, but in the wrong hands and irresponsibly used, actually dangerous.

Since it was the misinterpretation of Price's position that had started the debate, Price felt it his duty to set the record straight by restating his conciliatory position. In a paper to a meeting of Section F at Bath in 1888[36] he stated in a direct reference to the Ashley–Cannan exchange: 'A treatise on industrial conciliation . . . cannot be written "unaided" by economic theory; and yet it is none the less true to maintain that "theoretic economics" cannot resolve the problem involved in the determination of the *exact* basis of a pacification settlement.'

The only actual criticism levelled against Price in the Ashley–Cannan exchange had been from Cannan concerning Price's neglect of existing theory with which the arbitrator could resolve the precise point of wage compromise. Price, in return, argued that theory, at best, could determine the upper and lower limits of such a compromise. Settling for wages outside the limits defined by theory would mean that one or both

---

[36] L. L. Price, 'The Relations between Industrial Conciliation and Economic Theory', reprinted in his *Economic Science and Practice* (London, 1896).

of the parties was indifferent to its economic interests. But, in order to determine the precise point of agreement, the arbitrator must seek guidance beyond theory.

As long as the debate on the nature of the study of economics at the national level remained dormant, Price, with his conciliatory position, may be said to have represented the midstream position of Oxford's young economists. Up to the end of 1890 his work contained all the elements that typified the approach of the young Oxford school. Price was a firm believer in evolutionary progress through gradual reform in preference to radical revolutionary changes, a view he expressed in dealing with particular cases such as the Cornish mines,[37] as well as when discussing the general issue of change. Gradual progress was on the whole safer and surer: 'It is better to advance by gradual stages, than by a sudden and extensive change to incur the risk, if not to ensure the certainty, of reaction.'[38] Price maintained that moral reform was an essential part of all social and industrial reforms. In particular, he saw the organization of labour in trade unions as a great moral achievement. Where moral progress had been achieved, social industrial progress would soon follow.[39] On similar grounds he supported the Dockers' strike and, with H. Ll. Smith, saw in the power exerted by public opinion during the strike a great moral force which had, and would in future, serve to sanction and encourage the meeting on equal footing of employers and workers for the discussion of their differences to their mutual benefit.

In the wake of the Dockers' strike, these views were at the time quite controversial. General sympathy towards the strike had been expressed by Oxford's young economists, as well as by other students of social and moral questions (e.g. Sidney Ball's Social Science Club). However, the developments praised by Price and Ll. Smith were condemned by others. The *Journal of the Statistical Society* saw fit to publish in its December 1889 issue three letters which had previously been published in

---

[37] Id., 'West Barbary', in the *Journal of the Statistical Society*, 1888.
[38] Id., 'The Position and Prospects of Industrial Conciliation', read before the Statistical Society, May 1890, In the *Journal of the Statistical Society*, September 1890.
[39] Id., 'The Relations between Industrial Conciliation and Social Reform', read before Section F, Newcastle upon Tyne 1889, in the *Journal of the Statistical Society*, June 1890.

The Times, strongly condemning the Dockers' strike[40] and its supporters. In these attacks on the sympathy extended from various quarters towards the Dockers it was argued that 'the casual dock labourers are as little entitled to public sympathy as any class that can be named'. Public sympathy was considered an indulgence at the expense of the community. The community had gained nothing by the strikers' achievements, since the casuals would not change their habits, whilst the employers would in the future prefer regular to casual workers, because of the increase in the casuals' wages. Public opinion had sanctioned a dangerous attack on private property, on law, and on 'the elementary right of engaging willing labourers upon terms accepted'. Inadvertently, it had facilitated a well-planned and well-executed plot against social order.

These views in opposition to the strike represented a dying, though still well-represented, creed within Section F and the Statistical Society.[41] The blind acceptance of the orthodox 'laws of Political Economy' was an anathema to many of the new generation of English economists. Marshall had recognized the growing importance of public opinion in the settlement of wage disputes and his hope was that it would develop into an educated and independent force. He envisaged a public opinion that would force industry and labour to pursue policies that expressed the public interests rather than narrow class interests. On the other hand he regarded the current manipulation of various sectors within society by rival sides in an industrial dispute in order to rally public support to reinforce their claims as likely to lead to a dangerous escalation in industrial strife.[42] In their support of the Dockers' strike Ll. Smith and Price were taking an active part in promoting class interests, although in their view these were identical with the interests of society as a whole. Some years later, writing on the correct way in which a student should approach trade

---

[40] The letters appeared in *The Times* on 26 Sept., 29 Sept. and 9 Oct. 1889.

[41] e.g. the presidential address of Lord Bramwell at the Bath meeting of Section F in 1888, printed in the *Journal of the Statistical Society*, December 1888.

[42] A. Marshall, 'Some Aspects of Competition', Presidential Address to Section F, Leeds 1890, reprinted in A. C. Pigou (ed.), *Memorials of Alfred Marshall* (London, 1925), pp. 285-9.

unionism, Marshall argued that: 'when the academic student takes on himself the role of preacher, he is generally less effective than when he treats the problems of life objectively; that is when he assumes no major premises based on his own view of duty, his own ideals of social life'.[43]

Thus, although Price and Ll. Smith did not come into direct conflict with Marshall who, in turn, did not entirely oppose the intervention of public opinion as an agent in wage negotiations, their actions and views on the matter could not be described as representative of an economists' consensus or of the line of action approved by Marshall.

Price's extension lectures reveal at least a partial acceptance of the relativistic approach to the evaluation of past theories. A paper read in 1890 at the meeting of Section F at Leeds,[44] where the final concentrated effort towards the establishment of the British Economic Association and the *Economic Journal* was launched, expressed mistrust of theory with the ultimate 'Oxford' test — its applicability to practical affairs. Price considered it one of the faults of social reformers who relied heavily on theory, that they did not realize that 'we cannot expect to discover in practice the nice distinctions which can be established in theory, and that, so far as our conclusions are based on the nicety of these distinctions, so far they are, *ipso facto*, inapplicable to practical affairs.' Specifically he referred to the impossibility of distinguishing in practice between earned and unearned increment, a point similar to Cannan's argument differentiating between productive and unproductive labour.

Curiously enough, in retrospect Price was to argue that his practical experience as Oriel College Treasurer had made him realize that the theory of rent 'held good on its main lines in concrete fact though it had been deemed a specimen of extremely abstract speculation.'[45] Yet, although Price was elected Assistant Treasurer in 1887 and Junior Treasurer in April 1888, the change in his position did not occur until after 1890.

For as long as Ashley remained at Oxford as a college tutor and lecturer in modern history, his views as expressed in the

---

[43] Marshall to Bishop Westcott, 23 Jan. 1901, ibid., pp. 396-7.
[44] L. L. Price, 'Some Typical Fallacies of Social Reformers', reprinted in *Economic Science and Practice*.
[45] Id., 'Miscellaneous Reminiscences'.

Oxford Magazine remained unchanged. In the first part of the first (and only) volume of his *Introduction to English Economic History and Theory* written at Oxford and dedicated to Arnold Toynbee, he presented in the Preface, signed April 1888, an uncompromising view concerning the time-limit applicability of theories. In his description of the existing approaches to the study of economics he described the theoretical and historical schools as distinct and separate. The approach of his own—the historical—school, he presented in Comtist terms, claiming that it was

> no longer worth while framing general formulas as to the relations between *individuals* in a given society, like the old 'laws' of rent, wages, profits; and that what they must attempt to discover are the laws of social development—that is to say, generalizations as to the stage through which the economic life of society has actually moved. They [historical economists] believe that knowledge like this will not only give them an insight into the past, but will enable them the better to understand the difficulties of the present.[46]

Something of these convictions prevailed in Ashley's introductory lecture at Toronto, delivered on 9 November 1888[47] and dedicated to Gustav Schmoller. In it he informed his students that 'the method of study which we shall probably find most profitable will be largely *historical* and *comparative*,' and that 'the direction for fruitful work is no longer in the pursuit of the abstract deductive method which has done as much service as it is capable of, but in the following new methods of investigation—historical, statistical, inductive.'

However, Ashley was no longer a college history tutor and lecturer, but a professor in the newly established Chair of Political Science. Coming from the outside into a new position of authority and responsibility, he had to adopt a more conciliatory tone towards theory in order to prevent alienation and friction within the existing teaching staff. He eventually admitted that abstract theory was of some value in the university curriculum, because 'the tendencies which they [abstract theories] express do exist in society, with important consequences, and when the economist looks out upon the industrial world to study any specific question, the knowledge of what

---

[46] W. J. Ashley, *An Introduction to English Economic History and Theory*, part 1, vol. 1 (London, 1888).
[47] Id., *What is Political Science?* (Toronto, 1888).

well-informed and undiluted and unimpeded self-interest would produce will help to interpret the facts before him.' Nevertheless, he was quick to add: 'Having mastered this modicum of abstract theory—no difficult task—the important thing, it seems to me, is to directly tackle the pressing economic questions of the present.'

Within the next few years the change in circumstances and academic position strengthened the conciliatory line in Ashley's general statements. By January 1893, in his inaugural lecture at Harvard,[48] he had declared officially in favour of full reconciliation to the mutual benefit of both schools.

> There reigns just now a spirit of tolerance and mutual charity among political economists such as has not always been found within their circle . . . the followers of one method no longer maintain that it is the only method of scientific investigation . . . the believers in induction now recognize more fully the value of deduction . . . it is recognized that the most abstract sometimes refer to fact and the most concrete occasionally make use of abstraction.

The age of controversy, he declared, was over: 'The controversies which break the monotony of life of our German colleagues have not but a faint echo among English speaking economists.'

That the change in Ashley's views was more apparent than real, a result of necessity dictated by his academic position rather than conversion through conviction, is evident in his curiously revealing article on 'Economic History' in Part 6 of Inglis Palgrave's *Dictionary* (1893).[49] Ashley argued that the position he called 'the concurrent view', which he presented in his Harvard inaugural lecture, did not really decide the issue. It was 'appropriate to a period of compromise following upon one of controversy', but at the same time it left the question open, to be decided by future generations. How the question would be decided was revealed in the position he called 'the suppression view', which was basically the Comtist view of the absorption of theory by the study of society, not through confrontation but by a natural process. The future study of society based on historical investigation with a wider scope of enquiry

---

[48] Id., 'On the Study of Economic History', in the *Quarterly Journal of Economics*, January 1893. For the American background to his Harvard statement, see Joseph Dorfman, *The Economic Mind in American Civilization*, vol. 3 (New York, 1959), pp. 240–1.

[49] R. H. Inglis Palgrave (ed.), *Dictionary of Political Economy*, vol. 1, part 6 (London, 1893), pp. 675–6.

would produce general laws and generalizations derived by induction. The theoretical doctrines of economic development would be replaced by 'a philosophy of economic history: a view which is largely due to the influence of modern conceptions of evolution and the organic nature of society.' The pursuit of theory incorporated into the overall study of society would remain 'as a *minor* method of investigation and as a useful preparatory training, but it will no longer dominate the field of economic thought.' His sole concession to theory was in allowing that it would have some practical if minor role. Since Ashley considered such a development to be inevitable, conciliation did not mean capitulation. While each school was allowed to go its own way, the issue would be decided not through debate but by results. Conciliation was not a solution but a matter of convenience.

In Cannan's case, it may be said that neither did he change his preference for theory nor did he adopt Ashley's Comtist vision of the future of economics. Yet, probably under the influence of contemporary Oxford economists, he changed his priorities. It became obvious that a short textbook, however novel in its approach, could have no effect if it ignored existing and widely accepted doctrines.[50] Despite the deductivist position Cannan presented in the *Oxford Magazine*, he had, according to his own account, as an undergraduate at Balliol, been imbued with the historical spirit through A. L. Smith's teachings. Ideologically this led to a conversion in his social philosophy.[51] In his work in economics he occasionally applied historical relativism to observations on the evolutionary and constantly changing nature of society and its institutions.[52] As had happened in the past, his rejection of existing theories led him to formulate his own, some of which he based on historical analysis. But his main interest during the late 1880s had been directed towards the use of the historical approach in the critical analysis of economic theories. With this in mind he aimed 'to trace the development of general theory, showing it in its early crudeness as well as in the more plausible refine-

---

[50] Cannan, *The Economic Outlook*, p. 17.
[51] Ibid., p. 10–11.
[52] e.g. 'Economics and Socialism', read to the Fabian Society, 5 July 1889, in *The Economic Outlook*, pp. 53–86.

ments of later times, and explaining its connection with the circumstances in which it grew up.'[53] Towards the end of 1889 Cannan embarked on the work he eventually published in 1893 as *The History of the Theories of Production and Distribution*. He had set out to prove that the 'old economists' were primarily concerned with practical issues. The advancement of science through the formulation of their theories he considered to be a secondary matter. However, by the time the work was completed, circumstances had changed, and with them the structure and significance of Cannan's study of the 'old' doctrines.

[53] Ibid., p. 17.

6
OXFORD ECONOMISTS AND THE CHAIR

For twenty years, from 1868 until 1888, Bonamy Price was Oxford's Drummond Professor of Political Economy. His election was due mainly to the reaction within the University to Thorold Rogers's radical politics and the use he had made of the chair to propagate his views.[1] Coming to Oxford from a teaching post in Rugby, Price seems to have left no noticeable impression on the views of Oxford's young economists. He is not mentioned in any of their biographical works as a source of inspiration not are his opinions acknowledged as a positive contribution to political economy or condemned as fallacies. When the young economists, in their early works, present arguments in actual opposition to Price's views, he is not mentioned as a disputant. Such instances are usually points of minor significance in Price's work, in which he was merely voicing accepted maxims of contemporary economic thought.[2] At the same time, there were some major issues on which Price and the young economists were in complete agreement, the most important ones being his emphatic rejection of the wage-fund theory and its placing profits in an opposite relation to wages[3] and his singling out Ricardo for the strongest condemnation in terms

---

[1] N. B. De Marchi, 'On Early Dangers of being too Political an Economist; Thorold Rogers and the 1868 election to the Drummond Professorship', in *Oxford Economic Papers*, NS, vol. 28, 1976, No. 3. See also New College Archive, W. A. Spooner, 'Notes for Autobiography' (unpublished MS) No. 14356, ch. 5.

[2] e.g. when Cannan disputes the classification of labour as 'productive' and 'unproductive' in his paper to the Oxford Economic Society: 'The Capital of a Community' read on 1 Mar. 1887. Cannan papers, Balliol College. Cannan rejected the common dichotomy accepted by Price. The same applies to W. J. Ashley's analysis of the Canonist doctrine, in *An Introduction to English Economic History and Theory*, vol. 1, part 2 (London, 1893), ch. 6. Compare with Bonamy Price, *Chapters on Practical Political Economy; being the substance of lectures delivered in the University of Oxford* (London, 1878), pp. 108–44.

[3] Bonamy Price, *Chapters on Practical Political Economy*, pp. 121, 136.

reminiscent of Jevons[4] (although they precede those of Jevons). Yet even in their rejection of Ricardo and J. S. Mill, the young economists most often referred to Toynbee's lectures on the industrial revolution, whereas Price is never mentioned.

One possible explanation of Price's lack of influence may be found in the general lack of contact during that period between Oxford professors and students. It was the age of the college lecturers who enjoyed large classes through the new system of inter-college lectures. 'The Professoriate was almost dead, few Professors lecturing, still fewer having a respectable audience.'[5] It may accordingly be argued that since there is no mention of Price in the young economists' writings, it is possible that they did not even attend his lectures.

A different explanation may be found within the contents of Price's lectures. When one compares Price's views and those of the young economists on various economic issues, it becomes apparent that the points of disagreement either were trivial, of little interest to the young economists, or else merely reflected another authority's views. The points of agreement were simply components of a larger system for which they had little use but which seemed not to require a forceful refutation. Two examples may serve as illustrations.

On the question of method Bonamy Price was a revisionist. He sided neither with the theorists nor with the historians, but preached instead a return to the method of Adam Smith's *The Wealth of Nations*.[6] In substance he accepted Adam Smith with some corrections and modifications. Adam Smith was the subject of his lectures as well as a major part of the paper in political economy set for the Final Schools. Unlike those who referred to Adam Smith as the father of scientific political economy, Price rejected out of hand the possibility of

---

[4] Cf. ibid., p. 20, 'Let economical writers retrace their steps back beyond the point where Ricardo diverged into a wrong path'; and W. Stanley Jevons in the Preface to the second edition (1879) of *The Theory of Political Economy*, 'When at length a true system of economics comes to be established, it will be seen that the able but wrong headed man, David Ricardo, shunted the car of economic science on a wrong line.' Price was familiar with Jevons's views and in his book disputes Jevons's definition of value as well as the more general argument concerning the status of political economy as a science.

[5] Goldwin Smith, *Reminiscences* (New York, 1910), p. 99.

[6] Bonamy Price, *Chapters on Practical Political Economy*, p. 20.

establishing political economy as a science.⁷ He argued that the sole purpose of political economy was to expound everyday practices in the form of intelligible and clear truisms (thereby rejecting the use of mathematical formulae).⁸ On the subjects of rent and money he argued in favour of the use of induction as well as of a relativistic approach to economic theory,⁹ yet he took no definite stand on the use of historical research and its relation to abstract theory. Although the young economists were in agreement with some of his arguments, his failure to take a stand on what they considered the central issue probably determined their general indifference to his work.

A possibly more determinate factor was Price's politics. He was a staunch liberal of the old school, a strong believer in free trade, democracy, and progress, all of which were part and parcel of the young economists' politics. Furthermore, he accepted to a limited extent the necessity of state intervention in cases where wealth was sought by means injurious to the well-being of the people, in education, and in the control of the nation's currency.¹⁰ However, his confidence in a natural social harmony, and what he considered the irrefutable mutually binding nature of the interests of both capitalist and labourer led him to condemn trade unions as a destructive weapon of industrial war, a product of ignorance, suspicion, and hostility, whose sole effect was to set back the working men's cause as well as the welfare of society as a whole.¹¹ For similar reasons he rejected profit-sharing and productive co-operatives as economically unsound. Progress could only be obtained through free trade and a free labour market; and it was the task of education to prove to all classes the futility of the impediment through trade unionism to complete freedom of contact. His belief in the underlying unity of interests of all classes was not in conflict with that of the young economists or any disciple of Oxford Idealism. It was in essence the same belief that motivated their refutation of revolutionary socialism. But although the principle was (philosophically) sound, Price was

---

⁷ Ibid., ch. 1.
⁸ Ibid., p. 3.
⁹ Ibid., pp. 336, 361.
¹⁰ Ibid., pp. 245, 316, 415.
¹¹ Ibid., ch. 8.

felt to be mistaken in his analysis and understanding of trade unions and all forms of co-operativism and profit-sharing schemes and their positive and essential role in the progress of society. The young economists were primarily concerned with demonstrating the principle of social harmony as a viable and attractive alternative to the principle of inevitable class conflict as taught by revolutionary socialism. An attack on Price's interpretation of current developments in labour–capital relations would hardly serve any purpose while a more crucial struggle was at hand over the allegiance of the working class.

Bonamy Price lectured mainly on Adam Smith, using, with some reservations, J. S. Mill's *Principles*. His political views and his indeterminate position on controversial issues in the study of economics explain Thorold Rogers's silence on his successor in the chair. He was not without merit as an economist but his main field of interest—banking and currency — excited little attention at Oxford. He was probably best known for provoking Gladstone's 'banishment' of political economy to Saturn, but the remark seems to have survived its originator. (It appears frequently in arguments concerning ethics and economics.) Both Rogers and Price were members of the Oxford Political Economy Club. Although not friends, they maintained a formal and courteous relationship.[12]

During Price's life no known contender to the chair presented himself, even after the change in the statutes in June 1881 which transferred the responsibility of electing the Drummond Professor from Congregation to a Board of Electors. It was only after his death that the election became a contest once more. Then the nature of the study of economics in Oxford and the personality of the occupant of the chair emerged as issues of professional interest.

The twenty years of Rogers's retirement did little to mellow his manner. He was described by his friends as 'the son of thunder. He was a strenuous worker and really great in his line, though not perfectly judicial. Perfectly judicial he could hardly be as he was in politics a strong Radical.'[13] Those less impressed described his manner as 'ponderous, truculent and

---

[12] New College Archive, No. 14356. W. A. Spooner, 'Unpublished notes for an Autobiography'.
[13] Goldwin Smith, *Reminiscences*, p. 277. See also p. 84.

crushing like a railway train'.[14] During most of the twenty years he remained a resident of Oxford and in 1883 was appointed lecturer in political economy at Worcester College. Yet, although an 'insider', he could not muster within the University the wide support Bonamy Price enjoyed during his tenure of the chair. The following examples may serve to portray Rogers's style and his position on three major issues—the study of history and economic history, national politics, and university politics.

In a lecture on the 'Economic side of History' given in May 1887[15] he compared the importance of the usual historical research with economic history by arguing: 'At a time when historians of such different fibre as Greist, Froude and Stubbs have combined to mislead the student in his attempts to discover the proper position of that worthy Bluff King Hal in our history, a few economic facts about him will be of great service.' On another occasion, when describing historians such as Carlyle and E. A. Freeman as representative of the two extremes of historical research, he declared historians to be either blusterers or pedants.[16] He attacked their lack of relevance to the study of the problems of the present. It was this aspect of his work that became part and parcel of the basic concept of the Oxford school: the purpose of economic and historical research. In the words of W. J. Ashley, 'He [Rogers] has been regarded as the economist above all others who could claim to base his views as to the problems of today upon the knowledge of the history of the past.'[17]

In a political speech delivered, in the Banbury Exchange Hall, a few months after his election to the chair in 1888, he denounced the Tories in the following words: 'As the devil was the father of lies, so the Tories were the most legitimate descendents the devil ever had.' The *Oxford Magazine* described him as one who 'would not trust a Tory among the working classes, for a Tory was generally a sneak or a knobstick. A Tory

---

[14] Farnell, *An Oxonian Looks Back* p. 113.

[15] *Oxford Magazine*, 4 May 1887.

[16] This was in conversation with Jowett, who retorted: 'Do you not think, Professor Rogers, that they are sometimes both?' Letter of J. D. Rogers, 11 Feb. 1895, in the Jowett Papers, Balliol College, Oxford.

[17] W. J. Ashley, 'James E. Thorold Rogers', in the *Political Science Quarterly*, 1889, vol. 4, pp. 381-407.

in the Irish language meant a thief; and it was true.' 'Personally he would not trust a Tory with a twopenny piece.' A year later he is reported to have said: 'The Whigs were sneaks, the Unionists were liars and the Tories were thieves.'[18] Such phrases could not have gone down well with the large number of Tories in Oxford or with many of the Old Liberals who opposed Gladstone on the Home Rule issue and became Unionists. At the same time Rogers's radicalism in political as well as professional matters was more in line with the views of the young economists, all of whom had joined the Home Rule League during the Home Rule controversy.

His position in university politics was similar. At the end of 1889 he entered a debate on the merits of professors versus college lecturers, which started (though not for the first time) with an article published in the *Edinburgh Review* of October 1889,[19] by Herbert Henley Henson (1863–1947), then Fellow of All Souls. Henson argued that the existing decline in the functioning of the universities as centres of national education was caused primarily by the university professors and readers. Nobody attended their lectures. They did not much trouble preparing those lectures since they enjoyed security of position. On the other hand, the college tutors and lecturers carried practically all the burden of teaching despite being underpaid and overworked. Rogers retorted in an article in the *Contemporary Review*[20] that the blame should be sought in the tutorial system which he held to be 'indefensible and discreditable'. A rejoinder by the Examiners of the School of Modern History was published in the February edition of the *Contemporary Review*[21] proclaiming Rogers's criticisms to be 'inaccurate, ill founded and ill natured'. Here again Rogers shared the opinion of a group of young dons who formed themselves into a society (one of the many, named confusingly the Club[22]) at a meeting in Exeter College on 10 February 1889. The first ob-

---

[18] *Oxford Magazine*, 23 Jan. 1889, 2 May 1888.
[19] 'Oxford and Its Professors', in the *Edinburgh Review*, October 1889, pp. 303–27.
[20] 'Oxford Professors and Oxford Tutors', in the *Contemporary Review*, December 1889, pp. 920–36.
[21] With the same title as Rogers's article.
[22] Not to be confused with *The* Club—established in 1790—or The Club established c. 1862. See Falconer Madan, *Records of The Club at Oxford 1790–1917* (privately published at the University Press, 1917).

jective of the society, according to its programme as drafted by the historian F. York Powell, was 'to maintain the character of the University as a home of Learning and Science. With this view in the details of University politics, e.g. elections, etc., we wish to take the professional as distinct from the tutorial, and the University as distinct from the College point of view in questions of education.' The same society was later to be described as a caucus, organized by L. R. Phelps, 'that plied with postcards those, and those only who might be trusted in relation to a given measure to vote straight'.[23]

Thus, towards the end of his life, Rogers found that he enjoyed a greater rapport with a number of the younger dons and graduates within the University than with many of his own contemporaries. His name often appears alongside the names of much younger men in support of various political motions, social schemes, and suggestions for university reform.

The lack of solid support within Oxford for Rogers's re-election in 1888 drew a number of outsiders who considered their chances sufficient to make the effort worth while. At least one outsider—H. S. Foxwell—was under the false impression that the elections would still be conducted according to the original statute. He based his estimates of the odds of some of the candidates on the opposition within Oxford to Rogers's political views, especially in view of his career in Parliament and his stand on the Home Rule issue.[24] Marshall, on the other hand, realized that the Board of Electors, being of mixed membership, would not be as strongly influenced by Rogers's political views. Those who were outsiders did not necessarily share the internal dislike of his brand of radicalism,[25] and some of the Oxford men on the Board (e.g. Freeman) either sided with him politically or were indifferent (e.g. W. Wallace). He therefore tried to dissuade J. N. Keynes from standing as a

---

[23] R. R. Marett, *A Jerseyman at Oxford* (Oxford, 1941), p. 148. Some material on the various 'Clubs' may be found in the Bodleian Library, Oxford. On Phelps's part as a 'University Whip', see *Oriel Record*, vol. 7, 1937–39, pp. 160–6. Another activist in the same society was Sidney Ball who was made Honorary Secretary in December 1891.

[24] Marshall Library, Keynes papers, Foxwell to J. N. Keynes, 15 Jan. 1888.

[25] The positions on the outside were not as well defined as those on the inside. Thus, though Lord Goschen was opposed to Rogers's views on Home Rule, they were both in agreement on Free Trade.

candidate, pointing out that 'feeling in Oxford is against Rogers, but outside [it] is in his favour and a . . . responsible body of electors may pay more attention to outside opinion than to local opinion.'[26] There was little doubt as to Rogers's professional qualifications. His treatment of economic subjects was generally preferred in Oxford, and the only other external candidate who was, at least methologically, of the same school as Rogers was William Cunningham.[27]

Other outsiders who presented themselves and were considered, at least in Cambridge, to have reasonable chances were F. Y. Edgeworth, J. N. Keynes, and Inglis Palgrave.[28] Of the Oxford men the most serious contenders were Phelps and L. L. Price. Phelps had the advantage of professional recognition within Oxford. He was asked by the Hebdomadal Council, just before the elections, to give the lectures in political economy (including the general course based on Mill's *Principles*). This was during Hilary Term while the chair was still vacant.[29] In politics he had remained a mainstream Liberal during the Home Rule controversy and therefore in the same political camp as Rogers. On the basis of personal friendship he could probably depend on the support of the Regius Professor, E. A. Freeman, and Lord Goschen was approached on his behalf by James Bryce.

Price's youth reduced his chances considerably, but he had already established the beginning of a professional reputation. He was a popular Extension lecturer in political economy (having given eight courses in two years) and the first Toynbee Trust Lecturer. In December 1886 the results of his research at Newcastle were read in a paper on sliding scales to the Royal Statistical Society and published in the Society's *Journal* the following March. Another paper on the subject was read in the Hall of Trinity College on 16 February 1887,[30] and later that year *Industrial Peace* was published (including the Royal

---

[26] Keynes papers, A. Marshall to J. N. Keynes, 7 Feb. 1888.
[27] Keynes papers, Foxwell to J. N. Keynes, 14 Feb. 1888. But they were far from being in agreement on the value of each other's work. See the *Academy*, 20 and 27 May 1882.
[28] Keynes papers, Foxwell to J. N. Keynes, 15 Jan. 1888, Marshall to J. N. Keynes, 7 Feb. 1888.
[29] *Oxford University Gazette*, 13, 17 and 24 Jan. 1888.
[30] *Oxford Magazine*, 23 Feb. 1887.

Statistical Society paper) with a preface by Marshall.[31] It is likely that Marshall was instrumental in securing Price's Toynbee Trust Lectureship, possibly through his influence with Sidgwick and Foxwell—both trustees of the Toynbee Trust.[32] For the elections he was promised the support of Foxwell[33] and it was at the same time that he was considered as a possible candidate for the editorship of the planned *Economic Journal*.[34] However, his professional position was still of little weight and his chances were considered by Marshall himself to be slim.[35] No other Oxford candidate,[36] not even W. J. Ashley, is mentioned in the correspondence of Foxwell or Marshall on the matter.

Eventually Rogers was elected. His position *vis-à-vis* the Oxford economists was summed up by Spooner, a fellow member of the Political Economy Club:

> His book on the history of prices was a work of monumental learning and great industry employed in the examination of original sources. It led the way in that more inductive treatment of economic questions which has found an increasing charm [?] with the younger School of Economists who have so largely abandoned the more deductive treatment of the subject advocated by the great men of the middle of the last century, Ricardo and Cairnes and Mill. Yet in theory Thorold Rogers belonged himself to that earlier school.[37]

After his election Rogers wrote to Phelps:

> I cannot in the course of nature expect to be long the occupant of this office. But I certainly shall be glad of the opportunity which is given me, of stating those views which a long study of facts has put very cogently before me— views which differ materially from much which has hitherto been accepted and in my opinion with dangerous consequences to society.[38]

The general direction of Rogers's work was the same as that of Oxford's younger economists' and Phelps's description of it in Rogers's obituary was also representative of their own choice of direction: 'He set himself the task . . . of tracing to its source in

---

[31] Price, *Industrial Peace. Its Advantages, Methods and Difficulties. A report of an inquiry made for the Toynbee trustees.*
[32] Their position within the Trust is also mentioned by Price in 'Memoires and Notes', MS in the Royal Statistical Society, London.
[33] Marshall Library, Keynes papers, Foxwell to J. N. Keynes, 14 Feb. 1888.
[34] Keynes papers, A. Marshall to J. N. Keynes, 17 Mar. 1888.
[35] The same, 7 Feb. 1888.
[36] Other candidates are mentioned in the *Oxford Magazine*, 7 Mar. 1888.
[37] W. A. Spooner, 'Notes for Autobiography', ch. 5.
[38] Phelps papers, Thorold Rogers to Phelps, 15 Mar. 1888.

history the existing state of society. Only by a thorough knowledge of the past, of the actual daily life of our forefathers can the present be understood and interpreted.'[39] The study of history and economics were for Rogers the prerequisite information required for the curing of social and economic evils, a subject on which as a scholar he felt it was his duty to take a stand.

Despite a similar direction in research and politics, Rogers never became (nor was it ever argued that he did) the leader of Oxford economics in the sense that Marshall led the way in Cambridge. There are two explanations—his personality and his orthodoxy on economic theory. Although as a lecturer he was said to be amusing and instructive,[40] he was a poor teacher when it came to personal instruction. He had a tendency to keep most of his work to himself.[41] Age and experience made him sceptical where younger men were enthusiastic. In his *Apologia*[42] Hewins describes two encounters with the ageing Rogers. In the first, just before taking his degree in mathematics and having decided 'to devote myself entirely to economics as a career', Hewins came to Rogers for advice. He outlined to him the faults of orthodox economics and presented his own vision of 'political economy based upon the study of society and pursued in accordance with the modern historical and scientific method'. In essence Hewins's vision was no different from Rogers's concept of the subject, yet, instead of blessing the young convert, Rogers tried to dissuade him from a futile fight against well-established dogmas which he thought would inevitably wreck his career. About a year later, on the basis of his experience in extension work, Hewins asked Rogers's advice about a series of textbooks in political economy as part of an overall scheme to utilize extension work 'for the purpose of organizing economic teaching throughout the country'. Again Rogers tried to talk him out of it, possibly relying on his experience with his *Manual of Political Economy* which was meant to serve as a textbook for 'schools and colleges'.

---

[39] *Oxford Magazine*, 22 Oct. 1890.
[40] Yet his lectures were not widely attended. *Oxford Magazine*, 4 May 1887.
[41] N. S. B. Gras, 'The rise and development of Economic History', in the *Economic History Review*, January 1927.
[42] Hewins, *The Apologia of an Imperialist*, pp. 18-19, 20.

The same *Manual* provides the second explanation as to Rogers's position within Oxford economics. Despite being a rebel by nature and as such 'a tower of strength to those rebellious economists who, during the decade 1870–1880 began to criticize accepted doctrines',[43] his work in economic theory is well within those 'accepted doctrines'. In the words of Hewins: 'He objected to the method and to many of the conclusions of the Ricardian school of economics, but he never shook himself free from their conception.'[44] It was the same inability to shake loose the orthodox concepts that kept his historical explanations in line with the cataclysmatic school. In his *Six Centuries of Work and Wages*, first published in 1884, he presented the fifteenth century and the first quarter of the sixteenth as the golden age of the English labourer.[45] The subsequent deterioration was the result of a historical conspiracy on the part of landowners who sought to increase their profits through manipulation of government. Although by then Rogers rejected the wage-fund theory,[46] his explanation of the history of wages was dominated by the concept of an endless (though theoretically unnecessary and harmful) conflict of interests between the classes. He saw the future of the working class in the 'revivals of ancestral practice' in the form of guilds: 'the guild of labour, the guild of production and trade, and the guild of mutual help'.[47] These concepts could hardly be adopted by the younger economists who belonged to the evolutionary school and preferred to describe historical developments as resulting from 'ordinary individuals following ordinary motives'. They did not look back to a golden age for precedents for present action nor did they even believe in the existence of one. Their solutions for contemporary problems, although in essence the same as Rogers's, were found to be peculiar to an industrial society. Although Rogers fanned the

---

[43] W. J. Ashley, 'James E. Thorold Rogers', in the *Political Science Quarterly*, 1889, 4. 389.

[44] W. A. S. Hewins is the biographer of Thorold Rogers in the *DNB* vol. 17. pp. 123–6.

[45] See in *Work and Wages* the chapter entitled 'Wages of labour after the rise in prices'.

[46] Ibid., in the chapter 'The English Poor Law'.

[47] W. J. Ashley, 'James E. Thorold Rogers', in *Political Science Quarterly*, 1889, 4. 389.

flames of the younger economists' rebelliousness and in his lectures on J. S. Mill[48] pointed the way to a relativistic approach to past theories, he had no new system to offer them instead. A tribute to Rogers's work may be seen in the younger economists' praise of the work invested in the collection of material for the eight volumes of Rogers's *History of Agriculture and Prices*, of which Hewins said 'no similar record exists for any other country'.[49] It was even argued[50] that Cannan's particular reference to 1868 in his *History of the Theories of Production and Distribution* was due to its being the year of publication of the first edition of Rogers's *Manual* which heralded a new age in economic theory. But the younger generation never regarded Rogers as their mentor and the remaining Oxford economists, after the departure of W. J. Ashley and H. Ll. Smith, developed independently of his influence.

During the last years of the 1880s interest in social enquiry continued to grow in Oxford. The Social Science Club continued to function, but its activity was confined to occasional meetings which took place whenever Sidney Ball, the leading spirit of the 'Club', managed to induce an outside speaker to come to Oxford.[51] There was also some research on social ques-

---

[48] e.g. a lecture entitled, 'The Criticism of Mr. Mill's Political Economy; The place of Mr. Mill in the history of Political Economy and the influence under which he was brought', *Oxford University Gazette*, 12 June 1888, 12 Oct. 1888. He called the general lecture for Michaelmas 1888 'Adversia to Mr. Mill's Principles of Political Economy'.

[49] Hewins in the *DNB*, loc. cit.

[50] D. G. Ritchie's review of Cannan's *A History of the Theories of Production and Distribution* in the *Economic Review*, vol. 3, July 1893, p. 439. For other comments by Oxford economists on Thorold Rogers's work, see Hewins's review of Rogers, *The Industrial and Commercial History of England*, in the *Economic Journal*, vol. 2, September 1892; L. L. Price's review of the seventh volume of Rogers's *A History of Agriculture and Prices in England* in the *English Historical Review*, July 1903; L. L. Price, *A Short History of Political Economy in England from Adam Smith to Arnold Toynbee*, 14th edn. (London, 1931), p. 215. Price made the same sort of use of College records in his paper on the agricultural depression as Rogers in his *History of Agriculture* in which he used documents saved from destruction at Merton College. D. J. Medley, review of *The Economic Interpretation of History*, in the *Economic Review*, 1892, p. 138, and *England's Industrial and Commercial Supremacy*, ibid., pp. 416–18.

[51] Samuel, *Memoirs*, p. 13. See also two notices in the *Oxford Magazine*, 13 Feb. and 6 Mar. 1889, referring to meetings of the Club to hear papers by Sidney Webb and W. Clarke. In the discussion after Clarke's paper Ritchie, Ball, Hobhouse, and Hewins took part. A curious comment is included in the account of the discussion following Webb's paper: 'a discussion followed which terminated . . . in a fierce controversy between the lecturer and an Oxford economist as to which of the two was the more orthodox exponent of the Ricardian faith.'

tions as part of the Extension work. But outside the small Oxford Economic Society and the exclusive Political Economy Club, there was no organized body within the University that could offer its members a framework for reading, listening to papers, or conducting discussions on matters of social interest. Something to fill this need was done when the Oxford Branch of the Christian Social Union was formed on 16 November 1889 at a meeting held in Pusey House and chaired by Canon Henry Scott Holland. Its programme, adopted during the first meeting, expressed the direction in which the young Oxford High Churchmen were heading:

> The Union consists of Churchmen, who have the following objects at heart:—
> (i) To claim for the Christian Law the ultimate authority to rule social practice.
> (ii) To study in common how to apply the moral truths and principles of Christianity to the social and economic difficulties of the present time.
> (iii) To present Christ in practical life as the living master and king, the enemy of wrong and selfishness, the power of righteousness and love.[52]

The first president of the Branch—Canon Scott Holland—as well as two (out of six) of its first vice-presidents—The Revd. Charles Gore and Canon Aubrey Moore—were of the *Lux Mundi* group. It was their influence that was responsible for the combination of radical reformism and High Church dogma. The ideological forerunner of the Branch's programme can be found in Campion's article in *Lux Mundi* (first published in November 1889) on 'Christianity and Politics' and in the appendix 'on some aspects of Christian duty'.[53] One of the conclusions of the appendix states:

> A vast field of inquiry and study is . . . evidently open to economic moralists; and it has been opportunely suggested that the effort to study 'in the light of the revealed will of God, the intricate problems of society', might be a common bond between different sections of Christendom, and might promote that unity of God's Church, which is the true condition of effectual social reform.

The Branch's programme combined the need for social enquiry with Christian ethics and with the ideal of a universal united Church. Although membership was restricted to clergymen, it

---

[52] Pusey House, Oxford, Minutes of the Oxford Branch of the Christian Social Union.
[53] Charles Gore (ed.), *Lux Mundi* (15th edn., London, 1909), pp. 383-6.

did not exclude Broad and Low Churchmen.

An example of the radicalism of the views voiced by the Branch may be found in the proceedings of its third meeting held on 5 February 1890. A resolution concerning dwellings of the poor included sections in favour of tax upon unearned increment of the owners of the land, compulsory sale of land 'in a more simple and less costly manner than under the London County Council', state interference to provide dwellings for the poor, as well as points on environment and planning factors such as rapid transport and open spaces.[54]

By 1890 three of the Branch's officers—John Carter, T. C. Snow, and W. J. H. Campion— were members of the Oxford Economic Society. It was John Carter's idea, some time during the first half of 1890, that the Branch should start a quarterly periodical on economics. This was an entirely innocent proposal, made without any knowledge of similar plans being made in Cambridge. The Executive Committee of the Branch were won over to the idea and it was decided that a Board of Editors would be elected consisting of Snow, Campion, and Carter. By about June it was probably felt that one of the editors should have better qualifications as an economist. Since there was no such person in the High Church group centred at Pusey House, on 14 June 1890 Carter wrote to Phelps:

> The C.S.U. is proposing to start a quarterly Economic Journal. W^d you help us?
> Outside the society we have been promised the support of Mr. Ball of St. John's, Mr. Sadler of Ch.Ch., and Dr. Cunningham of Trinity, Cambridge. As you know we are not committed to any partisan attitude and as there is no such magazine published in England, we think it w^d be useful in many ways.[55]

The approach to Phelps, a Broad Churchman, demonstrated the relative ascendancy agreement in economic and social matters had over disagreements on church dogma. Carter and Campion saw nothing wrong in Phelps's becoming a member of the Christian Social Union, so that he might represent it on the editorial committee. A further appeal in this spirit was made by Campion on 30 June. He informed Phelps that work

---
[54] Pusey House, Minutes of the Oxford Branch of the Christian Social Union.
[55] Phelps papers, Carter to Phelps, 14 June 1890.

on the first issue had already begun and that a number of articles and reviews had been received:

> I think there is something to be made of Carter's plan of an Economic Review run by the X^n Social Union. Marshall and Palgrave's proposed Review w^d be on a larger scale and Carter's would be more distinctly X^n though taking any articles not anti-Christian, and dealing with social as well as economical matters.
>
> What I want to ask is whether you w^d join the X^n Social Union and act on the Editorial Comm^{ee}, the other members being Carter and myself.[56] Carter is [a]strong radical and socialist but if you will act, I think we could secure that the Review did not take too strong a colour that way. He is tremendously keen, and will do all the secretarial business.[57]

In mid July Phelps accepted the invitation and joined the Union and the Editorial Committee.

One of the venture's most enthusiastic supporters from its outset was Cunningham who, with barely suppressed glee, wrote to Carter on 21 June 1890:

> Everything seems to be shaping itself nicely for the *Review*. I cannot ask anyone here for articles at present because of this—in connexion with the *Brit. Ass. Commitia* a move is being made to start an *Economic Review*, which will appear in January, I fancy. There is to be a preliminary meeting about it next month; I know that Marshall will be much disappointed at finding his scheme frustrated, and I know he does not think there is room for *both* ventures . . . I shall be very glad to do what I can for your venture here. I believe there is plenty of room for you and for the more *ponderous* affair which Marshall means to run . . . It seems to me it will be very important for you to make quite clear what your line is; Marshall will be to some extent analytic and mathematical and I fancy you could be definitely Christian, and chiefly interested in the Ethical side of social questions.[58]

Without quite realizing the issues involved, the Oxford initiators of the *Review* wrote to Marshall who, after all, had been, although for a short period only, an Oxford don, asking for his support.[59] They were somewhat taken aback by his less than enthusiastic response, but were nevertheless determined to continue with the venture.

Campion wrote to Phelps on the matter:

---

[56] There is no known reason for T. C. Snow's leaving the editorial committee. There is certainly no evidence of any kind of a disagreement.

[57] Phelps papers, Campion to Phelps, 30 June 1890.

[58] Ibid., Cunningham to Carter, 21 June 1890.

[59] Ibid., Campion to Phelps, 9 July 1890.

I am very sorry that Marshall sh^d at all feel that we are taking the wind out of his sails. I do not think we shall touch more . . . people likely to support him. We shall of course, if we succeed, take away some of his possible subscribers. But the advantage of moving the people whom we shall touch and he would not (especially clergy) outweighs any lesser friction between the two.[60]

The editors of the *Review* do not seem to have realized that Marshall's lack of enthusiasm was the result of an issue more fundamental than mere commercial competition, i.e. the establishment of an image on a unified science. To assuage what they saw as Marshall's fear of competition they made some concessions. One was to drop from the original circular[61] the statement 'The Review will be concerned chiefly with modern economic difficulties as they bear on the whole of life' and replace it with 'The Economic Review will be concerned chiefly with the moral and social bearings of economic problems'.[62] This would define the difference in emphasis between the *Review* and the planned *Journal*. Another move which may have been intended as a gesture to Marshall was the postponement of the publication of the *Review's* first issue from October 1890 to January 1891 when, according to plan, the first issue of the *Journal* was to be published. It would not then seem as if the *Journal* was published as the *Review's* rival. (In the event, publication of the *Journal* was delayed by a couple of months so that the *Review* was still the first to be published.)

Marshall was concerned that the appearance of the *Review* might be regarded as a countermove to the foundation of the British Economic Association and the publication of its *Journal*. If so, the appearance of unity and the authority of the Association and the *Journal* as representatives of English economics would be challenged. One cause for annoyance was Carter's choice of name. On 31 October 1890 Marshall wrote to Phelps:

I am sure you have done what you thought was the best for all. But I had thought that in mentioning . . . that I thought it was important both for you and for us that the difference between our aims should be emphasized, I had indicated a hope that you would take some such title as 'The Journal of Social Reform'. I really believe you would have succeeded better if you had. But if you think your title is best for your purposes we ought not to ask you to change it.[63]

[60] The same, 26 July 1890.
[61] Phelps papers, appended to Campion to Phelps, 30 June 1890.
[62] Printed in the *Economic Review*, 1 (1891).
[63] Phelps papers, Marshall to Phelps, 31 Oct. 1890.

In a later letter he told Phelps that it would have been 'easier for us if you had been able to adopt a title which itself suggested that the two journals are designed to meet different wants, to supplement one another and not to compete with one another.'[64]

The Cambridge economists were also perturbed by Carter's choice of name because they had always considered it the most appropriate name for their own periodical. Discussing the issue with Phelps, Foxwell confirmed that the starting of the periodical was not merely a technical move aimed at creating a forum in which economists could voice their views: 'Our great difficulty was to secure a catholic and representative character for the review. That we have at length secured by the foundation of an Economic Association.'[65] However, Foxwell did not share Marshall's concern with the image of unity. His worry was that the two ventures might be confused—a possibility he did not consider to be of special importance.[66] Unlike Marshall, he welcomed a 'friendly rivalry' between the two ventures.[67] and was not over-concerned with the immediacy of establishing the differences between them: 'Both Marshall and I hope that your suggestion as to some division of labour between the two Journals may be ultimately carried out. We had better perhaps let each Journal assume its natural character before we attempt to make any precise division of functions and subjects.'[68]

The phrasing of the final circular on the *Review*[69] demonstrated the editors' determination to proceed with the venture while avoiding unnecessary friction with the Association. The Review, it stated, would deal primarily with the social and moral aspects of economic problems and would publish technical articles on specific aspects of the English industrial system and on 'the historical condition and development of some particular period'. Their hope was to maintain a balance between the moral aspects of economic issues, in which the members of the Christian Social Union were naturally in-

---

[64] Ibid., Marshall to Phelps, 5 Nov. 1890.
[65] Ibid., Foxwell to Phelps, 26 Oct. 1890.
[66] The same, 29 Oct. 1890.
[67] The same, 26 Oct. 1890.
[68] The same, 29 Oct. 1890.
[69] *Economic Review*, i, 1891.

terested, and material dealing with contemporary and pertinent historical issues, with which the Oxford economists were mainly involved.[70] No mention was made of economic theory and it was stated that the *Review* was intended for 'the increasing number of people who are feeling the burden of responsibility in regard to the stress of existing social problems'.

Economic theory was mentioned in the editorial of January 1891[71] as the subject matter for work in the history of economic theory in the manner demonstrated by the work of Oxford's economists in the Extension. Theory was mentioned again when the line was drawn between those who used historical methods and those 'who believe in the possibility of a body of Economic teaching based in large part on the labours of bygone Economists'. It is quite clear that the latter category was of outsiders whose opinions the *Review* was prepared to publish in the belief that both approaches were tenable within 'a new and larger Economics, using history and not abusing theory'. The editorial made it clear that the emphasis would be on subjects of present relevance and more specifically 'the condition of the labourers' and schemes of social reform, including the more radical ones.

The editorial, unlike the circular quoted above, did not put one aspect of the work in front of the other. It saw practical and moral conclusions as inseparable from the professional study:

> It is impossible . . . to draw a sharp line between the spheres of the Economic Moralist and the scientific Economist. If the Economic student cannot altogether put aside the practical bearings of his conclusions, and must therefore allow their due weight to other than purely economic considerations, still less, can the Moralist afford to dispense with a clear knowledge of the facts in forming a judgement on his duty with regard to them.

Thus the concept of 'duty in relation to social life' was the central theme of both the editorial and the circular.

That it was by nature an Oxford publication can be deduced not only from the editorial but from the list of contributors as well. There were only two Cambridge names on the list and

---

[70] Phelps papers, Campion to Phelps, 3 Aug. 1890, describing Ashley's suggestions for the *Review*.

[71] *Economic Review*, January 1891. The editorial is dated December 1890 and was drafted by Phelps with some additions by Campion. Phelps papers, Campion to Phelps, 7 and 15 Aug. 1890.

both were clerics—the Revd. A. Lyttleton, Master of Selwyn College (a *Lux Mundi* man), and the Revd. William Cunningham who, although not a member of the Christian Social Union, was in contact with the Oxford Branch from its inception and addressed its first meeting. As for the Oxford economists, sixteen members of the Economic Society (including the Editors) were listed as supporters of the *Review*. The list included all the Society's active economists except L. L. Price.

The initiative for the publication of the *Economic Review* was clearly independent of the Cambridge effort to launch a periodical. The manner in which it developed, the people who supported it within and outside the University, and the final form it assumed reflect a basic difference in attitude towards economic matters between Oxford and Cambridge. This difference did not go unnoticed. One rather acute observation is found in a letter from Foxwell to J. N. Keynes written by the end of 1894:

> Last time I advertised a course on Socialism* [in Cambridge] not a soul attended. There seems to be no real interest taken in Cambridge in any practical Economic question and only a few seem to interest themselves in theory . . . I don't know what is wrong here, but the contrast between Cambridge and Oxford is very striking. Whenever I go to Oxford I am struck by the general interest in Economics there. They seem to regard it as all of the subjects with which every intelligent person should concern himself.[72]

After protracted deliberations the Cambridge initiative, probably stimulated by the advanced stage of plans for the *Review* reached by mid 1890, finally got under way. The scheme calling for the foundation of an association to sponsor a periodical was launched at the annaul meeting of Section F of the British Association at Leeds, presided over by Marshall. By November sufficient support was mustered and the British Economic Association was inaugurated at a meeting on 21 November

---

* In London it draws the largest class.

[72] Marshall Library, Cambridge, Keynes papers, Foxwell to J. N. Keynes, 14 Dec. 1894. It is of interest that a Cambridge Branch of the Christian Social Union was not founded until the end of 1892—see the *Economic Review*, 1893. And that in an earlier letter to Keynes (15 Jan. 1888) Foxwell gives as one of the reasons why he had no intention of applying for the Drummond Professorship: 'I don't like the Oxford habit of mind so well as ours.'

1890, in University College London, with Goschen presiding.[73] According to the circular distributed by Marshall, the Association, by way of the *Journal*, would rectify the lack of means for academic and professional communication between economists. The *Journal* would serve the 'advancement of economic knowledge' and through it a central core of economic science would develop. Although all those present emphasized the inclusive nature of the Association (it embraced 'every school of economics which was doing genuine work'), it was quite clear that Marshall and Goschen were still not happy with the Oxford initiative which resulted in publishing the *Review* before the first issue of the *Journal* despite the delay in the publication of the *Review*. Apart from its threat to the image of unity, it is possible that there was also a fear of competition, since the *Review* was offered at the price of 10*s*. a year for subscribers, whereas the *Journal* cost a guinea a year.

During the meeting Marshall clearly underplayed the significance of the *Review*. It was described as a publication that would deal 'with problems in which ethical and religious questions took the first place, but which had a certain kernel of economic difficulty in the background'. He generously conceded that there was room for the Christian Social Union's own journal. However, during the proceedings an unnamed group of economists came under attack. Marshall referred to economists who had wasted time in useless controversies 'based upon a perversion of the words of some writer, the critic interpreting them in the most foolish manner possible, and then writing long articles to prove that they were absurd when misinterpreted'. In support of Marshall's resolution, Goschen mentioned certain quarters in which he saw men 'who called themselves political economists but who had not the slightest idea what economics were' and 'certain groups of men who seemed to disbelieve in the possibility of any economic science whatever'.

There can be little doubt that at least part of the attack was directed against Oxford economists and the *Review*. The list of members active in the administration of the Association shows the pattern even more clearly. The Association was to be

---

[73] The proceedings of the meeting are to be found in the first issue of the *Economic Journal*, March 1891.

administered by a Council of thirty-two members, of which only three were Oxford men—L. L. Price, L. R. Phelps, and H. Ll. Smith. A fourth Oxford man— A. H. D. Acland—was nominated, but not elected.

By 1890 Price's ties with Marshall and Cambridge economics had strengthened considerably. In 1888 he became one of the secretaries of Section F, the other secretaries including Edgeworth and Foxwell. He was being considered as one of the possible candidates for the editorship of the *Journal*. During 1890 he was given, with J. N. Keynes, the honour of reading the proofs of the first edition of Marshall's *Principles*.[74] Although he was not chosen to edit the *Journal* he was appointed, with Foxwell, Joint Honorary Secretary of the British Economic Association, a position which originally was to be of considerable importance, similar to that of Honorary Secretary to the Royal Statistical Society.[75] As a result he chose to refrain from supporting the *Review* and instead concentrated his efforts on ensuring the *Journal's* success. Ll. Smith had also moved away from Oxford economics and by 1890 was closer to Charles Booth and like-minded social investigators, members of the Statistical Society. He promised his support to both ventures but was active in neither.

In the case of Phelps the situation was markedly different, for on 12 October 1890 James E. Thorold Rogers died and Phelps—in common with a number of Oxford men—considered the chair to be rightly his. Phelps was not a brilliant economist. Whatever research he had done was mostly into the conditions of the poor, but little else. Ashley considered him 'a most undistinguished and unoriginal college tutor'.[76] But he was a popular lecturer and drew large classes to his lectures on political economy for Pass men and probationers of the Indian Civil Service.[77] He was described by one of his students as a 'remarkably eloquent' lecturer who 'poured out his material beautifully arranged in what amounted to a speech lasting fifty minutes. He absolutely refused to allow any note taking but the

---

[74] L. L. Price, 'Memoirs and Notes', ch. 2.
[75] J. N. Keynes, 'Herbert Somerton Foxwell 1849–1936', *Economic Journal*, 1936.
[76] Marshall Library, W. J. Ashley to Seligman, 13 Apr. 1891 (copy).
[77] See his biography in the *DNB*; *Oriel Record*, vol. 7, 1937–9. Price, 'Miscellaneous Reminiscences'.

last ten minutes of the hour he spent in dictating a most carefully worded summary of what he had been saying.'[78] It was the same student—Henry Sanderson Furniss—who singled out Phelps as the one lecturer to whom he owed a lasting debt of gratitude 'for he awoke what has been one of my main interests in life—Economics'.

Phelp's interest in the poor was manifested practically in his service on the Oxford Board of Guardians. During the one term in 1888 in which he filled in for the Professor of Political Economy, he lectured twice a week on 'English and Foreign Systems for Poor Relief'[79] and was to write some articles and reviews on the subject in the *Review*. During the years 1905-9 he was to serve on the Royal Commission which reviewed the Poor Laws, having enjoyed the reputation of being something of an authority on the subject. He had been a member of the Oxford Political Economy Club since 1883, the Tutors' Club (a dining club originally founded by Thomas Arnold), the Social Science Club, the (University Reform) Club, and of course the Oxford Economic Society. He loved wire-pulling and combined this 'hobby' with his work in the cause of university reform on centralized lines. Politically he was a Liberal and on the Home Rule issue he remained a Gladstonian.

Phelp's candidacy enjoyed some powerful support from within the University. References in his support were submitted by G. Brodrick (the Warden of Merton), William Markby (Reader in Indian Law and Curator of the Indian Institute), A. Robinson and W. A. Spooner of New College, and H. Reeve[80] who wrote in his testimonial: 'You have been a steady and uncompromising champion of sound economic principles, in opposition to many of the dangerous fallacies which are but too current amongst us.' Finally, and probably most importantly, he was supported by his friend E. A. Freeman, who wrote to him on 29 November 1890: 'I hear a strange rumour . . . that you are *not* going to stand for the

---

[78] Henry Sanderson Furniss, *Memoirs of Sixty Years* (London, 1931), p. 52.
[79] *Oxford University Gazette*, 13 Jan. 1888.
[80] Phelps papers, Brodrick to Phelps, 20 Nov. 1890; Markby to Phelps, 21 Nov. 1890; Robinson to Phelps, 22 Nov. 1890; W. A. Spooner to Phelps, 20 Nov. 1890; Reeve to Phelps, 18 Nov. 1890.

place vacated by the death of the late Rogers. I hope this is not true, for several reasons, one's that if it be so I shall have to think about somebody else to vote for, and I don't want the trouble.'[81] It was generally assumed at Oxford that he was the most likely successor to 'Old Rogers'.[82]

As decreed by the 1881 statute,[83] the Drummond Professor was to be elected for a five-year renewable period by a Board of Electors consisting of:

1. The Chancellor of the University.
2. The Chancellor of the Exchequer for the time being.
3. The Regius Professor of Modern History.
4. Whyte's Professor of Moral Philosophy.
5. A person nominated on each occasion by the Warden and Fellows of All Souls College to act as an elector.

By the end of 1890 the Board consisted of the same electors who elected Rogers to the chair in 1888. They were the Marquis of Salisbury, Goschen, E. A. Freeman, William Wallace, and John H. Doyle.

Thus Phelp's presence at the inauguration of the British Economic Association, probably as the representative of the group behind the *Review*, placed him in an extremely delicate position. This was not solely due to Goschen's presence in the chair. Within days of Rogers's death, Edgeworth wrote to Jowett asking for his support in the elections.[84] It was soon realized that Edgeworth enjoyed powerful support within and outside the University. He was also to be Editor of the *Journal* and Secretary to the Council of the Association. Therefore, even if Phelps detected an odious anti-Oxford current in Marshall's or Goschen's words he had no choice but to keep a straight face. At the end of the meeting he was to propose a vote of thanks to Goschen's chairmanship, lauding the latter's distinction 'as an economist, as a financier and as a statesman'.

A third candidate was W. J. Ashley. In 1888, frustrated with

---

[81] Ibid., Freeman to Phelps, 29 Nov. 1890.

[82] Ibid., G. W. E. Russell to Phelps. The same may be deduced from the surprise shown in Oxford when Edgeworth was elected.

[83] The statute is of 16 June 1881. Appropriate changes were made at the same time in the Statutes of All Souls.

[84] Jowett wrote as much to Marshall in a letter of 20 Oct., eight days after Rogers's death. Marshall papers, Marshall Library, Cambridge.

his duties as college tutor and lecturer and wishing to marry, Ashley resigned his Fellowship. After Rogers's election Ashley accepted the offer of the newly established Chair of Political Science at the University of Toronto. Upon his acceptance the name of the chair was changed to Political Economy and Constitutional History, in accordance with Ashley's academic interests, and he was given the task at Toronto of organizing the new Department of Political Science which by 1890 had more than 100 students. The Toronto chair was in a number of ways a considerable improvement on his position as a college tutor and lecturer, but it also meant that by 1890 he had hardly any support for the candidacy in England.

Ashley's decision to stand as candidate was based on his hopes that the choice of the Board would be made on grounds of professional competence and suitability. In asking the American economist, E. R. A. Seligman for a testimonial he wrote: 'I have determined to stand, though it looks presumptious. If there were any senior man of obviously preeminent claims, I should not put myself forward; but there will not be; and the candidates ought really to be very much on a level. I know I have little chance.'[85] He had demonstrated his ability as a scholar in his *English Economic History and Theory*, as well as in numerous articles and reviews, and as a teacher and administrator in his Oxford and Toronto posts. Accordingly he based his application[86] on testimonials attesting his success in these various spheres and on his ideas for the reorganization of the study of economics at Oxford. His administrative and teaching abilities were vouched for by Edward Blake (Chancellor of the University of Toronto), G. W. Ross (Minister of Education for the Province of Ontario), and Sir Daniel Wilson (President of the University of Toronto). B. E. Walker (General Manager of the Canadian Bank of Commerce) praised Ashley's introduction of the study of public finance into the university curriculum, and a student, J. M. McEvoy, attested his ability as a teacher.

[85] Marshall Library, Misc. 2(18), Ashley to Seligman (copy), 3 Nov. 1890. A similar statement by Ashley was made in a letter to Brentano, 16 Oct. 1890, H. W. McCreedy, 'Sir William Ashley; Some Unpublished Letters', *Journal of Economic History*, 1, 1955.

[86] Bodleian Library, 232 e. 641, 'Testimonials in favours of Mr. W. J. Ashley', Toronto, 20 Nov. 1890.

McEvoy's testimonial was probably also intended to dispel any fears of Ashley's political radicalism. In it he stated that Ashley 'succeeded in driving all the rancor of political party feeling, which is so prevalent here, from the minds of his students, and in getting them to bring to the study of all political questions calm and unbiassed judgement'. As for his personal qualities as a teacher, McEvoy testified that Ashley 'is a man of strong character and personal magnetism which have had an influence upon me and others of the younger graduates.'

In support of his scholarly achievements, Ashley presented an impressive array of references from economists, historians, and historical economists including K. Kneis, G. Schmoller, Émile de Laveleye, Gustav Cohn, E. R. A. Seligman, Luigi Cossa, Paul Vinogradoff, Lujo Brentano, and two English historians—F. Seebohm and F. W. Maitland,[87] both of whom supported his plan for the reorganization of Oxford economic studies. The emphasis in these references was on Ashley's proven ability as a historical economist. Brentano added to his praise of Ashley's scholarly work his view that Ashley's election would secure the continuity of Toynbee's work: 'Now as I know no disciple of Toynbee's who has come to such eminence by his writings as you have, I think the University of Oxford which cherishes the memory of that excellent man, cannot but give to your claim a fair consideration.'

Ashley's plan for the reorganization of Oxford economics combined the approach of the historical-relativists with his experience at Toronto in adapting the university curriculum to the needs of society:

There are two directions in which, as it appears to me, it is most desirable to promote economic study in Oxford. Of these one is Public Finance; it might not be impossible to secure for men who are about to enter into public life, the civil service, or the higher branches of business, a training similar to that provided by some foreign universities. The other is the history of Economic Phenomena and of the parallel growth of Economic Theory. While recognizing the value of recent work in further analysis of theory, there is, I think, reason to believe that the most fruitful field for economic work at the present time in Oxford is the historical. An effort in this direction would be in sym-

---

[87] Ashley added to the testimonials reviews of his work by K. Oldenberg and by Böhm-Bawerk.

pathy with one of the strongest intellectual forces in the University and it might reasonably be expected to enlist the interest of the students in the School of Modern History.

Ashley's hope of enlisting the support of Oxford's historians demonstrated one of the main weaknesses of his application—the lack of support from any of England's economists. Furthermore, he had no serious support within Oxford. Fully aware of the weakness of his position, he wrote to Seligman on 13 December 1890: 'I imagine they will elect Edgeworth; and Oxford will be doomed for its sins to unlimited psycho-mathematical economics.'[88]

In view of Ashley's proven abilities and his views on the development of Oxford economics, he was probably the candidate most suitable for Oxford's needs at the time. His election might have ensured a continued development of Oxford economics within the School of Modern History, drawing on the available group of young graduates actively interested in the subject. Indeed, such a choice would have indicated recognition by the University of the value of developing the curriculum in that direction, but that recognition was yet to come.

Two other candidates who had hardly any chance of success were Inglis Palgrave,[89] and H. Ll. Smith. Both were aware of the unlikelihood of their election. Ll. Smith admitted to his sister that his reason for standing was that 'it placed one in the running for other things—that is if people do not resent the candidature of one so young.'[90]

F. Y. Edgeworth was elected to the chair on 21 February 1891. There is no conclusive evidence concerning the deliberations of the electors. However, circumstantial evidence points in two related directions: the national development in the profession and the Balliol connection. Edgeworth was a Balliol man (he matriculated in 1867) as were two of the electors—Doyle (1863)[91] and Wallace (1864). Although he was not

[88] Marshall Library, Misc. 2(19), Ashley to Seligman, (copy) 13 Dec. 1890.
[89] Phelps papers, Inglis Palgrave to Phelps, 22 Nov. 1890.
[90] Ll. Smith papers, Ll. Smith to his sister, 14 Nov. and 8 Dec. 1890.
[91] Although Doyle graduated the year Edgeworth matriculated, it is possible that they met, since Doyle remained in residence in Oxford and made 'many friends among a generation of Balliol men junior to himself'. Introduction by Sir W. Anson to W. P. Ker (ed.), *John Andrew Doyle—Essays on Various Subjects* (London, 1911).

considered an Oxford man by the young economists he would surely have qualified with an older generation. In previous years, when offering himself as candidate for the Chair of Moral Philosophy at Dublin and as Examiner in Political Economy at the University of London, he was supported by testimonials from Jowett and T. H. Green. Professionally, he came highly recommended by Marshall, to whom he was extremely deferential. H. Sidgwick, Foxwell, R. Giffen, and E. C. K. Gonner, had all provided him with testimonials in the past.[92] It is in the contact with Marshall and Jowett that the Balliol and the professional connections come together. In a letter dated 20 October 1890, in which Jowett invited Mr and Mrs Marshall up to Oxford, Jowett wrote: 'Who do you think is the best candidate for our Professorship of Political Economy? Is any one superior to Edgeworth? He has written to ask me to support him so far as I have any influence.'[93] There can be little doubt about Marshall's reply, especially considering who the other candidates were.

Marshall met Jowett when the former became the first Principal of University College, Bristol, while Jowett sat on the College Council. They became quite close friends, Marshall entertaining Jowett on his frequent visits to Bristol.[94] When Toynbee died Jowett offered Marshall Toynbee's position at Balliol and Marshall remained in Oxford for four terms. It was probably during that period that he first met Goschen who came up as a weekend guest at Balliol lodge. When Marshall left Oxford for the chair in Cambridge, vacated by Fawcett's death, he was in a position to ensure that J. N. Keynes would be offered the job he himself left at Oxford.[95] His ties with Jowett remained strong. Jowett went to Cambridge for annual visits and stayed with the Marshalls at their home named by Marshall 'Balliol Croft'. During the rest of the year they kept up a steady correspondence, with occasional visits by the Marshalls to Oxford. The tone of Marshall's letters was ex-

[92] The testimonials can be found in the Edgeworth Papers, Nuffield College, Oxford.
[93] Marshall papers, Jowett to Marshall, 20 Oct. 1890.
[94] Mary Paley Marshall, *What I Remember* (Cambridge, 1947), pp. 37–9; and 'Reminiscences', MS in the Jowett Papers, Balliol College, Oxford.
[95] Keynes papers, W. Markby to J. N. Keynes, 2 Jan. 1885; Marshall to Keynes, 28 Oct. 1885.

tremely deferential with endings such as 'goodbye for the present my Patron Saint' and 'Goodbye my own very dear master'.[96]

Jowett, who occasionally taught economics, was actively interested in the subject. His concept of the subject was very much in keeping with the common view in Oxford and his position on economics during the 1860s and 1870s foreshadows that of Toynbee and some of his generation. Statements such as 'Political Economists have really done more for the labouring classes by their advocacy of Free Trade etc. than all the philanthropists put together', 'I want to have all the humanities combined with Political Economy' (both made in 1861) or 'I should like to see a political economy beginning with the idea not how to gain the greatest wealth, but how to make the noblest race of men' (1877)[97] were not much different from the views within the Oxford school of economists during the eighties. However, on matters of economic theory Jowett was staunchly orthodox. In a letter to E. Harrison, dated 12 June 1875, he wrote:

> I always consider that the old fashioned Political Economy is right as a theory and is the best basis on which to work, though it may receive many modifications in practice from the political or philanthropic or trades union point of view. I have a great belief in Ricardo as an abstract thinker and am inclined to say with Mr Charles Austin 'That I know of no proposition in Ricardo rightly understood, from which I dissent'.[98]

He attached great merit to Marshall's *Principles* for having mediated between the old political economy and the new.[99]

Jowett's position on economic theory explains his ability to overlook the complete unintelligibility of Edgeworth's work to the layman (an issue frequently raised in his letters to the Marshalls, in which he implored them to leave mathematics

---

[96] Balliol, Jowett papers, Marshall to Jowett, 11 Oct. 1891. See also letter from Mrs Marshall to Jowett, 12 Oct. 1891 in which she says 'it had been one of the best things in our lives that you have allowed us to be your friends.'

[97] Evelyn Abbott and Lewis Campbell, *Letters of Benjamin Jowett* (London, 1899). Letters to Miss Cobb, 1861 and 1877.

[98] Jowett papers, Jowett to Harrison, 12 June 1975. The papers include, in a passage by Sir Alexander Grant from a manuscript notebook, an example of Jowett's teaching of the wage-fund theory. A letter from J. D. Rogers, 11 Feb. 1895, recalls a story of how Jowett lashed out at the critics of J. S. Mill as people who were unworthy of latching Mill's shoes.

[99] Marshall papers, Jowett to Marshall, 24 July 1890.

and professional jargon out of the text of the *Principles*) in support of a candidate who was to write a few months after his election:

> To what extent did the Ricardian method as depicted by the Historical School actually affect English policy injuriously? . . . Are we so certain that they |Fawcett and McCulloch| were wrong? . . . People talk of the old Ricardians, the high and dry school etc. but they do not condescend to particulars so much as we might expect from persons of *historical* proclivities.[100]

It is safe to assume that Jowett used his influence within Oxford on behalf of Edgeworth. In the case of Goschen it is doubtful whether any persuasion was needed. Goschen was the president of an association of which Edgeworth was secretary and the editor of its journal. Phelps was the editor of the rival *Economic Review*. Both he and Ashley were far from being identified with the economic centre that the Association and the *Journal* were meant to consolidate. Goschen may have hoped with Marshall that Edgeworth's professorship would eventually lead the stray Oxonians back to the fold of the mainstream of British economics.

The lack of a defined political position on the part of Edgeworth and the completely theoretical nature of the little they might have known of his works may have had a certain appeal to Wallace and Doyle. Wallace, who was to a large extent under the influence of Jowett, took no part in university matters. His suspicions of socialism may have led him into opposing Phelps on the basis of his involvement with the Oxford Branch of the Christian Social Union.[101] Doyle was averse to the application of academic studies to practical problems,[102] a position which, if applied to economics, could easily lead to a preference for Edgeworth. Edgeworth's apolitical nature may have appealed also to Salisbury and Goschen as well as to some of the Oxford men who wished to avoid another Thorold Rogers. Indeed it was said in retrospect that at the time of Edgeworth's election 'he was chosen as "a safe man", the electors being somewhat alarmed by the subversive doctrines

---

[100] Keynes papers, Edgeworth to J. N. Keynes, 12 Apr. 1891.

[101] On Wallace see E. Caird (ed. and introd.), *Lectures and Essays on National Theology and Ethics by William Wallace* (Oxford, 1898), including an essay on 'The Ethics of Socialism'.

[102] See his criticism of Seeley in 'Freeman, Froude and Seeley', in Ker (ed.), *Essays*.

taught by the younger economists of those days.'[103] Finally, Freeman, Phelps's most important supporter, was away from Oxford, because of bad health, for most of the period immediately preceding the election. He was therefore probably unable to promote Phelps's candidacy.[104]

The electors' choice was an extremely unfortunate one and the disappointment felt was expressed shortly afterwards in the *Oxford Magazine*. It had been hoped 'that the electors would have fixed their choice on a candidate better known to Oxford than Mr. Edgeworth and more closely associated than he is with the recent study and teaching of the subject in the University. But the compromises of the Electoral Board are apt to bring to the front an outside candidate, and so it has been once more.'[105] Oxford needed a central figure who would use his authority as an economist and the authority of his position in the chair to stimulate and co-ordinate the work done in economics in Oxford and at the same time apply continuous pressure from within the University for a change in the position of the study and teaching of political economy and of economic history in the University.

Oxford had the kernel of an active and productive school of economics. The potential was evident in the significant interest in social and economic matters which had resulted in the publication of the *Economic Review* and in the presence of a group of young economists, many of whom had already demonstrated their ability as teachers and their potential in research. No doubt can be cast on the excellence of Edgeworth's contribution to economic theory. But although he stands out as one of the most brilliant economists to hold the Drummond Professorship he was the last man to bring about the much needed change in the institutional status of economics in Oxford. His concept of the nature and method of economics was essentially different from the concepts of the young Oxford economists and his aversion to university politics was detrimental to any efforts to change the academic status of

---

[103] 'Francis Ysidro Edgeworth', *Oxford Magazine*, 25 Feb. 1925.
[104] W. R. W. Stephens, *The Life and Letters of Edward A. Freeman* (London, 1895), ii. 425-6.
[105] *Oxford Magazine*, 25 Feb. 1891.

the study of economics at a crucial period in the development of the young economists' careers.

The first misgivings about Edgeworth were concerned with the nature of his work, which was in a direction different from that pursued by practically all Oxford economists of the period. It was soon demonstrated that Edgeworth's use of mathematics and professional terminology was not merely a matter of style. He believed economics to be essentially a difficult subject which would not lend itself to popularization.[106] Once he started lecturing he soon outreached the capacity of his listeners. In small classes he avoided leading discussions since, unlike most Oxford economists, and in stark contrast to his predecessor in the chair, he generally shrank from expressing a strong opinion on all matters, whether in economic theory or in university policy. According to Cannan, the 'Edger' would avoid taking a position by arguing 'Well you know, my dear Cannan, there's something to be said on both sides etc. etc.'[107] In economics he was soon regarded in Oxford as a theorist who hid his opinion behind the cipher of mathematics. When forced to state a position, he would refer to the authority of others.[108] It was said that the books in his room at All Souls contained in their pages 'abundant slips of paper to facilitate speedy reference to views of others'. Any attempt on the part of a colleague to form a plain and firm position was bound to distress and shock him. His tenure of the chair as far as the study of the subject by younger students was concerned, resulted in an actual setback. His general course depended on Mill's *Principles* as a textbook.[109] His style of lecturing kept students away to the extent that during one course of lectures he had an audience of one student. The consequences were described by Cannan during a controversy with Foxwell through the pages of the *Review*:

> Oxford, in spite of its old reputation for conservatism, in these days delights in 'movements'. Its own professors, who assume the purely critical attitude and have no opinions, lecture to empty benches, while crowds sit at the feet of

[106] Price, *A Short History of Political Economy*, p. 274.
[107] C. R. Fay, 'Edwin Cannan, The tribute of a friend', in the *Economic Record*, vol. 13, June 1937 (MS in the Cannan Papers, LSE).
[108] E. Cannan, *An Economist's Protest* (London, 1927), p. 335. See also L. L. Price's, 'F. Y. Edgeworth', obituary in *Journal of the Royal Statistical Society*, March 1920, and Price, 'Memoirs and Notes'.
[109] *Oxford University Gazette*, 9 June 1891.

any outsider of distinction who is sufficiently in earnest to devote an afternoon or evening to the propagation of his views on some current question among undergraduates, dons, and lady residents.[110]

Cannan, as Secretary of the Oxford Economic Society, tried to revive it during 1891 by changing the rules so that the Drummond professor would be *ex officio* its president and thus be placed in a position that would enable him to direct and instigate the work done in Oxford by the members of the Society. Instead of rejuvenation his scheme brought death to the Society. The first and last meeting under the new professor as its president was held on 27 October 1891, during which Hewins read a paper on 'Artisans in the seventeenth century'. Besides Hewins and Edgeworth only Roberts and Snow were present.[111] The issue was summed up in Price's obituary of Edgeworth:

I must own at the outset that some ardent zealots in our number who longed to raise economics from the ignoble level, at Oxford, of a tolerating, grudged, subordination to other studies, to the prominent status of recognized autonomy, won at Cambridge through Marshall's influence and effort, sighed sometimes at the absence of pugnacity, and the dread of assertiveness, which Edgeworth courted. We should have liked spice, at least, of the fight that was in Rogers. I myself should not be candid if I did not mention here that I tried hard in our [Edgeworth's and Price's] weekly conversations to urge him generally forward and particularly, to persuade him that a golden opportunity for marked advance was offered, and alas was being missed, after the war . . . my councel . . . of stout aggressiveness did not avail.[112]

Although for some the significance of Edgeworth's election for the future of economics at Oxford became evident quite soon, not many career opportunities were available. Immediately after the election Hewins presented himself as candidate for the Tooke Professorship in London, but failed to secure it.[113] He tried lecturing without an official position in Pembroke College, Oxford, on political economy with the hope that it might change the University's policy, but to no avail. It may have been during these years that Cannan applied unsuccessfully for a position in Bristol.[114] Even Price, the Honorary Secretary of

[110] E. Cannan, 'Bimetallism: A Criticism', in the *Economic Review*, October 1893, pp. 457–74.
[111] Note in the Cannan Papers, LSE, vol. 905.
[112] Price, 'F. Y. Edgeworth'.
[113] Hewins papers, 43/51, 43/55.
[114] Mentioned in Fay's 'Edwin Cannan'.

the Economic Association, reached a point of despair in 1896 when it occurred to him that Edgeworth would be re-elected. Price tried unsuccessfully for the Glasgow Adam Smith chair which was eventually won by William Smart,[115] after which he decided to stay on at Oxford to fight for the University's recognition of the need for a lectureship and then a Readership in Economic History. Cannan and Hewins remained in Oxford until 1895 when they moved away professionally with the founding of the London School of Economics. (Cannan remained in residence for the rest of his life.)

During the ensuing years two areas of professional activity remained within Oxford after the discontinuation of the Oxford Economic Society and the Social Science Club—the social and semi-professional meetings at the Oxford Political Economy Club and the publications of Oxford men in the *Review* and the *Journal*. Although not all members of the Oxford Economic Society became members of the Oxford Political Economy Club it is safe to assert that those who were elected to the Club began, during the 1890s, to dominate an increasing part of its proceedings, as may be ascertained from the number and nature of the issues discussed by the Club.[116] It was noted at the time that the character of the questions brought forward furnished a fair index of the subjects that engaged the attention of Oxford economists in general: 'From the nineties onwards the old economics has been gradually passing away and their place . . . taken by questions relating to Socialism, to State interference . . . what constitutes a fair wage? How can it be secured? Can the State take ground rents or lay hands on the unearned increment?'[117] The Club was not, strictly speaking, an association of professional economists, but rather a gathering of Oxford men interested in economic and social problems, including some professional economists. Though it was lively and not ill informed and indeed well worth attention, it could

---

[115] Cannan papers, Smart to Cannan, 14 May 1896. Also see Price, *Memoirs and Notes*.

[116] A probably incomplete collection of invitations to Club meetings can be found in the Bodleian Library. The invitations include subjects for discussion and their proposers. The number of subjects raised by OES members for the years under study are three out of six in 1891, two out of three in 1892, four out of nine in 1893, none out of six in 1894, five out of five in 1895.

[117] W. A. Spooner, 'Notes for Autobiography'.

strictly be regarded as comparatively amateur.'[118] Nevertheless, the standard of at least the opening statements must have been up to the standard of the Economic Society whenever one of its ex-members raised an issue based on a subject on which he was working. Nor was it merely a social gathering for intellectual exercise: among the subjects can be found issues that were at the centre of professional and political controversies. In 1901, for instance, Price raised the question of economic history in Oxford as part of his effort to bring about a change in the subject's status. In 1906 he raised the question of the tariffs and in 1900 Cannan presented as an issue 'Why is superiority of Free Trade over Protection not yet always obvious even to apparently intelligent persons?'

In the Club Edgeworth usually avoided submitting issues for debates. When he did on rare occasions present an issue it was phrased in extremely cautious and technical terms which made it practically impossible to debate the matter in the Club's usual semi-professional manner.[119] Price describes a reaction to one such 'Edger' during a Club meeting:

I still remember the look passing slowly but inevitably from perplexed bewilderment to manifest disgust or despairing abandon, on the face of a very able and informed, but also very sensible and just member of our body, as he listened, trying in vain to follow Edgeworth's subtly intricate if not tortuous statement of nice refinements of the case in hand.[120]

As for the *Review* and the *Journal*, any sincere hope for a spirit of co-operation and amiability to prevail, was soon disappointed. The contents of the two publications from 1891 to 1895 (when the new London School of Economics changed the institutional map of British economics) reveal the demarcation lines. Price and H. Ll. Smith, both members of the Council of the British Economic Association, published only in the *Journal* (in the case of H. Ll. Smith it was merely a review and an

[118] Oriel College, Price, 'Supplementary Memoirs.'
[119] 4 Mar. 1893, 'Are the following arguments relating to International Trade of weight:
(1) That if the output of an exported commodity be reduced (e.g. in consequence of a limitation of working hours) the advantage which the exporting country derives from foreign Trade will be diminished.
(2) That the industry of a country cannot be injured by foreign pauper labour.
(3) That a country cannot benefit itself at the expense of foreigners by taking imports.'
Compare this advocacy of free trade with Cannan's question mentioned above.
[120] Price, 'Memoirs and Notes'.

article). Phelps, the third Oxford member of the Council, published only in the *Review*, as did some other Oxford men who were members of the Association. Hewins, Cannan, and Ashley published most of their work in the *Review* and other periodicals. Over the period Hewins published two reviews of books by Thorold Rogers and Cunningham in the *Journal*. Ashley published one article in the *Journal* (in 1891) and Cannan four articles (one in two parts), a note, and a review, whereas in the *Review* he had in every issue a report on 'Legislation, Parliamentary Inquiries of Official Returns' and in addition ten reviews, three articles, and two notes. The contents of Ashley's and Cannan's articles in the *Journal* contain their views on the history of economic theory which were part of their attack on Marshall's interpretation of Ricardo. Some of the early animosity between the two publications was slow to die. In 1931 Cannan used a remark he had made privately on the argument between J. M. Keynes and T. M. Robertson over Keynes's theory of money as a generalization in his Sidney Ball Memorial Lecture (13 November 1931)—the only time in his life he held an official appointment in the University of Oxford. He opened his lecture on 'Balance of Trade Delusions' by saying:

This lecture is going to be a very elementary one. I do not think the founders of the Sidney Ball Lecture intended it for the kind of discussion of which we see examples in the *Economic Journal* when the inmost circle of experts dispute about imaginary phenomena with all the fervour of Roman augurs interpreting the meaning of the entrails of a sacrificed goose.[121]

The differences between the *Review* and the *Journal* went beyond actual economic issues. Since the *Review* was the only mouthpiece of what was left of the Oxford economists, through it, their independent line was repeatedly asserted, as the following examples will show.

In the second issue of the *Journal* (June 1891) Edgeworth lauded J. N. Keynes's *The Scope and Method of Political Economy* as a brilliant triumph. 'We wish for it', he concluded his review, 'a monopoly of favour, and such finality as in political economy is attainable.' In the October 1891 issue of the *Review* Phelps reviewed the same book in a manner that was both a

---

[121] E. Cannan, *Balance of Trade Delusions. Sidney Ball Memorial Lecture* (Oxford, 1931).

manifestation of the *Review's* position and an attack on the position held by Keynes and Edgeworth. He argued that the book was analytical in character, whereas what was wanted was a synthetic 'Scope and Method'. He found the style lacking in humour 'which whilst it helps . . . steer past the Scylla of paradox, runs . . . dangerously near to the Charybdis of Commonplace.' He found it careful, accurate, clear, and devoid of any distinguished ideas. The commonplace argument used by Keynes about induction and deduction, being each inadequate as methods, would do nothing for the progress of science:

> The deductive and the inductive economist start each with an equipment, a predisposition, a prejudice of his own—the hopes and the aims, no less than the history, of the one differ *toto caelo* from the hopes and aims of the other, and the difference is not confined to the field of economics. . . . the progress of science . . . will be mainly the work of men who are one sided.

In other words, it was doubtful whether effort should be channelled continuously towards finding a synthesis of the two methods. Phelps thus rejected the purely analytic study of economics and declared his faith in the scientific value of commitment to well-defined positions.

If the differences still needed spelling out, this was done by Edgeworth's inaugural lecture on 23 October 1891[122] in which, adapting Walker's maxim of 'teach, not preach', Edgeworth maintained that 'the teacher's opinion upon some burning question of the day should not be communicated to his pupils.' Edgeworth's views must have had on the Oxford men the effect of a red rag to a bull. In the first issue of the *Review* after Edgeworth's inaugural lecture, D. J. Medley wrote in a review of Richard T. Ely's *Introduction to Political Economy*: 'Careful definition and rigid logical argument are of the utmost importance in that they guard against loose thinking; but the essence of economic study consists in the fact that under all the mere facts with which it ostensibly deals, there lies a solid moral foundation which the economist neglects at his peril.'[123]

---

[122] Published as 'An introductory lecture on Political Economy', in the *Economic Journal*, December 1891.
[123] *Economic Review*, December 1891. Compare T. C. Snow's review of Montague's edition of Bentham's *Frament on Government* in the *Review*, 1891, pp. 289–92; S. Ball, 'Nicholson's Principles of Political Economy', in the *Economic Review*, 1894, pp. 526–36; and 'Nicholson's Historical Progress and Ideal Socialism', in the *Economic Review*, 1895 pp. 242–3.

The need for subjectivity appeared repeatedly in reviews written by Oxford men. It was an aspect of differences regarding the nature of the study of economics that stems from a world view beyond the narrow confines of the 'scientific objectivity' debate. It was, therefore, appropriate that Ritchie, in 1895, regarded the establishment of the London School of Economics as 'a well founded reproach that our economists "in the chair" do not pronounce authoritatively on current events.' In his view, Oxford's teachers had neglected their duty by allowing 'a large number of men to leave our Universities, to take an active part in a life which is full of economic problems, and we have given them no help towards their solution.'[124] The School would do what Cambridge refused, and Oxford failed, to do.

Apart from the active young economists who eventually managed to secure professional appointments of one sort or another, the *Review* represented a group of relatively young dons actively interested in economic and social issues. The failure of Oxford economics to develop on the lines they favoured and advocated in the *Review* left them isolated from the mainstream of English economics. Their own development in the field of economic and social enquiry gradually stopped. What had during the eighties and early nineties been a lively and active interest remained at best a semi-professional pursuit limited in scope and soon outdated. These efforts were not entirely futile,[125] but, as Ashley noted in the case of Ball, their professional frustration was nevertheless acute.[126]

[124] D. G. Ritchie, note in the *Economic Review*, July 1895, pp. 404–5.
[125] e.g. Asa Briggs, 'Social Welfare, Past and Present', in A. H. Halsey (ed.), *Traditions of Social Policy. Essays in Honour of Violet Butler* (Oxford, 1976).
[126] W. J. Ashley, *Scientific Management and the Engineering Situation* (Oxford, 1922).

7
THE DEBATE — MARSHALLIANS AND DISSENTERS

Up to the formation of the British Economic Association and the publication of the *Economic Journal*, which shortly followed, the general issues concerning the nature of the study of economics were left smouldering beneath the surface. The issues did emerge occasionally, but in the guise of dealing with specific issues. One such instance was Cunningham's article 'What did our forefathers mean by rent?', published at the beginning of 1890.[1] In it he criticized the tendency of modern economists to use the Ricardo and Jevons theories of rent, which were applicable only to modern economic conditions, for the explanation of the entirely different economic reality of the Middle Ages. At the same time he detected an inverse trend in the use made by statesmen in applying, out of context, the medieval principle of fixed rent to the contemporary situation in Ireland. Cunningham's arguments, if generalized, advocated a relativistic application to economic theory. However, they were not presented in their generalized form and were therefore strictly a historian's criticism of misleading statements and observations made by economists and statesmen who tended to misapply their knowledge of history.

The situation changed dramatically with the foundation of the British Economic Association and the firm establishment of Marshall and his supporters as the dominant school of thought, the representatives of the central core of the science, the essential consensus. Cunningham found himself isolated from the mainstream of Cambridge economics and in his endeavour to counter the emerging Marshallian dominance, he concentrated his efforts on creating a counter camp. He had actively supported the publication of the *Economic Review* which managed to take some of Marshall's supporters by surprise.[2] But, perhaps

[1] W. Cunningham, 'What Did Our Forefathers Mean by Rent?' in *Lippincott's Monthly Magazine*, February 1890.
[2] Palgrave papers, J. B. Martin to R. H. Inglis Palgrave, 14 July 1890.

contrary to expectations, the *Review* initiative hastened the publication of the *Journal* rather than upset it. Early in 1891, having for the moment despaired of producing any change at Cambridge, Cunningham offered himself as a candidate for the Tooke Professorship in London, vacated by Edgeworth's election at Oxford. For a while Cunningham considered this as a possible step towards migration to London, a move which was understandably supported by Marshall and Edgeworth, both of whom submitted references on his behalf.[3] However, Cunningham's mood of despair did not last. His election to a Fellowship at Trinity (Cambridge), with its demonstration of support, raised his spirits, and with the added authority of the Tooke Professorship he decided to continue the struggle from Cambridge.

Cunningham took advantage of the opportunity offered by his presidency of the 1891 meeting of Section F in Cardiff. In his address he described his view of the demarcation lines between Oxford and Cambridge, intending it more as an attack on Cambridge economics than as a sober description of the differences between the two emerging camps. Thus his address is representative of his own position rather than an authoritative expression of the Oxford camp. Nevertheless, it may be considered the first major public statement of the camp opposed to Marshall to follow the formation of the Association.

In Cunningham's view,

> The 'Review' bears on the forefront that it hails from Oxford; while the 'Journal' and its destinies have been often talked over at Cambridge, and it seems to me, at least, to be full of the Cambridge spirit. The old contrast between these two Universities comes out strongly and distinctly. The intense interest which Oxford has always shown in the study of man and of conduct has put her practically in touch with many sides of actual life, and has caused her to be the mother of not a few great movements. But in Cambridge we are so engrossed in the study of things that we have not time to spare for trying to know ourselves. If we ever do give our thoughts to man, we like to think of him as if he were a kind of thing; so that we may apply the same methods which we are wont to use in the study of physical phenomena. . . . of course we may always attain to precision in our statements on human affairs so long as we are content to be superficial, and are not at pains to penetrate to the very heart of the matter.

---

[3] Audrey Cunningham, *William Cunningham: Teacher and Preacher*, pp. 69-70.

Although the fullest account of the Marshallian position on the nature of economics had been present in Marshall's *Principles*,[4] Cunningham chose to direct his attack against Marshall's less elaborate statement of 1885 ('Present Position') with a vehemence absent from his previous comment on the same statement. He accused Marshall of considering human nature to be a constant, and of applying modern theories of rent to medieval historical realities (the subject of his 'What did our forefathers mean by rent?' article). On a note of personal antagonism, he added that 'perhaps [Marshall's position] is meant as a sort of scientific witticism; it is not always easy to tell when a Professor of the dismal science is making a joke.' By pursuing a relativist line of argument Cunningham demonstrated his suspicion of all economic theories, maintaining that each should state clearly its hypotheses so that no mistake could be made as to its range of application. Application he considered to be limited both in time and in space. Thus a working hypothesis applicable to Western Europe was invalid in a different period as well as at the same time if applied to the Russian steppes, and vice versa. In his opinion, unclear statement of hypotheses, i.e. a theory's conditions of applicability, had been the source of the errors of the theories of Ricardo and Senior, as well as of the works of some of their followers. They had no relevance to economic situations other than the ones in which they were formed.

A different line of attack, revolving round an often debated issue, considered the position of the self-interest motive in economic theory. Cunningham argued that since self-interest did not in any way reign supreme, the study of economics should re-examine its main premisses. Instead of concentrating solely on measuring the power of self-interest—the quantifiable motive (a practice defended by Marshall)—an effort should be made 'to distinguish the cases where self interest coincides with family welfare and national prosperity, and those where it does not.' This should be done with an eye to 'qualitative as well as

---

[4] It is possible that Cunningham had not, at the time, read the newly published *Principles*, in which both the question of changes in human nature and the use of modern methods of analysis for the understanding of historical economic realities are dealt with in a more elaborate and less controversial manner than in the 1885 'Present Position'.

quantitative distinctions in discussing the motives which influence men in their material concern', going beyond the use of money as a means for measuring motives.

Marshall's *Principles* had already dealt with many of the issues raised by Cunningham. In his efforts towards conciliation he had managed to blend into the work most of the issues raised by the various factions in a way that theoretically could have satisfied all. Yet one issue, as far at the relativists were concerned, could not but remain controversial: Marshall, while aiming at establishing the continuous and cumulative nature of economic theory,[5] argued that 'the foundations of the theory [of cost production in relation to value] as they were left by Ricardo remain intact',[6] and that the doctrine 'though unsystematic and open to many objections, seems to be more philosophic in principle and closer to the actual facts of life than had been argued by his critics.' Ricardo had been an anathema to the economists Marshall called the ethico-historical school[7] and although Cunningham would have to re-state some of his arguments in view of the new articulation of the *Principles*, Ricardo remained a constant target.

Marshall tailored most of his arguments concerning the nature of economics to fit the Comtist definition of science. Cunningham did not accept the Comtist definition and in an attempt to offer a counter-reconstruction scheme presented a somewhat outdated, mechanistic model. In a paper read to the London Economic Club,[8] shortly after his attack on Marshall at the Section F meeting, Cunningham presented a vision of a clear dichotomy between theory and history. Theory would aim at creating a precise language not unlike formal logic or geometry, quite contrary to the general preference (including Marshall's[9]) for the use of common language. Through the use of a formal language the theorist would work out all the logi-

---

[5] In the Preface to the first edition of *Principles* he described the economic science as 'one of slow and continuous growth', and the purpose of his treatise as the presentation of 'a modern version of old doctrines'.

[6] In the first edition, 'Note on Ricardo's Theory of Cost of Production in Relation to Value' at the end of ch. 6, book VI.

[7] See Preface to the first edition of Marshall's *Principles*.

[8] W. Cunningham, 'A Plea for Pure Theory', read 13 Oct. 1891 and published in the *Economic Review*, January 1892.

[9] *Principles*, II. i. 33-4.

cally possible forms of exchange, all the possible types of bargains, etc., to create a technical apparatus which would enable the historian to classify and name historical phenomena, somewhat like a botanist classifying a plant. Such an apparatus would exclude any mention of causes or laws of causation since, in Cunningham's view, 'the attempt to treat economics as a science of causation has been most unfortunate, and has introduced hopeless confusion.'

Determining causation would remain the historian's task, but here again the vision of the historian's work was non-Comtian. The historian would not seek the formation of general historical laws of social development, as envisaged, for instance, by Ashley. Instead Cunningham declared: 'We do not need to assume uniformities or to discuss what is normal or to state our results as laws on phenomena . . . . We merely wish to note the condition which brought about a given event.' It was the vision of a historian secure in the validity and efficiency of his method and wishing to repel various external attacks by redrawing somewhat outdated demarcation lines. Finally, in the same way in which he rejected the use of theory in historical analysis, he rejected the infusion of ethics into the consideration of economic problems. The economic calculus could not take heed of right and wrong distinctions.

Cunningham's affiliation to the ethico–historical camp was based mainly on his criticism of Marshallian economics; his own views placed him in complete isolation. The other ethico—historians were by and large Comtists who could not accept Cunningham's dichotomy. They were not interested in separating causal enquiry and inductive or deductive generalizations from the science whether it was called economics or sociology. It is therefore not surprising that Cunningham's scheme came under attack from within the Oxford camp from David Ritchie in the *Economic Review*.[10]

Ritchie argued that the exclusion of causal investigation from economics was practically impossible. Rent, for instance, could not be defined without its cause. Just as impossible would be a separation of theory from history, with the latter preserving its meaning. The practical approach was not separation but

---

[10] D. G. Ritchie, 'What are Economic Laws?', in the *Economic Review*, July 1892.

combination. However, the positive position adopted by Ritchie indicates a certain misunderstanding of the issues at stake. He adopted a clearly relativist approach to theory: 'The attempt to escape history in dealing with human phenomena makes the restoration of the particular historical background of the theorist essential to the understanding of the professedly abstract theory.' He claimed to represent the growing tendency towards reconciling the abstract and the historical schools, a position he believed he shared with Marshall. Yet his position, both relativistic and moralistic, was far removed from the conciliation Marshall had in mind, although it is a fine tribute to the catholic phrasing of his views in the *Principles*.

Ritchie considered theory from the point of view of the historian, i.e. determining the importance of theory in the historian's work — the exact opposite to Marshall's point of view. Ritchie conceded that hypotheses, being theoretical presuppositions, were essential in the historian's work but nevertheless they were no more than an implement which might prove to be false and require replacement. No mention was made of continuity. Ritchie also argued that economic investigations were inseparable from the consideration of moral factors since economic issues, such as demand for commodities, 'are not permanently fixed by the nature of things, but are partly dependent on moral causes'. In this respect, Ritchie stopped short of the 'preach and teach' argument of L. R. Phelps and Sidney Ball, since he admitted the need to consider moral factors only in the process of investigation but did not argue for their inclusion in the choice of a subject of investigation or in the presentation of its conclusions.

Cunningham had not been the only economist to voice an opinion contrary to the views of Marshall's 'central core'. F. J. Mouat, in his inaugural address as President of the Statistical Society, delivered on 18 November 1890,[11] emphasized the importance of using knowledge gained in economic investigations for the education of public opinion. What was required was greater publicity for the work of the members of the Society, not for intra- and inter-professional reasons, but in order to dispel 'fads, fallacies and economic heresies' and to be able to

---

[11] *Journal of the Statistical Society*, December 1890.

guide 'the public opinion of the country in all social and economic questions'. Such an approach to the use of the findings of economic investigations would not in any way jeopardize their scientific impartiality and would, at the same time, insure them against the fate of past theories which, unable or unwilling to change with the times, were left behind 'the van of progress' to stagnate and eventually to die forgotten.

There was a strong body of opinion within the Statistical Society[12] that opposed the separate formation of the British Economic Association and the publication of the *Economic Journal*. It was in agreement with the Marshallian advocacy of the separation of ethics from economics but argued that there was a present need for less theory and more inductive analysis of current facts as well as a duty to make use of the findings thus obtained, mainly through the education of public opinion.

The opposition to the Marshallian position from within the Statistical Society did not go as far as adopting the Oxford 'teach and preach' position. Yet this position was not exclusively held by Oxford. A similar position was stated by William Smart of Glasgow in the August issue of the *Fortnightly Review* in 1891.[13] Akin to Oxford both in meta-theory and in its ideological connotations, Smart firmly advocated, in the spirit of Ruskin's teachings, the inalienability of morals from economics: 'We dare not any longer present the gulf in practical life between morality and economics . . . it is at his peril as a Teacher if he [the Economist] does not show that, where morality cannot be applied and followed in business, there is something wrong whether with the morality or with the business.' Economic theory, according to Smart, was neither universal nor eternal, but of relative applicability only. 'Old' political economy was, therefore, of no use in the analysis of the present industrial reality which was significantly different from its previous phases of development. With the change of times the focus of economic enquiry had switched from wealth

---

[12] These views are presented by Charles Booth, President of the Society 1892–3, and Lord Farrer, President of the Society 1894–5, in their Presidential addresses published in the *Journal of the Statistical Society*, December 1892, December 1893, December 1894.

[13] W. Smart, 'The Old Economy and the New', in the *Fortnightly Review*, August 1891.

to labour and distribution: 'What we are now called on to do is to write the Political Economy of a rich nation, whose wealth has all run to one end, and where the masses of the people are . . . still very far from what we might have expected.'

Smart approved of Factory Acts and the growth of trade unions as means 'to restore the independence of the labourer and make free contract possible again'. His vision of a future society envisaged the voluntary subordination of individual liberty 'to the realisation of a common life whose interests do not conflict but co-operate' — a collectivist vision not much different from that described by Marshall at the Industrial Remuneration Conference.

Smart was not a historical economist. Rather like Cannan, he combined theory and relativism in his approach to economics (hence the inaccuracy of the term ethico–historical as descriptive of the opposition to the Marshallian position). Smart and Cannan considered economic theory to be of immediate application and validity only. Smart emphasized to a larger extent than Cannan the place of morals in his work, so that although he did not produce a work comparable to Cannan's *Theories of Production* in proof of relativism, his moral approach brought him into close alliance with the Oxford position.

All in all, relativism of past theories, especially Ricardo's, remained the central issue of the debate. Relativism disputed the validity of the continuity argument, whereas the linkage of morals and economics argument did not. The relativist argument against Ricardo had two parallel forms: (1) Ricardo's theories had been a product of circumstances particular to his age and were not intended for universal application; (2) whether Ricardo intended his theories to be applied universally or not, they were inaccurate and invalid when applied to present economic circumstances. It was generally agreed that Ricardo's theories were in the main true as far as they went, i.e. structurally valid and of limited application.[14] J. N. Keynes pointed out, in a review of Gonner's 1891 edition of Ricardo's *Principles*, that that '[Ricardo] did pre-eminently excel as a

---

[14] See Marshall's reply to Ashley's criticism in App. I, 32,fn of the 3rd edition of *Principles*.

deductive economist need not be denied; but to imply that he left deductive political economy in anything like a complete or final form is to play into the hands of those who minimise the importance of deduction in economic theories.'[15] Thus the argument presented by the theorists was not one of complete adoption of Ricardian doctrines but of their correction and modification for current usage.

The first direct attack on Marshall's treatment of Ricardo in his own *Principles* came from W. J. Ashley in the first volume of the *Economic Review*.[16] Marshall was not the sole subject of criticism. Ashley identified a group he called the rehabilitationists which included Marshall, Sidgwick, and J. N. Keynes, who, through generous interpretation, qualification, and supplementation, pronounced Ricardo's theories to be of permanent value. Marshall argued that Ricardo's theory of value had been misunderstood by Marx and Rodbertus and therefore misused. Ashley contested Marshall's presentation of the facts. Ricardo, he argued, presented his theory of value 'in terms indistinguishable from those employed by Rodbertus and Marx' and had been accordingly interpreted by James Mill, De Quincey, McCulloch, and Malthus. They had all interpreted Ricardo in a reasonable manner and if one wished to interpret him 'generously', the same could be done for the socialist adaptation of his theories: 'It is surely possible to do this, and yet, like the present writer, to think no better of Socialism because it can fairly claim Ricardo's authority, and to think no worse of Ricardo because his teaching received so unexpected an application.'

Ashley's article was not intended as an all-out attack on Marshall. He had submitted to the expediency of conciliation and was careful to soften his criticism by proclaiming Marshall 'the *doyen* of English economists and his *Principles* as a viable compromise which would allow all schools to work together'. Nor did Marshall wish to develop the issue into a full-blown controversy. In his reply to Ashley's criticism in the third edition of his *Principles* he pointed out that since Ricardo had not left a clear statement of his theory 'each reader must decide

---

[15] *Economic Journal*, December 1891.
[16] W. J. Ashley, 'The Rehabilitation of Ricardo', in the *Economic Review*, 1891.

for himself according to his temperament.' The issue could not, therefore, be decided by argument.

In contrast, Cunningham had nothing to gain by conciliation. The rebuke his 'Pure Theory' had received at Oxford, although comparatively mild, led him to discontinue that line of argument. Oxford economists and supporters, of the *Review's* line were careful in their criticism of him,[17] and Cunningham understandably decided in favour of resuming his attack on Marshall. Cunningham's next, and perhaps best-known, attack on Marshall was in the form of a paper read during March 1892 to the Royal Historical Society, of which Cunningham was a prominent member, and printed in the September issue of the *Economic Journal* later that year.[18] It was a historian's paper addressed to fellow historians and its tone was one of urgency and alarm. Citing Marshall's somewhat overused, 'Present Position' and the use Marshall made of historical facts in his *Principles* as targets, Cunningham denounced theoretical economists as a threat to historians. Their use and application of Ricardo's theories beyond the historical confines of time and space meant that they believed themselves to possess knowledge of the universal laws of society, a belief which allowed them to belittle the value of investigating the actual facts. 'If they understand the real motive forces already, it seems mere pedantry to bother about the precise form in which they were garnished.' Such an attitude created a vicious circle: 'From the point of view of economic theory neglect of patient study of actual fact seem excusable; from my point of view, it is disastrous, because it prevents the economist from finding out the narrow limits within which his generalizations are even approximately true.'

In order to demonstrate to his fellow historians the immediacy of the danger, Cunningham chose five cases from Marshall's *Principles*, in which he argued that facts had been neglected in pronouncing on historical issues. At the same time he wished to make it clear that his concern was not with the specific cases but with the phenomenon in general:

[17] Hewins papers, 43/107, C. Firth to W. A. S. Hewins, 2 Nov. 1892.
[18] W. Cunningham, 'The Perversion of Economic History', in the *Economic Journal*, September 1892.

THE DEBATE—MARSHALLIANS AND DISSENTERS

When critics speak of this book as authoritative on points of history, or tell us that the historical school of economists made a useful protest but implicitly deny that they have necessary work to do in supplying a basis for positive economic doctrine, one cannot but feel that there is a time not only for silence but for speech; lest silence should be mistaken for acquiescence. At least, it is well to draw attention to the risks which even a very able man runs in attempting to construct history from general principles, instead of submitting to build it up bit by bit from definite data of fact.

Cunningham's paper was not exclusively directed against Marshall. The second part consisted of an attack on what Cunningham considered to be similarly dangerous tendencies in Thorold Rogers's work—specifically, his over-emphasis of economic motives and the consideration of economic factors in isolation from the other circumstances of their age. But Rogers had died in 1890 and few, if any, were prepared to defend his method. Not so with Marshall. Cunningham had placed the dispute outside the boundaries of the economists' community, wishing to turn it into a confrontation between the theoretical economists and the academically powerful historians. It was a dangerous manoeuvre which threatened Marshall's position within Cambridge and one Marshall could not afford to ignore or leave to be dealt with by proxy. The same issue of the *Journal* containing Cunningham's attack included as an immediate response 'A Reply' by Marshall.[19] Marshall countered Cunningham's manoeuvre by reducing their disagreements to the person-to-person level of a professional dispute within Cambridge, rather than admitting to a difference of views at the general level of theoretical economists versus historians.

In answer to the examples Cunningham had presented of his misuse or disregard of historical facts, Marshall admitted in some cases to having been mistaken. In others, he argued, he had been misunderstood by Cunningham: 'His criticisms proceed on assumptions that I hold opinions which in fact I do not hold, and which I believe I have not expressed; while in several cases I think I have definitely expressed opposite opinions.'

Other instances of disagreement which Cunningham declared to be both basic and dangerous, such as the contemporary position of Ricardian theories, Marshall chose, as in his

---

[19] A. Marshall, 'A Reply', in the *Economic Journal*, September 1892.

reply to Ashley, to describe as mere differences of individual interpretation:

> Ricardo's teachings on rent do not appear to him [Cunningham] to have the same general import they do to me. For I regard them as containing a living principle applicable, with proper modifications, to the income derived from almost every variety of Differential Advantage for production; and applicable also under almost every variety of rights as to property, dues, and freedom of action, whether those rights be upheld by law or by custom.

Having dealt with Cunningham's specific criticisms, Marshall turned to the historians in general, reassuring them that Cunningham's was a false alarm. He did attribute great importance to facts, and he did not assume either universality of laws or historically unchanged human motives. He had merely suggested that modern theory could prove helpful in filling gaps in historical research where facts were unobtainable. He had no claim over the historian's domain since he considered the task of economics to be limited to the investigation of contemporary economic conditions.

The publication of both Cunningham's criticism and Marshall's reply in the same issue of the *Journal* helped to defuse Cunningham's attack by means which, though efficient, were considered by some (including Foxwell) as unfair editorship.[20] Cunningham tried to induce Edgeworth to print a reply, but to no avail.[21] Rather than let Marshall have the last word, Cunningham managed to get a reply printed both in the *Academy* and in the *Pall Mall Gazette*.[22] In it he addressed what he considered as the main issue: 'the applicability of Ricardo's theory of rent to Tudor times in England'. But despite his description of the issue as a disagreement on the technical question of the application of Ricardo's theory, he did not wish it to be understood as a retraction of his attack on theorists in general. In his view those who practised this form of misapplication were 'in danger of deducing statements about facts from the principle, instead of studying the actual facts as they existed.'

Cunningham did not accept Marshall's explanation nor did he admit of any misinterpretation:

---

[20] Phelps papers, Foxwell to Phelps, 17 Aug. 1893.
[21] Audrey Cunningham, *William Cunningham*, p. 66.
[22] *Pall Mall Gazette*, 29 Sept. 1892 and *the Academy*, 1 Oct. 1892.

These facts are so well known that I did not think it necessary to state them explicitly in my note; but it seems that Prof. Marshall was not aware of them . . . He relies on Ricardo's principle and tells us what must have happened, but his statement conflicts with the evidence as to what actually did occur. Ricardo's principle appears to be saved, but it is so much the worse for facts. This may serve to show why I record Prof. Marshall's attitude and influence, despite his real interest in and appeals to history, as antagonistic to the serious study of history. *Le mieux est l'ennemi du bien.*

Finally, realizing the purpose of Marshall's manoeuvre in concentrating on technical differences, Cunningham concluded: 'I cannot but feel it is a pity, when Prof. Marshall has broken silence that he should content himself with insisting on some verbal trivialities, instead of dealing with the real difficulties in regard to his writings which many of us have felt and which I have ventured to point out.'

The historians may have been mollified by Marshall's reply, but Cunningham remained relentless. Shortly after the publication of his paper to the Royal Historical Society and Marshall's answer in the *Economic Journal*, he resumed the attack in an introductory lecture at King's College, London, published in the American *International Journal of Ethics* in January 1893.[23] This time Cunningham added a new element, the 'Oxford' criteria of applicability. Economic theory, he claimed, was practically inapplicable while possessing pretensions of universality. In a direct reference to Marshall's 'Reply' he argued:

> The new school, of which Professor Marshall is the acknowledged head, devote themselves to expressing principles in their widest form. Ricardo's doctrine of rent is expanded into a form in which it becomes applicable not merely to land, but to every variety of differential advantage for production. In the same way economic theory is treated, not as concerned with material wealth . . . when economic doctrine is formulated thus, it does not serve so readily as a guide in practical difficulties; it is harder to frame maxims with its help. And thus . . . the new school are inclined to give economic doctrine a character in which it is divorced from actual life, and are, to my mind, themselves to blame for the general apathy they sometimes deplore.

Having adopted the criteria of practical application, Cunningham was forced to present the value of historical

---

[23] W. Cunningham, 'Political Economy and Practical Life', an introductory lecture to the students of the Evening Classes at King's College, London, 7 Oct. 1892, in the *International Journal of Ethics*, vol. 3, January 1893.

research in a form significantly different from that of his 'Pure Theory'. Arguing the utility of historical economics necessitated the use of the Comtist and moralist arguments. The problem of understanding the present he stated in Comtist terms: 'If we wish to understand what is sometimes called the play of social forces we shall have to turn to the past rather than to the present', whereas economics 'studies the operation of human powers and is pre-eminently a moral rather than a physical science'. Cunningham may therefore be said to have moved into the 'Oxford' camp, not merely in terms of a practical alliance as had been the case up to 1892, but also in adopting the 'Oxford' position on practical application and morals. Like Ashley, he pronounced theory to be, at best, of limited application and, adopting Marshall's 'Present Position' argument, he agreed that it was of use as a negative guide to practical schemes.

Although, in retrospect, the Cunningham–Marshall exchange was to become the best-known part of the debate concerning the nature of economics, in terms of the camps they were made out to represent it is a misleading one. Cunningham's position on the issue as depicted in 'Pure Theory' was peculiarly his own, unrepresentative of the views held by other historical economists or relativists. Add to that Marshall's reluctance to enter such an inevitably (in his view) harmful debate, and an incomplete and inaccurate view of the debate and the issues involved may be easily construed. The main defence of Marshall's position was conducted by proxy, so that simultaneously with the Marshall–Cunningham exchange, a less one-sided debate was conducted with the historical and relativist issues somewhat better presented than in Cunningham's occasionally inconsistent and emotionally charged attacks.

In 1891 Price published the first edition of *A Short History of Political Economy in England*, which he had completed late in 1890, before the new phase of the controversy had erupted.[24] It was intended as a non-controversial textbook, based on his Extension lectures and produced for Extension usage.[25] In it

[24] L. L. Price, *A Short History of Political Economy in England from Adam Smith to Arnold Toynbee* (London, 1891). The preface is dated 8 Dec. 1890.
[25] It was first published in the Extension Series, edited by Professor J. E. Symes.

Price had somewhat qualified his previous position on relativism, for although he aimed at describing past theories and the circumstances in which they were formed, he added in the case of each economist, a consideration of the relation his work bore 'to more recent economic thought'.[26] Marshall's influence is discernible in some of Price's pronouncements on general issues. He clearly adopted Marshall's position on the separation of the scientific enquiry from questions of practical application: 'The science of economics, like other sciences, investigates the relations betwen cause and effect, and states what is the case; and the art of philanthropy or statesmanship discovers how the knowledge furnished by science should be used as a guide in practice.'[27] This position was inconsistent with the prescriptive nature of some of his past and future, works.

Price re-stated his belief that the age of conciliation had arrived and that the deductive–inductive controversy had abated.[28] However, he reduced the role of the historical method to testing and correcting the work of the abstract-deductive school: 'It [the historical school] shows that the theories of the older economists were sometimes stated too universally, at any rate by more extravagant followers, and that they require modification when employed as explanations of actual fact.'[29] Nevertheless, Price had retained something of the historical approach in his analysis of some of the 'old' economists,[30] including his final comment on Ricardo: 'It is only by a liberal interpretation that the Ricardian theory can be considered adequate, whether we regard it as an explanation of the past, or a statement of the present, or a prediction of the future.'[31]

Price had also repeated his previously stated comment on the inapplicability of over-refined theory.[32] At the same time, in his treatment of Ricardo, he had laid the basis for a disagreement with Ashley by arguing that 'Ricardo is not alone, or entirely,

---

[26] Price, *A Short History*, preface; and p. 126 in the 1937 edition. Page numbers in earlier editions are in close proximity.
[27] Ibid., p. 12.
[28] Ibid., p. 128.
[29] Ibid., p. 125.
[30] e.g. on Malthus; ibid., p. 43.
[31] Ibid., p. 78.
[32] Ibid., p. 84.

responsible for the misunderstanding or misapplication, of his views by unpractical or unscientific followers.'[33]

A short while after the completion and publication of his book, with the commencement of the new round of criticisms of Marshall's defence of Ricardo, Price moved even closer to Marshall's position. In an article published in the first issue of the *Economic Journal*,[34] he pointed out:

> The criticisms of economists of the historical and inductive school have been chiefly directed against his [Ricardo's] doctrines. If the theories of any one economist were to be selected as an illustration of divergence from fact, the choice of many persons would at once fall on Ricardo . . . The criticism may be erroneous, or, it may be unduly severe.

In this article Price quoted extensively from Marshall's treatment in his *Principles* of Ricardo's concept of rent as payment for differential advantages. Yet the 'rehabilitation of Ricardo' was not the sole subject of the article. Price repeated some of his previous observations concerning the importance of the knowledge of the circumstances in understanding Ricardo's theories, the problem of applying his theories under different circumstances, and the difficulties of application caused by the theory's refinements.

In his article on the 'Standard of Comfort', for Inglis Palgrave's *Dictionary*, written some time during 1891 or early 1892,[35] Price repeated another component of the 'rehabilitation' argument, which by now had clearly become a controversial issue following Ashley's 'Rehabilitation' article. He adopted Marshall's position in greater detail than in his *History of Political Economy*, arguing that the socialists had misinterpreted Ricardo to mean by 'standard of living' the bare necessities of life, excluding life's decencies and luxuries which change from age to age and from environment to environment. As for the Iron Law: 'The origin of the socialist law of wages has been ascribed to Ricardo's theory of the natural price of labour, but Ricardo's own language is sufficiently elastic and comprehensive.'

---

[33] Ibid., pp. 84, 68.
[34] L. L. Price, 'Some Aspects of the Theory of Rent', in the *Economic Journal*, March 1891.
[35] R. H. Inglis Palgrave (ed.), *Dictionary of Political Economy*, vol. 1, part 3 (London, 1892), pp. 337–8.

Whether by then Price still had any reservations about the 'liberal interpretation of Ricardo' they were completely submerged in his grand eulogy of Marshall's *Principles* in an article 'A Recent Economic Treatise', published in March 1892 in the *Economic Journal*. It was almost as if Price had run out of words of praise to describe Marshall's work. He kept referring to it as epoch-making, comparable only to Adam Smith's *Wealth of Nations* in its scope and in its achievement of unification after years of bitter controversy. He was admittedly not objective, nor did he conceal the fact that he found it difficult to consider the book in a critical and detached manner, having been one of Marshall's proof readers: 'From the outset he must confess that his attitude is one of admiration. Which has deepened as he has withdrawn from immediate proximity of the proof reading, and contemplated from a distance in its entirety what he knew first in its separate parts.'

Price regarded Marshall's *Principles* as the much anticipated synthesis of the various contentious theories and approaches developed since Adam Smith. The *Principles* joined together all streams and schools of thought — the historical and the mathematical, the continental, the English, and the American. All had been fairly dealt with, creating 'an orderly systematic unity, where the different work of different writers is assigned its own place, and its merits are duly appreciated, without being allowed to thrust out another from its rightful position, or to appropriate to itself the recognition, which should properly be bestowed in other quarters.' With the achievement of this unity, a new age of constructive work would ensue, replacing the long period in which so much effort was wasted in controversy. Price even went as far as comparing the work of Marshall and Sidgwick, to the decided advantage of the former.

Part of the article dealt with the first wave of criticism directed against the *Principles*. Cunningham was not mentioned by name, but Price made much of Marshall's use of historical facts and pointed to the 'distinct traces of the influence of the historical school'. Ashley's criticism was dealt with more directly, although Price attempted to sidestep the criticism by attempting to change the issue. Ashley had argued that Ricardo had been correctly understood by his contemporaries and by socialist interpreters. Marshall had admitted that Ricardo's words were inconclusive and open to various interpretations. Price argued that Ricardo's importance was not so much based on the manner in which he had been interpreted by his contemporaries or by the socialist interpreters, but rather on his position in the overall development of economic thought, viz. the place allotted to him by Marshall regardless of whether Marshall's interpretation had been entirely accurate or not. Generally speaking, he argued, 'the older economists have often been so unfairly and indiscriminately attacked, and so grossly misrepresented or misinterpreted, that even an extreme movement in the opposite direction might be welcome. But we do not believe that Professor Marshall has erred [in overstating his case].' (The question of Marshall's faithful defence of the 'older' economists brought out an interesting difference in character between Price and Cannan, since whereas Price found it laudable, Cannan considered it absurd and referred to it as 'intellectual ancestor worship'.[36])

In his reference to Ashley's criticism, Price touched upon the crux of the relativists' argument. Ashley had argued that there was no question of unfair treatment of Ricardo on the part of his contemporaries. The relativists in general readily conceded that the 'old' economists' theories were quite applicable to their circumstances and it was only the change of circumstances that had rendered them obsolete. Two articles demonstrating the point were published by Cannan during 1892, making use of his research for *Theories of Production*. Price had complained of the lack of consideration amongst 'the more extreme supporters of historical methods'[37] for the special circumstances in which theories were formed, when they came to pass judgement on them. Cannan's articles on the Law of Diminishing Returns and on Malthus[38] aimed at disproving Price's allegation.

Cannan used the case of the Law of Diminishing Returns to disprove the continuity argument: 'The early nineteenth-

---

[36] E. Cannan, 'Alfred Marshall 1842–1924', in *Economica*, No. 12, November 1924.
[37] L. L. Price, 'A Recent Economic Treatise', in the *Economic Journal*, March 1892.
[38] E. Cannan, 'The Origin of the Law of Diminishing Returns 1813–1815', in the *Economic Journal*, 1892, and 'The Malthusian Anti-Socialist Argument', in the *Economic Review*, 1892.

century English economists obtained the law of diminishing returns, like most of their doctrines not from study of the work of their predecessors, but from the actual experience of England during the war.' Price could not accuse him of being entirely unjust, since he argued that under the circumstances 'West and Ricardo were quite right as to the practical questions at issue.' What had rendered their theories obsolete was the unanticipated direction in which society had developed: 'Few historical facts can be better established than that with progress of wealth and population in the present civilized world, the labour of providing raw produce has been performed by a steadily decreasing proportion of the whole population . . . we may take this as sufficient proof that the returns have increased and not diminished.'

In his article on Malthus, Cannan adopted an argument similarly structured to Ashley's argument on the interpretation of Ricardo. Malthus, Cannan argued, had not, in any way, been misunderstood by his socialist critics: 'Malthus was really an anti-socialist, and it is almost entirely from him that the anti-socialist reputation of the English classical school of economics is derived.'

Cannan did not confine his article to the consideration of theoretical traditions. His interest in Malthus stemmed from a growing interest in the rate of population growth in general, which he eventually summed up in his paper for the meeting of Section F at Ipswich in 1895: 'The Probability of a Cessation of the Growth of Population in England and Wales During the Next Century'.[39] Cannan used his research for *Theories of Production* to disprove any claims of the misinterpretation of Malthus. He then proceeded to use his research into the rate of population growth in order to argue that there was no contradiction between prudential checks, which he considered to be in evidence, and various schemes usually identified with state socialism. Thus Cannan aimed in the same article at

---

[39] Published in the *Economic Journal*, 1895. Cannan's observations on the rate of population growth include 'The Growth of Manchester and Liverpool 1801–1891', in the *Economic Journal*, 1894, and observations in his 'Legislation, Parliamentary Inquiries and Official Returns', in the *Economic Review*, April 1891, October 1891, October 1892, and October 1894.

refuting Malthus on a contemporary basis as well as on a historical one.

In his article on Marshall's *Principles* Price had continually pointed out the close resemblance it bore to the *Wealth of Nations*. His address to Section F during its meeting at Edinburgh in 1892[40] contained an attempt to describe the value of the *Wealth of Nations* by the same arguments used to describe the value of Marshall's *Principles*. Price maintained that the greatness of Adam Smith's work was due to his flexible use of both the deductive and the inductive methods. Since both schools claimed him as their founder, his work proved that a clash between the two was not inevitable and that a synthesis was possible. Another aspect of the same argument claimed that it was due to this flexible and unifying approach that Adam Smith's theories were still full of relevance and validity, the core of the living tradition of economic theory, the existence of which the 'relative dissenters' refused to recognise. What Price probably found difficult to argue in the case of Ricardo he did with ease in describing the contemporary value of the *Wealth of Nations*:

The surprising fact remains how little is really unimportant now, and how much is supplied in germ in the *Wealth of Nations*, which later investigation has done no more than develop into the maturer plant.

[And elsewhere in the same paper:]

The first two books of the *Wealth of Nations* may be said to contain a theory of production, exchange, and distribution, which presents in essence the fuller development of later criticism and speculation.

Price found Adam Smith's theories to be not only of current value, but also of contemporary applicability as well, as his arguments concerning free trade demonstrated.

Relativist attempts at disproving the 'living tradition' claim of the Marshallians had so far produced fragmentary arguments attacking specific theorists which did little to shake the edifice built by Marshall and loyally defended by Price. In 1893 Cannan completed and published his *Theories of Production*

---

[40] L. L. Price, 'Adam Smith and Recent Economics', in the *Economic Journal*, June 1893.

and Distribution[41] — a major thesis against the continuity argument. Cannan's style had something of an 'over-kill' effect. Jevons's comment on the 'wrong headed Ricardo' is well remembered for a poignancy rare in academic controversies. Cannan's work included comments just as harsh, and much more frequent, dealing practically with all the luminaries of the 'old' school, as may be illustrated by some of the following examples.

'It can scarcely be denied that Adam Smith left the whole subject of "capital" in the most unsatisfactory state.'[42] 'It would be idle to pretend that this account [by Adam Smith] of the causes which determine the rate of profits is, as a whole, entitled to any great respect.'[43]

Malthus, a favourite target, was 'seldom blessed with a clear cut opinion on any subject'.[44] 'No one confounded capital and produce more helplessly than he did.'[45] On Malthus's use of Great Britain as a universal model—'He refused to believe that subsistence in Great Britain could be made to increase faster than in an arithmetical ratio. This was leaving experience and soaring into prophecy, and, like most prophets, Malthus turned out to be wrong.'[46]

On Ricardo Cannan repeated a criticism he made in a draft for an article on 'Definitions' for Palgrave's *Dictionary*[47]:

> Like most people who have not had the advantage of literary education, Ricardo was apt to think that a word ought to have whatever sense he found convenient to put upon it. Ricardo's attempt to show that improvements must temporarily lower rent, whether we apply it to his first or his second class of improvements, and whether we suppose him to mean money rent or corn rent . . . ends in complete and hopeless failure.[48]

And in an echo of Ashley's argument on the interpretation of

---

[41] E. Cannan, *A History of Theories of Production and Distribution in English Political Economy from 1776 to 1848* (London, 1893). The Preface is signed April 1893.
[42] Ibid., p. 89.
[43] Ibid., p. 278.
[44] Ibid., p. 7.
[45] Ibid., p. 99.
[46] Ibid., p. 142.
[47] Cannan papers, LSE, vol. 908. In the draft Cannan wrote at first, 'owing to the insufficiency of his [Ricardo's] literary education'. The sentence is crossed out and replaced by 'owing to the peculiar bend of his mind'. In the *Theories of Production*, p. 195, Cannan returned to the original wording.
[48] Ibid., p. 331.

Ricardo by the socialists—'Ricardo's view, adopted by Marx, plays a part in the history of Socialism; in the history of Economics it is not important.'[49]

On Senior, there is an allusion to Marshall—

> It is rather amusing to see that, after having . . . made havoc of the old classification, and created a new totally different one, Senior finds it convenient to use the old one, and only to make occasional reference to the new. His extraordinary attempt is only interesting as an example to be avoided, and as an anticipation of that desire to call everything rent which is a marked feature of English economics at the present time.[50]

And on a different matter — 'On the question, as on many others, Senior begins by exciting great hopes of a clear exposition, and then miserably disappoints these hopes.'[51]

On the Mills — 'J. S. Mill taught by so confused and vacillating a tutor as his father, could scarcely be expected, at the age of twenty-three, to contribute much towards the solution of the question as to the causes which determine the rate of profit.'[52] Similar treatment was awarded to practically all the economists dealt with.

Something of Cannan's intention was stated with an obvious reference to the Marshallians, in the book's preface:

> It has been constantly supposed that 'abstract theory' must be defended at almost any cost against the attacks of the 'historical school' and the result has been a creation of a mythical Ricardo and Malthus, who never wrote anything which cannot be 'limited and explained' till it ceased to be in conflict either with recognised fact or accepted modern opinion. With such idealisation I have no sympathy . . . My object is simply to show what the various theories concerning production and distribution were and to explain how and why they grew up and then either flourished or decayed.

If the full extent of Cannan's positive intention was phrased somewhat vaguely, it was stated more clearly in chapter 9, 'General Review. Politics and Economics', in the summing up of the findings of the first eight chapters:

> Judged then, by what we may, perhaps, using the term in a sense which has very often, though not very accurately, been given to it, call the 'abstract method', the theories of production and distribution arrived at in the first half

---

[49] Ibid., p. 363.
[50] Ibid., p. 199.
[51] Ibid., p. 357.
[52] Ibid., p. 298.

of the nineteenth century must be visited with almost unqualified condemnation. But if we try them by the historical method, and inquire how far they met the practical needs of their time, they must obtain a much more favourable verdict.⁵³

Cannan aimed at proving the 'living tradition' to be a fiction through a detailed study of each of the theorists whose work constituted the said tradition. He argued that past theories, usually adequate for the purposes of their age, when examined on the basis of modern theory and present-day circumstances, proved to be riddled with flaws, inconsistencies, and mistakes. For contemporary needs they were useless, indeed some had proved to be dangerous when used out of context. By implication, if a contemporary economist insisted on using 'old' theories he was either mistaken in misinterpreting them or untruthful in claiming to read into them what they did not contain.

Cannan was clearly not a universalist. Theories formulated in the past were not just technically faulty but by definition could not be applied to the present. The best theories for explaining the present were the theories formed in the present. Cannan clarified the point in the two sections he added to the second (1903) edition of *Theories of Production* in which he wrote: 'I have attempted to indicate the relation of the theories of today to those of the period under review, and to show that the old theories have been replaced by others stronger from a scientific point of view, and equally suitable for the practical needs of their own time.'⁵⁴

Much of Cannan's reputation in later years was based on his contribution to *Dogmengeschichte*. Two of his future students—Hugh Dalton and T. E. Gregory—in later years described his method as tradition-making rather than dogma-making. He inspired his pupils with his own complete lack of reverence for any dogma in existence and his insistence on the critical examination of each theory on the basis of practical needs. His approach became highly conducive to a critical methodology but it also explains why Cannan was never hailed as the creator

---

⁵³ Ibid., p. 383.
⁵⁴ Ibid., Preface to second (1903) edition, p. vi.

of a school of thought in terms of establishing a tradition of dogma.[55]

The criticism of past theories led Cannan occasionally to express a positive position on some of the issues dealt with, or to point to spheres in which he thought better theories were needed — an approach demonstrated in his treatment of Malthus and the rate of population growth. Thus, although his positive theoretical suggestions were not the subject of *Theories of Production*, the book contains a good measure of his own theoretical work. However, these contributions were dwarfed by his critical onslaught, which caused his critics to denounce his work as destructive. His approach was strongly condemned, yet little could be offered in the way of a complete refutation of his argument point by point. As Price wrote in 1931,[56] Cannan 'turned his formidable ruthless rifle against Marshall':

> We are constrained to doubt whether any author, however wary, could pass triumphantly through so minute and close animadversion, or would emerge untarnished, without some apparent stain at least, whether removable or not. And we are impelled to voice regret that, however persuasive such inspection can be made, search for desert to praise should not be generously mingled with almost unvarying blame. Marshall's recoil from negative criticism is relevant here. At the best, work, which must be onerous, does not promise to be very helpful; at the worst, it runs serious risk of doing grave injustice. It is obviously destructive rather than constructive in result, if not in intent.

and so on in the same vein.

The work, which Cannan claims to have embarked upon quite innocently, became a 'hostile and uncharitable' survey directed against Marshall.[57] Its contribution to the debate was acknowledged by a reviewer in the *Daily Chronicle*. Under the title 'An Economic Iconoclast'[58] he linked Cannan's book with recent developments in English economics:

---

[55] Hugh Dalton, 'Professor Cannan's General Contribution', in Hugh Dalton and T. E. Gregory, *London Essays in Economics in Honour of Edwin Cannan* (London, 1927). T. E. Gregory, 'Edwin Cannan's Work; A Personal Impression', in the *Observer*, 14 Apr. 1935, and id., 'Edwin Cannan; A Personal Impression', in *Economica*, November 1935.

[56] In the enlarged edition of *History of Political Economy in England*, pp. 295–6.

[57] See Edgeworth's review of the second edition in the *Economic Journal*, 1903.

[58] *Daily Chronicle*, 29 May 1893.

THE DEBATE—MARSHALLIANS AND DISSENTERS 233

Professor Marshall too often followed the same path [as Cairnes and J. S. Mill] of filial reverence, and the operation of 'making sense' of Ricardo has now provoked a not unnatural reaction. At a British Association meeting not long ago, a dissatisfied auditor was heard to declare that the process of whitewashing has been carried too far. Professor Ashley has since been provoked into the remark that if the Historical School of Economists have sometimes neglected deduction, The Deductive School has perverted history.

The reviewer noted the characteristics of the two camps involved in the controversy:

> There appears to be an almost feverish desire in some economic circles that the 'solidarity' of the body of economic doctrine should be maintained in face of a Philistine world. Unless the economists stand shoulder to shoulder it seems to be thought political economy will lose its hold on a sceptical democracy, which, deprived of this sheet anchor will inevitably drift on the rocks of dreaded Socialism. There are those, on the other hand, who see in the exaggerated respect for the memories of the classic economists a timid and somewhat unworthy lack of faith in science.

The origins of Cannan's feud with Marshall are unclear. Cannan attested[59] to having known Marshall by sight when Marshall was Principal of University College, Bristol. Because of his sea cruise to New Zealand, he missed studying under Marshall at Balliol, and maintains that the next time he saw him was when Marshall was President of Section F during its meeting at Leeds in 1890. According to his own testimony, Cannan could neither abide nor understand Marshall's reverence for the 'old' economists. Nor did he see much point in attempting 'a complete exposition of general economics', a task which Cannan argued 'has long ceased to be possible for mortal man':

> [Marshall] would have done better for himself and for economics if he had given his life to advancing and defending and developing what was fresh and new in his doctrine instead of including it very slowly and awkwardly among a mass of uninteresting attempts to rehabilitate traditional and often obsolete doctrines . . . He could not bear to say or even think that he had improved anything in the work of the masters, to say nothing of washing it out.

Cannan's continuous fight against Marshall and Cambridge ecnomics over an impressive array of subjects included the use

---
[59] Cannan, 'Alfred Marshall 1842-1924'.

of some unconventional tactics[60] and a unique parody of Marshall in an article 'The Division of Income' (published in the American *Quarterly Journal of Economics*, 1905, and not in England, perhaps because of the unusual form of criticism used in it[61]). It is clear that Cannan thoroughly enjoyed the fight, as he had enjoyed many of his other professional clashes. A Cannan family tradition attributes importance to knowing how to be 'a good hater',[62] a quality in which Edwin Cannan excelled. He did not suffer fools gladly and he revelled in exposing fallacies, 'trusting always in calm certainty to justifiable self-confidence'.[63] The language he used for such 'exposures' was always harsh. In that respect his comments on the 'old' economists in *Theories of Production* were not reserved for dead economists alone but used unsparingly for live ones as well. C. R. Fay[64] records him as having said at one time or another: 'Keynes will be in a mental asylum before he's done, if he goes on like this' (after the publication of *A Treatise on Money*). 'That fellow Hayeck has corrupted them all [at the LSE], and ought to be deported' etc., language which was by no means restricted to private correspondence. Nevertheless, his feud with Marshall was unique in its duration and although it was boosted along the way by various incidents, not the least of which was Marshall's misquotation of Cannan in the third edition of the *Principles*,[65] it seems to have begun with Marshall's defence of Ricardo.

Cannan was ideologically committed to disproving revolutionary socialist solutions to present social and economic pro-

[60] See C. R. Fay, 'Edwin Cannan; A Tribute to a Friend', in the *Economic Record*, June 1937.

[61] The article was reprinted in E. Cannan, *The Economic Outlook*, in which Cannan commented (p. 29) 'several professors have told me privately that they did not think that my portrait of the Professor in the article resembled them, but it was not intended for them, but for others who have given no sign.'

[62] I owe this bit of information as well as many insights into the Cannan family to Mrs D. Farr.

[63] L. L. Price, 'Memoirs and Notes on British Economists 1881–1947', MS in the Royal Statistical Society, London.

[64] Fay, 'Edwin Cannan; A Tribute to a Friend'.

[65] Marshall misquoted Cannan's *Economic Journal* article of 1894, 'The Growth of Manchester and Liverpool 1801–1891', in the third edition (p. 280 n.), attributing to Cannan a conclusion opposite to the one he actually reached. The sentence was changed in the fourth edition (p. 278 n.) and deleted from the fifth. See Marshall to Cannan, 6 Nov. 1895, in the Cannan Papers, LSE.

blems. Like Ashley, he saw a direct link betwen Ricardo and revolutionary socialist theories. Defence of one was therefore defence of the other. He could not see the advantage in Marshall's sticking to the 'continuity' argument since he did not accept the application of the Comtist definition to theoretical economics. His condemnation of Marshall's stubborness as an impediment may have had nothing to do with the actual contents of Marshall's modifications of Ricardo. The feud would probably have followed a very different course had Marshall forgone the use of Ricardo as an authority and presented the modified theories as his own. Cannan objected to the claim of Ricardo as an authority more than to Marshall's reinterpretation of Ricardo's theories, which was admittedly different from the socialist interpretation. Since both Ricardo and his socialist interpreters were invalid, Cannan could not see the point of claiming him as an authority.

Although Ricardo was considered by Cannan to be a 'prime target', he was not unkind to him or to any of the other 'old' economists when judging them on the basis of the circumstances of their age. T. E. Gregory has said of Cannan's work: 'He may have stripped Smith, Malthus and Ricardo of the mantle of infallibility, but he has clothed them instead with the attributes of humanity.'[66]

The critical nature of *Theories of Production* clearly overpowered any 'kind' references to Ricardo and his work (including Cannan's acceptance of the interpretation of Ricardo according to which wages tended towards an ever-changing standard of living instead of merely the bare necessities). Yet, such 'kindness' was apparent in Cannan's articles 'Ricardo in Parliament', printed in the June and September 1894 issues of the *Economic Journal*. These articles traced Ricardo's career in Parliament in a manner not only devoid of condemnation but in some cases even complimentary, pointing out Ricardo's lack of consideration for his own financial interests in his hostility towards protection. Elsewhere, Cannan went so far as to wonder whether Ricardo's solution for the National Debt, usually considered impractical, would not have resulted in a much more rapid increase in the material welfare of the nation

---

[66] Gregory, 'Edwin Cannan; A Personal Impression'.

in the next seventy years. No 'kinder' appreciation of Ricardo by Cannan was possible than the consideration of his theory on a certain issue as immediately practical.

Marshall's answer to Cunningham's denunciation of theoretical economists did not persuade Cunningham to abandon his line of argument. Instead he chose to restate the 'danger' issue, and once again to challenge Marshall with it. At an introductory lecture at King's College, London, on 13 October 1893,[67] later printed in the *Economic Review* under the title 'Economists as Mischief Makers', he accused Marshall of promoting class hatred. He argued that in the past economists had caused grave harm by wrong analysis and the rash application of invalid theories to practice. Nevertheless 'It may suffice for us to recognize that the economists were in error; we need not assume that they were deliberately aiming at the evil results which came about from the measures they advocated. Yet this seems to be the view which is taken by Professor Marshall of the extreme advocates of laissez faire.'

As before, Cunningham concentrated on the sections in Marshall's *Principles* dealing with the development and nature of the study of economics.[68] However, this time Cunningham did not confine himself to pointing out what he considered to be inaccuracies and mistakes. He argued that Marshall had irresponsibly promoted class bitterness and hostility by presenting class strife as a historically continuous phenomenon. One cannot help feeling that Cunningham was grasping at straws. At one point, where his criticism was directed against a footnote in the *Principles*,[69] he complained: 'It is the indefiniteness of Professor Marshall's language that makes it a matter of complaint . . . a serious charge should surely be put in as definite a form as practicable, so that it may be possible to see at once, how far and of whom and in what place and time it is true.'

Doubtless, Cunningham felt strongly on the issue of presenting class struggle as a historical and therefore possibly an inevitable phenomenon. After all, this was precisely the argu-

[67] W. Cunningham, 'Economists as Mischief Makers', in the *Economic Review*, Jan. 1894.
[68] In the first four editions, Book I, chs. 2 and 3.
[69] In ch. 2, p. 36.

ment the reformist economists hoped to disprove by rejecting Ricardo. Nevertheless, his attack on Marshall was misdirected, since, as he himself admitted, Marshall did not intend that his work should be thus interpreted and the cases of 'careless use of language' for which Cunningham criticized him were few and comparatively unimportant.

By 1894 the controversy slackened. Its eruption was largely due to reaction to the organizational developments which determined the balance of power within the economists' community and indicated the direction of the future. The issues dealt with in the debate concerning the nature of economics could not be decided through discussion at a time when the lines between camps had already been drawn organizationally. Both sides presented their cases to the best of their ability while doubtless remaining convinced, after the various exchanges had taken place, that they were still in the right. Yet on the whole, indulgence in a debate on these issues seemed a luxury at a time when it was felt that extensive research was needed on various problems. Most pronouncements on the subject, after the initial spate of statements, were confined to inaugural and introductory lectures, or to general surveys of the type of Marshall's *Principles*. Cannan could afford to indulge in the pursuit of the various issues raised since he did not have to earn a living as a teacher, whereas those who taught were expected to occupy themselves in the pursuit of different questions. Cunningham's dedication to the cause of disproving Marshall can be gauged by his insistence on using the various introductory and inaugural lectures he gave for continuing the debate and by his ability to get them published.

Both Cannan and Cunningham had invested in the debate something of their own personal dislikes and private grudges. Their tenacity placed them by the mid-1890s in a minority within their own camp. Their fellow relativists and historians, without changing their own views, came to consider the controversy as counter-productive and pointless. Ashley argued that the Cunningham–Marshall exchange was 'almost an anachronism',[70] since unlike Cunningham, he did not accept

---

[70] W. J. Ashley, 'On the Study of Economic History', in the *Quarterly Journal of Economics*, January 1893.

that there was a real threat to historical economics. There were more important things than continuing the debate: 'We might well cry a truce to controvesy as to economic method, if only a band of fit scholars could be attracted into a field which cries out for labourers.'[71]

Similarly the *Economic Journal* showed less and less interest in allocating space for the continuation of the argument. As long as the dispute remained unsettled, it would only serve the enemies of economics in proving that no real consensus existed as to a central core. Accordingly, the attacks on Marshall were to a growing extent published in the *Economic Review*, in book form, and in the American *International Journal of Ethics, Quarterly Journal of Economics*, and *Annals of the American Academy of Political and Social Science*.

The debate on historical relativism was petering out — mainly because of the nature of the debate and the organizational changes of the period, namely, Marshall's camp consolidating its hold on the British Economic Association as the representative body of English economists. Yet the issue of economics and morals still attracted attention. Organizational changes could not decisively determine the issue of economics and morals since, much of it was concerned with the popular image of the science. Thus, in the same work in which Ashley cried for an end to controversy on method, he argued that it was by no means inevitable that political economy should be studied as a 'pure science', as it had been since Adam Smith. He found that 'even English economists have of late found it impossible to restrict themselves to purely "scientific" exposition.' He pointed to the recent example of a group of influential German economists who 'are ready to allow that political economy ought to "treat material interests as subordinate to the higher ends of human development"; and, although the modern definition of these "higher ends" may differ from the mediaeval, in recognizing the need of an ethical standard they occupy substantially the same ground as their theological forerunners.'[72] Although the issue of economics and morals was one of scope and contents, it was not accidental that most of

---

[71] Id., *An Introduction to English Economic History and Theory*, vol. 1, part 2, preface.
[72] Ibid., p. 380. The reference quoted by Ashley is from Brentano.

those who, on these questions, argued for the preservation of 'political economy' rather than replacing it with the Marshallian 'economics' were relativists, whether historians or theoreticians.

The issue was dealt with at the same time as the methodological debate, and in some cases by economists who chose to avoid involvement in the methodological debate although they held strong views on the matter. One such was William Smart in his articles 'The Effects of Consumption of Wealth on Distribution' and 'The Place of Industry in the Social Organism', both published in American journals.[73]

Because the moral issue was strongly linked with the bad public image of their science, economists who were concerned with that image could not very well emphasize the separation of one from the other, a separation which was at the same time considered essential for the scientific status of economics. G. J. Goschen, whose political position made him well aware of the delicacy of the issue, chose it as the subject of his presidential address to the third annual meeting of the British Economic Association on 14 June 1893.[74]

As a politician Goschen could not present the separation of ethics from economics purely on the basis of method and scientific status. Instead, he attacked the moralists as emotionalists who really had no knowledge of the issues they haphazardly dealt with. The cool-headed scientific approach was vital to save the emotionalists from themselves: 'In modifying that younger, that more ethical teaching which if allowed to run riot without the sober, unimpassioned influence of the older school, might in its turn be discredited and be refused even that influence which it deserves.' The bad popular image of economics was, he claimed, mainly due to misunderstandings of the significance of technical devices such as hypotheses or the use of the 'economic man' concept. For in truth 'the attitude of the economist is no less ethical than that of the emotionalist—it is more far seeing, more social. It looks to the good of the community. It is called hard, but it is wise, and it deserves the

---

[73] W. Smart, 'The Effects of Consumption of Wealth on Distribution', in *Annals of the American Academy*, November 1892, and 'The Place of Industry in the Social Organism', in the *International Journal of Ethics*, July 1893.

[74] G. J. Goschen, 'Ethics and Economics', in the *Economic Journal*, September 1893.

general interest.' It was, in fact, the ethical duty of the economist 'to curb the rush of the impatient and the gush of the emotionalist', thereby preventing rash action which might aggravate existing problems, since the economist, in matters such as the poor laws or wage regulations, could see beyond the philanthropist and the amateur.

Seconding a vote of thanks to Goschen, Marshall developed the theme further. He stated that the economist, when weighing human motives, considered moral as well as baser ones. But when it came to the choice of subject for investigation the economist was no more than a technician. It was the student of ethics who set for the economist the problems requiring his attention. In that sense ethics was the mistress of economics — clearly a pose meant for Cambridge internal consumption.

A similar dichotomy was visible within the Statistical Society. However, the secure status of statistics as a recognized and accepted discipline, concerned with the analysis of current problems, freed the leading scientists in the field from the need to explain the separation of statistics from ethics. In his inaugural address as President of the Statistical Society, on 20 November 1894,[75] Lord Farrer found Goshen too apologetic for his taste. In his view, the two subjects could not conflict because they never met. One dealt with what ought to be done, while the other was concerned with what could be done. Yet, Farrer was not a Marshallian, for he was an advocate of induction and of the relativism of theory; he regarded with disapproval the separate establishment of the British Economic Association as well as the publication of the *Economic Journal*. It was incidental that Farrer's statement on method made it clear why the establishment of a separate association was necessary.

Like the question of method, the issue of economics and ethics remained unresolved and was to re-emerge periodically.[76] The Association and the *Journal* became the

---

[75] The Rt. Hon. Lord Farrer, 'The Relations Between Morals, Economics and Statistics', in the *Journal of the Statistical Society*, December 1894. During the period 1887–90 Farrer directed a series of attacks against Goschen's policies as Chancellor of the Exchequer in Lord Salisbury's government. His articles in the *Contemporary Review* were collected and reprinted in 1891, and were made use of in the General Election of 1892.

[76] e.g. J. S. Nicholson in the 1896 meeting of Section F.

recognized representatives of the central core of English economics. Even the Statistical Society soon chose to overlook its original opposition to the economists' declaration of independence. Statisticians came to consider the economists' methodological questions as an external dispute, a sentiment expressed by Sir Rawson Rawson in 1895:[77]

> Whether we claim for our studies the position of a science, an art, or a method, whether political economy be or not be the handmaiden of ethics, whether economics be an abstract science or altogether dependent on statistics for the data on which it depends as a foundation whereon to build its laws, the changing conditions of society will always furnish to statistics problems whose solutions must be uncertain unless it be based on the evidence not solely of *a priori* reasoning but also on ascertained facts.

Thus, by the mid-1880s, the historical relativists and the moralists gradually found themselves in an increasingly isolated situation, both organizationally and methodologically.

[77] In the *Journal of the Statistical Society*, 1895.

8
THE ALTERNATIVES FACING THE DISSENTERS

By the end of 1894, the struggle of relativists and historical economists against the increasing dominance of the Marshall school over English economics seemed more futile than ever. Their frustration was expressed by Cunningham in his article 'Why had Roscher so little influence in England?',[1] printed in the United States. In a revealing passage he described the plight of the dissenting economists, coloured, no doubt, by his own bitterness:[2]

> Those who choose to refuse to conform to the reigning fashion in the community in which they live, must expect to be ostracized, and the tryanny of intellectual fashions is even more supercilious than that of Bond Street and Savile Row. Anyone who has refused to follow the economic fashion of recent years in England must have been greatly hampered in his efforts to pursue his own studies or guide those of others; boards of studies would exercise a galling control, and editors and publishers would view his writing with suspicion. That is the natural fate of those who do not swim with the stream.

Cunningham denounced conciliation as a sham:

> the more recent English economist likes to make references to history and airy remarks about history. Mr. Price seems to think that in this way the results of the work of the historical school can be incorporated into the main body of economic tradition, [but] theorists, who are satisfied with doctrines that are curiously unreal for the present day, can hardly be expected to take much pains to be true to life in their explanations of the past.

Summing up his objections to the 'new' theory, Cunningham returned to the criteria of applicability. The 'old' theories had a limited and well-defined application, viz. to conditions of completely free competition. There was no doubt as to when and where they were to be used, since it was obvious that under some circumstances the theories were of no use at

---

[1] W. Cunningham 'Why has Roscher so little influence in England?', in *Annals of the American Academy of Political and Social Science*, November 1894.
[2] One consequence of his frustration was his move in 1895 to St. Andrews.

all, while under other circumstances they were of only partial use. In contrast, the new form of analysis—Marshall's organon—was presented as a universal tool: 'but it gives no guidance to show for what particular place or time any given result is true or untrue . . . the relations . . . with actual life are more vague and indefinite than ever.' The universal form of the 'new' theory did not guarantee universal applicability. Marshall and his disciples were confusing formal validity with factual truth. Despite the soundness of the structure, it was useless for present purposes as well as impractical in the study of the past. While conveniently overlooking his 'Pure Theory' argument, Cunningham complained that the historian's position regarding theory had been greatly misrepresented. Despite what L. L. Price or Marshall might have said, no historian claimed to discard theory as valueless. Theories, either as hypotheses or as general laws, were indispensable. But that did not hold for theories such as Marshall's organon, which Cunningham found to be inapplicable to the historian's work. Although Cunningham showed signs of weariness, he refused to admit total defeat: 'Intellectual fashions are changeful too, and the reaction against the dominant English school has already set in.'

In retrospect, one of the major problems facing the dissenters' camp, apart from the lack of an organizational base, was lack of leadership. There was no figure of unquestioned professional authority in their camp who could bring unity and cohesion to their arguments and at the same time co-ordinate the struggle over academic recognition and the establishment of university posts. Ashley, who had proved his ability at Toronto, might have filled such a position had he been elected to the Drummond Professorship in 1891, but his failure kept him well removed from the debate both physically and in his work. Two other dissenters established themselves in London professorships—Foxwell at University College and Cunningham at King's College. Here again, one might speculate, a chance was missed when Cunningham was preferred to Hewins in the elections to the Tooke Professorship in 1891. Whatever Cunningham's qualities may have been, he was not the person to inspire or lead a school.

Cunningham's professional eminence was readily admitted

by fellow historical economists. In 1891 Ashley wrote:[3] 'Any one who is acquainted with recent English political economy knows that for the last decade, Mr. Cunningham has been the sturdy and even aggressive critic of the dominant abstract school, the advocate of a more historical or "empirical" study of social phenomena.' Yet, as his 'Pure Theory' suggestions revealed, Cunningham's methodological position was very different, and only considerable manoeuvring made it compatible with that of his colleagues. In the review quoted above, Ashley pointed out that Cunningham's main fault was his failure to incorporate in his work the concept of the evolution of institutions and ideas. This led Ashley, in a later review of Cunningham's work,[4] to point out what to a Comtist would seem obvious and serious faults:

> We are throughout confronted with details of new projects, new manufactures, new legislation. There is little description of the broad features of the industrial organization of each period; little attempt to disentangle the larger and more stable conditions from the minor and temporary . . . , the narrative . . . creates a sense of confusion, an impression of perpetual flux, which is probably far from the truth.

In a review of the same work Hewins[5] concentrated on the problem of applying Cunningham's 'Pure Theory' to historical research:

> It may be said at once that, as a method of scientific investigation of the countless problems of economic and social history, the course which Dr. Cunningham has proposed to adopt is worthless. It would lead to nothing more than a chronicle of events with perhaps a summary of contemporary arguments for and against any proposed change. This would be interesting . . . but would explain nothing we wish to understand.

Fortunately, as Hewins pointed out, Cunningham had not been consistent and did not actually adhere, in his work, to his own methodological scheme.

As an economic historian Cunningham was hailed by Ashley as a guide rather than as a leader, an attitude reminiscent of

---

[3] W. J. Ashley, 'Cunningham's Growth of English Industry', in the *Political Science Quarterly*, March 1893.
[4] Id., review of Cunningham's *The Growth of English Industry and Commerce in Modern Times*, in *Political Science Quarterly*, March 1893.
[5] W. A. S. Hewins, review of Cunningham's *Growth of English Industry*, in the *Economic Review*, September 1892.

Oxford's young economists' attitude towards Thorold Rogers. The importance of his work lay not in his conclusions, which were debatable, but in its direction: 'To a small but growing body of students who are interested in economic history, it is the utmost service that a competent scholar should have sketched out for them a rough plan of the area to be examined, should have drawn up a programme to guide them.'[6] It was a tribute, despite major disagreements on the interpretation of historical facts such as Cunningham's acceptance of the Mark theory, which was fiercely rejected by Ashley.

Another major flaw in Cunningham's character was his temper. A regrettable lack of courtesy towards professional disputants prevailed throughout his work. He had, without doubt, strong feelings on the issues he debated, but he was unable to curb his use of what was often offensive language. He was not able, like Marshall, to avoid unnecessary confrontations. In the review quoted above, Hewins pointed to Cunningham's lack of courtesy towards the dead Thorold Rogers:[7] 'I am not sure that he would attach much weight to the opinion of the late Professor Thorold Rogers, but surely he should have taken the trouble to allude to him in a footnote.'

Cunningham took two years to answer the criticism contained in Hewins's review.[8] Whilst rejecting some of the accusations of inaccuracy as groundless, he wrote rather testily: 'Is it possible that it was the critic who wrote in haste? It is a pity, but it seems to be the common experience of authors who look to reviews for something else than indiscriminate praise or unintelligent fault finding that they often look in vain.'

A similar show of bad temper can be found elsewhere in a review of Ashley's work[9] in which Cunningham revealed his resentment of Ashley's adoption of a conciliatory position while removing himself from the methodological debate:

[6] W. J. Ashley, review of Cunningham's *Growth of English Industry* in the *Political Science Quarterly*, 1893.

[7] Reflecting Rogers's lack of consideration of Cunningham in his review of Cunningham's first edition of 'English Industry and Commerce', in the *Academy*, 20 May 1882.

[8] W. Cunningham, 'Dr. Cunningham and his Critics', in the *Economic Journal*, September 1894.

[9] Id. 'A New Contribution to Economic History; Ashley's English Economic History', in the *Political Science Quarterly*, 1891.

In the freer atmosphere of the New World |Ashley| can even allow himself the luxury of bestowing good advice on fellow workers who are forced to engage in controversies on method . . . So long as practical influences exclude those who devote themselves to political economy as an empirical science from taking part in teaching or writing on modern affairs, the controversy about method is likely to continue.

Such remarks may have antagonized some of Cunningham's Cambridge contemporaries but they were not taken too seriously by his fellow historical economists. The tribute they paid to his work remained unchanged[10] and they seem to have been careful not to manifest their disagreements unnecessarily.[11]

Like Ashley, Hewins chose to avoid involvement in the methodological debate although he was clearly unhappy with the inferior position allotted to economic history. In January 1892 he wrote to his brother Fred:[12] 'Economic history as a rule bears as much relation to what it ought to be as a dead goose prepared for cooking to the glorious creature that fed on the Common.' Nevertheless, he could not afford to enter the fray, since he had not yet secured an academic position. He was becoming increasingly disenchanted with the Extension movement, realizing that it was unlikely to achieve the aims he and his fellow Oxford economists had hoped for during the mid-eighties. He was unable to persuade Pembroke College to give him a teaching position. He had tried unsuccessfully for the position of Bursar at St. John's College and for the job of Secretary to the Publishing Department of the National Liberal Federation.[13]

By the mid-1890s, while still an Extension lecturer, Hewins had begun to build up an academic reputation. In 1892 his book *English Trade and Finance* (which Ashley promised 'to sound his trumpet for' in Germany and in America[14]) was published, followed by an increasing number of articles for Palgrave's *Dictionary*, mostly on sixteenth- to seventeenth-English economic history. In 1894 he was appointed Public

---

[10] e.g. W. J. Ashley's article, 'The Historical School', in R. H. Inglis Palgrave (ed.), *Dictionary of Political Economy*, vol. 2 (London, 1893), p. 313.
[11] Hewins papers 43/104, C. Firth to W. A. S. Hewins, 21 Nov. 1892.
[12] Hewins papers 43/87–8.
[13] Ibid. 43/45–9, 41/253.
[14] Ibid., 10/27.

Examiner for the University and in the same year he became a member of Section F and was asked to read a paper at its annual meeting.[15] Taking a strong public position in the debate might have jeopardized any future chances for an academic position. But although he did not advertise it, his position remained basically unchanged throughout the debate.

By 1894 the institutional position of the young dissenting economists seemed hopeless. At Oxford the History Studies Board prevented any change in the status of the study of economics.[16] Edgeworth, the Drummond Professor, would not be prodded into action on the matter. Elsewhere in England the situation seemed much the same. Few jobs were available, but whenever an academic position was vacated it went, more often than not, to one of Marshall's followers. Change, however, did come from an unexpected quarter when on 29 March 1895 Hewins was approached by Sidney Webb on behalf of the Hutchinson Trust with the offer of the Directorship of the planned London School of Economics and Political Science at a salary of £300 per annum.[17]

The Hutchinson Trust was set up in September 1894, with Sidney Webb as its chairman, to deal with the manner in which nearly £10,000 left to the Fabian Society by the eccentric Hutchinson should be used. At first there were serious doubts as to the legal validity of Hutchinson's will. The Trust was concerned with the possibility that the family might claim it to be null on the grounds of Hutchinson's possible insanity (he had committed suicide).[18] Webb was also concerned with the uncertainty as to the legal standing of the Fabian Society and the specified use of the estate for the promotion of socialism. Haldane set his mind at rest on the legal aspects[19] and the family raised no objections to the will, the Trust having moved to increase the sum left in the will to members of Hutchinson's immediate family.[20]

[15] Ibid., 10/38-9.
[16] Hewins, *The Apologia of an Imperialist*, p. 24.
[17] Hewins papers 43/131. See also LSE School Archives, Hutchinson Trust Minute Book, vol. i.
[18] Nuffield College, Oxford, Fabian papers, A. F. Constance Hutchinson to E. R. Pease, 23 Aug. 1894, A2, S. Webb to Pease, 3 and 25 Aug. 1894
[19] For a detailed account, see Sir Sidney Caine, *The History of the Foundation of the London School of Economics and Political Science* (London 1963).
[20] Fabian Papers, Executive Committee Minutes C5, 28 Sept. 1895.

Nevertheless, Webb decided to try to keep the Trust's existence as secret as possible. It was his feeling from the start that the money must not be wasted on the routine operation of the Fabian Society. On 25 August 1894 he wrote to E. R. Pease, the Society's secretary and a fellow trustee:

> The view that I take very strongly is that . . . the Trustees ought to make it a strict rule not to help the ordinary current purposes of the Society (or else we shall merely dry up all other contributions and thus gain nothing at all) but that my fund should be kept exclusively for special work of a large kind . . . I should like to attract the clever young economists to the working out of Collectivism and thus get some 'research' done.
>
> After all, the lecturing and tract distributing comes to naught unless there is some solid work of costly but not showy character going on behind it. Unless we can 'keep the sacred fire' there will be no sparks to carry about presently, and the whole thing will peter out.[21]

For a number of years the Society had been interested in attracting 'the clever young economists'[22] to its work. It had tried to do so through invitations to lecture at Cliffords Inn and Essex Hall, but with limited success. Therefore, if the setting up of an active research body was indeed of primary importance, it necessitated a different organizational approach.

The idea of the School probably came to Webb through his interest in organizing a lecture scheme through the Technical Education Board which he chaired. The TEB had been set up as a result of the adoption by the London County Council, through a committee set up to consider how the Council should proceed under the 1890 Technical Instruction Act, of a report compiled by Hubert Llewellyn Smith,[23] then Secretary of the National Association for the Promotion of Technical Education. Having secured the right to promote the teaching of practically any subject,[24] the TEB in 1894 went beyond promotion and co-ordination, and instituted a course of lectures given by William Cunningham for clerks of subscribers and held under the auspices of the Chamber of Commerce at its rooms in

---

[21] Fabian Papers, Executive Committee Minutes C5, 28 Sept. 1895.

[22] Ibid., C5, 31 Aug. 1895. For the autumn 1894 courses the Executive Committee considered E. C. K. Gonner, J. Bonar, W. M. Acworth, and E. Cannan.

[23] See H. Ll. Smith, 'The Teaching of London; A Scheme for Technical Instruction', in the *Contemporary Review*, May 1892.

[24] Beatrice Webb, *Our Partnership* (London, 1948), p. 80.

Eastcheap.[25] It was probably for the purpose of extending the courses that Webb first consulted Hewins.

According to Beatrice Webb,[26] the Webbs first met Hewins at Oxford while they were gathering material for *The History of Trade Unionism*. They had come up to Oxford as the guests of David Ritchie and were hoping to find material in the Bodleian Library. When they found the librarian unco-operative, Hewins, who at the time was reading in the library, offered his help. It may have been the first time the Webbs had noticed Hewins, but it was clearly not the first time he had encountered them. They were frequent visitors to Oxford and at least twice had addressed the Oxford Social Science Club. On one of these occasions Hewins was present in his capacity as secretary.[27] When approached by Webb in 1894 he was probably asked for advice on organizing lectures on the basis of his Extension experience. Some of that experience may be detected in the scheme drawn up for the London School of Economics.

When Sidney Webb conceived the idea of the School late in 1894, he sought to start it as a development of the TEB lecturing scheme. He felt that he had to conceal its ideological purposes when he presented the scheme to the TEB and the Chamber of Commerce. At the same time he hoped to reassure the Fabian Society that the money of the Trust was being used for its stipulated purpose. Partly in order to pre-empt objections to the School within the Fabian Society, a part of the Trust was used to finance a scheme of Fabian lectures in the provinces. These occasional lectures, given before 1895, bore a close resemblance to the Extension lectures given by the Oxford economists. Their purpose was:

> ... to encourage and assist the study of questions connected with the industrial and social organization of Society. They treat these subjects both from a historical and from a comparative standpoint. They are primarily educational in character, and are only propagandist to this extent, that the

---

[25] Hutchinson Trust Minute Book, Excerpt from the Agenda of TEB 6 May 1895; Report of Finance and General Purposes Committee.

[26] *Our Partnership*, p.8

[27] One meeting was held in Sidney Ball's rooms at St. John's on 9 Feb. 1889. Hewins was one of the signatories on the invitation which is in the Bodleian Library. Another meeting is noted in Hewins's pocket diary on 25 Jan. 1890 in the Hewins Papers Box 203. See also Hewins, *Apologia*, p. 16.

lecturer will not merely state the problem and explain its difficulties, but also indicate the manner in which he considers it can best be solved.[28]

Thus the scheme did not suffer from two handicaps Hewins had detected in the Oxford Extension system—it was avowedly political and it did not aim at the systematization and development of academically more advanced studies.

Like the Extension lectures, each Fabian lecture included a syllabus and a book box which could be lent to local societies and organizations. It even offered the option of correspondence classes. The lectures were intended for co-operative societies, trade unions, political associations and clubs, socialist societies, or committees formed specifically for the purpose of organizing such lectures. Finally, thanks to the Hutchinson Trust, the lectures and the syllabuses were free of charge. Ideally, Webb argued, the whole work of educating the nation towards the adoption of collectivism should be done by nationwide lecturing of the Extension type. However, there was no staff of lecturers available, and it was one of the purposes of the planned school to create such a staff. Like many of the Oxford Extension lecturers, the Webbs believed that a rational person presented with the facts and the tools to analyse them could not but reach inevitable conclusions (in their case, collectivism[29]). They conceived the influence of Fabianism to be directly related to their ability to present their case and attract the right audience, to collect and analyse the facts, and to make their findings known.

On 8 February 1895 Sidney Webb presented the Hutchinson Trustees with a set of proposals[30] which, when adopted by the Trust, became the platform of the London School of Economics and Political Science. Discussing the needs and the future of the collectivist movement, Webb argued that political change and the transformation of society would come about through the education of society as a whole:

The greatest needs of the Collectivist movement in England appear to me: (a) An increase in the number of *educated* and able lecturers and writers, as apart from propagandist speakers.

[28] LSE, the Hutchinson Trust Minute Book I.
[29] LSE Archives, Herbert Samuel, 'Reminiscences of former students'.
[30] The Hutchinson Trust Minute Book I.

(b) The further investigation of problems of municipal and national administration from a Collectivist standpoint. This implies original research, and the training of additional persons competent to do such work.
(c) The diffusion of economic and political knowledge of a real kind—as apart from Collectivist shibboleths and the cant and claptrap of political campaigning.
All this means attracting and training clever recruits, setting them to do work on social problems, and then using them to educate the people. Ten years of this work might change the whole political thinking of England.

The first choice for the Directorship was Graham Wallas who as unanimously appointed by the Trustees on 8 February 1895. However, by 28 March he had notified them that he was unable to accept the appointment and after a discussion it was agreed to offer it to W. A. S. Hewins, who until that point had been consulted by Webb on the organization of the School. Hewins was offered the position of Director, with pay to start on 1 April 1895. The job would entail one or more courses of lectures, the editorship of a series of books consisting of original studies and, possibly, translations and reprints, and the assurance that as the School grew his position as Director would grow with it. Unless Hewins accepted, so he was told, the whole scheme would probably have to be abandoned.[31]

At that point it was clear to Hewins that Oxford Extension lecturing had not, and could not, live up to earlier expectations. Operating on its own, it had failed to establish thorough or systematic courses where they were most needed—in England's large industrial centres. It was unable to stimulate even the best students to continue their studies and was unable to popularize advanced courses. What was needed were centres in which advanced studies would be pursued. This concept was clearly stated in the first prospectus Hewins drew up for the School, which he presented the Trustees with on 29 July 1895. In it he included in the class of students which the School hoped to attract 'Those students who have already, by means of University Extension Lectures or otherwise, gained some acquaintance with economic and political science will be able to pursue their studies under the direction of experts'. A small number of scholarships was offered to Extension students and indeed the very first students included five women who fol-

---

[31] Ibid. S. Webb to W. A. S. Hewins, 29 Mar. 1895 (copy).

lowed Graham Wallas from the Extension.[32] As in the Extension, the first courses were given after regular working hours to enable working men and women to attend. The public was offered various courses with fees charged for each course separately.

The lessons of the failure of the Extension's course certificate system may have been partly responsible for the School's orginal avoidance of any university connection.[33] It did not intend to fill the gap in the curriculum of the older universities, and its courses were not intended as preparation for a University of London degree. Past experience had taught Hewins how difficult it was to reform the curriculum of a university through campaigning for a change in its examination system. In any event academic qualifications were not the initial purpose of the School's training. The School was primarily intended as a research training centre in social problems, aimed at creating a cadre of trained social researchers and serving as a centre for such research. Accordingly, Hewins's proposal of the ideally qualified teacher was not confined to academic qualifications but added to them 'special acquaintance with one subject, a thorough grasp of economic theory, and the history of at least English industry and commerce, some knowledge of the world, experience in investigation and research, ability as a lecturer, and some capacity for organisation'.[34]

From the outset it was clear that the School would become the centre of the dissenting economists. Reflecting on the School's early days, Sidney Webb commented, 'I was in revolt against one Professor of Economics; I wanted a lot of Professors.'[35] One of his reasons for choosing Hewins was that 'he was not a Cambridge orthodox person', while W. M. Acworth and Cunningham were brought in 'to counteract Marshall'. It was believed by some that the intellectual resources of economic dissent would be the School's main source of strength.[36]

---

[32] Introduction by W. H. Beveridge to *The London School of Economics and Political Science Register 1895–1932* (London, 1934), p. vii.
[33] Ibid., and S. Webb, 24 Nov. 1932 in 'Reminiscences of former students'.
[34] Hewins, 'The Teaching of Economics', *Journal of the Society of Arts*, 4 Dec. 1896.
[35] S. Webb, 24 Nov. 1932 in 'Reminiscences of former students'.
[36] e.g. Hewins papers 43/188, W. S. Bauer to W. A. S. Hewins, 14 May 1895.

THE ALTERNATIVES FACING THE DISSENTERS 253

At the same time it was Webb's concern that the School should not be closely identified with the Fabian Society lest it should acquire an image of a body dedicated to radical propaganda and undermine any chance of being accepted as a serious institute of scientific research. His instructions to E. R. Pease on the matter were:

> I think that the Fabian Society had better be kept *quite* out of it for the moment; hence please be absolutely discreet. The right answer is to say that it is done by trustees, of whom Webb is Chairman. It is better not even to give the names of trustees . . . It is vital to get started without any compromising suspicion.[37]

Giving the School a clear ideological character could undermine the whole project in a number of other ways. During its early stage of development a neutral image was essential in order to secure the co-operation of the Chamber of Commerce.[38] It was also feared that a radical image might scare away potential middle-class students and staff. Some years later, when the School assumed a more academic character, such an image might have jeopardized academic recognition and incorporation into the reconstituted University of London. This concern for the School's neutral image, despite some strong misgivings from within the Fabian Society,[39] resulted in the creation of a separate body of Trustees, identical in membership to the Hutchinson Trustees but officially independent of the supervision of the other members of the Fabian Society's Executive Committee.[40]

Discretion was also evident in the School's recruitment of support. For instance, when Cunningham, who was in turn concerned with recruiting Foxwell for the Technical Education Board and Chamber of Commerce lectures, was told about the School and asked by Hewins for his support, he wrote that he was delighted with the scheme and promised to keep silent about the whole project.[41] Support from Cunningham and Foxwell[42] was secured at quite an early stage when the School

---

[37] Fabian Papers, A2, S. Webb to Pease, 9 June 1895.
[38] Hewins papers 43/194, the Chamber of Commerce to W. A. S. Hewins, 17 May 1895.
[39] LSE Passfield papers, G. B. Shaw to S. Webb, 1 July 1895.
[40] The Hutchinson Trust Minute Book, entry for 10 Feb. 1896.
[41] Hewins papers 43/143, W. Cunningham to W. A. S. Hewins, 14 Apr. 1895.
[42] Hewins papers 43/207, Foxwell to W. A. S. Hewins, 25 May 1895.

was still being discussed in terms of an extension of the TEB courses. About the same time Hewins brought in H. Mackinder from the Oxford Extension movement.[43] A. L. Bowley recorded a meeting on 8 June 1895 in Oxford where Hewins told him, Ashley, and some others about the scheme.[44] It was probably around the same time that Edwin Cannan and L. T. Hobhouse was recruited.

The scheme offered the dissenters a unique and enticing opportunity despite uncertainty about its future. Instead of teaching to prepare students for an antiquated examination system which would qualify them for a useless degree, they were offered an opportunity to teach the subjects they were most interested in to students who would seek to utilize their knowledge. A flexible curriculum meant that they could continue research and publish their results via the School and the Trust. In view of the professional and ideological attractions of the School, it is no surprise that its regular staff from 1895 included Foxwell, and Cannan. Hobhouse, who was an occasional lecturer during the years 1896–7 became a regular lecturer in 1904. Occasional lecturers (who were not regular members of staff) included W. J. Ashley (1898–9),[45] W. Cunningham (1895–6, 1900–1, 1913–15), J. A. Hobson (1896–7, 1914–16), H. Ll. Smith (1897–8) and Hewins's Oxford tutor Charles Firth (1896–7). In later years F. S. Marvin (1915–16) and M. E. Sadler (1903–13) were added.

Marshall was naturally suspicious of the School. Although some of his suspicions were allayed, he could not refrain from the disparaging remark, on seeing the School's programme, that it was compiled to suit the lecturers who were available, and did not present a systematic organization of subjects.[46] This basic difference in approach was soon to disappear when the School adopted in 1898, as one of its purposes, the preparation for a University of London BA degree. Over the next few years Marshall remained suspicious of the Webbs,[47] although

---

[43] S. Webb, 24 Nov. 1932 in 'Reminiscences of former students'.
[44] A. L. Bowley, 'Early Days of the L.S.E.', Hewins papers 44/94, W. J. Ashley to W. A. S. Hewins, 19 Sept. 1895.
[45] At the time Ashley was on a sabbatical from Harvard where his courses were given by Cunningham.
[46] LSE, A. L. Bowley, 'Early Days of the L.S.E.'.
[47] See Fay, 'Edwin Cannan; The Tribute of a Friend'.

his suspicion was not shared by all the economists who accepted his leadership in professional matters. Occasional lecturers during the School's early years included F. Y. Edgeworth (1896–1900), Robert Giffen (1898–9), E. C. K. Gonner (1896–8), and R. H. Inglis Palgrave (1900–1). Minimal exposure of its dissenting character during its early years and academic and financial independence ensured that whatever misgivings Marshall and his supporters may have had they could not ignore its existence or the value of its contribution to the study of economics in England, although an anti-Cambridge bias survived, at least on Webb's part, for some years to come.[48]

During the School's first year traces of its original purpose could still be found. At a meeting of the Hutchinson Trustees on 29 July 1895 it was agreed that members of the London Fabian Society would be granted tickets to any of the courses at half the fees, the Trustees making up the difference to the School.[49] During the School's first year the ratio between Fabians and non-Fabians was 1 to 6[50]; however, after a few years the arrangement lapsed through lack of interest.[51] Sidney Webb had anticipated that since the first few years of the School would be dedicated to research and the training of a young team of research students, the benefits to the cause of collectivism would not immediately be noticed. Nevertheless, once teaching began it must have become obvious that more would be required if the working classes were to be drawn towards the School. During September 1895 Webb passed on to Hewins a suggestion made by S. G. Hobson of the Independent Labour Party[52] that the School should capitalize on the fact that Oxford would not be holding an Extension summer meeting in 1896. The School should hold one in London and draw 'some hundreds of Co-opertaors, Trade Unionists and Socialists from the provinces' to extend its own influence to the working-class leadership in the provinces. By the time the

[48] S. Webb, 24 Nov. 1932, in 'Reminiscences of former students'. Discussing the question of appointing a Director after Mackinder, he commented: 'We did not want a Cambridge economist.'
[49] Hutchinson Minute Book, entry for 29 July 1895.
[50] Fabian Papers, W. A. S. Hewins to E. R. Pease, 29 Oct. 1895.
[51] E. R. Pease, Sept. 1943 in 'Reminiscences of former students'.
[52] Hewins papers 44/91, S. Webb to W. A. S. Hewins, 9 Sept. 1895.

meeting's prospectus was written, the intention of reaching the provincial working-class leadership was diluted into an opportunity offered 'to those who live at a distance from centres of systematic study . . . of obtaining guidance in their work'.[53] The School was becoming increasingly introverted, and the other two purposes described in the prospectus for the summer meeting were the supplementation of the School's work and an informal conference on the best means of promoting the scientific study of the subjects taught at the School.

The nature of the shift in emphasis was expressed early in 1896 by Beatrice Webb in her diary:[54]

> Now we collectivists have to assert ourselves as a distinct school of thought, taking up each question separately and reviewing it in the light of our principles. But the first need of a school of thought is to think. Our special mission seems to be to undertake the difficult problems ourselves, and to gather round us young men and women who will more or less study under inspiration.

The change in emphasis also meant a change in the class of students the School hoped to attract. From the outset the School was intended to cater for two different classes—the working-class advanced student who sought the knowledge that would assist him in advancing the cause of his class and the lower-middle-class professional men who sought technical and commercial training. It was for the second class of students that the original TEB and Chamber of Commerce courses were started. Courses on railway economics and commercial law survived the disappearance of the aspiration to reach a working-class audience.

The disappearance of the 'education of a working-class élite' cause was due partly to the School's actual inability to attract a significant number of working-class students. When Hewins came to describe the School's student population after one year's work[55] no mention was made of the working class. Instead, it consisted of:

---

[53] The prospectus is in the Oxford Extension Movement Archive, Rewley House, Oxford.
[54] *Our Partnership*, p. 128.
[55] The report is quoted in Hewins, 'The Teaching of Economics'. Other observations on the early student population may be found in Bowley, 'Early Days of the L.S.E.' and in Beveridge's introduction to *The L.S.E. Register 1895–1932*.

those who desire the guidance of experts on particular subjects. The students consist of graduates of British and foreign universities, women students of the universities, and are mainly engaged in the research department of the school, and of civil servants, local government officials, young men and women engaged in business, bank managers and clerks, teachers and other persons engaged in public work.

At least on the part of the Webbs, the change was also due to a change in policy. Frustration and disappointment in the policy adopted by the ILP during the General Election of 1895, and despair of the Liberal Party, led Beatrice Webb to reflect in a diary entry for 8 July 1895:[56] 'The Labour men are mere babies in politics; judging from our knowledge of the Labour Movement we can expect *no* leader from the working class. Our only hope is in permeating the young middle-class men — catching them for collectivism before they have enlisted on the other side.' And in an entry later that year:[57] 'We have turned our hopes from propaganda to education, from the working class to the middle class.' The recruiting and training of promising middle-class men and women in the cause of collectivism was one of the purposes of the LSE as understood by Beatrice Webb.[58] The need felt to create an alternative programme of social reform based on careful scientific research, coupled with the training of young teams of scholars in research and its applications, explains some of the changes in the School's direction during its first year of existence.

Hewins's change in attitude towards the Liberal Party appears to have coincided with that of the Webbs. Like most of his fellow members in the Oxford Economic Society, he had been an ardent Liberal when at Oxford. In April 1891, in the by-elections for the mid-Oxfordshire seat, he had campaigned on behalf of G. R. Benson (the future first Baron Charnwood) — an Oxford contemporary, a Gladstonian Liberal, and a staunch Home Ruler. Benson's last-minute campaign (he had been in Spain when the vacancy was declared) relied heavily on young Oxford volunteers. Hewins was part of a larger party of young Liberals which included G. B. Dibblee (then at All Souls), H. E. A. Cotton (of Jesus College), and Herbert L.

---

[56] *Our Partnership*, p. 125.
[57] Ibid., p. 125.
[58] Ibid., p. 92.

Samuel and Louis Stuart (both of Balliol).[59] During the next few years he continued to support the Liberal Party and as late as January 1894 he became a member of the Oxford Liberal Association. This was changed by the General Election of 1895, after which he wrote to his mother: 'Five years ago it was not difficult to see that unless the Liberal party mended its ways it must be sooner or later destroyed. The catastrophe has come more quickly than I anticipated.'[60]

The failure of the Liberal Party caused Hewins to begin a political transition which would eventually lead to his resignation as the School's Director in order to serve the cause of tariff reform. Why he did not move in the other direction towards the ILP becomes fairly clear when his early political ideals are examined. His Extension work was from the outset seen as a way of countering the cause of revolutionary radicalism among the working classes. He was a supporter of gradual social reform and by 1895 it seemed that the means previously employed to draw the working classes away from revolutionary radicalism had failed. It was previously believed that trade unionism and the co-operative movement would lead the working classes to abandon revolutionary solutions in favour of a gradual transformation of society. But although the new unionism supported by Hewins and other Extension lecturers was thriving, the young labour movement did not consider means such as co-operation and trade unionism as final. The passing in 1893 and 1894 of the socialist resolution by the TUC to support only candidates pledged to 'the collective ownership and control of the means of production, distribution and exchange'[61] and the rejection by the ILP of any co-operation with the Liberal Party, meant that despite co-operation, unionism, and the various other solutions offered by liberalism to the plight of the working classes, the latter were still drawn to seek redress by revolutionary means.

[59] *Oxford Chronicle*, 18 and 25 Apr. 1891. Hewins is reported to have addressed a rally at Beckley in the course of which he referred to parish councils (the cause of the National Church Reform Union) and allotments as the issues requiring immediate attention. The seat was won by the Tory candidate G. H. Morrell.
[60] Hewins papers 10/42, W. A. S. Hewins to his mother, 19 July 1895.
[61] Henry Pelling, *A History of British Trade Unionism* (3rd edn., London, 1976), p. 107.

Hewins did not share the Webbs' suspicions of Chamberlain's social reform schemes. Like the rest of the young Oxford economists, he opposed Chamberlain on the Home Rule issue during the mid-eighties, but the political issues of the mid-nineties were significantly different. Chamberlains' programme for reform provided a political alternative to the Liberal Party, which seemed unable to produce a similar comprehensive reform programme. For the young economists a comprehensive programme was as essential then as it had been during the early 1880s with the re-emergence of the threat of political class antagonism. However, whereas in the past they had laid emphasis on working-class self-help, while arguing that state intervention should be kept minimal, they now shifted emphasis to assign greater importance to state intervention. Reforms were to be initiated by the state and financed by the nation through various means, one of which was imperial preference. This, it was argued by its advocates, would bring in much needed revenue to finance reform, revitalize home and colonial production, and promote the strength and solidarity of the Empire.

Imperial preference as presented by Chamberlain at the time[62] was a rejection of free trade on practical grounds. He argued that the principle of free trade was at present inapplicable to international commerical circumstances—the failure of most of the world to adopt it and Britain's growing isolation. The establishment of a modified form of free trade throughout the Empire would be a step towards a possible future of universal free trade. It would be one more way in which the Empire would serve as a model for the future development of the rest of the world. Hewins's shift towards emphasizing the future role of the state in social reform is demonstrated in his plans to contribute to the studies in economics and political science, published by the School, a collection of documents illustrating state regulation of wages.[63] The change in his position on free

---

[62] e.g. in his speech, 'Commercial Union of the Empire', to the Congress of Chambers of Commerce of the Empire, London 9 June 1896, in C. W. Boyd (ed.), *Mr. Chamberlain's Speeches* (London, 1914).

[63] Advertisement, in Edwin Cannan, *The History of Local Rates in England* (London, 1896)—the first study published in the series edited by Hewins.

trade and the tariff is revealed in his article in Inglis Palgrave's *Dictionary*.

In his article 'English Early Economic History', published in 1894[64], Hewins wrote: 'The vast increase in the wealth of the country, and the greater ease with which large sums can be raised by taxation, have made inapplicable to the present age the practical suggestions of the mercantilist writers.' In 1896 he was to write:[65] 'It is conceivable . . . that . . . so far as England . . . is concerned there might be some return to mercantilist principles if a definite attempt were made to carry into effect a scheme of imperial federation.' In the same article he pointed out the similarities between the mercantile system and state socialism. The main difference between the two was their respective purposes. The mercantile system aimed at national self-sufficiency, whereas the end of state socialism was 'the improvement of the lot of the wage earners'. If the nation were to adopt as an ideal the aims of state socialism it could still employ many of the means advocated by the mercantilists, including the regulation of industry and commerce 'with a view to national interests as distinct from those of the consumer'.

The argument employed by Hewins reveals an attempt to preserve the premises of his social ideology with a shift of ground on the question of its practical implementation. In later years he was to argue[66] that the imperial movement represented a 'revolt against the individualist conception of society in this country and an effort to express in a practical form new social conceptions in their application to the . . . British Empire'. In terms of Hewins's educational work the change meant that the Extension ideal of educating the working class was outdated. It was unrealistic in practical terms and since the ideal of self-help had in reality fallen short of the hopes entertained during the eighties, it was also politically pointless. Change would be sought instead through the state on the basis of plans worked out and executed by the middle classes.

[64] W. A. S. Hewins, 'Early English Economic History', in the *Dictionary of Political Economy*, vol. 1, part 6 (London, 1894), p. 726.
[65] 'Mercantile System', ibid., vol. 2 (London, 1896). In the article Hewins refers to Ashley's translation of Schmoller's 'Mercantile System', published in 1896 so that the article must have been written during 1896.
[66] Hewins, *The Apologia*, p. 3.

During roughly the same period Ashley, who, since moving to Canada and then to the United States, had become increasingly interested in local economic developments, revived an old interest in imperialism. By his own admission[67] he had first become interested in the imperial cause while at Oxford, but after his move to Canada his imperialism became temporarily dormant:

> At Oxford I read Seeley and paid 2/6 to the Imperial League. In Toronto it seemed absolutely hopeless; the rising generation of Canadians were as a matter of fact brought too little into contact with England to really think about her. Of late my residence in the U.S. has worked up the John Bull within me, so that I feel a keener desire for British unity. And the recent Canadian tariff had made me feel more hopeful.

Caution dictated by his academic position prevented Ashley from stating the case in a controversial manner. Instead, in 1896 he chose to publish his translation of Schmoller's *Mercantile System*. He presented this as Schmoller's most characteristic work, while carefully pointing out that the work deserved attention 'whatever judgement may be arrived at concerning the validity of the argument'.[68] One of the points made by Schmoller was that 'historical progress had consisted mainly in the establishment of ever larger and larger communities as the controllers of economic policy in place of small.'[69] Translated into imperial-preference terms, the adoption of a common commercial policy by all the members of the imperial system was a progressive move in that it manifested a recognition in common economic interests. Progress, Schmoller maintained, led through such developments to an age of universal free trade:

> That age could begin to think and act in the spirit of free trade, which had left so far behind it the toilsome work of national development; that it regarded its best results as matters of course and forgot the struggle they had cost; an age which, with cosmopolitan sentiments, with great institutions and interests of international traffic, with a humanised international law . . . was already beginning to live in the ideas and tendencies of a world economy.[70]

---

[67] LSE Graham Wallas papers, Ashley to Wallas, 21 July 1897.
[68] Gustav Schmoller, *The Mercantile System and its Historical Significance*, translated by W. J. Ashley (New York, 1896).
[69] Ibid., p. 77.
[70] Ibid., pp. 61–2.

Once Ashley became an active supporter of the tariff he described his brand of imperialism in terms similar to those of Hewins—'a Democratic Imperialism with a genuine Social Amelioration intent and content'.[71]

In its issue of 15 August 1903 *The Times* published the free-trade manifesto organized by Edgeworth, together with a letter from L. L. Price to Edgeworth, explaining why he found himself unable to join him, Marshall, Pigou, and the other signatories in their rejection of the tariff. Instead, Price chose to side on this political and economic issue with Ashley, Hewins, Foxwell, and Cunningham. During 1904 he became President of the Oxford University Tariff Reform League. Price's position on the tariff was preceded by a gradual shift on theoretical issues which placed him, during the mid-nineties, in opposition to Marshall. Coupled with a change in views was a change in his academic position. Within a few years of the foundation of the British Economic Association, Price must have realized that the position of Joint Honorary Secretary of the Association, which he shared with Foxwell, was mainly a titular one, despite the original intention that it should develop into a position of some prominence.[72]

Joining Marshall's camp had proved less beneficial to Price's career than he might have expected. Edgeworth's position as the Drummond Professor had had no bearing on Price's academic position within Oxford. During 1895 there seems to have been some hope that because of ill health,[73] Edgeworth would not offer himself for another term in the chair. When it became known that he would be a candidate after all, and would certainly be re-elected, Price anxiously sought a chance to leave Oxford and offered himself as a candidate for the Glasgow Adam Smith Chair which, as anticipated, was given to William Smart.[74] Price's own work suggests that the Marshallian position he so tenaciously defended was not independently arrived at. As the debate died down and Price's hopes for an academic position resulting from his alliance to

---

[71] Anne Ashley, *William James Ashley*, p. 000.

[72] J. N. Keynes, 'Herbert Somerton Foxwell', *Economic Journal*, December 1936.

[73] See J. Bonar to R. H. Inglis Palgrave, 31 Mar. 1895, in the Palgrave family papers.

[74] LSE, Cannan papers, W. Smart to E. Cannan, 14 May 1895..

Marshall's camp diminished, his work returned to his old interests — industrial peace and industrial reform. Ever conciliatory when dealing with such matters, Price strove to present an optimistic picture of the militancy of new unionism and the failure of productive co-operatives to transform society.

Following Beatrice Webb's lead, Price argued[75] that in the case of both trade unionism and the co-operative movement, a new concept of their aims had been introduced. Co-operatives had become essentially a distributive democratic movement aiming at the regulation of consumption on as wide a scale as possible. Their former exclusive nature and faith in the ability to transform industrial society had been discarded. At the same time, trade unionism had emerged as an essential and indispensable factor in achieving industrial peace. Thus, whereas the movements had in the past been ideological rivals offering very different, if not opposing, solutions to the unequal distribution of wealth, they were transformed over the years and had become two important complementary forces in the more general trend towards progress.

Price was still much concerned with impressing his audience with the value of gradual and diversified reform incorporating various solutions and means. Since his aim was to present trade unionism as a positive and progressive movement, he argued, when addressing a non-trade-unionist audience, that the radical resolutions adopted by the TUC in 1893 and 1894 were no more than emotional outbursts 'abstract resolutions, begotten, it is true, of a real disapproval of the more obvious evils of the existing economic order, but intended rather as an expression of sentiment than as a preliminary to actual action.'[76]

Price did not change his earlier view of the balance between self-help and state intervention. He supported the fifth report of the Labour Commission,[77] which argued that state intervention in industry should be kept to a minimum and that in industrial disputes, the state should act as a 'counsellor and

[75] L. L. Price, 'Methods of Industrial Reform', read to the London Branch of the Christian Social Union, and 'Co-operation and its Relations to Trade Unionism and Socialism', read to the Oxford Co-operative Society, March 1896. Both printed in his *Economic Science and Practice*.
[76] Id. 'Co-operation and its Relations to Trade Unionism'.
[77] Id. 'The Report of the Labour Commission', read to Section F at its 1894 Oxford meeting. In the *Economic Journal*, September 1894.

encourager rather than . . . compulsory peacemaker'. Nevertheless, having realized that trade unionism and co-operatives could no longer be offered as comprehensive solutions, Price chose the cause of bimetallism.

Price did not stop at adopting a technical position to which Marshall was opposed. In his presidential address to Section F at its meeting in 1895, he practically recanted in the presence of his fellow economists some of the Marshallian views he had previously defended.[78] He rejected the definition of economics as a pure science and declared it to be an applied one: the insistence on the economists' neutrality in practical matters was idle and misleading:

> The student must be more or less than human, who, dealing with a department of knowledge so intimately related to the welfare of humanity, can avoid, as the result of his scientific inquiry, forming a favourable view of one course of conduct, and an adverse opinion of another, and endeavouring to promote the former and to hinder the latter, both by advice and by act. He cannot be content to observe the connection of cause and effect without trying to set in motion the cause or to restrain its action. He cannot contemplate the misery due to bad economic arrangements without seeking to devise and supply a remedy.

Price criticized professors who avoided their duty and would not take part in economic affairs. At one point in his address, he came close to accepting Cannan's view of the 'old' economists, pointing to their preoccupation with the practical issues of their day and the gaps and inconsistencies in their work discovered by later analysis.

His own practical suggestion was bimetallism, which he tried to support by backing deductive reasoning with historical evidence.[79] As a cause, although it was by definition a state-initiated measure, it did not require further state intervention. Price blamed the instability of the gold standard for stationary wages, falling profits, and the failure of the economy to recover from temporary depressions caused by credit fluctuations. He

---

[78] Id. 'The Relations of Economic Science to Practical Affairs', reprinted in his *Economic Science and Practice*.

[79] Id. 'International Bi-Metallism', read to the Economic Society of Newcastle upon Tyne, November 1895, in his *Economic Science and practice*; id., *Money and its Relations to Prices; The Newmarch Lectures at University College, London 1895* (London, 1896). H. S. Foxwell, a fellow Bimetallist and by then a 'dissenter', was the Political Economy Professor at University College.

argued that many of the faults of the economic system would disappear with the stimulus created by rising prices, which in turn would be a result of the switch to bimetallism. Rising prices would, he claimed, operate greatly to the advantage of the working classes and contribute significantly to a shift in the distribution of wealth. In fact he identified progress with such a shift: 'The broad tendency of progress in the modern world inclines to an alteration in the distribution of wealth in favour of the workmen, and to advance in wages.'[80] Elsewhere he argued that 'one of the most important advances of recent economics consists in the emphasis given to the influence of distribution on production.'[81]

Price's move away from the Marshallian position, a position he never renounced as such, led him eventually to define himself as a historical economist,[82] a partisan of the school he had previously criticized for its attacks on Marshall. His adoption of the bimetallist cause went beyond a technical difference of opinion with Marshall. It was a clear stand on a controversial issue, and at that an unpopular one which may have contributed to his failure to secure the Adam Smith Chair.[83] Some years later, when Price took up the cause of tariff reform, Marshall's reaction was to chide him 'like an irate dominie flogging a naughty schoolboy'.[84]

Price remained at Oxford, but despite repeated efforts could not induce Edgeworth to take action to change the academic status of economics within Oxford. In retrospect,[85] he described the feelings that led him in 1902 to take the unusual step of publishing an open letter to the University's Vice-Chancellor—D. B. Monro, Provost of Oriel College (whom he may have sounded out beforehand): 'I fear that I shared a view very generally entertained that Economics in Oxford looked like slumbering quietly or in effect at least must languish comparatively as it rested, so to say, inert in Edgeworth's keeping.

---

[80] Price, *Money and its Relations to Prices*, p. 75.
[81] Id. 'The Relations of Economic Science to Practical Affairs'.
[82] See the enlarged (14th) edition of *A Short History of Political Economy in England* (London, 1931), p. 211; and *A Short History of English Commerce and Industry* (London, 1900), ch. 1.
[83] Cannan papers, Sir Matthew Pollack Fraser to E. Cannan, 10 Sept. 1896.
[84] Price, 'Memoirs and Notes'.
[85] Ibid.

There was no active stir of a resonant hive of busy students gathering honey under his helping regime.' In his letter Price described the dismal state of Oxford economics. Relegated to a secondary position in the curriculum, it was, he argued, clearly at a disadvantage compared to Cambridge's continuous production of capable young economists, compared to the LSE whose success attracted English as well as foreign students, and compared to the younger universities where new programmes were incorporated with the aim of training students for business life. The standard of economic knowledge attained by Oxford students and the standard demanded by Oxford examiners were low. It was essential that economics be given a more prominent position.

> as a preparation for engaging with wise competence in the solution of those 'social questions' which confront all who are anxious to improve the condition of the masses of the people, as one of the means of enabling Englishmen to overcome the difficulties which will attend the commercial and industrial future of the Empire.[86]

Price did not go into the details of a revised curriculum; he merely described it as 'a department of learning which is full of human interest, and has shaken itself free of the dry and barren logomachies which once hindered its advance.'

Price's letter was intended for the meeting of the Hebdomadal Council on 20 February 1902, during which the issue was forced by Phelps's motion, calling the Council's attention to the tenure of the Political Economy Professorship. It is unclear whether Phelps actually hoped to carry a motion that would prevent Edgeworth's re-election or whether he merely intended to force the Council to deal with the issue. The motion was dropped, but as a result of its pressure the Vice-Chancellor circulated a letter requesting the Heads of Institutions and Departments, the Boards of Faculties, the Professors and the Readers, to state their views on the University's needs in their fields.

In an answer to the Vice-Chancellor's letter dated 6 June 1902[87], Edgeworth conceded that 'it will be thought desirable,

---

[86] Id. 'The Present Position of Economic Study in Oxford', 14 Jan. 1902, MS in the Bodleian Library, Oxford.
[87] *Statements of the Needs of the University* (Oxford, 1902), pp. 114–17.

for reasons which are forcibly urged in the petition [by Price] . . to afford some fresh incentive to the study of Political Economy' (thereby disassociating himself from the actual petition). Despite his previous inaction, Edgeworth was not an obstructionist. He accepted the desirability of a Readership in English Economic History, but by pointing out that 'the connexion is not very close between my subject and Modern History' he hinted at some of the reasons for his inaction. The Drummond Professorship had been technically attached to the School of Modern History, an attachment he had been unhappy about but did little to change. Now the Vice-Chancellor's letter gave him an opportunity to state his views. Instead of the commonly accepted bond between economics and the School of Modern History at Oxford, Edgeworth saw another affinity between 'his' brand of political economy—abstract theory—and the School of Literae Humaniores. Theoretical economics was: 'the one branch of knowledge, outside mathematics and mathematical physics, which has realized in any considerable degree the ideal of a demonstrative science to which Greek Philosophy aspired in vain'. Thus he was clearly uninterested in developing economics within the School of Modern History, but would rather see it strengthened independently of history within the School of Literae Humaniores, presumably on lines similar to the development of economics as envisaged by Marshall. He was not one to initiate reform, much less if it was not in accordance with his own concept of the study of economics. But he was not averse to change: he did not block the establishment of Price, first as the first University Lecturer, and then as the first University Reader in Economic History. Furthermore, he lent his support to the young LSE, where he occasionally lectured during the period 1896–1900, to Ruskin Hall, later to become Ruskin College, and to Barnett House, which was started in 1914 as a centre of social and economic study and research.

Price's bitterness led him to declare that Edgeworth's tenure of the Drummond Professorship had been, in terms of the development of the study of economics at Oxford, a barren one. He confessed that he found himself unable to judge Edgeworth's contribution to mathematical economics. But since, in opposition to Edgeworth, he believed that economics could, and indeed should, be made, easily understandable, he confessed to being greatly comforted when towards the end of his career he observed that most students could 'still master economics without expert or amateur mathematics'.[88] Despite his professed ignorance, and admitting the usefulness of mathematics as a technical aid, he warned, when summing up Edgeworth's contribution to economics,[89] that 'the facile employment of a polished tool can betray the user into the belief that he has more power than he really commands, or even perhaps into the assurance that he has solved a problem when he has only stated it neatly or correctly.' Using Marshall and J. N. Keynes as his authorities, Price claimed that only the most basic elements of economic theory could be expressed mathematically, and that the mathematics required for the purpose was 'so easy as to beguile those with not much technical training'.[90] Needless to say, if his view on the matter had any impact, it was solely within Oxford.

Edwin Cannan began teaching at the LSE during the autumn of 1895 – the School's first term. Like his fellow Oxford economists, he had had some contact in the 1880s with Sidney Webb. In February 1889 he wrote to Webb 'complaining that the collectivisation of the means of production was no cure for extreme poverty'.[91] Webb answered[92] that he did not think that the Fabian position differed from Cannan's. The exchange of views was followed by an invitation to Cannan to address the Fabian Society.[93] His paper 'The Bearing of Recent Economics on Individualism, Collectivism and Communism', read to the Fabian Society on 5 July 1889,[94] is one of the fullest statements by an Oxford economist of Cannan's generation on the ideological aspect of their economic positions. Of the response to his paper all he could recall in later years was that 'Sidney Webb declared that I was qualified to be a Fabian, and that

[88] Price, 'Memoirs and Notes'.
[89] Id. *A Short History of Political Economy*, p. 278.
[90] Ibid., p. 279.
[91] Cannan, *The Economic Outlook*, p. 15.
[92] Cannan papers, S.Webb to E. Cannan, 14 Feb. 1889.
[93] Ibid., S. Oliver to E. Cannan, 8 Mar. 1889.
[94] Cannan, *The Economic Outlook*, pp. 16, 53–86.

Bernard Shaw and, I think, other speakers, repudiated me in more or less violent terms.'[95]

During the early 1890s Cannan's quarterly reports on 'Legislation', 'Parliamentary Inquiries', etc., for the *Economic Review* led him to develop an interest in local government.[96] He had regarded the work of the London County Council with approval and in 1894 and again in 1895 used the opportunity of reviewing the *London Statistics* to defend its policies. Reviewing the 1892–3 volume[97] he argued:

> Those who can discern no merit in the London County Council are not wise, and are not addicted to research. Instead of reading the Council's annual volume, and finding out what its work actually is, they prefer to abuse it for going outside its province when it is performing duties entrusted to it by Parliament, and to complain that it is neglecting its proper business when it is simply not attempting to usurp the functions of other authorities.

Some months later, in a review of the LCC's next volume of *London Statistics*,[98] Cannan singled out a common adversary for special treatment:

> When the President of the British Economic Association [Lord Goschen] sneered at the last County Council as a parcel of enthusiasts who believed that they were rapidly producing an earthly paradise, he probably had the 'New London' of the *Daily Chronicle* in his mind. Had some modern Jeannie Geddes[99] risen in wrath and successfully aimed the *London Statistics* at his head he would have fared ill both morally and physically. For the book is large, heavy and hard, and there is something excessively incongruous between its prosaic contents and 'fantastic schemes' . . . for earthly paradises.

Cannan's interest in local government and his objection to the single-tax scheme as a total solution to the problem of unequal distribution led him to take up the defence of the local rating system. Early in 1895 he published an article considering the inequalities of local rates in various districts.[100] He

---

[95] Ibid., p. 17.
[96] e.g. the *Economic Review*, April 1891, July 1891, and July 1892.
[97] In the *Economic Review*, 1894.
[98] Ibid., 1895.
[99] Jeannie or Jenny Geddes is supposed to have inaugurated the riot in St. Giles Church, Edinburgh, when she prevented an attempt to read the Lord's service book on Sunday, 23 July 1637, by flinging a stool at the head of David Lindsay, Bishop of Edinburgh, *DNB* vol. vii, s.v.
[100] E. Cannan, 'Inequality of Local Rates and its Economic Justification', in the *Economic Journal*, 1895.

argued that in some cases inequality was due to a difference in services performed by local government or a difference in its past or present fiscal policy, and therefore entirely justifiable since higher rates were in such cases counterbalanced by superior benefits to the ratepayer. Where higher rates were due to other differences and were not counterbalanced by benefits, they could, and by implication should, be equalized through appropriate legislation such as the redivision or amalgamation of Poor Law areas so as to make them coterminous with local government districts and the administrative counties. Cannan concluded the article with a relatively mild general statement: 'Though we cannot decide between hostile factions we ought at least to make some attempt, however inadequate, to provide them with better arguments than those which they employ at present.'

The article presented the results of Cannan's enquiries into the contemporary situation. Nevertheless, he did not feel it to be a sufficient answer to the single-tax argument. To provide such an answer he turned, with some assistance from Hewins and Cunningham, to the origins and development of local rates. Cannan did not seek a precedent. As a historical evolutionist, he wished to show not only how local taxation developed but the rationale behind its development. As a social institution it was not an inflexible dictate imposed on society once and for all, but a continuously modified system undergoing constant alterations according to changing circumstances, aimed at confining and channelling individual activity so that it might forward the interests and welfare of the community. The value of such a social institution at any point in time depended on its ability to fulfil that function.[101] The earlier article gave part of the contemporary rationale behind the system of local taxation. The historical survey was intended to draw the general principles on which the system was based and to show their continuous adaptability to changing circumstances and their adequacy at fulfilling their function.

Cannan chose the subject for his first course of lectures at the LSE. It was a subject well suited to the new School, based as it

[101] Although this position is at the basis of Cannan's work on local rates, it is fully stated only in the second edition of his *History of Local Rates in England* (London, 1912), p. 176.

was on historical analysis and dealing with the practical and controversial issue of reform on which Cannan had a definite position. As in the earlier article, he included in the course a general statement about the purpose of economic investigation. However, the language he used was more appropriate to the character of the young LSE:

> Laborious students whose investigations have interested scarcely any one but themselves have been known to seek comfort in the assertion that truth is valuable for its own sake. I do not believe that this is the case. A great deal that is true is not worth knowing. The most inveterate bore is often the most truthful man. All history should, I think, have some practical aim. Some moral, some lesson of guidance, should be offered by it. Even if this is not true of all history, it is surely true with regard to economic history. It would be absurd to study a subject so dry, not to say odious, as local rates except with a view to practical aims. We do not study such subjects from a love of truth in the abstract or to while away a wet Sunday afternoon, but because there are practical controversies about them and we hope that we may learn something which may be of assistance in these controversies.[102]

Cannan discerned two basic types of taxation—that based on the ability of the taxed to pay, and that on the basis of the benefit derived by the taxed from the actions of the taxing body. He found that at the national level the general tendency was towards taxation according to ability, and at the local level towards taxation according to benefit. It was impossible, he argued, to distinguish clearly between benefit and ability, while it was clear that the two criteria were not interchangeable, so that one principle could not fully replace the other. Nor could it be expected that the national and local spheres of taxation would merge. There was a limit to the capability of local authorities to expand geographically and their work could not be replaced by a national central agency. Therefore, apart from some minor reforms of the type indicated in his article in the *Economic Journal*, the two systems of taxation should remain separate. 'The complete solution of the problem must not be expected till a short time before the commencement of the millenium.'[103] Once again, Cannan had reached the conclusion in line with one of the main themes of

---

[102] Cannan, *History of Local Rates in England* p. 1. The book is the first in the Studies in Economics and Political Science edited by W. A. S. Hewins. The Preface is dated January 1896.

[103] Ibid., p. 136.

the Oxford economists' work and ideology—there was no single, total alternative to the existing and slowly evolving system. Effective reform was a constant and steady process rather than a drastic, revolutionary undertaking.

Although Cannan joined the regular staff of the LSE in the School's first term, he did not leave Oxford. He lectured at the School twice a week, careful to end his lectures by 6.57 p.m. so that he might catch the 7.30 p.m. train back to Oxford.[104] He avoided staying in London overnight and, except for lecturing, did not allow his London appointment to change his daily Oxford routine, which was mainly one of solitary work in his study, gardening, and country cycling. Although the LSE provided him with his first academic position, it did not change his way of life. Unlike the Oxford economists who left Oxford, he was not drawn into national politics. With changing political and social circumstances, he became more interested in local government than in national government. In December 1896 he was first elected to the Oxford City Council as member for the University (in 1901 he was joined in the Council by John Carter). The principle of involvement was similar. Within the limits of self-help, his attention was focused on the activity of government in the cause of progress.

Another factor which contributed to Cannan's avoidance of some national controversies was his attitude towards Foxwell. From the first years of the LSE Foxwell lectured on banking and currency, whereas—with the School becoming more academic—over the years Cannan taught elements of economics for first-year students, to which were added more advanced courses on production and distribution. Not till the First World War did he begin to write extensively on matters of currency and prices.[105] It seems that Cannan consciously avoided a dispute with Foxwell, despite the fact that they disagreed on the issue of bimetallism.[106]

That a clash between these two short-tempered economists on the question of bimetallism was avoided is a testimony to

---

[104] Bowley, 'Early Days of the L.S.E.', and interview with Lord Robert Hall, 13 Mar. 1979.
[105] A. L. Bowley, 'Edwin Cannan', in the *Economic Journal*, June 1936.
[106] H. S. Foxwell, 'Bimetallism: Its Meaning and Aims', in the *Economic Review*, July 1893 and E. Cannan, 'Bimetallism; a Criticism' in the *Economic Review*, October 1893.

Phelps's role in the affair. After Foxwell's paper on bimetallism, delivered at Oxford during February 1893 and published in the July issue of the *Review*, Cannan wrote to Phelps:[107]

> As recriminations about facts are rarely profitable I have not attempted to deal with his [Foxwell's] mis-statements . . . These of course are mistakes made in good faith but I think John Carter's article on Commercial Morality might well be followed by one on the Morality of Writers on Economic subjects. Just as Marshall tries to give the impression that all recognised economists are very slightly modified Maltho-Ricardo-Millians and Sidney Webb that they are all Socialists so Foxwell would have his hearers believe that they were all bimetallists. The average bagman praising his wares isn't in it.

After this unburdening of himself to Phelps, Cannan's published criticism of Foxwell's bimetallism was devoid of any personal invective, although there were a few passing comments on Oxford professors (such as Edgeworth) who 'have no opinions'. Foxwell did not find it unduly provocative. Upon receiving the proofs of Cannan's article from Phelps before its publication he wrote to Phelps:[108]

> Cannan reminds me of William Sidgwick [brother of Henry and Arthur]. He can write smartly on any subject, and his effectiveness is not impeded by any slavish regard for facts or respect for authorities. There is nothing in the article to which I do or could object but it is what we used to call at school 'cheeky'. I should have preferred an attack from an opponent of heavier metal, though no doubt I should have suffered more; but I am quite satisfied that the question is kept alive in any way.

Phelps's even-handed editorial policy on the matter contrasts favourably with Edgeworth's policy in the Marshall–Cunningham exchange. Not only did he send Foxwell the proofs of Cannan's article, he also offered him the option of a reply, which Foxwell declined. He did not show either of them the full correspondence, thereby allowing the two to reach a cordial agreement to disagree.[109]

Over the years Cannan maintained a careful attitude towards Foxwell, similar to that of Ashley and Hewins towards both Cunningham and Foxwell.[110] The two were important

[107] Phelps papers, Cannan to Phelps, 30 July 1893.
[108] Ibid., Foxwell to Phelps, 17 Aug. 1893.
[109] LSE, Cannan papers, fo. 909, Foxwell to Cannan, 27 Oct. 1893.
[110] For Foxwell's position on the institutional and methodological issues, see J. M. Keynes, 'Herbert Somerton Foxwell'.

allies of the dissenters. Their common criticism of Marshall was of more note than any differences they may have had with the Oxford economists on comparatively minor issues. Thus when he wrote on the subject of currency, Cannan was to criticize the works of Lord Farrer[111] for what he regarded as a dubious defence of the gold standard, rather than to attack bimetallism.

Like many other contemporary Oxford liberals, Cannan did not find it necessary to question his belief in free trade and internationalism and adopt the cause of imperial preference. In common with some of the tariff reformers, he considered the Empire to be a step on the way to a united global community. In 1909 he wrote to J. S. Nicholson:

> I cannot believe in the permanence of an institution like the British Empire . . . But I think it is eminently desirable that it should be maintained till the time comes . . . when some form of union between European and American peoples make it or most of it part of a larger whole. Till then it is useful because it does to some extent reduce the number of supposed separate interests in the world.[112]

Devoid of any sentiment towards imperial unity and disinclined to take Britain's isolation too seriously, Cannan could not see the point in adopting what he regarded as the regressive measure of the tariff. In his view it was economically unsound and of no military value. Nor would it advance the cause of imperial unity. Like Hewins, he insisted that his position on the tariff did not denote a change in his social ideology. Where Hewins found a resemblance between state socialism and imperial preference, Cannan argued that 'the fact that a man may believe that sound reasons can be given in favour of factory legislation or municipal enterprise does not in any way debar him from believing that good reasons have not been given in favour of interference with foreign trade.'[113]

Free trade was one of the few issues on which Cannan's feelings were strong enough to make him join a political organiza-

---

[111] E. Cannan, reviews of Lord Farrer's, 'The Quantitative Theory Money and Prices', in the *Economic Journal*, March 1898, and of Lord Farrer's 'Studies in Currency', in the *Economic Review*, October 1898.

[112] Cannan papers, E. Cannan to J. S. Nicholson, 21 Dec. 1909.

[113] E. Cannan, 'Colonial Preference', in the *Independent Review*, October 1905, reprinted in *The Economic Outlook*.

tion. In November 1903 he became a member of the Committee of the Trade League of the University, City, and County of Oxford, alongside F. Y. Edgeworth, A. J. Carlyle, L. R. Phelps, and H. A. L. Fisher.[114] He was also one of the signatories to the manifesto, 'Professors of Economics and the Tariff Question', organized by Edgeworth and published in *The Times* on 15 August 1903.[115]

The tariff controversy placed Cannan in a curious situation. At Oxford, Price, as a tariff reformer, was in a minority amongst his fellow economists (L. R. Phelps also signed Edgeworth's manifesto). However, at the LSE the situation was reversed, with Cannan in a minority, while Hewins, Foxwell, Cunningham, Mrs Lilian Knowles, and H. J. Mackinder, as well as W. J. Ashley and H. Ll. Smith, supported tariff reform. An indication of Cannan's probable unease may be seen in his comparative restraint in publishing his views on the matter—one article and three reviews in the 1903 volume of the *Economic Journal*. It must have been awkward for him to find in the December 1903 issue of the *Economic Journal* two of his reviews against tariff alongside Edgeworth's criticism of Ashley's *The Tariff Problem* as well as Edgeworth's rebuke of Cannan's second edition of *Theories of Production and Distribution*.

[114] The League was also supported by S. Ball, A. L. Smith, and A. Sidgwick.
[115] The other signatories were C. F. Bastable, Leonard Courtney, F. Y. Edgeworth, E. C. K. Gonner, A. Marshall, J. S. Nicholson, L. R. Phelps, A. Pigou, C. P. Sanger, W. R. Scott, W. Smart, and Armitage Smith.

9
SOME CONCLUSIONS

In retrospect, the group which this study has dealt with offers an example of lateral scientific development expressed organizationally by the redemarcation of the boundaries of political economy as an academic discipline. In its lifetime the group of Oxford economists was regarded as a school of thought in confrontation with the group referred to as the Marshallians. Despite what may be said about the differences being more apparent than real or about the two groups arguing at cross purposes, the controversy was a conscious struggle between the proponents of two rival concepts of the definition of the nature of economics. Today such a debate over these two would be almost technically and conceptually impossible. What were then two conflicting concepts within the same science would today be considered as belonging to two separate and independent departments—economic history and economics. An economist may use historical data and the economic historian may use economic theory, but one may not question the basic concepts, indeed the *raison d'être*, of another department. Therefore the definition and description of the controversy as a methodological one—deductive theory versus the historical method—is misleading. For although some of the differences were expressed in methodological terms, the issue was not the tools of the economist but the more fundamental issue of the nature of economics, an issue which has a methodological aspect to it. Hence the difficulty of producing a coherent description of the Oxford group and its supporters in methodological terms. Cannan and Smart were not historical economists (at least not mainly) and even the application of the label to Price is questionable, yet they all consciously belonged to the same camp, commonly referred to in previous research as 'the historical economists' and placed outside the main tradition of English economic theory. (This might explain the relative lack of interest in their work.)

SOME CONCLUSIONS

In the 1880s and 1890s economics was taught at both Cambridge and Oxford as part of the study of modern history. Within such an organizational framework a clash between the two concepts was made more likely. To this was added the sense of threat felt by the relativists when faced with an attempt to define and organize the science of economics in a way that would place them apart from the mainstream of English economics. If Marshall's concept was to become the general consensus they could not define themselves as economists. Yet once the science of economics was redepartmentalized the threat to some extent disappeared. Since both sides remained convinced that theirs was the best approach, once the direct threat to their position was removed they felt certain that facts and history would prove them right.

A certain parallel may be drawn between the outcome of the controversy following the secure institutional establishment of the two approaches and the change in attitude of most members of the Royal Statistical Society to the claims of the economists led by the Cambridge camp. While the economists were arguing for a reorganization of the Society they were considered a threat. When they eventually founded the British Economic Association there was a sense of resentment and the fear of a possible loss of authority. However, once the conciliatory nature of the Association became known and its existence an obvious success, the Society accepted the theoretical rationale for its separate existence although theoretically nothing had changed.

The foundation of the London School of Economics to a large extent saved the careers of some of the dissenters and allowed them to develop their own independent lines of enquiry. Nevertheless, the dissenters sorely lacked a Marshall to help to establish their academic independence. As a result, the departmental status of economic history is yet to reach its final form. In some universities it is part of the study of history, in others of economics, and in a few it is wedded to social history to create an independent department.

The source of the actual differences between the camps, as well as the inter-camp similarities which create its cohesion, have been regarded as mainly biographical. The basically similar *Weltanschauung* of the members of the Oxford Economic

Society reflects a combination of the similar, though not identical, cultural and social backgrounds of a number of young Oxford men of roughly the same age who came up to Oxford with the same financial handicaps and experienced the same influences at roughly the same time. Not only did their intellectual development at Oxford progress on parallel lines, but through actual association they became a corporate entity. The existence of an Oxford camp is not a matter of retrospective analysis based on a comparative examination of their work. During their professionally formative years they consciously constituted a group, and some of the similarities in their work (as in the case of Cannan) may be attributed to this conscious association. Similarly, none of the other groups referred to was a theoretical entity. The cohesion of a school of thought in this study is not solely dependent on a theoretical consensus. A school is also a social entity held together by ties of friendship and loyalty.

The presence of a strong religious sentiment combined with radical liberalism in upper-working-class and lower-middle-class families was not unique. What was unique was the first appearance of members of such families in any significant numbers at Oxford. That an Oxford education should be considered at all be the families of Ashley, Hewins, or Ll. Smith indicates a shift in class attitude towards higher education which came with the development of social aspirations. This ambition to improve one's social position by means of an Oxford education was even stronger in the families of Sadler and Price which, although not well off financially, had in the past known better times; some members of those families had gone to the University. Oxford was to open up for them new and social and professional options which otherwise were beyond their reach.

With the exception of Cannan, all our economists suffered at Oxford from a similar financial handicap of which they were constantly conscious. An Oxford education put a severe financial strain on their families and a dependence on scholarships and exhibitions in order to cover the expense. This early concern with material want may or may not have stimulated their interest in social problems in general and in distribution in particular, but it clearly shaped their way of life at Oxford. It dictated their attitude towards their studies, which they knew could not be supplemented with an additional course of studies such as reading for the Bar. The lack of a public-school education (except in the cases of Sadler and Cannan) imposed a limited choice of social sets and clubs. Lack of interest or money excluded them from some sets, while membership in some clubs (e.g. the Palmerston) came virtually naturally. Their financial situation also limited their career options while personal inclination and newly formed ideological beliefs ruled out the 'traditional' options of the church and school teaching.

The fact that despite their scholarly achievements, the young economists could not hope for the same opportunities as most of their Oxford contempories was not a source of resentment, nor did the limits of social mobility cause noticeable frustration. Initially, their social aspirations were limited and they felt highly privileged to have been at Oxford. Rather than resent the system for its inequality they were grateful for the opportunities it opened up for them. It was Ashley's view[1] that 'No sensible man who has gained from Oxford what I have gained could think of grumbling because in earlier years hopes more than once went astray.'

This attitude was reflected in an eagerness to make higher education in general, and Oxford in particular, more popular among the lower classes. While striving to change the academic status of their subject the economists did not seek to change the whole system. As young graduates their immediate instinct was to generalize from their own personal experience to the national level. In their initial enthusiasm, coloured by faith in knowledge and reason, they could not perceive that their sentiments might not be representative of the general attitude of the working classes towards adult education. It was only after the relative failure of the Extension to popularize systematic higher education that Price, Ll. Smith, Hewins, and even Sadler, sought new ways in which they might contribute individually to the course of progress.

When considering the young economists' social background, the lack of certain patterns might be considered as significant as the presence of others. One is the absence of a definite link between religious and party politics. In all the families under

[1] W. J. Ashley, *Scientific Management and the Engineering Situation* (Oxford, 1922).

consideration there is evidence of a strong religious sentiment and a tendency towards radical liberalism, in some cases bolstered by the economists' schooling. However, in church politics the families cover virtually the whole range from dissent to High Church. Religious dogma had been replaced by a strong faith in a Christian society as the desirable end of all progress. As conscious Christians they emphasized the essential link between material and spiritual progress. In their view material prosperity would be purposeless without a spiritual vision. Similarly, at Oxford radical reform cut across church party lines. There is no evidence to suggest that disagreement on dogma obstructed co-operation on social reform.

Unlike church politics, party politics do provide a pattern, although support of the Liberal party did not necessarily entail a coherent political ideology. As young men the Oxford economists shared the belief in continuous progress through the removal of all obstructions to free competition and free trade and through the encouragement of self-help, bolstered, where the working classes were at their weakest, by cautious state intervention. When they began to develop a more comprehensive ideology these fundamental beliefs remained an integral part of it. Indeed their original interest in liberal politics had brought them, at Oxford, into contact with men such as Toynbee, A. L. Smith, A. Sidgwick, Sidney Ball, and others whose influence was important in extending their basic ideological beliefs into a fuller ideology from which they derived the rationale for their choice of career.

The combination of religious, social, and political factors in their background made the group receptive to a certain type of message. Developments at Oxford during the seventies, its size, and the small number of colleges involved created a certain uniformity in their exposure to this message. It was not only a uniformity in contents derived to a large extent from T. H. Green's Idealism and other current trends; there was also a uniformity in their coming under the influence of a small number of young inspiring dons active within certain limited circles. This often had nothing to do with the young men's initial choice of academic studies so that, from the start, entering a young don's 'zone of influence' was in most cases an ideologically motivated act. Beyond the transference of ideas and beliefs, the young dons' influence extended towards their pupils' actual choice of various social schemes for direct involvement, largely through personal example. It was only with the passage of time and the accumulation of experience that some of the young men began independently to seek other forms of action which would express their ideological beliefs.

The choice of economics as a career was an outcome of the combined effect of an intellectual and ideological development and material circumstances. The choice was clearly one of intellectual and ideological preference since it was a profession that at best offered a very uncertain future, a problem demonstrated by the divergence of the careers of Hewins, Sadler, Ll. Smith, and Price after the relative failure of the Extension. Thus careers in this instance have been examined in the light of early aspirations rather than from the perspective of their final form. Often there is little resemblance betwen the two. The choice, when made, did not consist solely of a technical decision. It entailed a concept of the nature of the subject, its place within a *Weltanschauung*, and a scholar's first indpependent research programme. Such a programme brought together academic training, which more often than not was sorely lacking in post-Millian economics, various ideological notions including one's individual duty towards society and commitment to non-revolutoinary progress, and certain intellectual influences, most notably the historical evolutionary approach to the study of society and some aspects of Jevonian theory and methodology. The initial choice of subjects for research reflects an inclination to seek scientific proof for what the economists already believed to be true and although some of these issues (e.g. the status of Ricardo's theory) concern certain internal controversies, the motive behind their choice is scientifically external. The usual exception in this case is Cannan, whose choice was initially the result of a somewhat isolated development with a gradual expansion of scope as he came into close contact with other Oxford economists.

Beyond their wish to prove certain preconceptions scientifically, the young economists were interested in determining the means that would serve to strengthen the progressive trends detectable in society. Thus Price did not merely hope to prove that industrial peace was increasingly attainable and that trade unions contributed to it, but also to provide the best means for ensuring peaceful resolutions of wage disputes. Ashley hoped not only to prove that progress was continuous but also to determine the regulative laws of progress which would serve as guides for current policies. The concepts they set out to prove were at first relatively simple and straightforward, and they seem to have expected fairly uncomplicated prescriptive conclusions. However, although the basic ideology from which they derived their preconceptions remained largely unchanged, research experience and changes in circumstances (internal and external) led to changes in research directions, as is demonstrated by Price's interest in bimetallism and Cannan's work on the history of theory.

Changes in the direction of their research came about largely as a result of the development of the economists's careers. Scientifically internal influences were brought to bear on their work, relations of loyalty and rivalry were developed, and various practical considerations were taken into consideration. Nevertheless the basic ideology remained unchanged even if occasionally some aspects of it were temporarily compromised. Ashley's conciliatory statements at Toronto and Harvard cannot be considered as reflecting an actual conversion, as indeed his article in Palgrave's *Dictionary* demonstrates. Price's attacks on the Oxford historical approach may be regarded more as a matter of expediency when seen in the light of his later career.

The history of the early years of the Oxford Extension movement is not merely a chapter in the early careers of Price, Hewins, and Ll. Smith. Beyond its demonstration of a process in which preconceptions about society were confronted with social reality, the Extension was one of the practical expressions of an ideology of social action shared by the Oxford economists and reflected in their work. It is therefore significant that this embodiment of the ideology should lead to a confrontation with other extension organizations. In some respects this confrontation is of relevance to the understanding of the debate on the nature of economics. In the history of the Oxford Extension, principles were translated into means of action which brought the Extension into conflict with the Cambridge and London extension bodies. In the debate on the nature of economics ideological and conceptual differences were translated into methodological issues. Thus in both cases the differences on means were but an expression of differences on more fundamental issues. Technical conciliation, even when possible, could not resolve the basic differences.

As in the extension disputes, the course of the debate on economics was greatly influenced by organizational and institutional developments. The foundations of the British Economic Association and the publication of the *Economic Journal* and the *Economic Review*, all of which were embodiments of definite concepts as held by certain camps, determined the timing and the form of the controversy. Although the differences between the camps were independent of this organizational expression, it may be argued, as it had been argued in economics, that theoretically the two basic concepts could develop side by side. Indeed in retrospect, given a different organizational arrangement, they coexisted in that manner before the foundation of the BEA as their heirs do today. The main cause of the clash was the fear that the Marshallians, through the BEA and the *Journal*, were aiming at a monopoly of economics in a manner that would exclude the dissenters. It is therefore significant that the Oxford economists constantly (and unjustly) attacked Marshall's catholicity as a sham and a distortion of facts. They were fighting to ensure that independent existence of their 'brand' of economics and it is somewhat ironical that the plans for the publication of the *Economic Review* may well have provided the final required stimulant to prod the Marshallians into action over the Association and the *Journal*.

The main ideological issues in the Oxford position were:

1. The *historical–evolutionary approach* to the study of all social phenomena: the belief that society is constantly undergoing a process of progressive change along certain lines, such as the gradual development towards conscious corporate action replacing in importance individual impulsive action. The key, therefore, to the understanding of current social reality was in the understanding of the general laws of progress and social change, which were laws of motion rather than laws of a static state. Furthermore, since progress took the form of growing

conscious corporate action, it was essential that society as a whole should come to understand progress in order to develop. Hence the importance of both the investigator and the educator.

2. *Relativisim*. Since society was in a constant state of change any static theory providing regulative laws for a certain aspect of social activity at a certain place and time was applicable only to that place and time. Static state analysis was of some use since the general course of social progress could be divided for practical purposes into a sequence of static states of development. Therefore, static analysis was useful but of only limited application in space and time. Any attempt to apply it beyond its contextual boundaries was false and could be dangerous in that it created a false image of reality.

3. *Applicability*, an issue closely linked with the wider ideological issues of the individual's civic duty towards society and the belief in conscious corporate action as an aspect of progress. The object of economic investigation—or any social investigation—was practical results. Accordingly methods should be evaluated on the basis of their attainment of such results. Knowledge was not to be pursued for its own sake and unless the scientist used his knowledge for the benefit of social progress, viz. in prescribing forms of conscious corporate action, he was shirking his civic duty.

4. *Ethics*, which with applicability dictated both the choice of subject for investigation and the choice of practical forms of action to be prescribed. Hence, ethical considerations determined the means as well as the ends of social action. The economist, having investigated a certain pertinent social phenomenon, was expected to provide a course of action which would be in itself both practical and ethical. Thus trade unions were regarded as a positive development not only because they led to the improvement of the material conditions of the working man, but also because by joining a union the worker had already progressed in that he was willing to sacrifice his own narrow interests in favour of corporate interests. Within this ideological system it was assumed that the most practical course of action would also be the ethical one. Therefore the abolition of material inequality by means of revoluton was both impractical and morally wrong, whereas gradual scientifically

directed reform provided a practical and ethical course of action.

Since each ideological system which is at the basis of the differences on the nature of economics should be considered independently, it would be misleading to define one on the basis of its rejections of the other's arguments. Describing the ideology behind the Marshallian position as the opposite of the views expressed by the dissenters is as misleading as confining it to a methodological dispute. Such descriptions are the result of the common inclination towards the linear account in the internal history of economics. Once it has been assumed that the history of economics is essentially the history of a sequence of economic theories, various theoretical concepts are considered in their relation (continuation or reaction) to previous and contemporary concepts. The sole importance of the dissenters for the internal historian, interested in the development of the main tradition of economic theory, may be in their internal opposition to Marshall, but their views cannot be explained or described solely on the basis of reaction to Marshall or vice versa.

Since the differences were not technical (and in view of the disputants' frame of mind), they could not be decided by argument. There was no question of one side converting the other in a conflict that was regarded by some (notably Cunningham) as a fight for the academic survival of their subject and by others as involving fundamental principles. While the controversy was in progress efforts were being made at Cambridge and later at Oxford to improve the academic standing of economics. As a matter of expediency a certain approach to the study of economics had to be agreed upon and under the circumstances it was impractical to allow two or more approaches to be given an equal and mutually independent status in the campaign. The adaptation of one single approach which would allow the existence of other approaches an auxiliary position in the proposed new curriculum made a concentrated effort possible. Had Marshall agreed on an equal status for economic history at Cambridge, and had the Oxford camp agreed to direct their campaign towards the establishment of economics as a major subject in the School of Literae Humaniores (as suggested by Edgeworth) and of economic history in the School of

Modern History, their chances for success would have been considerably diminished. Furthermore, in Marshall's case, the image of internal unity was an essential component of his vision of a reorganized science. Under the circumstances he could not very well maintain the image of unity while allowing an equal autonomous position to economic history, as long as advocates of the latter claimed that it rendered economic theory relatively unimportant. Having started the controversy from a position of advantage, Marshall therefore tried to conciliate, belittle the differences, and reduce the issues to technical disagreements while the more militant dissenters tried to do the opposite.

In view of the fundamental nature of the differences between the two camps it is difficult to decide (if one is not an internal historian) the objective superiority of either one. Even if one were to use present-day criteria to decide between the two he would find that the members of each camp are hailed separately by two different academic departments as pioneers in their own right,[2] from the perspective of two separate scientific traditions. However, the same observation does not apply to the internal development within each camp. It can hardly be disputed that within his own camp Marshall derived much of his authority from the unrivalled excellence of his work, a fact readily acknowledged by many of the dissenters. Objective merit may well remain the most important criterion for the internal historian of a tradition in explaining the ascendancy of a Marshall over his contemporaries within the same scientific discipline.

Technically the dissenters suffered from some serious disadvantages. To begin with they were younger than Marshall and his close supporters so that not only were they handicapped by challenging a relatively mature theoretical corpus but also by opposing economists in well-established positions and of considerable prestige. Whereas Marshall was the acknowledged doyen of current economic theory, the opposition lacked a recognized leader of comparable stature as well as a clear sense of direction beyond local action. The dissenters were unable to

[2] For the position of Ashley, Cunningham, Toynbee, etc. in the development of economic history, see R. M. Hartwell, 'Good Old Economic Theory', in *Journal of Economic History*, March 1975.

produce a generally accepted standard work to serve as a textbook for training a new generation in their subject. Furthermore, while Marshall was faced, on the matter of a standard text, with the relatively simple task of bringing the universities to replace one book of *Principles* (Mill's) by another (Marshall's) the dissenters were promoting a new type of textbook of a form still to be established.

The relativists were finally saved by the entirely unpredictable foundation of the London School of Economics, which gave them a secure institutional base for their own research, with publication facilities and access to a new generation of students, all of which ensured the survival of their concepts of economics. Their contribution, largely through the foundation of the School, was of major importance in preserving the heterogeneity of economics in Britian.

The Oxford economists' fundamental concept of economics, derived from a wider *Weltanschauung*, and containing a basic research programme and a methodology, may be regarded as a paradigm of some interest to historians of scientific thought in general. It has been observed that this paradigm owes its formation to the effect of a combination of various types of external and internal stimuli on the intellectual development of certain individuals. Some of these stimuli originate from general, social, political, and cultural conditions, others from developments and trends within the scientific community, while the internal state of the science is of influence on the formation of the paradigm only after the *Weltanschauung* of the various individuals is largely formed. Hence one might consider the rejection of J. S. Mill's economics as a response to a general trend prevalent at Oxford at the time to replace Mill's philosophy by Green's Idealism,[3] transformed into an internal issue and strengthened by the criticism of Mill by Toynbee, Rogers, and Jevons. It is doubtful whether any of the views on internal issues were a purely spontaneous reaction by a purely intellectual process of theoretical analysis and study.

The rejection of various aspects of J. S. Mill's work demonstrates the nature of the intellectual environment in which the Oxford paradigm was formed. Simultaneously various paradigms in various fields of scientific enquiry were

[3] Described in Farnell, *An Oxonian Looks Back*, pp. 43-4.

being rejected while the criticism of past theories contained the suggestion of alternatives.[4] There is therefore no clear-cut process of disintegration and rebirth, nor is the term 'revolution' entirely appropriate since, despite their own insistence, Marshall's claim of continuity and the Oxford claim of a break with the past were largely overstatements. That the criticism of the past contained the indication of alternatives is demonstrated in the influence of Rogers. During the eighties he had rejected his previously held orthodoxy but was unable to offer an alternative body of theory, yet his own work in history suggested an alternative approach to economics and had been acknowledged as such. The Oxford economists formed their paradigms in an initial atmosphere of reaction towards previously held theories, while following specific suggestions of alternative approaches to economics.

Paradigms in this case were neither externally imposed nor were they internally produced through spontaneous regeneration. The Oxford paradigm was the result of a combination of responses to various external and internal stimuli in which the individual economist created his own structure by using the building blocks provided by his academic training. The causes of diversity and similarity in paradigms might therefore, best, be sought in the individual processes in which they are formed. The differences between Marshall's concept of economics and Ashley's may be sought largely in their being two different individuals of different ages, temperaments and backgrounds, with different intellectual and professional biographies, responding to different stimuli. At the same time, the existence of an Oxford paradigm indicates the significance of similarity in background, age, and the environment in which the paradigm is formed. Cross-fertilization, the national or even the international nature of various trends, and the similarity in response to some stimuli seem to suggest some of the reasons for similarity in paradigms, for instance, between the Oxford camp and some of its allies.

---

[4] The relevant developments in constitutional history and in philosophy seem to suggest that a case might be made for a comparative examination of the reasons for which various paradigms in a number of fields were rejected at roughly the same time and of the alternatives suggested.

Within the limits of this study there is no case of radical conversion of a mature economist from one paradigm to another. This does not exclude the possibility of such a conversion. An economist might regard his paradigm as inadequate, as Rogers did in his later years, or even change some of it as Cunningham seems to have done in the course of the controversy over the nature of economics. Yet the process of conversion is not a creative one. The convert does not create a new paradigm to replace an inadequate one but rather adopts an existing alternative.

A change of paradigm should be distinguished from such minor changes such as those in the prescribed policy. Our economists proved to be reluctant to admit that a change in prescribed policy in any way indicated a change in their basic ideology. Hence both Cannan and Ashley argued that their opposite positions on tariff were consistent with basically identical social ideologies. The nature of conversion and the reluctance to abandon or change fundamental concepts seem to suggest, at least in this case, that the individual's creative process at the most fundamental level is limited to the creation of one paradigm which is a derivative of his basic *Weltanschauung*.

This paradigm consists of the individual's first comprehensive concept of the nature and scope of his profession and it, in turn, is expressed in his first independent research programme. If this can be shown to be the case in similar instances, it may be argued that within a given scientific field the sequence of paradigms might be considered as a sequence of generations of scientists. One paradigm replaces the other as one generation of scientists replaces the other, and the cause of the relation of one paradigm to another should therefore be sought in the initial process of each generation's intellectual development.

Finally, to return to the first conclusion, the study suggests a possible pattern of scientific lateral development. When two paradigms compete for the central position within a field while, at the same time, aiming at the replacement of an older paradigm, or alternatively if the sense of inadequacy of a 'veteran' paradigm is not commonly shared and its position is challenged by only some of the scientists in the field, and if it is believed, not necessarily for objective reasons, that the two paradigms cannot coexist within the same field as currently defined, one paradigm need not necessarily disappear while the other triumphs. Instead the competition may result in the redepartmentalization of the field in such a way that the two paradigms may develop separately as two mutually autonomous scientific departments. Such a development depends to a large extent on external circumstances such as the 'muscle' of each camp and the academic position of its members within the scientific community in general. In any event, it may be assumed that voluntary submission to the authority of a rival paradigm for external reasons is not likely to be the scientist's natural preference.

APPENDIX

Members of the Oxford Economist Society
1886–1891
Academic Record

MEMBERS OF THE OXFORD ECONOMIC SOCIETY 1886–1891—ACADEMIC RECORD

Name	Year of Birth	Matric.	College	Status	Mods.	Class	Final School	Class	Prize	BA	MA	First Fellowship
J. J. Bickerton	1840	23.5.1866	Charsley Hall				Law & Mod. Hist. 1870	3rd		1870	1876	
P. F. Willert	1844	20.10.1862 trans. 1864–7	Balliol C.C.C.	Taylorian Scholar Scholar	Cl. Mods. 1864	2nd	Lit. Hum. 1866	1st		1867	1869	Exeter 1867
W. A. Spooner	1844	18.10.1862	New Coll.	Scholar	Cl. Mods. 1864	1st	Lit. Hum. 1866	1st		1867	1869	New Coll. 1867
R. Ewing	1846	16.10.1866	Balliol	Exhib.	Cl. Mods. 1868 Math. Mods. 1868	2nd 1st	Lit. Hum. 1870	1st	Junior Greek Test. 1869	1870	1873	St. John's 1870
St. G. W. J. Stock	1850	26.10.1868	Pembroke	Scholar	Cl. Mods. 1870	1st	Class. 1872	2nd		1873	1875	
W. J. H. Campion	1851	10.6.1870	Univ.	Exhib.	Cl. Mods. 1872 Math. Mods. 1872	2nd 1st	Lit. Hum. 1874	2nd		1875	1875	Keble 1882
A. W. Roberts	1851	25.10.1869	Lincoln		Cl. Mods. 1871	3rd	History 1873 Jur. 1873 B.C.L. 1875	1st 2nd 2nd		1873 B.C.L. 1875		
T. C. Snow	1852	19.10.1870	C.C.C.	Scholar	Cl. Mods. 1872	1st	Class. 1874	1st		1874	1877	St. John's 1875
L. R. Phelps	1853	22.10.1872	Oriel	1) Scholar 2) Exhib.	Cl. Mods. 1874	2nd	Class. 1876	2nd		1877	1879	Oriel 1877
D. G. Ritchie	1854	26.5.1874	Balliol	Class. Exhib.	Cl. Mods. 1875	1st	Lit. Hum. 1878	1st		1878	1881	Jesus 1878
S. Ball	1857	19.10.1875	Oriel	1) Scholar 2) Ireland Exhib. 3) Robinson Exhib.	Cl. Mods. 1877	1st	Class. 1879	2nd		1879	1883	St. John's 1882
O. M. Edwards	1858	15.10.1884	Balliol	Brackenbury Scholar			History 1877	1st	Stanhope 1886 Lothian 1887 (Arnold His. Essay 1888)	1888	1889	Lincoln 1889

APPENDIX

Name	Matric.	College			Mods.	Cl. or Class	Final School	Cl. or Class	Scholarships/Prizes			Fellowship
W. J. Ashley	19.10.1878	Balliol					Mod. His. 1881	1st	Shakespeare 1880 Lothian 1882	1881	1885	Lincoln 1885
M. E. Sadler	19.10.1880	Trinity	Scholar		Cl. Mods. 1882	1st	Class. 1884	1st		1884	1887	Ch. Ch. 1890
E. Cannan	29.1.1881	Balliol			Cl. Mods. 1882	2nd	Pass 1884		Lothian 1885	1884	1887	
D. J. Medley	19.10.1880	Keble					History 1883	1st		1883	1887	Keble 1884
A. J. Carlyle	18.10.1883	Exeter		Exhib.			Mod. His. 1886 Theology 1887	1st 2nd		1886		Univ. 1893
J. Carter	18.10.1882	Exeter		Exhib.			Class. 1887	2nd		1887		
L. L. F. R. Price	15.10.1881	Trinity	Scholar		Cl. Mods. 1882	3rd	Lit. Hum. 1885	1st		1885	1888	Oriel 1888
J. Tracey	18.10.1881	Brasenose	Scholar		Cl. Mods. 1883	1st	Lit. Hum. 1885	1st		1885	1888	Keble 1887
F. S. Marvin	14.10.1882	St. John's	1) Scholar 2) Senior Scholar 1887		Cl. Mods. 1884	1st	Class. 1886 History 1887	1st 2nd		1886	1889	
L. T. Hobhouse	19.10.1883	C.C.C.	Class. Scholar		Cl. Mods. 1884	1st	Class. 1887	1st		1887	1890	Merton 1887
H. Ll. Smith	19.10.1883	C.C.C.	Scholar		Math. Mods. 1884	1st	Math. 1886	1st	Cobden 1886	1886	1889	
H. W. Blunt	31.10.1882	Oriel	Scholar		Cl. Mods. 1883	2nd	Class. 1886	1st	Arnold 1887	1886	1889	Ch. Ch. 1889
W. G. Smith	14.10.1882	St. John's	Scholar		Cl. Mods. 1884	1st	Class. 1886 History 1887	1st 1st		1886	1889	St. John's 1889
H. L. Withers	10.10.1883	Balliol	Scholar		Cl. Mods. 1884	1st	Lit. Hum. 1887	1st		1887	1894	
W. A. S. Hewins	27.10.1884	Pembroke	Scholar		Math. Mods. 1885	1st	Math. 1887	2nd		1887		

LIST OF ABBREVIATIONS

Matric. — Matriculation
Mods. — Moderations
Cl. or Class. — Classics
Math. — Mathematics

Lit. Hum. — Literae Humaniores
Mod. His. — Modern History
Jur. — Jurisprudence
Exhib. — Exhibitioner

C.C.C. — Corpus Christi College
New Coll. — New College
Ch. Ch. — Christ Church

Source: A. Kadish, 'Oxford Economists and the Young Extension', in Trevor Rowley (ed.), *The Oxford Region* (Oxford, 1980).

BIBLIOGRAPHY

A. MANUSCRIPT SOURCES

1. Cambridge
    (a) Cambridge University Archives
    (b) Marshall Library
        1. J. N. Keynes papers
        2. Marshall papers
        3. Miscellaneous economists' papers
2. GLC Record Office
    A/Toy
3. Lambeth Palace, London
    Barnett papers
4. Leeds University, Brotherton Library
    L. L. Price papers
5. London School of Economics and Political Science
    (a) Cannan papers
    (b) Giffen papers
    (c) Passfield papers
    (d) School archives
        1. Hutchinson Trust Minute Books
        2. Material related to the early history of the LSE,
    (e) Wallas papers
6. Oxford
    (a) Balliol College
        1. Cannan notebooks
        2. Jowett papers
        3. A. L. Smith papers
    (b) Bodleian Library
        1. Papers related to the activities of various Oxford societies and clubs, including the Oxford Economic Society and the Oxford University Political Economy Club.
        2. Papers related to the activity of various Boards of Studies.
        3. F. S. Marvin papers
        4. M. E. Sadler papers
    (c) Corpus Christi College
        1. C.C.C Debating Society Minute Books
        2. The Pelican Club Minute Books
    (d) Magdalen College
        Thorold Rogers papers

(e) New College
    Spooner MSS
(f) Nuffield College
    1. Edgeworth papers
    2. Fabian papers
(g) Oriel College
    1. Phelps papers
    2. Price MSS
(h) Pusey House
    Oxford Branch of the Christian Social Union Minute Book
(i) Rewley House
    Oxford University Extension Lectures Archive
(j) Trinity College
    L. L. Price chapter from autobiographical MS
7. Private Papers
   (a) Cannan family papers c/o Mrs Diana Farr
   (b) Gell family papers c/o Mrs P. V. W. Gell
   (c) Inglis Palgrave papers c/o Mrs Barker
   (d) Llewellyn Smith family papers c/o Dr S. Llewellyn Smith
8. Royal Statistical Society
   L. L. Price MS
9. Sheffield University Library
   Hewins papers

B. ORAL SOURCES

Information has been obtained through interviews from Mrs Diana Farr, Lord Hall, Dr S. Llewellyn Smith and Lord Robbins.

C. PRINTED SOURCES
    1. Primary Sources
   (a) Periodicals, newspapers, yearbooks, etc.

British Association for the Advancement of Science, Reports of Annual Meetings
Cambridge University General Almanac and Register
Co-operative Congress, Annual Report
Economic Journal
Economic Review
Journal of the Royal Statistical Society
Oriel Record
Oxford Chronicle
Oxford Gazette
Oxford Magazine
Oxford University Extension Gazette
Proceedings of the Oxford University Union Society
Pelican

   (b) Books and articles. The entries by W. J. Ashley, S. Ball, Edwin Cannan, W. Cunningham, W. A. S. Hewins, L. L. Price, and H. Ll. Smith are in chronological rather than alphabetical order.

ASHLEY, W. J., *James and Philip van Artvelde* (London, 1833).
——, various articles in Sidney J. Low and F. S. Pulling, *The Dictionary of English History* (London, 1884).

——, 'Feudalism', in H. O. Wakeman and A. Hassal, *Essays Introductory to the Study of English Constitutional History* (London, 1880).
——, 'Modern History' in A. N. N. Stedman (ed.), *Oxford, Its Life and Schools* (London, 1887).
——, *The Early History of the English Woollen Industry* (American Economic Association, September 1887).
——, Review of L. L. Price, *Industrial Peace, Oxford Magazine,* 1 Feb. 1888.
——, 'Industrial Peace; Our Reviewer Replies', *Oxford Magazine* 7 Mar. 1888.
——, *Surveys Historic and Economic* (London, 1900): contains most of Ashley's important reviews and articles of the period published outside Britain.
——, *What is Political Economy?* (Toronto, 1888).
——, *An Introduction to English Economic History and Theory,* vol. i, part i (London, 1888), part ii (London, 1893).
——, 'Introductory chapter on the English Manor' in Fustel de Coulanges, *The Origin of Property in Land* (London, 1891).
——, 'The Destruction of the Village Community', *Econ. Rev.* July 1891.
——, 'The Rehabilitation of Ricardo', *Econ. J.* September 1891.
——, Review of Goldwin Smith, *Canada, Econ. Rev.* October 1891.
——, 'Methods of Industrial Peace', *Econ. Rev.* July 1892.
——, 'The History of English Serfdom', *Econ. Rev.* April 1893.
——, Reviews on German and English Medieval History in the *Econ. J.* June 1893, December 1893, June 1894, June 1895, September 1895, and December 1895.
——, Introduction to G. Schmoller, *The Mercantile System and its Historical Significance,* trans. by W. J. Ashley (New York, 1896).
——, *Social Legislation* (Oxford, 1909).
——, J. S. Mill, *Principles of Political Economy,* edited by W. J. Ashley (London, 1909).
——, *Scientific Management and the Engineering Situation* (Oxford, 1922).
——, *The Christian Outlook; Being the Sermons of an Economist* (London, 1925).
——, The Place of Economic History in University Studies', in *Econ. Hist. Rev.* January 1927.
ASHTON, ARTHUR, *As I Went on My Way* (London, 1924).
BALL, SIDNEY, 'A Plea for Liberty; A Criticism', *Econ. Rev.* July 1891.
——, Review of the Duke of Argyll, *The Unseen Foundations of Society, Econ. Rev.,* April 1893.
——, Review of N. P. Gilman, *Socialism and the American Spirit, Econ. Rev.* October 1893.
——, Review of A. Watt, *An Outline of Legal Philosophy, International Journal of Ethics,* January 1894.
——, 'Socialism according to Bebel', *Econ. Rev.* April 1894.
——, Review of G. B. Wilson, *Drunkenness, International Journal of Ethics,* April 1894.
——, Review of L. T. Hobhouse, *The Labour Movement, International Journal of Ethics,* July 1894.
——, 'Nicholson's "Principles of Political Economy",' *Econ. Rev.* October 1894.

——, Review of Luigi Cossa, *An Introduction to the Study of Political Economy*, *Econ. Rev.* October 1894.
——, 'Nicholson's "Historical Progress and Ideal Socialism",' *Econ. Rev.* April 1895.
——, Review of F. Dolman, *Municipalities at Work*, A. Shaw, *Municipal Government in Great Britain*, and F. J. Goodnow, *Municipal Home Rule*, *Econ. Rev.* October 1895.
——, Review of J. G. Brooks, *Compulsory Insurance in Germany*, *Econ. Rev.* October 1895.
BARNETT, HENRIETTA, *Canon Barnett; His Life, Work and Friends*, (London, 1918).
BARNETT, S. A. and H., *Practicable Socialism; Essays on Social Reform* (London, 1888, 2nd edn., revised and enlarged 1894).
BLUNT, H. W., 'A Footnote to Ruskin', *Economic Review*, July 1900.
BOOTH, CHARLES, (ed.), *Life and Labour of the People of London*, vol. i (London, 1889); vol. ii (London, 1891).
——, 'Presidential Address', *Journal of the Royal Statistical Society*, December 1891.
BORWICK, F., *Clifton College Annals and Register 1862–1912* (Bristol, 1912).
BOYD, C. W. (ed.), *Mr. Chamberlain's Speeches*, 2 vols. (London, 1914).
BRYCE, JAMES, 'The Future of English Universities', *Fortnightly Review*, March 1883.
CAIRD, E., 'Political Economy Old and New', *Quarterly Journal of Economics*, January 1888.
CANNAN, EDWIN, *The Duke of Saint Simon* (Oxford and London, 1885), Letters to the *Oxford Magazine*, 26 May, 9 June, 23 July 1886.
——, ' "Industrial Peace": Our Reviewer Reviewed', *Oxford Magazine*, 8 Feb. 1888.
——, *Elementary Political Economy* (Oxford and London, 1888).
——, Legislation, Parliamentary Inquiries and Official Returns, *Econ. Rev.* 1891–1902.
——, Review of Say and Chailley, *Nouveau Dictionnaire d'Économie Politique*, *Econ. Rev.* April 1891, July 1892, January 1893.
——, Review of Bowker and Iles (edd.), *The Reader's Guide in Economic, Social and Political Science*, *Econ. Rev.* July 1891.
——, Review of O. Mühlbrecht, *Uebersicht der gesammten staats und rechtwissenschaflichen litteratur des Jahres 1890*, *Econ. Rev.* July 1891.
——, 'The Malthusian Anti-Socialist Argument', *Economic Review*, January 1892.
——, Note, 'What is one pauper?', *Econ. Rev.* April 1892
——, Review of C. F. Bastable, *Public Finance*, *Economic Review*, October 1892.
——, 'Bimetallism; A Criticism', *Econ. Rev.* October 1892.
——, *The History of Theories of Production and Distribution 1776–1848* (London, 1893).
——, Review of P. Mayet, *Agricultural Insurance*, *Econ. Rev.* January 1894.
——, Note, 'The Growth of Manchester and Liverpool 1801–1891', *Econ. J.* March 1894.

——, Review of *Industries of Russia*, *Econ. Rev.* April 1894.
——, 'Ricardo in Parliament', *Econ. J.* June and September 1894.
——, Note, 'The Eight Hours Day at Salford Ironworks', *Econ. Rev.* July 1894.
——, Review of *London Statistics 1892–93*, *Econ. Rev.* July 1894.
——, Review of Dodd, *The Parish Councils' Act Explained*, *Econ. Rev.* July 1894.
——, Review of E. Helm, *The Joint Standard*, *Econ. Rev.* October 1894.
——, Review of W. Brough, *The Natural Law of Money*, *Econ. Rev.* January 1895.
——, 'Inequality of Local Rates and Its Economic Justification', *Econ. J.* March 1895.
——, Review of R. S. Wright and H. Hobhouse, *An Outline of Local Government*, *Econ. J.* March 1895.
——, Review of *London Statistics 1893–94*, *Econ. Rev.* April 1895.
——, Review of A. Shaw, *Municipal Government*, *Econ. J.* 1895.
——, 'The Stigma of Pauperism', *Econ. Rev.* July 1895.
——, 'The Probability of a Cessation of the Growth of Population in England and Wales during the next Century', *Econ. J.* December 1895.
——, *The History of Local Rates in England* (London, 1896, 2nd edn. 1912).
——, Review of Lord Farrer, *The Quantitative Theory of Money and Prices*, *Econ. J.* March 1898.
——, Review of Lord Farrer, *Studies in Currency*, *Econ. Rev.* October 1898
——, 'The Practical helpfulness of Economic Theory', read to Section F, September 1902, in R. L. Smyth (ed.), *Essays in Economic Method* (London, 1962).
——, Review of Jevons, *The Principles of Economics*, *Econ. Rev.* April 1906.
——, *The Economic Outlook* (London, 1912).
——, 'Alfred Marshall 1842–1924', *Economica*, November 1924.
——, *An Economist's Protest* (London, 1927).
——, *Balance of Trade Delusions* (Oxford, 1931).
CANNAN, GILBERT, *Little Brother* (London, 1912).
CANNAN, MAY WEDDERBURN, *Grey Ghosts and Voices* (Kineton, 1976).
CARTER, J., *The Christian Social Union* (Oxford, 1910).
CHRISTIE, O. F., *Clifton School Days 1879–1885* (London, 1930).
——, *The Claims of Labour* (Edinburgh, 1886).
——, *Co-operative Life* (London, 1889).
CREIGHTON, MANDELL, 'Prefatory Note', *EHR* January, 1886.
CUNNINGHAM, W., 'The Progress of Socialism in England', *Contemporary Review*, January 1879.
——, *Growth of English Industry and Commerce* (Cambridge, 1882).
——, 'English Industry and Commerce, Reply to Professor Thorold Rogers', *Academy*, 27 May 1882.
——, 'On the Statement of the Malthusian Principle', *Macmillan's Magazine*, December 1883.
——, 'Repression of the Woollen Manufacture in Ireland', *EHR* April 1886.
——, 'The Comtist Criticism of Economic Science', read at Section F, Newcastle upon Tyne 1889, *Proc. Brit. Assoc.* (London, 1889).
——, 'What did our Forefathers mean by Rent?,' *Lippincott's Magazine*,

February 1890.
——, 'Nationalism and Cosmopolitanism in Economics', read at Section F meeting, Cardiff 1891, *Proc. Brit. Assoc.* (London, 1891).
——, 'A Plea for Pure Theory', *Econ. Rev.* January 1892.
——, 'The Relativity of Economic Doctrine', *Econ. J.* March 1892.
——, 'Perversion of Economic History', *Econ. J.* September 1892.
——, 'The Perversion of Economic History; A Reply to Prof. Marshall', *Pall Mall Gazette*, 29 Sept., and *Academy*, 1 Oct. 1892.
——, 'Political Economy and Practical Life', *International Journal of Ethics*, January 1893.
——, 'Economists as Mischief Makers', *Econ. Rev.* January 1894.
——, 'A Living Wage', *Contemporary Review*, January 1894.
——, 'Dr. Cunningham and his Critics', *Econ. J.* Sept. 1894.
——, 'Why has Roscher so little influence in England?', *Annals of American Academy of Political and Social*, November 1894.
——, 'The General Election—Prospects of Social Legislation', *Econ. Rev.* October 1895.
EDGEWORTH, F. Y., 'An Introductory Lecture on Political Economy', *Econ. J.* December 1891.
ELLIOT, IVO, *The Balliol College Register 1833–1933* (2nd edn., Oxford, 1934).
FARNELL, LEWIS R., *An Oxonion Looks Back* (London, 1934).
FARRER, LORD, 'Inaugural Address', *Journal of the Royal Statistical Society* December 1893.
——, 'Presidential Address', *Journal of the Royal Statistical Society*, December 1894.
FAWCETT, M. G., *Political Economy for Beginners* (London, 1876).
FISHER, H. A. L., *An Unfinished Biography* (Oxford, 1940).
FOXWELL, H. S., 'Bimetallism; Its Meaning and Aims', *Economic Review*, July 1893.
——, 'The Economic Movement in England', *Quarterly Journal of Economics*, October 1887.
——, 'What is Political Economy?', *Eagle*, No. 79 (1885).
FREEMAN, E. A., *The Growth of the English Constitution from the Earliest Times* (London, 1872).
——, 'Oxford after Forty Years', *Contemporary Review* 1887.
FURNISS, HENRY SANDERSON, *Memories of Sixty Years* (London, 1931).
GORE, CHARLES (ed.), *Lux Mundi* (London, 1889).
GOSCHEN, G. J., 'Ethics and Economics', *Econ. J.* September 1893.
——, *Guide to the Co-operative Congress of 1882* (Oxford, 1882).
[HENSON, HERBERT HENLEY], 'Oxford and Its Professors', *Edinburgh Review*, October 1889.
HEWINS, W. A. S. 'The National Debt; Its Origin, Growth, and the Methods which have been adopted from time to time for its reduction', in *The Co-operative Wholesale Society Ltd. Annual and Diary* 1889 (Manchester, 1889).
——, Review of Wells, *Recent Economic Changes*, *Econ. Rev.* January 1891.
——, Review of Mummery and Hobson, *The Physiology of Industry*, *Econ. Rev.*

January 1891.
——, 'The Co-operative Movement', *Econ. Rev.* October 1891.
——, Review of Thorold Rogers, *The Industrial and Commercial History of England*, *Econ. J.* September 1892.
——, Review of Cunningham, *The Growth of English Industry and Commerce*, *Econ. J.* December 1892.
——, *English Trade and Finance; Chiefly in the Seventeenth Century* (London, 1892).
——, 'Ashley's Economic History', *Econ. Rev.* April 1895.
——, 'The Teaching of Economics', *Journal of the Society of Arts*, 4 Dec. 1896.
——, 'The London School of Economics and Political Science', in *Education Department Special Reports on Educational Subjects*, vol. 2 (HMSO 1898).
——, *Trade in the Balance* (London, 1924).
——, *The Apologia of an Imperialist* (London, 1929).
HOBHOUSE, L. T., *The Labour Movement* (London, 1893).
——, Review of Howell, *Conflicts of Capital and Labour*, *Econ. Rev.* January 1891.
HOPE, ANTHONY, *Memories and Notes* (London, 1927).
——, *Industrial Remuneration Conference* (London, 1885).
JEPSON, EDGAR, *Memories of a Victorian* (London, 1933).
JEVONS, W. STANLEY, *The Theory of Political Economy edited by R. D. Collison Black* (Pelican edn., Harmondsworth, 1970).
——, *The State in Relation to Labour* (London, 1882).
KADISH, A., 'Oxford Economists and the Young Extension', in Trevor Rowley (ed.), *The Oxford Region* (Oxford, 1980).
KEYNES, J. N., Review of Ricardo, *Principles*, *Econ. J.* December 1891.
LAURIE, ARTHUR P., *Pictures and Politics; A Book of Reminiscences* (London, 1934).
LESLIE, T. E. CLIFFE, *Essays in Political Economy* (London and Dublin, 1888).
MACAULAY, LORD, *Reviews, Essays and Poems* (London, 1875).
MCCREADY, H. W., 'Sir William Ashley; Some unpublished letters', *J. Econ. Hist.* 1955.
MARSHALL, ALFRED, *The Economics of Industry* (London, 1879).
——, *Elements of Economics of Industry* (London, 1892).
——, Preface to L. L. Price, *Industrial Peace* (London, 1887).
——, *The Present Position of Economics* (London, 1885).
——, 'The Present Position of Economics', *The Times*, 2 June 1885.
——, *Principles of Economics*, ed. C. W. Guillebaud (9th edn. London, 1961).
——, 'Progress and Poverty', reprinted by G. J. Stigler, in *Journal of Law and Economics*, April 1969.
——, 'A Reply to "The Perversion of Economic History" by Dr. Cunningham', *Econ. J.* September 1892.
——, 'Some Aspects of Competition', address to Section F, Leeds 1890, reprinted in A. C. Pigou (ed.), *Memorials of Alfred Marshall* (London, 1925).
——, 'Theories and Facts about wages', *The Co-operative Wholesale Society Ltd. Annual 1885* (Manchester, 1885).
——, 'Two Early Articles', reprinted by L. Royden Harrison in *Econ. J.* 1963.

——, 'Wages and Profits', *Quart. J. Econ.* January 1888.
MARSHALL, MARY PALEY, *What I Remember* (Cambridge, 1947).
MEARNS, ANDREW, *The Bitter Cry of Outcast London* (London, 1883).
MEDLEY, D. J., Review of Cunningham, *The Growth of English Industry and Commerce, Econ. Rev.* January 1893.
——, Review of R. T. Ely, *An Introduction to Political Economy, Econ. Rev.* October 1891.
——, Review of J. E. Thorold Rogers, *The Economic Interpretaton of History, Econ. Rev.* January 1892.
——, Review of J. E. Thorold Rogers, *England's Industrial and Commercial Supremacy, Econ. Rev.* July 1892.
——, *Socialism as a Moral Movement; A Short Consideration of its Value and its Dangers* (Oxford, 1884).
MOUAT, F. J., 'Inaugural Address', *Journal of the Royal Statistical Society,* December 1890.
NICHOLSON, J. S., *The Effects of Machinery on Wages* (2nd edn. London 1892).
——, 'A Plea for Orthodox Political Economy', *National Review,* December 1885.
——, *Political Economy as a Branch of Education* (Edinburgh, 1881).
——, 'Profit Sharing', *Contemporary Review,* January 1890.
——, 'The Reaction in Favour of the Classical Political Economy', *Journal of the Royal Statistical Society,* December 1893.
OMAN, CHARLES, *Memories of Victorian Oxford* (London, 1941).
ORMISTON, THOMAS LANE, *Dulwich College Register 1619–1926* (London, 1927).
Oxford Tutor, An, 'Young Oxford', *Fraser's Magazine,* May 1881.
'Oxford Professors and Oxford Tutors', *Contemporary Review,* February 1890.
Oxford University Extension Lectures, Report of a Conference of Representatives of the Local Committees, Oxford, April 20–21 1887 (Oxford, 1887).
PALGRAVE, R. H. INGLIS (ed.), *Dictionary of Political Economy* (London, 1891–6).
PASCOE, CHARLES EYRE, *Where Shall I Educate My Son?* (London, 1884).
PHELPS, L. R., 'The Economy of High Wages', *Edinburgh Review,* January 1894.
——, Review of Keynes, *Scope and Method, Econ. Rev.* October 1891.
——, 'Population', *Edinburgh Review,* October 1892.
——, 'The Wages of Labour', *Edinburgh Review,* January 1890.
——, 'Present Position', *The Times,* 30 May 1885.
PRICE, BONAMY, *Practical Political Economy* (London, 1878).
PRICE, L. L. F. R. *Industrial Peace; Its Advantages, Methods and Difficulties* (London, 1887).
——, 'West Barbary or Notes on the System of Work and Wages in the Cornish Mines', *Journal of the Royal Statistical Society,* September 1888.
——, 'The Relations between Industrial Conciliation and Economic Theory', read at Section F, Bath 1888, and reprinted in L. L. Price, *Economic Science and Practice* (London, 1896).
——, 'The Relations between Industrial Conciliation and Social Reform', *Journal of the Royal Statistical Society,* June 1890.

—— 'Some Typical Fallacies of Social Reformers', read at Section F, Leeds 1890, reprinted in *Economic Science and Practice* (London, 1896)
——, *Journal of the Royal Statistical Society*, September 1890.
——, *A Short History of Political Economy in England from Adam Smith to Arnold Toynbee* (London, 1891).
——, Review of Smith, *Emigration and Immigration*, *Econ. J.* March 1891.
——, 'Some Aspects of the Theory of Rent', *Econ. J.* March 1891.
——, Review of Ely, *An Introduction to Political Economy*, *Econ. J.* September 1891.
——, Review of C. Booth, *Life and Labour*, *Econ. J.* September 1891.
——, Review of Howell, *Trade Unionism*, *Econ. J.* September 1891.
——, Review of Social Science Series, *Econ. J.* September 1891.
——, Review of J. Mavor, *The Scottish Railway Strike*, *Econ. J.* September 1891.
——, Review of Palgrave, *Dictionary of Political Economy*, *Econ. J.* September 1891.
——, Review of Stanton Coit, *Neighbourhood Guilds*, *Econ. J.* December 1891.
——, Review of B. Potter, *The Co-operative Movement*, and Holyoake, *The Co-operative Movement*, *International Journal of Ethics*, January 1892.
——, 'The Recent Depression in Agriculture as shown in the Accounts of an Oxford College 1876–1890'. *Journal of the Royal Statistical Society*, March 1892.
——, 'Notes on a Recent Economic Treatise', *Econ. J.* March 1892.
——, Review of Gide, *Principles of Political Economy*, *Econ. J.* March 1892.
——, Review of Cook Taylor, *The Modern Factory System*, *Econ. J.* March 1892.
——, Review of Mahain, *Étude sur l'Association Professionelle*, *Econ. J.* March 1892.
——, Review of Marshall's, *Elements of Economics*, *Econ. J.* June 1892.
——, Review of Schloss, *Methods of Industrial Remuneration*, *Econ. J.* June 1892.
——, Review of C. F. Bastable, *The Commerce of Nations*, *Econ. J.* June 1892.
——, Review of Perry, *Principles of Political Economy*, *Econ. J.* June 1892.
——, Review of Booth, *The Darkest England Social Scheme*, *International Journal of Ethics*, October 1892.
——, Review of Cunningham, *The Use and Abuse of Money*, *International Journal of Ethics*, October 1892.
——, 'Profit Sharing and Co-operative Production', *Econ. J.* September 1892.
——, Review of Giffen, *The Case Against Bimetallism*, *Economic Journal*, December 1892.
——, Review of *The Proceedings of the Bimetallic Conference*, *Econ. J.* December 1892.
——, Review of Bastable, *Public Finance*, *Economic Journal*, December 1892.
——, Review of Wise, *Industrial Freedom*, *Econ. J.* December 1892.
——, 'Methods of Industrial Reform', 1893, reprinted in *Economic Science and Practice*, op. cit.
——, Review of Nicholson, *The Effect of Machinery*, *Econ. J.* March 1893.
——, Review of Ross, *Sinking Funds*, *Econ. J.* March 1893.

——, Note, 'The National Agricultural Conference', *Econ. J.* March 1893.
——, 'Adam Smith and his Relations to Recent Economics', *Econ. J.* June 1893.
——, Review of the Duke of Argyll, *The Unseen Foundations*, *Econ. J.* June 1893.
——, Review of Bonar, *Philosophy and Political Economy*, *Econ. J.* June 1893.
——, Review of Pearson, *National Life*, *Econ. J.* September 1893.
——, Review of Clare, *The ABC of Foreign Exchanges*, *Econ. J.* September 1893.
——, Review of de Molinari, *Précis d'Économie Politique*, *Econ. J.* September 1893.
——, Review of Shaw Lefevre, 'Agrarian Tenures', *Econ. J.* September 1893.
——, 'On Some Objections to Bimetallism', *Econ. J.* December 1893.
——, Review of Nicholson, *Principles of Political Economy*, *Econ. J.* December 1893.
——, Review of de Molinari, *Les Bourses du Travail*, *Econ. J.* December 1893.
——, Review of L. T. Hobhouse, *The Labour Movement*, *Econ. J.* March 1894.
——, Review of Shaw Lefevre, *The English Commons*, *Econ. J.* June 1894.
——, Review of Morris and Bax, *Socialism*, *International Journal of Ethics*, July 1894.
——, Review of Mallock, *Labour and Popular Welfare*, *International Journal of Ethics*, July 1894.
——, 'The Report of the Labour Commission', *Econ. J.* September 1894.
——, Review of Kidd, *Social Evolution*, *Econ. J.* September 1894.
——, Review of Rae, *Eight Hours*, and Brentano, *Hours and Wages*, *Econ. J.* September 1894.
——, Review of Jones, *Co-operative Production*, *Econ. J.* December 1894.
——, Review of J. A. Hobson, *The Evolution of Modern Capitalism*, Cooke-Taylor, *The Factory System*, and Jeans, *Trusts, Pools and Corners*, *Econ. J.* December 1894.
——, Review of Rae, *Life of Adam Smith*, *Econ. J.* June 1895.
——, Review of Cunningham and McArthur, *Outlines of English Industrial History*, *Econ. J.* June 1895.
——, 'The Relations of Economic Science to Practical Affairs', read at Section F, Ipswich 1895, reprinted in *Economic Science and Practice*, op. cit.
——, 'International Bimetallism', read to the Economic Society, Newcastle upon Tyne, November 1895, reprinted ibid.
——, Review of Nicholson, 'Treatise on Money', *Econ. J.* December 1895.
——, *Money and its Relations to Prices* (London, 1896).
——, 'Co-operation in its Relations to Trade Unionism and Socialism', read to the Oxford Co-operative Society, March 1896, reprinted in *Economic Science and Practice*, op. cit.
——, Review of Smart, *Studies in Economics*, *International Journal of Ethics*, April 1896.
——, *A Short History of English Commerce and Industry* (London, 1900).
——, Review of Ashley, *Surveys*, *Econ. J.* March 1901.
——, *Letter to the Vice Chancellor; The Present Position of Economic Study in Oxford* (Oxford, 1902).

——, Review of Thorold Rogers, *History of Agriculture*, *EHR* July 1903.
——, 'Letter to Edgeworth', *The Times*, 15 Aug. 1903.
——, 'The Fiscal Question; Retrospect and Prospect', *Econ. Rev.* April 1906.
——, *The Position and Prospects of the Study of Economic History* (Oxford, 1907).
——, 'Obituary; F. Y. Edgeworth', *Journal of Royal Statistical Society*, March 1926.
——, 'Obituary; W. A. S. Hewins', *Econ. J.* March 1932.
Q[UILLER-COUCH, A. T.], *Memories and Opinions; An Unfinished Autobiography* (Cambridge, 1974).
RITCHIE, D. G., Review of C. Booth, *Life and Labour*, *Econ. Rev.* April 1893.
——, Review of Cannan, *A History of Theories*, *Econ. Rev.* July 1893.
——, Note, 'The London School of Economics and Political Science', *Econ. Rev.* July 1895.
——, *The Moral Function of the State* (London, 1887).
——, 'The Social Contract Theory', *Political Science Quarterly* December 1891.
——, *The Ultimate Value of Social Effort* (London, 1890).
——, 'What are Economic Laws', *Econ. Rev.* July 1892.
ROGERS, J. E. THOROLD, 'A Century-and-a-half of English Labour', in the *Co-operative Wholesale Society Ltd. Annual 1885* (Manchester, 1885).
——, *A Manual of Political Economy* (3rd edn. Oxford, 1876).
——, 'Oxford and its Professors', *Edinburgh Review*, October 1889.
——, *Six Centuries of Work and Wages* (5th edn. London, 1908).
RUSKIN, JOHN, *Unto this Last* (London, 1862).
SADLER, M. E., *The Economic Force of Combination* (Oxford, 1889).
——, 'Introduction' to W. F. Moulton, *Richard Green Moulton; A Memoir* (London, 1926).
——, 'Oxford University Extension Lectures', in A. M. M. Stedman, (ed.), *Oxford; Its Life and Schools* (London, 1887).
——, 'Owen, Lovett, Maurice and Toynbee', *University Review*, July 1907.
——, 'Rugby' in C. E. Pascoe, *Everyday Life in our Public Schools* (London, 1881).
——, *Three Lectures on the Beginnings of Modern Socialism* (Oxford, 1889).
SADLER, M. E., and H. J. MACKINDER, *University Extension Past, Present and Future* (London, 1891).
SAMUEL, VISCOUNT, *Memoirs* (London, 1945).
SCHMOLLER, G., 'The Idea of Justice in Political Economy', *Annals of the American Academy*, March 1894.
——, *The Mercantile System and its Historical Significance*, trans. by W. J. Ashley. (New York, 1896).
SELBY-BIGGE, L. A., 'Practical Oxford—A Reply to Professor Goldwin Smith', *Contemporary Review*, May 1894.
SICHEL, WALTER, *The Sands of Time* (1923).
SIDGWICK, H., *The Principles of Political Economy* (London, 1883).
——, 'The Scope and Method of Economic Science', read at Section F, Aberdeen 1885, *Proceedings of the British Association* (London, 1885).
SMART, W., 'The Dislocation of Industry', *Contemporary Review*, May 1888.
——, 'The Effects of Consumption of Wealth on Distribution', *Annals of the American Academy of Political and Social Science*, November 1892.

——, 'Glasgow and its Municipal Industries', *Quart. J. Econ.* January 1895.
——, 'The Old Economy and the New', *Fortnightly Review*, August 1891.
——, 'The Place of Industry in the Social Organism', *International Journal of Ethics*, July 1893.
——, *Studies in Economics* (London, 1895).
SMITH, GOLDWIN, *Reminiscences* (New York, 1910).
SMITH, H. Ll., *Economic Aspects of State Socialism* (Oxford, 1887).
——, *Two Lectures on the Books of Political Economy* (London, 1888).
——, 'Influx of Population', in C. Booth (ed.), *Life and Labour*, vol. i (London, 1889).
——, With Vaughan Nash, *The Story of the Dockers' Strike* (London, 1889).
——, *Modern Changes in the Mobility of Labour* (London, 1890).
——, 'Migration', in C. Booth (ed.), *Life and Labour*, vol. ii, part iii, (London, 1891).
——, Review of J. A. Hobson, *Problems of Poverty*, *Econ. J.* September 1891.
——, 'The Teaching of London; A scheme for technical instruction', *Contemporary Review*, May 1892.
——, 'Chapters in the History of London Waterside Labour', *Econ. J.* December 1892.
——, 'The Food of London', *Quarterly Review*, October 1899, January 1900.
SMITH, W. G., Review of L. T. Hobhouse, *The Labour Movement*, *Econ. Rev.* October 1893.
SNOW, T. C., Review of Bentham, *Fragment on Government*, *Econ. Rev.* April 1891.
——, Review of Lord Brassey, *Papers and Addresses*, *Econ. Rev.* October 1895.
——, 'Liberal Theology in the Church of England', *Contemporary Review*, January 1892.
SORLEY, W. R., *Mining Royalties and their Effect on the Iron and Coal Trade* (London, 1889).
Statements of the Needs of the University (Oxford, 1902).
STRACHEY, JOHN ST. LOE, *The Adventure of Living; A Subjective Autobiography* (London, 1925).
STUBBS, WILLIAM, *The Constitutional History of England*, vol. i (4th edn., Oxford, 1883).
TOYNBEE, ARNOLD, *Lectures on the Industrial Revolution* (Popular edn. London, 1908).
——, *Progress and Poverty; A Criticism of Mr. Henry George* (London, 1885).
WAINEWRIGHT, JOHN BANNERMAN, *Winchester College 1830–1906; A Register* (Winchester, 1907).
WALLACE, WILLIAM, *Lectures and Essays edited by E. Caird* (Oxford, 1898).
WEBB, BEATRICE, *Our Partnership* (London, 1948).
WILLERT, P. F., Review of Thorold Rogers, *The Economic Interpretation of History*, *EHR* July 1889.
WRIGHT-HENDERSON, P. A., *Glasgow and Balliol and other Essays* (Oxford, 1926).

2. Secondary Sources

ABBOTT, EVELYN and LEWIS CAMPBELL, *Letters of Benjamin Jowett* (London, 1911).

ANNAN, N. G., 'The Intellectual Aristocracy', in Plumb, J. H. (ed.), *Studies in Social History* (London, 1957).
ASHLEY, ANNE, *William James Ashley; A Life* (London, 1932.).
BALL, OONA H. *Sidney Ball Memories and Impressions of an 'Ideal Don'* (Oxford, 1923).
BEVERIDGE, W. H., *Introduction to The London School of Economcis and Political Science Register 1895–1932* (London, 1934).
BOWLEY, A. L., 'Edwin Cannan', in the *Economic Journal*, June 1935.
BRYCE, JAMES, *Studies in Contemporary Biography* (London, 1903).
CAINE, SIDNEY, *The History of the Foundation of the London School of Economics and Political Science* (London, 1963).
CHRISTIE, O. F., *A History of Clifton College 1860–1934* (Bristol, 1935).
COATS, A. W., 'The Classical Economists and the Factory Acts—A re-examination', in A. W. Coats (ed.), *The Classical Economists and Economic Policy* (London, 1971).
——, 'The Historist Reaction in English Political Economy 1870–1890', *Economica*, May 1954.
——, 'The Origins and Early Development of the Royal Economic Society', *Econ. J.* June 1968.
——, 'Sociological Aspects of British Economic Thought', *Journal of Political Economy*, vol 75, 1967.
——, 'Political Economy and the tariff reform campaign of 1903', *Journal of Law and Economics II* (1968).
CORDER, PERCY, *The Life of Robert Spence Watson* (London, 1917).
CUNNINGHAM, AUDREY, *William Cunningham; Teacher and Priest* (London, 1950).
DALTON, HUGH, and T. E. GREGORY (eds.), *London Essays in Economics in Honour of Edwin Cannan* (London, 1927).
DE MARCHI, N. B., 'On Early Dangers of Being Too Political an Economist; Thorold Rogers and the 1868 Election to the Drummond Professorship', *Oxford Economic Papers*, vol. 28, 1976.
DORFMAN, JOSEPH, *The Economic Mind in American Civilization*, vol. 3 (New York, 1959).
FABER, GEORGE, *Jowett*, (London, 1957).
FARR, DIANA, *Gilbert Cannan; A Georgian Prodigy* (London, 1978).
FAY, C. R., 'Edwin Cannan; A Tribute of a Friend', *Economic Record*, June 1937.
FRASER, W. HAMISH, *Trade Unions and Society* (London, 1974).
FREEDEN, MICHAEL, *The New Liberalism; An Ideology of Social Reform* (Oxford, 1978).
GRAS, N. S. B., 'The Rise and Development of Economic History', *Economic History Review*, January 1927.
GREGORY, T. E., 'Edwin Cannan; A Personal Impression', *Economica*, November 1935.
——, 'Edwin Cannan's Work; A Personal Impression', *Observer*, 14 Apr. 1935.
HALSEY, A. H. (ed.), *Traditions of Social Policy; Essays in Honour of Violet Butler* (Oxford, 1976).

HARTWELL, R. M., 'Good Old Economic History', *Journal of Economic History*, March 1973.
HAYEK, F. A., 'The London School of Economics 1895–1945', *Economica*, February 1946.
HAYTER, WILLIAM, *'Spooner: A Biography'* (London, 1977).
HILL, C. P., *The History of Bristol Grammar School* (London, 1951).
HOBSON, J. A., and M. GINSBERG, *L. T. Hobhouse; His Life and Work* (London, 1931).
HORN, PAMELA, 'Agricultural Trade Unionism in Oxfordshire', in Dunbabin, J. P. D. (ed.), *Rural Discontent in Nineteenth Century Britain* (London, 1974).
HUTCHISON, T. W., *On Revolutions and Progress in Economic Knowledge* (Cambridge, 1978).
JAMES, D. G., *Henry Sidgwick* (Oxford, 1970).
KER, W. P. (ed.), *John Andrew Doyle, Essays on Various Subjects* (London, 1911).
KEYNES, JOHN MAYNARD, *Essays and Sketches in Biography* (Paperback edn. New York, 1956).
LAWRENCE, ELWOOD P., *Henry George in the British Isles* (East Lansing, Michigan, 1957).
LOCKHART, J. G., *Cosmo Gordon Lang* (London, 1949).
LYTTELTON, E., *The Mind and Character of Henry Scott Holland* (London, 1926).
MACKAIL, J. W., *James Leigh Strachan Davidson* (London, 1925).
MADAN, FALCONER, *Records of the Club at Oxford 1790–1917* (Oxford, 1917).
MALONEY, JOHN, 'Marshall, Cunningham and the Emerging Economic Profession', *Economic History Review*, vol. 24 1976.
MALLET, CHARLES E., *Anthony Hope and His Books* (London, 1935).
——, *A History of the University of Oxford*, vol. 3 (reprint London, 1968).
MARRIOTT, STUART, 'Dr. Welch on "Oxford and University Extension": A Critical Note', *Studies in Adult Education*, April 1979.
NORMAN-BUTLER, BELINDA, *Victorian Aspirations; The Life and Labour of Charles and Mary Booth* (London, 1972).
Oxford Co-operative and Industrial Society Ltd.; An Historical Sketch From 1872 to 1909 (Manchester, 1909).
PELLING, HENRY, *A History of British Trade Unionism* (3rd edn. Harmondsworth, 1976).
——, *Origins of the Labour Party* (2nd edn. Oxford, 1965).
PETRIDIS, A., 'Bilateral Monopoly, Tariff Reform and the Teaching of Economics; The Neglected Contribution of Langford Price', *History of Political Economy*, Spring 1979.
PRESTIGE, G. L., *The Life of Charles Gore* (London, 1935).
REMPEL, RICHARD A., *Unionists Divided* (Newton Abbot, Devon, 1972).
RICHTER, MELVIN, *The Politics of Conscience; T. H. Green and his Age* (London, 1964).
ROBBINS, LIONEL, *Autobiography of an Economist* (London, 1977).
——, 'A Student's Recollections of Edwin Cannan', *Econ. J.* June, 1935.
SADLEIR, MICHAEL, *Michael Ernest Sadler; A Memoir by his Son* (London, 1949).
SIMEY, T. S. and M. B., *Charles Booth, Social Scientist* (Cambridge, 1960).
SIMON, BRIAN, *Education and the Labour Movement 1870–1920* (London, 1974).

SMITH, MARY FLORENCE, *Arthur Lionel Smith* (London, 1923).
STEPHENS, W. R. W., *The Life and Letters of Edward A. Freeman*, vol. 2 (London, 1895).
TEMPLE, WILLIAM, *Life of Bishop Percival* (London, 1921).
WHITAKER, J. K., *The Early Economic Writings of Alfred Marshall* (Cambridge, 1975).
WINCH, DONALD, *The Emergence of Economics as a Science 1750–1870* (London, 1971).
YORKE, PAUL, *Ruskin College 1899–1909* (Ruskin College, Oxford, 1977).

D. UNPUBLISHED SECONDARY SOURCES

DAVIDSON, ROGER, 'Sir Hubert Llewellyn Smith and Labour Policy 1886–1916' (Cambridge University PhD Thesis 1971).
JESSOP, FRANK, 'Oxford and Adult Education', paper presented at the International Graduate Summer School, 12 Aug. 1976.
KOOT, GERARD M., 'English Historical Economics and Neo-Mercantilism, paper presented at the History of Economic Thought Conference, Loughborough, September 1978.
——, 'The English Historical School of Economics 1870–1920' (State University of New York at Stonybrook PhD Thesis 1972).
MORGAN, P. T. J., 'Jonkers under Bellamy', essay read at St. John's College Essay Society, 22 Mar. 1960.

INDEX

Acland, Arthur Herbert Dyke, 14 ff., 21, 24 f., 27 n., 28, 67 n., 77 ff., 89, 92, 114 n., 192
Ashley, William James, 1 ff., 20 f., 28, 29, 35 f., 39 ff., 48 ff., 58, 60, 67 n., 71, 73, 97, 103, 117, 120, 125, 148, 152 ff., 158 f., 161 ff., 167 ff., 172 n., 176, 180, 182 n., 189 n., 192, 194 ff., 206, 213, 217, 220, 222 ff., 229, 233, 237 f., 243 ff., 254, 261 f., 273, 275, 278 f., 282, 286 n., 288 f.

Bagehot, Walter, 44
Ball, Sidney, 16, 21, 23, 25 ff., 32, 36, 43, 53, 97, 165, 178 n., 183, 185, 207 n., 214, 249 n., 275 n., 280
Barrett, Revd. Samuel Augustus, 23 ff., 43
Blunt, H. W., 28
Bonar, James, 23, 248 n.
Booth, Charles, 70, 75, 93, 124 f., 192, 215
Brentano, Lnjo, 44 n., 196
Bristol Grammar School, 19
British Association for the Advancement of Science, Section F, 90, 127, 134 f., 141 f., 150, 156, 164, 165 n., 166 f., 190, 192, 210, 212, 227 f., 233, 240 f., 247, 264
British Economic Association, 130, 152, 167, 187 f., 190 ff., 204 ff., 209, 215, 238 ff., 262, 269, 277, 283

Caird, Edward, 147
Cairnes, John Elliott, 48, 58 f., 153, 157, 180, 233
Campion, W. J. H., 28, 34, 53, 55, 94 n., 97, 103 n., 117, 184 ff.
Cannan, Charles, 6 ff., 10, 17, 156
Cannan, Edwin, 5 ff., 20 f., 29, 35 n., 42 f., 53, 55 ff., 67 n., 71, 73, 97, 117, 126, 153, 156 ff., 167, 170 f., 172 n., 183, 202 ff., 216, 226 ff., 248 n., 254, 264, 268 ff., 276 ff., 281 f., 289
Cannan, Gilbert, 9, 159
Carter, John, 34, 185 ff., 272 ff.
Chadwick, Edwin, 6 f., 11
Cliffe Leslie, Thomas Edward, 44, 153, 155
Clifton College, 8 f., 18
communism, 56 ff., 10
Comte, Auguste and Comtism, 36, 39, 42, 44, 127 ff., 150, 155, 161, 168 ff., 212 f., 222, 235, 244
Co-operative Congress, (1882) 78 f., (1883) 82, (1885) 83, (1885) 83
Cunningham, William, 28 n., 96 n., 99, 127, 143, 148 ff., 155, 179, 185 f., 190, 206, 209 ff., 218 ff., 225, 235 ff., 242 ff., 248, 252 ff., 262, 270, 275, 285, 286 n., 289

Docker's Strike, the, 24, 72, 123, 165
Dulwich College, 30 f.

Economic Journal, 125, 130, 167, 180, 186 ff., 204 ff., 209 ff., 215, 218 ff., 224 f., 235, 238, 240, 271, 275, 283
Economic Review, 28, 55, 125, 152, 161, 185 ff., 200 f., 204 ff., 209 f., 213, 217 f., 236, 238, 269, 273, 283
Edgeworth, Francis Ysidro, 99, 145, 179, 192, 194, 197, 199 ff., 210, 220, 232 n., 247, 255, 262, 265 ff., 273, 275, 285
Edwards, Owen Morgan, 21, 26, 28, 97, 103 n.
Ely, R. T., 54, 207
Engels, Friedrich, 71
Ewing, Robert, 34, 53, 97, 103 n.

Fabian Society, 57, 129, 170 n., 247 ff., 253, 255, 268
Fawcett, Henry, 55, 130, 148, 150, 157 f., 200

INDEX

Firth, Charles Harding, 35, 99, 254
Foxwell, Herbert Somerton, 27 n., 28 n., 89, 129 n., 133, 139 ff., 178, 180, 188, 190, 192, 198, 202, 220, 243, 253 f., 262, 264 n., 272 f., 275
Freeman, Edward Augustus, 36, 39 f., 176, 178 f., 193 f., 201

Gell, Philip Lyttleton, 22 n., 25, 43
George, Henry, 22, 41, 62 ff., 125, 139, 146, 157
Giffen, Roberts, 75, 129 n., 143, 198, 255
Gonner, E. C. K., 142 f., 198, 216, 248 n., 255, 275 n.
Goschen, George Joachim, 112 ff., 121, 178 n., 179, 191, 194, 198, 200, 239 f., 269
Green, Thomas Hill, 16, 24, 26, 36, 38, 42, 47, 77, 161, 198, 280, 287

Hewins, William Albert Samuel, 4, 15, 21, 28, 32 ff., 42, 48, 53, 96 ff., 101 ff., 105, 107, 117 ff., 161, 181 ff., 203 f., 206, 243 ff., 249, 251 ff., 269, 270, 273 f., 278 f., 281 f.
Hobhouse, Leonard Trelawny, 14, 17 ff., 21, 28, 97, 123, 254
Hobson, John Atkinson, 98, 105, 124 n., 254
Holland, Henry Scott, 23, 79, 184
Home Rule (Ireland), 20 f., 177 ff., 193, 257, 259
Hudson Shaw, W., 14, 17, 96, 98, 99 n., 102, 103 n., 104 n.

Inglis Palgrave, Robert, 141 f., 144 f., 169, 179, 186, 197, 224, 229, 246 n. 255, 260, 282

Jevong, William Stanley, 55, 58 f., 67 ff., 74, 117, 160 n., 173, 209, 229, 281, 287
Jones, Benjamin, 80 ff.
Jowett, Benjamin, 2 n., 3, 21, 35, 76, 95, 198 f.

Keynes, John Neville, 130, 145, 152, 178 f., 190, 192, 198, 206 f., 216 f., 268

Lang, Cosmo Gordon, 13 n., 17, 27, 28 n.

Lassalle, Ferdinand, 46, 71, 154
London School of Economics and Political Science, 107, 204 f., 208, 234, 247 ff., 266, 268, 270 ff., 275, 277, 287
Lux Mundi, 34, 79 n., 184, 190

Maine, Henry, 41
Malthus, Thomas Robert, 58, 134, 217, 226 ff., 235, 273
Marshall, Alfred, 32, 53 f., 61 ff., 77, 89, 123, 125 f., 129 ff., 155, 157, 159 f., 162 f., 166 f., 178, 180, 186 ff., 198, 203, 206, 209 ff., 242 f., 245, 247, 252, 254 f., 262, 264 f., 267 f., 273 f., 275 n., 276 f., 283, 285 ff.
Marvin, F. S., 96, 254
Marx, Karl, 46, 48, 71, 73, 125, 146, 154, 217, 230
Mazzini, Giuseppe, 36, 42
Medley, D. J., 14, 17 ff., 21, 28, 97, 123, 254
Mill, James, 125, 217, 230
Mill, John Stuart, 55, 58, 74, 76, 148, 154, 156 ff., 159, 173, 175, 179 f., 182, 199 n., 202, 230, 233, 273, 281, 287
Milner, Alfred, 22 n., 25, 27 n., 89

National Association for the Promotion of Technical Education, 92, 248
National Church Reform Union, 23, 43, 258 n.
Nettleship, Richard Lewis, 38, 79
Nicholson, Joseph Shield, 129 n., 130, 139, 143, 207 n., 240 n., 274, 275 n.
Oxford Co-operative and Industrial Society, 78, 263 n.
Oxford University,
  colleges, All Souls, 194, 202, 257
    Balliol, 1 ff., 9, 14, 17, 24, 27, 28, 36, 37 n., 38, 64, 170, 197 f., 235, 258
    Christ Church, 17, 28, 84
    Corpus Christi, 8, 10, 17, 19, 31, 47, 51
      Adam Smith Club, 21, 70, C.C.C. Debating Society, 19 ff.
      Pelican Essay Club, 17 f., 21
    Exeter, 177
    Jesus, 38, 257
    Keble, 28

INDEX

Lincoln, 35, 43 n., 51
Magdalen, 28
New, 28 ff.
Oriel, 32, 77 n., 167, 265
Pembroke, 31 ff., 99, 203, 246
St. John's, 26, 99, 246
Trinity, 8, 10, 13, 17, 28, 31, 84, 162 n., 179
   Gryphon Debating Society, 15
Worcester, 176
Extension Movement, 13, 32, 55, 66, 73 f., 77, 83 ff., 115 ff., 246, 249 ff., 255, 258, 260, 279, 281 ff.
Societies, Christian Social Union, Oxford Branch, 34, 55, 184 ff., 200
   Oxford Economic Society, 28, 35, 52 ff., 59 n., 72 f., 96 f., 103, 117, 154, 159, 172 n., 184 f., 190, 193, 203 ff., 257, 277
   Oxford Union Society, 14 f., 19 f., 29
   Oxford University Political Economy Club, 52, 175, 180, 184, 193, 204 f.
   Palmerston Club, 4, 15 f., 24, 29, 279
   Russell Club, 15, 26
   Social Science Club, 25, 27 n., 28, 32 ff., 165, 183, 193, 204, 249
Pease, Edward Reynold, 248, 253, 255 n.
Percival, John, 8, 10, 14, 31 f., 79, 87, 92, 99 n., 103
Phelps, Lancelot Ridley, 20 f., 22 n., 23 f., 25 n., 28, 34, 43, 52 f., 54 n., 79, 84, 94 n., 97, 101 n., 143, 178 f., 180, 185 ff., 192 f., 200, 206 f., 214, 266, 273, 275
Price, Bonamy, 76 n., 145, 172 ff.
Price, Langford Lovell Frederick Rice, 13 n., 14 f., 21, 29 ff., 35 n., 61, 63 ff., 75, 77 n., 89 ff., 94 n., 96 f., 99, 101 n., 103 n., 107, 117 ff., 125 f., 145, 160 ff., 179 f., 183 n., 190, 192, 202 n., 203 ff., 222 ff., 232, 242 f., 262 f., 275 f., 278 f., 281 f.

Ricardo, David, 45, 48, 58, 64 f., 71, 73 f., 134, 151, 153 f., 156 f., 159, 163, 172 f., 180, 183 n., 199 f., 206, 209, 211 f., 216 f., 219 ff., 223 ff., 229 f., 233 ff., 237, 273, 281.

Ritchie, David, 38, 183 n., 208, 213 f., 249
Rogers, James Edwin Thorold, 19 f., 40, 52, 77, 96, 99 n., 125, 172, 175 ff., 192, 194 f., 200, 203, 219, 245, 287 ff.
Royal Statistical Society, 70 n., 90 f., 127, 142 ff., 162 n., 165 n., 166, 179, 192, 214 f., 277
Rugby, 8, 12 f., 17, 51, 92, 172
   Oxford Old Rugbeians, 14
Ruskin, John, 47, 49 n., 76, 147, 215

Sadler, Michael Ernest, 4, 11 ff., 21, 22 f., 24, 27 f., 29, 31 f., 42, 48, 53, 79, 83 ff., 94 n., 97 f., 101 n., 103, 105, 106 n., 111 f., 117, 122 n., 123, 126, 185, 254, 278 f., 281
Schmoller, Gustav, 168, 196, 261
Seligman, E. R. A., 51 n., 53, 195 ff.
Senior, N., 125, 211, 230
Shaw, George Bernard, 129, 253 n., 269
Sidgwick, A., 16, 17, 23, 24 n., 25, 79, 82, 114 n., 275 n., 280
Sidgwick, Henry, 27 n., 89, 133, 135 ff., 141 f., 150, 157, 161, 180, 198, 217, 225
Smart, William, 147, 204, 215 f., 239, 262, 275 n., 276
Smith, Adam, 55, 74, 76, 131, 134, 156, 173, 225, 228 f., 235, 238
Smith, Arthur Lionel, 4 f., 22 n., 23 f., 35 ff., 42 f., 50, 56, 79, 170, 275 n., 280
Smith, Hubert, Llewellyn, 11, 14, 18 ff., 28 f., 32, 34, 42, 51 f., 54, 70 ff., 91 ff., 94 n., 96 ff., 100 f., 107, 117 ff., 122 ff., 161, 165 ff., 183, 192, 197, 205, 248, 254, 275, 278 f., 281 f.
Snow, T. C., 16, 21, 28, 85, 186 n., 203, 207 n.
socialism and socialists, 45 f., 48, 58, 64 f., 73, 116, 122, 153, 174, 217, 224, 226 f., 236, 233 ff., 247, 273
Spencer, Herbert, 44 f.
Spooner, William Archibald, 20, 24, 29 n., 52, 180, 193
Stubbs, William, 35, 39, 176

Taylor, Sedley, 44, 89
Toynbee, Arnold, 6 n., 15 f., 22 ff., 36, 42 ff., 50, 57 f., 63, 73, 78 n., 79 ff., 87, 94, 117, 119, 121, 125,

140 n., 145, 159 f., 168, 173, 196, 198 f., 280, 286 n., 287
Toynbee Trust, 66, 74 f., 88 ff., 93 f.

University Settlements, 22, 24 ff.
   Oxford House, 22, 28 f., 32
   Toynbee Hall, 22, 27 ff., 32, 75, 87 f., 94, 99, 124

wage-fund theory, 22, 54, 157, 159, 172, 182, 199 n.
Walker, F. A., 22, 44, 54, 125 f., 159, 207
Wallas, Graham, 251 f.
Webb, Beatrice, 248 n., 249, 256 f., 263
Webb, Sidney James, 57 n., 183 n., 247 ff., 266, 273
Willert, P. F. 96
Winchester School, 29